Beyond Coal and Steel

Beyond Coal and Steel

A Social History of Western Europe after the Boom

Lutz Raphael

Translated by Kate Tranter

polity

Originally published in German as *Jenseits von Kohle und Stahl: Eine Gesellschaftsgeschichte Westeuropas nach dem Boom* © Suhrkamp Verlag Berlin 2019. All rights reserved by and controlled through Suhrkamp Verlag Berlin.

The translation and production of this book were enabled by a grant from the Deutsche Forschungsgemeinschaft (German Research Foundation).

Deutsche
Forschungsgemeinschaft

German Research Foundation

Polity Press
65 Bridge Street
Cambridge CB2 1UR, UK

Polity Press
111 River Street
Hoboken, NJ 07030, USA

ISBN-13: 978-1-5095-5437-9 – hardback
ISBN-13: 978-1-5095-5438-6 – paperback

A catalogue record for this book is available from the British Library.

Library of Congress Control Number: 2023933992

Typeset in 10.5 on 12 pt Sabon
by Fakenham Prepress Solutions, Fakenham, Norfolk NR21 8NL
Printed and bound by CPI Group (UK) Ltd, Croydon, CR0 4YY

The publisher has used its best endeavours to ensure that the URLs for external websites referred to in this book are correct and active at the time of going to press. However, the publisher has no responsibility for the websites and can make no guarantee that a site will remain live or that the content is or will remain appropriate.

Every effort has been made to trace all copyright holders, but if any have been overlooked the publisher will be pleased to include any necessary credits in any subsequent reprint or edition.

For further information on Polity, visit our website:
politybooks.com

CONTENTS

PART II CLOSE-UPS

Fields of experience and horizons of expectation in times of upheaval

LIST OF FIGURES

LIST OF TABLES

ACKNOWLEDGEMENTS

This book has been long in the making. The idea originated in 2008 when work began on a research programme entitled 'After the Boom – Studies on the History of Western Europe after 1970' led by Anselm Doering-Manteuffel and myself. We were a group of historians at the universities of Trier and Tübingen who wanted to discover the specific essence of the last three decades of the twentieth century. In particular, we wanted to understand the structural transformations that changed societies in Western Europe during this period. The research association was and still is funded by the German Research Foundation (Deutsche Forschungsgemeinschaft, DFG), initially within the framework of a combined application of the two universities of Tübingen and Trier and since 2013 as a DFG Leibniz Research Group at the University of Trier.

I have profited immensely from numerous conversations with Tobias Dietrich, Anselm Doering-Manteuffel, Raphael Dorn, Maria Dörnemann, Fernando Esposito, Tobias Gerstung, Hannah Jonas, Martin Kindtner, Christian Marx, Silke Mende, Arndt Neumann, Morten Reitmayer and Wiebke Wiede. They supported this project from the outset with critical comments, discussed my ideas with me and always provided me with references to current studies and new results. I would like to express my sincere thanks to them all for their intellectual interest and support.

Both Nicole Mayer-Ahuja and Serge Paugam provided me with generous support for the analysis of important documents and social data by providing access to the archives of the research institutes they direct, the Centre Maurice Halbwachs in Paris and the Soziologisches Forschungsinstitut (SOFI) at the University of Göttingen. I am deeply grateful to them for their kind and unbureaucratic assistance.

ACKNOWLEDGEMENTS

The wealth of useful information available in the database of the Socio-Economic Panel (SOEP) would probably have remained hidden to me if it had not been for the helpful advice of Christoph Weischer, and I was able to access and use it thanks to the help of Raphael Dorn. After the latter had successfully solved the various problems of restructuring the presentation of the data, we were both able to use new methods of collective biographical evaluation in our analyses. For this and for our joint work with the SOEP, I am extremely grateful.

This book would not have been able to take shape as it did after 2010 were it not for the support I received through a whole chain of fortunate circumstances. A fellowship at the International Centre 'Work and Human Lifecycle in Global History' at the Humboldt University in Berlin permitted me to immerse myself from October 2010 to August 2011 in the topic from a comparative German–French perspective. The subsequent period of research as visiting fellow of the European Studies Centre at St Antony's College in Oxford encouraged me to include Britain in my study. I would like to thank both institutions and their directors at this point. It would not have been possible for me to carry out this research and write the book at the same time as my university teaching and other research projects if I had not been fortunate enough to receive the Gottfried Wilhelm Leibniz Prize from the DFG in 2013. I am extremely grateful to all the judges for this honour and generous financial support for my research. It was finally the Gerda Henkel Foundation which enabled me to take up a guest professorship at the London School of Economics and at the German Historical Institute in London in the academic year 2015–16. This gave me the opportunity to bring my research on the British perspective to a provisional close and present first drafts. I am indebted to all my colleagues at both these institutions for their hospitality and for their numerous criticisms and suggestions, which I hope I have been able to accommodate adequately. I am particularly grateful to Jane Caplan, Andreas Eckert, Andreas Gestrich and Jürgen Kocka.

I had the opportunity of presenting the first draft of some chapters in various places as talks or lectures and always benefited from the subsequent discussions. I would like particularly to thank David Gugerli, Ulrich Herbert, Ariane Leendertz, Nicole Mayer-Ahuja, Ute Schneider and Jacob Tanner for their interest and critical support. A true intellectual act of friendship was provided by Brigitta Berner, Clelia Caruso, Anselm Doering-Manteuffel, Andreas Gestrich, Christian Marx, Arndt Neumann, Martin Reitmayer and Christoph

Weischer. They were prepared to read first drafts and comment on them critically, a process which also ironed out many smaller and larger deficiencies. I am extremely grateful to them all. I am equally grateful to Niklas Penth and Pascal Licher for their masterful work on the notes and the bibliography as well as their help with various searches. Arndt Neumann developed the design and the text for the illustrations and demonstrated a special flair in choosing them. I am very grateful to him for this.

The book finally profited vitally from the fact that I was given the opportunity of presenting its ideas and aims in summer 2018 in the Frankfurt Adorno Lectures, organized and hosted by the Institute for Social Research at the Johannes Wolfgang Goethe University in Frankfurt in cooperation with Suhrkamp publishers. My thanks go to Axel Honneth for bestowing me with this honour and his team for the perfect organization and support at these events.

Last but not least, I would like to thank Eva Gilmer. Her careful and patient editing did not allow the slightest linguistic inaccuracy or stylistic peculiarity to go undetected and she quietly and competently insisted on a concise and reader-friendly text. My final thanks, however, are reserved for Kate Tranter. With her meticulous translation of the original edition, she competently transformed this typically German text into an equally concise and reader-friendly English version.

INTRODUCTION

Perspectives on a history of Western European society after the boom

Between 1970 and 2000, every country in Western Europe was affected by profound and structural change which was propelled by various crises. This book is concerned with the circumstances and consequences of this change, whose main characteristic is the multi-faceted decline of the industrial sector in the different national economies or economic areas. As a result, it is often defined as 'deindustrialization' and described as a transition from an industrial society to a service society. The 'old' industries, the steelworks, coal mines, dockyards and textile factories, which had been the backbone of these economies during the decades of the postwar economic boom, disappeared during this process of change, taking away millions of jobs. Industrial employment decreased, but at the same time, and closely linked to this, the industrial sector experienced a significant increase in labour productivity. As far as technology is concerned, these decades were marked by the spread of electronic and computerized data processing in all areas of industry, from production to customer services, with far-reaching consequences. On the whole, the structural change described in this book was a long-term trend which we in Western Europe have become accustomed to, much as we would to any natural phenomenon. From a historian's point of view, this is a basic process, comparable to the increase in life expectancy or the diversification of lifestyles.

This process had numerous and serious social consequences. While in most countries in Western Europe in the mid-1970s industrial workers made up by far the largest social group, both by profession and by status, nowadays most people in these countries work in a wide variety of jobs in the service sector. This caused major changes in Western European societies over the last three decades of the

1

twentieth century, which still reverberate today. Whereas in the boom years industrial expansion in the three countries in this comparative study – Britain, France and West Germany – was accompanied by full employment, from the beginning of the 1970s there was a return of the mass unemployment of the interwar period, especially of youth unemployment and the long-term unemployed. At the same time, industrial knowledge was either devalued or redefined, careers had to be reinvented and life plans revised. Flexibility became the buzzword of the period.

Bidding farewell to the industrial labourer also meant bidding farewell to the industrial futures that still inspired the collective imagination of Western European societies around 1970. They now restyled themselves as 'post-industrial' or 'service' societies, eagerly assisted in this redefinition by social scientists, political advisers and journalists. Industrial society immediately began to be given its own history as a phase of Western European modernity that had come to an end. Museums and monuments began to be built or extended to commemorate the first era of industrialization; sometimes this structural change was even accompanied by whole regions being turned into museums.

A history 'from below'

Tracing such a fundamental, long-term and comprehensive process always runs the risk of slipping into a narrative pattern whose rhetoric implies a more or less inherent inevitability. It is a pattern preferred by politicians and contemporary analysts, then as now, to cloak their current pragmatic goals in a gold-leaf mantle of historical philosophy. To avoid this risk, I have chosen a different narrative perspective for this book, focussing on the lives and experiences of industrial workers. The protagonists of my social history of industrial labour are the workers themselves, male and female, skilled and unskilled, who found themselves increasingly sidelined and to a certain extent invisible to the public eye when future opportunities and risks were being discussed. The advantage of this perspective for writing a critical history is obvious: it is easier to discover the 'cost of progress' – that is, the processes of social decline and the increase of social inequality and marginalization – than if I were to adopt the position of those who emerged from this long transformation as 'winners', such as the employers and employees in the information technology (IT) and finance sectors, in marketing and consultancy

2

or in research and development. A social history written from the perspective of these groups would no doubt bring out the undeniably impressive opportunities and potential of a new 'post-industrial' order far more strongly than it does here. On the other hand, it would offer fewer insights into the dynamics of the growing social inequality linked to these structural changes, which has become increasingly evident since the turn of the century.

By the mid-1990s, the issue of social inequality had more or less disappeared from the socio-political academic debate in Western Europe. It returned all the more intensely nearly twenty years later, not least because of Thomas Piketty's acclaimed studies.[1] With it came a heightened interest in the negative social effects of the post-industrial order. It suddenly became clear how limited the opportunities for participation were (and still are) for those with little or no income or possessions. It also became clear how little social recognition they received for their work and skills, and still do receive from the media and the public in everyday social interaction. One of the aims of this book is to show how this increase in the imbalance of economic, political and social inequality was seen from the point of view of 'ordinary people' in the reality of their daily lives. Another aim is to examine the forces that were mobilized and the institutional barriers that were erected to counteract the social consequences of this trend. The book also aims to contribute to the understanding of the current crisis of liberal democracy. The roots of this crisis can now be traced back clearly to the topic of this book: the decades of upheaval in the industrial societies of the West. Structural transformation led to tangible changes in social conditions in Western democracies.[2] I again use the perspective 'from below' to examine whether the way these basic conditions were transformed for workers meant that basic forms of 'social relational equality'[3] were eroded.

A history 'from yesterday'

When the 'fat years' of the economic boom after 1948 came to a definitive end in Western Europe a quarter of a century later, sections of the industrial workforce suffered the same fate as farmers and craftspeople had several decades earlier. During their own lifetime, they became part of a future past, with no prospects in the present, let alone in the future. They were to a certain extent overtaken by events. In their attempts to understand processes of structural transformation, historians rarely take the perspective of such actors seriously. In this book, I aim to combine the perspective 'from below' described above with the less familiar perspective 'from yesterday'. In this way, I attempt to counteract the effects of a common professional disease that often seems to afflict contemporary social history, which is to follow a sociological view of future-oriented trends and so to discover the beginnings of anything new primarily in the social phenomena of the immediate past. This is ultimately based on an obsession with narratives relating to progress or growth, whereas narratives relating to the decline or disappearance of social groups or entities tend to be met with silence or indifference.[4] In contrast, I will devote the following chapters to examining the changes affecting the living and working conditions of a shrinking industrial workforce in order to bring to light aspects of living and working environments neglected even today. Depending on the country or region, this will reveal lines of continuity and forces of stability which have together contributed to give the three Western European societies in question their specific profile – a profile, incidentally, that in some respects entirely failed to meet the expectations of a post-industrial order.

My thesis is, therefore, that the upheavals in Western European societies can only be understood if we consider the tension between the spheres of experience of the existing industrial society and the horizons of expectation of the emerging 'service society'. These tensions had been mounting since the mid-1970s. The numerous protests, strikes and conflicts that accompanied the process of deindustrialization show, for example, that it, too, had a history of politicization, whose impact is still felt today. Looking at concrete occupational biographies also reveals how complex and disparate the real lives of those directly affected by structural transformation were. Ultra-stable and precarious worlds existed side by side, as did old and new patterns of order and different horizons of expectations specific to certain generations and groups. Some enjoyed repeated promotion and long periods of affiliation to one company; others faced unemployment and threats to their livelihood; others experienced labour migration or the power of local ties. The interpretive schemes that shaped politics and society in the three countries examined here were correspondingly diverse.

Reference points for a social history of deindustrialization

Around fifteen years ago, my colleague Anselm Doering-Manteuffel and I were involved at the start of a wider research programme in contemporary history. In this context, we drew up initial principles and research perspectives for a history of Western Europe in the three decades from 1970 to 2000.[5] Our thesis at the time was that during this period in Western Europe there were clear 'structural fractures' and simultaneously there was 'revolutionary social change'. By 'structural fractures' we mean striking discontinuities that were already clearly visible at the time. These include the demise of the older branches of industry and the crises in the old industrial regions as well as the rise of computer technology and financial market capitalism. 'Revolutionary social change', on the other hand, denotes the turning points resulting from the accumulation of change that gradually developed over a longer period and without the awareness of people at the time. This applies, for example, to the increase of women in paid employment, the growth of consumption and the opening and expansion of education systems. Structural fractures and the turning points of social change have transformed the contours of Western European societies and left their mark in a wide variety of spheres and fields of action. This is why a comprehensive history of these post-boom decades can only be conceived as a synthesis of a variety of different approaches, both methodological and thematic. The studies undertaken in our research network available so far and from which I draw in this book are correspondingly wide-ranging.[6]

These two categories of 'structural fractures' and 'revolutionary social change' also serve as a reminder that in this transition phase there was a certain openness to a variety of paths of development. This is a further reason for my decision to choose a comparative perspective for this book and to examine the transformation of the industrial worlds of France, Britain and West Germany. This approach makes it easier to recognize and describe the scope available to the actors and the idiosyncratic regional and national effects that link the economy, politics, culture and society. The following pages will repeatedly demonstrate that the basic process of deindustrialization never led to an erosion of the specific profiles of these three Western European countries and their regions, even in times of internationalization and globalization. On the contrary, national, regional and local differences in Western Europe tended to become more marked during this period. It also seemed to me that a comparative approach could be fruitful because since the 1980s there has been broad consensus amongst the political and economic elites of Western Europe on the means and goals of economic and social policies.

This consensus means that the history of ideas speaks of a (neo) liberal era and that the corresponding programmatic statements have sometimes been credited with an impact powerful enough to move mountains. It is true that the new spirit of (Western) capitalism had a profound influence on the process of European unification, not least in the 1990s. It is also true that between 1983 and 2008 there was a great deal of common ground in the government policy agendas of the three countries in question, from privatization to the opening up of international financial markets and the expansion and alignment of education systems right through to the cost-cutting restructuring of public social welfare systems.[7] Nevertheless, we must take extreme care with our methodology, for two reasons. On the one hand, a series of national singularities, mostly developed historically, have led to this 'new spirit' being 'materialized' in a way which is not identical in these three countries. On the other hand, the dwindling significance of national borders for the impact of economic trends, legal norms and cultural practices means that a single-country focus is inadequate. It may even be unproductive as the crucial processes as far as both similarities and differences are concerned were acted out on the regional or local level.

The question is why I chose these three countries, France, Britain and Germany, for my study and not, say, Spain, Italy or the Netherlands. Apart from purely subjective reasons to do with my previous knowledge and language skills, there are a number of objective reasons for this choice. These are the three largest economies in Western Europe and their development into industrial societies followed very different paths. During the period in question, they were members of the European Union and their national economies were integrated into the European single market. They also offer a broad spectrum of both specific national characteristics and typical choices in the political and social structuring of the transition period. This meant that I could draw on a wealth of empirical material for the analysis of the interaction between national path dependencies and processes of Europeanization and internationalization. One important constraint, however, should be mentioned. My Western European comparison encountered considerable difficulties in the case of the Federal Republic of Germany after 1990, since it was only then that the industry-based socialist society in the regions of former East Germany, the German Democratic Republic (GDR), collapsed, albeit with almost revolutionary character and speed. There was a completely different basis for this dramatic structural collapse than for the transformations taking place in Western Europe since the

1970s, which stretched over a period of at least three decades. For this reason, it has been necessary in some comparative cases to use or generate data series which refer solely to the old German Federal Republic, former West Germany, right up to the end of the period of study in the year 2000. It should also be noted that it was not possible to discuss the specifics of the upheavals in what were then the new German federal states in this book, even though there are many indications that a comparison with developments in a slightly different period in Britain, particularly the 1980s, could offer many new insights into the transformation process of the GDR.[8]

A 'history of society': the implications of a concept

This book is also an attempt to renew and update the concept of a 'history of society' that was developed by scholars studying the history of modern industrial societies in Europe. The original proposal by Eric Hobsbawm in 1971 saw 'history of society' as a concept which linked the historical study of population development, social structures, social classes or social groups and mentalities with the history of overarching social systems or spaces. Compared to classical social historical research, this meant a broadening of the scope of what it claims to explain but also of its subject matter and methodology. Hobsbawm accepted very different approaches and starting points for this kind of social history but adhered to the idea that any concrete historical analysis of a distinct phenomenon should be embedded in the larger framework of the transformation of social structures, for which the category 'society' is used. Its theoretical basis was provided either by typologies of social forma-tions based on Marx – that is, epoch-specific, transnational or global structural features – or by more narrowly defined typologies, such as the concept of moral economy for the early modern period. The concept of history of society was as open as its author was sceptical in the face of the considerable difficulties in its concrete empirical implementation.[9]

West German history of society (*Gesellschaftsgeschichte*), as pioneered by Hans-Ulrich Wehler, applied this approach less theoreti-cally while at the same time taking it in a decidedly national-historical direction: 'Modern *Gesellschaftsgeschichte* understands its subject to be the whole of society, in the sense of "society" and "société"; it thus attempts to capture as much as possible of the basic processes that have determined, and perhaps still do determine, the historical development of a large-scale system that usually lies within state and political boundaries.'[10] In doing so, however, it was condemned to perform a feat of synthesis that only seemed feasible at the macro level.

The idea of an overall or total history of European societies that were constituted politically as nations was admittedly ambitious and it was difficult to defend its methodology against the focussed attacks of structural-analytical microhistory or anthropologically informed cultural history. Accordingly, a good twenty years after the publication of the last volume of Wehler's *Deutsche Gesellschaftsgeschichte* (*History of German Society*), such attempts at historiographic surveys and descriptions of social bodies designated as 'nations' are largely met with scepticism. This kind of approach is also not suitable for my project, since nation-state demarcations increasingly lost their significance for the circulation of goods, capital, people and ideas in the course of European unification. The challenge this poses for a history of society approach can be illustrated by a simple example: in France and West Germany in the 1970s and 1980s, between 15 and 20 per cent of those working in industrial production were 'foreigners' or labour migrants who lived in at least two social, economic and cultural areas. Their social space was completely different from that of their indigenous colleagues, but in a social history focussed on national entities they are assigned solely to a national social 'container'. At the same time, the proportion of cross-border production processes in the industrial production of all three countries increased steadily and with it the proportion of employees who crossed borders for work. This also has to be taken into account by any history of contemporary society. Thus, when addressing concrete research questions, the term 'society' is redefined as a relational concept.[11]

A remaining key problem is that nation-state and society are often equated. I aim to avoid the pitfalls of a methodological nationalism without, however, ignoring the nationalizing effects that a good two hundred years of nation building have had on European societies. Capital and labour may not have changed their character at national borders, but nationally regulated education systems, national welfare systems and, above all, the nationally constituted arenas of political communication, with their specific political languages, shaped the living conditions and communication patterns of the British, French and Germans at the end of the twentieth century. This means that the 'nation as a container' does emerge at various points in my study, more or less clearly, and with a claim to provide explanations. At the same time, the numerous cross-border transfers and mutual

8

observations must also be considered. British, French and German companies that invested in their respective neighbouring countries tried to implement best practices and solutions there; politicians of all three countries hoped to learn from the mistakes and successes of their neighbours. Finally, all three countries were at that time in the process of making their legal regulations compatible as well as opening up their national markets in all areas of the economy.

At this point, it might seem that the best way to solve the key problem of a history of society outlined above and avoid the nation-state trap is to choose Europe as a reference point. However, existing social histories of Europe show that this merely shifts the problem to a higher level. In one respect, they even exacerbate the problem since they are condemned to remain at the macro level of major trends and highly aggregated social statistics to an even greater extent than their nation-state counterparts. As a result, the regional dimension again remains underexposed, and it is extremely laborious and hardly possible in such a framework to do justice to the political and cultural dimensions fundamental to a social history. However, in view of the advancement of European integration in the late twentieth and early twenty-first centuries towards the European single market and monetary union, it would be a mistake to omit the European dimension as a mere economic reality, administrative superstructure or political idea, because it has of course had long-term effects on the social realities of the member countries. I allow for this by making the industrial regions of Western Europe the wider frame of reference for my comparative study. Further studies will have to determine whether this is appropriate: that is, whether the insights gained here can also be applied to countries such as Luxembourg, Belgium or Sweden, or whether they will need revision.[12]

This book thus works with an open concept of 'society' and employs five quite different methodological approaches without weighing them against each other as such. The first uses political economy. It allows us to adopt an interdisciplinary perspective and relate transnational economic processes to attempts to direct them politically. This seems to me to be a promising approach which enables the basic process of deindustrialization to be grasped more precisely in its concrete forms. It will be applied in chapter 1. The second approach, which I will use primarily in chapter 4, focuses on legal regulations. It is concerned with the significance and specificity of legal patterns pertaining to labour, social relations and collective bargaining and their impact on social dynamics in this period of upheaval. The third approach, which will be applied in chapters 2 and 4, works with the history of knowledge. On the one hand, it is concerned with the changes in the interpretive schemes and representations of the social world that provided orientation for contemporary actors, not only for the decisions they made in the labour world and related conflicts but also for their everyday routines (chapter 2). On the other hand, this approach generates the question of changes in knowledge systems that were directly linked to the transformation processes in the industrial worlds of the time. It draws attention to the changing value of educational and professional qualifications and to the emergence of new bodies of knowledge and distributions of knowledge and competencies in an era that was shaped by the rise of the prominent new digital technologies (chapter 5).

The fourth approach focuses on events. 'History of society' ought not only to be concerned with trends and anonymous social change but also to assign relevance and significance to events. This applies on both a large and a small scale. Events that are media-staged formats of collective occasions represent the sphere of the political par excellence still today. While their precise consequences for society and the economy are far from clear, it seems evident to me that such events have a powerful impact. In addition to these 'loud' headline events, there are micro events far removed from the media that mark individual and collective biographies: career choice, leaving home and retirement are important as landmarks – they shape experiences and life courses. I will use an event-centred perspective in chapter 3 to examine the history of political protest movements, and in chapter 6, where I will look at working lives and biographies. The fifth aspect in this social history of deindustrialization is the socio-spatial dimension. Here I am particularly interested (especially in chapters 7 and 8) in the spatially bound forces of stability and dramatization effects that have led to all three countries studied here experiencing greater differences and a more striking distribution of inequality in their social spaces today than they did fifty years ago.

Methodology: the complications of close-up and bird's-eye perspectives, the effects of theory and the selection of sources

'History of society' is thus a perspective or a frame of reference that guides historians' attention, but it should not let the actual concept of society determine the objects and spaces to be studied. The early epistemological optimism of social history has been destroyed by another methodological insight, namely that findings from the macro and micro levels cannot simply be merged, and although the insights they provide can be generalized, they are not always congruent. This phenomenon was termed the 'law of levels' by Siegfried Kracauer, one of the first social and cultural theorists to engage with it systematically. It creates serious problems of representation, since constructions of the past which arise from individual levels of investigation do not (always) fit together in the end.[13] In this book, I try to make a virtue out of this necessity by confidently ignoring the 'law of levels' in order to reveal complexities and opportunities for action by repeatedly switching back and forth between micro and macro levels. Thus, for example, I examine the shifts within individual work biographies in the same way as the shifts that the rise of international financial markets caused in British, French and West German industrial companies. I combine this variation between close-up and bird's-eye perspectives with frequent moves between categories of comparison, now looking at countries, then at regions, now at companies, then at households or individuals.

Historians automatically encounter confusing traces of complex social worlds later than social scientists, for example. This is an advantage in one respect. The longer time frame preceding both longer and shorter chains of events enables historians to gain an overview that social scientists who are oriented to the present can usually only achieve by means of strong theory-based constructions and abstractions combined with precise methods. These explanatory models, theories and diagnoses developed by the social sciences have already been used by the historical actors in our period of study in their attempts to evaluate, correct and steer the course of events and the futures of their businesses, careers or nations. Social historians of the recent past constantly stumble across such 'theory effects'. These are maxims of action or figures of legitimation with practical implications. They stem from social science knowledge production and compel us to be theoretically vigilant.

Strictly speaking, a 'history of society' cannot do without a detailed history of knowledge. Or at least it cannot dispense with historicizing those social data and figures of thought from the social sciences which seemed to be relevant to behaviour and have a broad impact – in other words, which had left the esoteric circle of professional interpreters of society and social researchers and were circulating in the wider social world. For this reason, in the process of analysing the social 'realities' of workplaces, employment, occupational status and living quarters in this book, I have to deal repeatedly with this unverified 'knowledge' (*doxa*). In this context, I will frequently connect the two levels of social and symbolic structures, but in the initial two chapters I keep them analytically apart so as to first present the basic outlines of economic processes and perceptions of society in these three Western European societies.

Theoretical vigilance in this context also means taking contemporary social science research seriously and being prepared to consider its results and its explanatory models and theories as aids to historical analysis. In spite of their nature as constructs, it does not mean that having reconstructed their contexts of origin historically and critically, historians should simply dismiss them as historical artefacts with no practical contemporary relevance. A narrative that feigned ignorance would simply fall below the level of knowledge of the social sciences and would always run the risk of accepting unverified 'truths' (*doxa*) as the closest, apparently natural means of explanation. Social historians are also unable to avoid their own constructs. Being vigilant in this case means always laying open the theory-driven insights that have inspired or directed the creation of our constructs. In this respect, social historians must be in constant dialogue with their social science colleagues, their research ideas and explanatory models. Following Kracauer's concept of the 'historical idea', I consider 'research ideas' to be those hypotheses or theories that open up new research perspectives, highlight new research topics and reveal potential, previously overlooked connections. 'They introduce a new principle of explanation; they reveal – with one stroke, as it were – as yet unsuspected contexts and relationships of a relatively wide scope; and they invariably involve matters of great import.'[14] For this book, six such main research ideas have emerged.

The first idea comes from the American industrial sociologists Michael Piore and Charles Sabel, who in the early 1980s already predicted that there would be massive structural changes in the relationship between capital and labour in the course of the third industrial revolution.[15] They foresaw a move towards flexible quality production, accompanied by a redistribution of labour and knowledge, a shift to smaller industrial production units and the upgrading of regional solutions to enable new competitive industrial production. This hypothesis has helped me enormously in the effort not to lose sight of the big picture, even though the fields of industrial sociology and business research present such heterogeneous findings and research theses.

The second idea comes from the French sociologists Stéphane Beaud and Michel Pialoux. Given the dramatic upheavals in France, they pointed out the often-overlooked connection between social

12

disparities in 'democratized' education systems and transformations in the industrial world of work. In doing so, they paved the way to challenging one of the most powerful ideological tropes of this epoch, namely that all problems of inequality and discrimination would be eliminated by broadening access to general education and qualifications.[16]

My third research idea stems from the German industrial sociologist Hermann Kotthoff. His assumption is that in the world of work, specifically in companies, cooperation and conflict have not only institutional and economic aspects but also a genuine socio-cultural dimension. This was a major key to a better understanding of the corresponding dynamics in times of great change and constant uncertainty.[17]

This idea in turn points to two other crucial theoretical assumptions to which my study is committed. With the concepts of 'social recognition' and 'relational equality', Axel Honneth and Pierre Rosanvallon have provided fundamental reflections on the reciprocity of social relations, which I follow in this book.[18] Individual recognition and lack of discrimination as the norm is the fourth research idea. It denotes a fundamental dimension of social relations in the industrial societies of Western Europe, which were characterized by collective (class) structures and socio-economic inequality. Indeed, many disputes in the world of work were and still are, sometimes even primarily, about social recognition, even if this is often overlooked. I use this idea to gain a better understanding of how the relations between social groups developed in the course of the upheavals studied here.

Next I would like to highlight Pierre Bourdieu's reference to *effets de lieu*, site effects, as the fifth research idea that has guided me. By considering changes in social spaces, their symbolic value and the structures of inequality realized in them, my gaze was diverted from workplaces to housing and forms of settlement, which enabled me to make insightful observations.[19]

The sixth idea comes from the French ethnologist Olivier Schwartz. In his research on the private lives and cultural practices of blue- and white-collar workers in France, he uses the term *classes populaires*[20] to bring together two dimensions that are frequently separated and analysed from completely different perspectives using very different categories. These dimensions are socio-economic inequality and cultural distance or difference. What connects them, in Schwartz's view, is the relationship between the dominating and the dominated (*dominants–dominés*). It is only through this relationship that both socio-economic and cultural differences acquire social relevance and

13

meaning. Combining a perspective on inequality that was originally sociological with one that is culturalist seems to me a particularly suitable approach to do justice to the changes observed in the three countries during the period under investigation. *Classes populaires* is a term that permits us to link the formation of classes or social groups based on economic status with cultural dynamics and new considerations of cultural capital. It also permits us to recognize the deficits of traditional class analysis, which is unable to capture the dual logic of both cultural and socio-economic influences. For my purpose of writing a comparative social history, there are numerous benefits of using the term *classes populaires*. First, it enables the disparate national traditions of class formation (see chapter 2) to be seen as variations of one basic constellation. Second, it helps to account for cultural and economic factors in equal measure. And, third, it makes it possible to conceptualize the social and cultural convergence of previously separate occupational groups and social status groups.

In addition to these six research ideas, I draw on a multitude of theoretical insights of the most diverse provenance, thus taking an eclectic or – to put it more positively – pluralistic approach. This is not unusual for a historian. Readers will soon notice my preference for tracing actions, events and processes back to the specific logic of social fields of action. Indeed, I ascribe considerable significance to the way individual actors are embedded in such social configurations and repeatedly give more explanatory credit to the 'social' and its inherent logic than to the abstract, instrumentally rational logics of action favoured by methodological individualism. Whether such a holistic view is better suited to do justice to the complexity of the upheavals analysed here is for others to decide.

Lastly, in this book I adhere to yet another basic assumption of social theory that has long since ceased to be self-evident. I continue to regard work as a nucleus of the formation of social structure, both in the period under study and in the present. Now as ever, work both as gainful employment and as a profession defines not only socio-economic positions, but also social inclusion and participation. Work experiences shape the formation and position of cultural and political groups or are conversely influenced by them. My position differs from many others in the social sciences and history which consider work to have already lost its formative social power to shape consumption and leisure in the last three decades of the twentieth century.[21] I am adamant that work is pivotal to a socio-historical perspective. Whether this will take us far enough remains to be seen.

14

A few final remarks on sources, data and documents. A 'history of society' as attempted here has no preference for a certain type of source, knows no primacy of state archives or official statistics. It only finds traces of events, processes or ideas that it takes up, regardless of how they have been handed down and who has preserved them. In many cases, it uses the results of contemporary empirical social research for a critical secondary analysis. I have therefore reinterpreted sociological research documents, for example, and used them as historical sources many times in this book and have combined findings from very different sources, in full awareness of the methodological risks this entails. Expanding the source base in such a way is in my view to the advantage of socio-historical research and means it can effectively evade the common demand for methodological monogamy as proof of what is deemed to be professional rigour. However, I am, of course, also aware that the quantitative evaluation of social data originating from both official and social research is a different procedure from the historical-critical reading and interpretation of life testimonies, political documents, academic publications and legal texts.

In fact, no individual researcher would ever be able to completely examine and analyse all the available material relevant to this study. The critical selection of data and documents therefore plays a significant role and would have deserved to be fully presented and explained in each case. I have largely refrained from this for reasons of space, but hope, nevertheless, that debate amongst experts will bring to light the errors and misinterpretations that certainly exist and introduce new, better documents to further the argument. A list of the most important data series and archival materials used, along with official statistics and published documents, can be found at the beginning of the bibliography as an aid to the reader.

One point has to be mentioned here. It would have been easier to meet the aim of this book to present a perspective 'from below' if comparable data on the social spheres of the *classes populaires* had been available for all three countries. This was sadly not the case. For Germany, the Socio-Economic Panel (SOEP) provided the basis for a relatively comprehensive set of data for the social space of industrial workers, their partners, parents and children from 1984 to 2001.[22] However, data of this kind were not available for France and Britain for a similarly long period or with a similar amount of information. This means that data sets were differently generated and structured and had to be examined and repeatedly checked to see whether a quantitative comparison could lead to any kind of meaningful result.

15

— PART I —

A BIRD'S-EYE VIEW
Three national labour regimes in transition

— Chapter 1 —

INDUSTRIAL LABOUR IN WESTERN EUROPE AFTER THE ECONOMIC BOOM FROM THE PERSPECTIVE OF POLITICAL ECONOMY

By the mid-1970s, industrial workers accounted for more than half of the labour force in most Western European countries. Then, between 1975 and 2012, the number of industrial jobs shrank by half in Britain and France, and by a quarter in Germany.[1] As a result, the proportion of industrial workers in the working population fell to between 20 and 28 per cent. Behind these figures lie profound changes in the underlying structure of the economy and society. In the 1970s and 1980s when the manufacturing sector in Western Europe was experiencing profound crisis-driven structural change, many of the 'old' industries – the steelworks, coal mines, shipyards and textile mills – disappeared. In addition, the entire industrial sector declined in importance and the number of people employed fell significantly in most branches. Since many of those previously employed as industrial workers were unable to find new jobs after being laid off, especially between 1975 and 2000 the rise in the unemployment rate for industrial workers (including technicians and engineers) in Western Europe was correspondingly high.

Deindustrialization can be defined as the absolute and/or relative decline of the industrial sector of a national economy in terms of employment and/or value added.[2] In the case of Western Europe, it has been attributed to the critical long-term shifts arising from the rapid economic growth and increased productivity in the long twentieth century. Where it was characterized by a shift in employment structures, deindustrialization has been closely linked to an increase in labour productivity in the industrial sector. This increase enabled new jobs to be created in the service sector, in education and science, health and public administration. Together with other areas directly related to industry, such as financial services or research and

19

development, this led to the whole of the tertiary sector expanding to such an extent that today it employs more people and generates a larger share of gross domestic product than does industry. However, this process was and is by no means linear and uniformly structured in the way suggested by the three-sector model that Allen Fisher, Colin Clark and Jean Fourastié developed (independently of each other) in the 1930s and 1940s. Its course is characterized instead by regional and national variants. Deindustrialization cannot therefore be understood as a one-way street that leads everyone along the same clear track to a 'post-industrial' economy and society;[3] it has rather to be seen as a set of diverse services that retain 'a close attachment to the industrial core'.[4]

The fact that the tertiary sector in these three countries was growing faster than the industrial sector and that, as a result, its share of value added and employment increased in their national accounts was first observed in the 1960s. It then experienced a spectacular surge in Europe in the three decades between 1970 and 2000. In West Germany, for example, the relative share of manufacturing in value added fell from 53 per cent in 1960 to 30 per cent in 2012. At the beginning of the 1980s, the service sector was still on a par with industry, accounting for just over 40 per cent of value added.[5] The relative decline in value added observed in the three countries in this study during this period by no means indicated an absolute decline in industrial value added, except in times of recession. What it did indicate was that growth became disconnected from employment. This happened much earlier in Britain than in France and Germany. While industrial jobs were already being lost in Britain in the 1960s, this trend did not emerge in France and Germany until after 1975. At that time, rationalization resulted in the disappearance not only of individual jobs, but also of entire companies – indeed whole branches of production in the industrial economy – never to be seen again. The same trend accelerated in the former socialist industrial societies of Central and Eastern Europe after the political upheavals of 1989–90 and the collapse of the large industrial units of the socialist economies during the transformation phase.[6] Along with the former GDR, a particularly striking example of this shift in economic value added and employment from the secondary to the tertiary sector in a European comparison is provided by Britain, since there it took place extraordinarily quickly and was particularly profound. The extent of this structural change can only be revealed by studying its effects on labour markets and employment structures, industrial production and the transformation of capitalism in Western Europe.

Deindustrialization in Western Europe

First, we can establish that the economic conditions for deindustrialization in Britain, France and Germany were very similar. All three economies experienced recessions in 1973–4, 1980–2, 1992–4 and 2000–1. These economic crises led to a decline in production in most industrial sectors and resulted in bankruptcies, factory closures, job cuts and rationalization. At the same time, growth rates in the years between these recessions remained lower than during the long period of growth between 1948 and 1973, falling from annual rates of around 3 per cent in the second half of the 1970s to just under 2 per cent in the 1990s.[7] This meant that Western European industries entered a new phase of development in which many different kinds of industrial enterprises came under similar structural pressure to adapt. This was due not only to the decision to create a single market in Europe but also to the growing competition from non-European suppliers, mainly from East Asia, but also from North America. Deindustrialization in Western Europe thus went hand in hand with the rise of other industrial locations with significantly higher growth rates. From a global historical perspective, this was the first time since the beginning of the industrial revolution in the late eighteenth century that growth rates and wealth creation had shifted in favour of Asian countries. The rise of Japan as an important industrial manufacturer and exporter was followed by that of South Korea, Taiwan, the People's Republic of China and Singapore. At the same time, other Asian countries – from Indonesia to Pakistan – became important locations for various industries, but particularly for the textile industry as it spread its global network. The significant increase in the proportion of industrial employment in Asia was a mirror image of its decline in Europe, in both relative and absolute terms. This is illustrated by the three examples in table 1.1.

Table 1.1 Employment in industry (including construction) in Asia (in thousands)

Country	1970s*		2001		2012	
China	69,450	17.2%	162,337	22.3%	232,410	30.3%
South Korea	1,936	18.3%	5,928	27.5%	6,134	24.6%
Indonesia	4,736	8.9%	17,015	18.7%	n.a.	

*Figures for China for 1978; South Korea for 1972; Indonesia for 1976.
Source: ILO statistics by sectors and countries, *https://www.ilo.org/ilostat/*.

By the end of the three decades studied here, a dynamic and crisis-ridden process of readjustment had led to the establishment of new global divisions of labour between the various industrial locations. The enhanced global competition rested on two main factors: labour cost advantages and state support in the so-called emerging economies. Technologically simple but labour-intensive manufacturing processes were transferred to locations where labour costs were particularly low, a development which transformed the textile and garment industry in particular into a highly mobile, globally operating production network.[8] The emerging economies also profited from government subsidy policies which enabled the construction of container ships, the mass production of steel and the manufacture of electrical appliances and solar cells to be accomplished much more cheaply. What remained in North America, Western Europe and Japan were old and new branches of technology-intensive quality production as well as the research, development and planning centres of globally producing industrial companies and multinational corporations.

Some economists have tried to evaluate the comparative influence of individual factors on the overall process of deindustrialization in Western Europe. While their results may be contested, their figures provide a first impression of the most important factors. The following figures have been calculated for French industry in the period from 1980 to 2007. The first factor relates to employment and is in fact only a statistical distortion: numerous tasks that used to be carried out within manufacturing companies were increasingly outsourced to external companies or affiliates after 1980 and thus simply attributed statistically to the service sector. As a result, the relative share of employment in industry fell by about 10 per cent. This statistical effect 'explains' one-fifth to one-quarter of the job losses in French industry between 1980 and 2007.[9] Another quarter of the job losses resulted from rationalization and increases in productivity.

Attempts to calculate the effects that resulted from foreign competition or the relocation of industrial sites abroad reveal much greater fluctuations between countries and also depend on the method of calculation selected. For France, the calculations vary between 13 and 40 per cent, depending on the method. Foreign competition, popularly referred to as 'globalization', did not develop evenly over the period under study or in parallel in the three countries. The competitive conditions of domestic industrial enterprises, particularly in the case of small and medium-sized companies, were influenced by economic and monetary policy decisions and the ease of access to credit markets. In general, it can be said that West German industrial manufacturers succeeded more often than their British and French competitors in withstanding foreign competition, so that the external factor of deindustrialization was less important there than in the other two countries.[10]

These globalization processes are also closely linked to the creation of the European Economic Area and internal market. Globalization was carefully coordinated and regulated at the regional European level. It is important to remember that the European Commission did not simply pursue global free trade policies, but negotiated import quotas, tariffs and other trade restrictions for foreign industrial importers in a whole series of multilateral or bilateral trade agreements, thus protecting European suppliers in the internal market from international competition. Trade liberalization of the European market was often a gradual process, whose purpose was to give European companies time to adjust to the competition. This applied to the steel industry but above all to the entire textile industry. For almost three decades, a succession of agreements protected it from direct competition, especially from Asian countries, and so enabled it to develop niches for its own production.[11] More successful or newly emerging European industries such as the automobile industry and the manufacturing of semiconductors were also at least partially protected from the effects of globalization.[12] Even the reduction of the considerable excess capacity in the European steel industry was regulated within Europe, by means of a plan drawn up by the then EU Commissioner Étienne Davignon. It protected domestic producers (to some extent) from external competitors, provided for internal quotas and production agreements and restricted national protectionism.[13]

After the 1990s, the European Commission made the deregulation of markets of any kind – goods, services or capital – a major objective in its development strategy and became a leading advocate of this new 'deregulation philosophy'. Its concrete aim was to strengthen the financial sector by removing any legal and administrative barriers which hindered, for example, the transfer of capital. The European Economic Area gradually adapted to the neoliberal rules which already applied in the US and in some post-communist states in Eastern Europe as well as in many emerging and developing countries.[14]

The establishment of the single European Economic Area in 1992 led to non-European industrial groups setting up subsidiaries in EU countries or entering into strategic partnerships with European companies in order to establish a presence on the European domestic market. This applied chiefly to companies in the US, Canada and Japan, but in the 1990s also included some from Taiwan and South Korea, and mainly involved the automobile industry, consumer electronics and information technology. The number of subsidiaries of Japanese firms, for example, increased rapidly in the three countries studied here, especially in the 1980s, and had tripled by 2000.[15] At the same time, many West German, French and British firms expanded their presence in neighbouring European countries, founded subsidiaries there or bought up local companies. This led to a steady rise in the proportion of foreign firms or majority foreign-owned companies in the industries of the three countries.

In Britain and France in particular, the proportion of foreign industrial enterprises grew in the 1980s and 1990s, so that by 1997 they employed almost 18 per cent of workers in Britain and a good 28 per cent in France.[16] The figures for Germany at that time were still considerably lower, at 7 per cent of the workforce. In all three countries, European firms accounted for the lion's share, followed by US and Japanese firms, both of which were particularly strong in Britain.

This trend towards the internationalization of companies has accelerated further since the turn of the millennium, fuelled both by the increasing internationalization of markets for industrial goods of all kinds and by the deregulation of financial markets. The acquisition of companies or factories and plants abroad became an important part of the business strategies of institutional investors and globally operating corporations. The phrase used by British business journalist and company historian Nicholas Comfort to summarize economic developments in his country's industry during the years 1997 to 2012 was 'selling up and selling out'.[17] France similarly became a popular country for international investors, especially from the US, but also from Germany. Medium-sized industrial companies in particular, which wanted to hold their own in the environment of necessary adjustment and innovation after 1975, felt bound to invest internationally, either by acquiring plants or companies abroad or by founding new ones.

One example is a medium-sized West German machine tool company, TRUMPF, which used sales, service and production sites to systematically expand its international market presence. It had already founded subsidiaries in Switzerland and the US in 1963 and 1969 and it proceeded to invest in sites in Britain, Japan and France in the 1970s and Brazil, Sweden, Spain, Austria, Singapore, the Czech Republic and Malaysia by the mid-1990s. Nine of its total of seventeen subsidiaries abroad were also production sites.[18] In 2017, for all its divisions (laser technology, electronics, power tools and machine tools), the company website lists ten sites in Germany, thirty-six in Europe (including three in Britain and two in France), fifteen in Asia and eleven in North and South America, Africa and the Middle East.[19] TRUMPF is an example of a successful medium-sized company, mainly supplying manufacturers with machinery, where the geographical spread of its sites illustrates vividly the extent to which domestic industrial production has become international in recent decades. Deindustrialization at the national level was thus closely linked to the redistribution of production sites and to the success or failure of industrial companies as markets became more European and more international. Despite many similarities, it is possible to observe striking national differences, not only company-related, which lent deindustrialization in each of these three countries its own specific profile.

In Britain, the share of value added and employment deriving from manufacturing was already shrinking dramatically in the second half of the 1970s and the early 1980s. Between 1972 and 1982, 1.89 million (24 per cent) of jobs in industry were lost. This trend continued for the next ten years: by 1992, another 1.457 million jobs (again 24 per cent) had disappeared and it was not until the 1990s that this rate slowed. Between 1992 and 2002, employment in the industrial sector fell by only a further 544,000 workers (13 per cent).[20] British industry, therefore, shrank significantly even though, in a second stage beginning in the 1980s and increasing in the 1990s, there was a rise in investment, especially of foreign capital, in British industrial companies. Hardly a single branch of industry was spared. Not only did the 'traditional' or 'old' industries such as textiles, mining, steel and shipbuilding disappear, but typical sectors of the postwar economic boom such as the car industry and the consumer goods industry were also affected. In 2007, at the end of the period we are studying, the share of the industrial sector in national value added was 14.5 per cent, making Britain a country with one of the smallest industrial sectors in the European Union.[21]

In France, industry was never as dominant as it was in Britain. At the height of the policy of industrialization pursued mainly in the postwar period and in the Fifth Republic, it employed 38.6 per cent of the workforce.[22] Between 1972 and 1982, the industrial sector shrank much more slowly than it did across the Channel. In France, 394,000 jobs were lost in this period (7.2 per cent); in the following decade, between 1982 and 1992, this process then accelerated to a loss of 754,000 jobs (15 per cent), only to slow down again between 1992 and 2002 to lose 401,000 (9.4 per cent).[23] While the French steel industry suffered a considerable decline in capacity and jobs after 1982, the automobile, chemical and pharmaceutical industries remained largely intact. As a result, industry continued the path, already evident before 1970, towards a dualist structure. A small number of large, highly productive, capital- and research-intensive enterprises existed alongside many other mainly medium-sized businesses that were far more vulnerable to international competition than were their German counterparts.[24] Economists trying to discover why the experience of small and medium-sized industrial enterprises was so different in France find themselves forced to accept complex clusters of historical and social factors as possible explanations. In fact, it is primarily regionally specific combinations of business networks and ownership structures, work qualifications and work cultures that play an important role. In chapters 7 and 8, I will return to these details and look at the consequences and concomitants of deindustrialization at the micro and meso levels from a socio-historical perspective.

As in Britain, the initial figures for industrial employment in Germany started at a higher level than in France. After experiencing a much more dramatic job loss than there was on the left bank of the Rhine – between 1972 and 1982, 1.235 million jobs were lost in Germany (13.5 per cent) – by the 1980s and 1990s the figures then stood at 11 and 12 per cent respectively, and thus at a level comparable with France.[25] Here too, this could at best be described as a partial crisis of its industrial infrastructure, but it is more accurate to call it accelerated and crisis-driven structural change in all sectors. A handful of industries and locations disappeared almost completely, textiles, shipbuilding, mining and steel being those most affected. Typical for West Germany, however, was that in the 1970s and 1980s other sectors – the automobile, chemical, pharmaceutical and mechanical engineering industries – underwent a profound restructuring process but emerged overall in a much stronger position as regards the division of labour in a globalizing industrial world.

At the same time as this long decline in manufacturing jobs was taking place in all three countries, there was also a shift in the balance of the different industrial sectors within each country. Table 1.2 shows a snapshot of the six industries with the highest employment in Britain, France and Germany in 1989. It shows the six main sectors employing the majority of industrial workers in the three countries. The three largest sectors in West Germany (electrical engineering,

Table 1.2   Industrial sectors by number of employees in 1989 (in thousands)

	West Germany	Britain	France
Electrical engineering	1,195 (1.)	491 (2.)	528 (2.)
Mechanical engineering	1,141 (2.)	485 (3.)	448 (3.)
Automobile	982 (3.)	289 (6.)	358 (5.)
Chemical (inc. pharmaceuticals)	635 (4.)	331 (5.)	312 (6.)
Food	633 (5.)	568 (1.)	611 (1.)
Textile and garment	442 (6.)	467 (4.)	379 (4.)
As percentage of total employed in manufacturing	5,028 = 60.2%	2,732 = 53.8%	2,637 = 54.1%

Source: Data for Britain and Germany from Mary O'Mahony and Karin Wagner, *Wechselndes Glück: eine Studie zum Produktivitätswachstum der britischen und deutschen Industrie über drei Jahrzehnte*, Berlin, 1994, pp. 59 and 60. Data for France from *Annuaire statistique de la France 95* (1990), Tableau 2.01: 'Population active', p. 105.

mechanical engineering and automobile) employed three times as many people as the same sectors in France and Britain. This reflects the sustained export strength of these West German industries. The only industries to have a similar employment rate in all three countries were the textile, clothing and food industries. In France and Britain just as in Germany, these three classic consumer goods industries had survived as major employers after the dramatic reduction of jobs in the steel, shipbuilding and mining industries.

The table shows clearly that certain key sectors accounted for most industrial employment during this period of change. Although the car industry always attracts public attention, in this case it does not win first place. This goes to the electrical industry, which employs many more workers. In all three countries, workers continued to produce household appliances – washing machines, vacuum cleaners, tumble dryers, colour televisions, video equipment and telephones – mainly for the European domestic market, but also for export to third countries.

How does this picture from 1989 fit into the developmental process of industrial restructuring that took place during the three decades from 1970 to 2000? There seem to me to be eight aspects that stand out.

(1) In all three countries, the traditional industries of coal mining and iron and steel production lost their key roles in terms of both the national economy and the structure of employment (see figure 1.1).

Figure 1.1 Bernd and Hilla Becher, *Blast furnace, Homecourt, Lorraine, France*, 1980.

Bernhard and Hilla Becher are the most important contemporary artists to have dealt with deindustrialization. As early as the 1960s, they understood industrial buildings as something that would disappear. They documented countless factory buildings, especially in West Germany, France and Britain. Their photographs anticipated the romantic view that would later characterize the perception of industrial culture. The fact that there are practically no workers to be seen in their photographs was not for artistic reasons but reflects a socio-historical fact – they, too, belong to the past.

In Britain and Germany, another traditionally important sector also disappeared, namely the shipbuilding industry, which was highly concentrated in certain regions.

(2) It was the industries that produced first for the national domestic market and then the European domestic market that held their ground in all three countries. These were the food industry, the manufacture of electrical appliances and the clothing and textile industries, though with considerable job losses. The food and drink industries benefited from the further growth in the European agricultural sector, resulting from its industrialization, which occurred behind the safety barriers of European agricultural protectionism. At the same time, the emergence of the European single market and the establishment first of supermarkets and then of discounters profoundly changed the market conditions in this sector. It remained predominantly characterized by small and medium-sized enterprises, in spite of the fact that here as elsewhere after the 1990s a few large multinationals, such as Kraft, Danone, Nestlé and Unilever, became market leaders. The corporate concentration in the food trade allowed some large companies to gain a dominant position in the market and increasingly control production plants.

(3) The automobile industry, which had expanded continuously in all three countries in the 1960s and 1970s, subsequently entered a phase of considerable economic fluctuation, during which there was a radical restructuring not only of production processes but also of the range and marketing of products.[26] With the exception of the area of luxury and niche products (sports and racing cars), the British automobile industry lost its independence and since the 1990s has been almost completely dominated by Japanese, American, French and German corporations and their suppliers.[27] Britain, however, remained an important location for those automobile groups which wanted to extend their international presence as, in addition to the American groups Ford and General Motors (GM), Nissan, Toyota and BMW had been producing there since the 1980s. In France, the domestic automobile industry, whose success was mainly restricted to the home market, lost a considerable market share to its Japanese and German competitors, but was able to maintain its position in the 1980s through appropriate mergers and restructuring. Peugeot first merged with Citroën, then bought up Chrysler Europe at the end of the 1970s, and on this basis consolidated its position in second place behind Renault among France's carmakers. Renault, as a state-owned company, coped with the recessions of 1973–4 and 1980–2 by forging strategic alliances with Fiat and Peugeot,

and then secured its status through the acquisition of the Japanese car company Nissan. As a result, the French car companies Peugeot and Renault outstripped their British and Italian competitors and successfully placed themselves among the world market leaders at the beginning of the twenty-first century. This success also meant that France remained an important location for the components industry. By means of new acquisitions and start-ups, companies such as Valeo (75,000 employees in twenty-four countries) and Faurecia (50,000 employees) moved up in the early 2000s to join the circle of multinational suppliers to the small group of global automobile concerns.[28] The German automobile industry was even more successful in holding its own during the turbulent years of restructuring; indeed, in the late 1970s it attained a leading international position in the high-price segment of the market, especially in competition with the Japanese automobile companies. Three West German companies, Volkswagen (VW), Daimler and BMW, survived the mergers and acquisitions of this phase, while other heavyweights, Opel-GM, Ford and Peugeot, retained a presence in Germany as an industrial location.

(4) In all three countries, the chemical and pharmaceutical industries remained competitive. They were characterized by large market leaders (BASF, Bayer, Hoechst and Merck in Germany; Rhône-Poulenc, Roussel Uclaf and L'Oréal in France; Glaxo Wellcome and SmithKline Beecham – combined as GlaxoSmithKline from 2000 – ICI, Courtaulds, BP and Shell Chemicals in Britain).They had already grown into multinationals before 1970 and were particularly interested in acquiring shares in the growing and high-turnover North American market.[29] Following the recessions of 1973–4 and 1980–2, which drove up energy costs and intensified international competition, the chemical industry experienced a cost and sales crisis in its traditionally strong production segments such as petroleum-based chemicals and synthetic fibre production. This resulted in plant closures, production relocations and staff cuts. The 1980s and 1990s saw considerable changes in corporate structures in all three countries, with mergers, hostile takeovers and the break-up of large corporate groups. In the end, the historically evolved concept of integrated chemical parks (*Verbundchemie*), which had profited from being able to apply chemical research on-site, was largely abandoned in favour of new sub-sectors such as life sciences, basic chemicals and paint production. These were technologically more specialized and economically independent. The only notable exception to this was BASF.[30]

(5) The only country where the machine tool and plant engineering sector survived the recessions and intensified international competition was Germany. If British and French suppliers survived at all, it was only in specialized niches.[31] The international expansion of the West German machine tool company TRUMPF, described briefly above, exemplifies the rise of the so-called hidden champions.[32] These were world market leaders in highly specialized products, often machines for very different industrial sectors. In many cases, they were medium-sized companies, many of which were (and still are) family-owned.

(6) Not least as a result of government orders, but also of exports, the defence and aerospace industries consolidated in all three countries, all of which were and still are prominent members of NATO.

(7) At the beginning of the twenty-first century, the proportion of industrial workers employed in companies with fewer than 500 employees was higher than thirty years earlier. In all three countries, this proportion increased for small and medium-sized businesses. By the end of the 1970s, the long growth phase of large factories with more than 1,000 employees had stopped. Table 1.3 shows this trend for Britain and Germany.

No corresponding figures are available for the 1970s and 1980s in France. However, data for the 1990s show a similar trend with

Table 1.3 Distribution of industrial employees in Britain and Germany by company size (as percentage of employees)

	10–19	20–49	50–99	100–99	200–499	500–999	>1,000
	Britain						
1973	3.3	8.0	8.9	11.8	20.3	15.2	32.6
1985	5.7	10.3	10.7	14.1	21.0	15.0	23.0
1994	6.8	13.3	13.0	16.3	22.3	12.7	15.7
	Germany						
1972	9.3	8.8		30.2		13.9	37.8
1984		8.5	9.8	12.1	18.7	13.3	37.5
1994	3.4	21.2		47.8		31.3	

Source: My own calculations based on Statistisches Jahrbuch für die Bundesrepublik Deutschland 1976, pp. 234–5; Statistisches Jahrbuch für die Bundesrepublik Deutschland 1987, pp. 176–7; Statistisches Jahrbuch 1996 für die Bundesrepublik Deutschland, pp. 206–7; Annual Abstracts of Statistics 113 (1976), p. 169; 123 (1987), p. 123; 131 (1995), p. 115.

an overall larger share of industrial employees in small and medium-sized companies (categorized here as between ten and 199 employees). Between 1990 and 2000, their share in industrial employment increased by a further 1.4 per cent to reach 54.3 per cent.[33]

The reasons for this trend reversal away from large factories were the same in all three countries. Rationalization caused workforces to shrink, the outsourcing of production units and departments reduced the need for capital and labour to be combined and concentrated in one place, and new businesses rarely expanded beyond the medium employment range. Experiments with reorganization at company level also shifted individual decision-making and partial responsibilities to departments or subsidiaries, so that in the overall picture the large factory lost significance as an abstract point of reference for industrial labour relations. Smaller and medium-sized enterprises found suitable niches more easily by adapting quickly and smoothly to changing demand – this was true for the furniture and textile and clothing industries. Sectors with a traditionally high share of small and medium-sized companies gained in relative importance – one example is mechanical engineering in Germany.[34] And finally, the management strategies of large companies with their concepts of lean production and outsourcing led to an increase in the number and volume of orders and thus to an increase in the size of the companies supplying them.

(8) At the same time, however, the concentration of capital continued to grow. Large corporations, holding companies or foreign financial investors increasingly became the owners of formerly independent small and medium-sized enterprises during these decades. Many factories existed only as subsidiaries of large multinational corporations or were owned by holding companies and their management was by no means autonomous in terms of their entrepreneurial strategies. However, the complexity of capital relations and ownership makes this process less transparent, and as a consequence the statistical data from the different countries can hardly be compared in this respect. For France, official economic statistics show a clear trend towards higher concentration between 1983 and 2000, but with significant differences between sectors. On the one hand, there were highly concentrated industries such as automobile manufacture. Here, the four companies with the highest volume of sales employed 50 per cent of the total workforce in 1983 and 67 per cent in 2000. Similar figures can be found for the aviation and electronics industries. Other sectors, however, were far less concentrated. In mechanical engineering, the four companies with the

highest sales volume employed only 9 per cent of the total workforce in 1983 and 16 per cent in 2000. In the textile and clothing industry, the share of the four companies with the highest sales volume was still below 10 per cent in 2000.[35] Comparable figures are also available for Germany. Its Federal Statistical Office calculated the share of employees in the six largest companies per sector, revealing that as well as highly concentrated sectors such as the automobile industry (56 per cent of employees in 1984, 57.5 per cent in 2000), in the mechanical engineering, textile and clothing industries east of the Rhine it was medium-sized companies that were the norm.[36] This was the beginning of the age of interconnected companies which saw the emergence of complex hierarchies of suppliers and end manufacturers, firms delivering services and large corporations. In addition, the new business philosophy of shareholder value ensured that clearly separated profit centres were created whose profit rates could be calculated precisely and were no longer hidden in the overall accounts of a large company. Naturally this overarching trend continued to be crucially underpinned by the material and technical conditions of industrial production.

The application of new technologies in manufacturing

The most significant technological advance during the decades we are studying was the spread of computer-based communication and data storage. This in turn enabled ever greater numbers of numerical control (NC) systems in ever smaller formats. The key quality of the new information technology was not only that it opened up major opportunities for rationalization in manufacturing, but also that it boosted far-reaching structural changes in the organization of industrial companies as well as in their relations with customers, suppliers and authorities.

Although, as we know, the origins of the computer date back to the nineteenth century, it was the development of microelectronics and the emergence of the microprocessor in 1971 that triggered the innovations in information technology that have since then rapidly and fundamentally changed the overall framework of industrial enterprises.[37] The next stage of development was reached in the mid-1990s with the spread of the intranet and internet, which resulted in further links both within and between companies.

The list of technical innovations in these decades is long. The new industrial robots that replaced welders, painters and assembly workers in the production halls and packers and warehouse workers in the food and beverage industry were undoubtedly spectacular. In 1974, the Swedish manufacturer ASEA presented the first industrial painting robot to be controlled entirely by microprocessors (see figure 1.2).

The technology-related innovations in the departments for planning and design were equally spectacular. Computer-aided design profited from the IT revolution of the period and within a few years migrated from mainframe computers via the workstations of the early 1980s to personal computers (PCs). Gradually, more aspects of the design process in manufacturing were 'computerized', moving from geometric modelling through calculations and simulations to the point of handover to manufacturing and production. Just one example of the extraordinarily rapid acceleration in this field since the 1980s is the French aerospace company Dassault. They had begun developing computer-aided design programmes in 1967, had risen to market leader by 1981 and had been marketing their own programme Catia in collaboration with the US market leader IBM since 1981. Compared to 400 Catia users in 1985, this figure had leapt to 4,000 ten years later.[38] At the same time, the introduction of NC and CNC (computer numerical control) machines also fundamentally changed the types of machines used in industrial manufacturing. With the aim of modern control technology, these new machines were able to automatically produce components with very high precision, even in the case of complex shapes. This gradually reduced the need for constant supervision of production by auxiliary staff on many production lines. Soon only a few workers were employed directly at the machines, since the control systems made it feasible even for quality control to be integrated fully automatically into the production process. The complexity of the monitoring and maintenance tasks increased accordingly, as did the need for skilled workers trained in the use of these machines. The results of surveys for the West German machinery and capital goods industries show that while at the end of the 1970s these new machines were used only in a maximum of 10 per cent of companies, they then spread rapidly in the 1980s. A first saturation threshold was reached in the mid-1990s with a level of more than 70 per cent in the capital goods industry and over 80 per cent in mechanical engineering.[39]

The opportunities provided by this new electronically controlled and supported machine production also facilitated the numerous and varied product innovations that coincided with the waves of

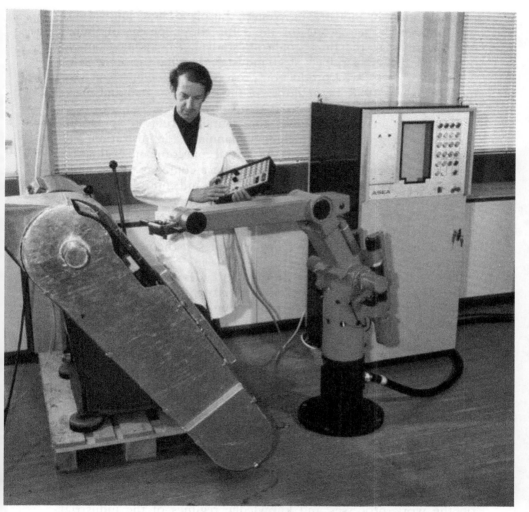

Figure 1.2 Photograph of the first industrial robot from ASEA (later ABB) with inventor Björn Weichbrodt.

In 1973, the Swedish company ASEA presented its first industrial robot to the public. It was developed by the engineer Björn Weichbrodt, seen in this photograph. A microprocessor from the US semiconductor manufacturer Intel enabled its control. In the following decades, automation penetrated more and more areas of industrial production, resulting in unskilled workers losing their former key role.

rationalization in industry in Western Europe. These innovations were immensely significant for the future development of industrial locations in the three countries studied. A striking example of this is the crisis-ridden steel industry. During the long sales crisis of 1974–85, steel production processes were comprehensively modernized. In 1988, the majority of the 2,500 patented and registered grades of steel were no more than six years old.[40]

As I have mentioned above, the digital revolution spread to every area of a company, including planning, administration and marketing. One key element was the central collection and evaluation of all data, which in turn made it easier for a company to introduce rationalization measures throughout. Checks and controls conducted by means of coding systems and digital registration of all operational processes led to the further expansion and standardization of the documentation system. Quality standards, such as ISO 9000, left a permanent imprint on the everyday workings of the new digitalized factories.[41]

The technical revolutions of these decades ultimately created entirely new opportunities for 'flexible automation'. It soon became evident that the structuring of production processes and company communication was not determined by the specifications of the new technologies. On the contrary, a 'disconnection between technology, company organization and work structures' could be observed.[42] The new information and communication technologies allowed not only a further division of work processes according to Taylor's blueprint but also the integration of tasks and functions. This meant that the range of solutions in which computer-assisted machines and systems could be implemented was correspondingly wide and the consequences for the structure of the actual tasks carried out by industrial workers similarly complex and diverse. This is one reason why chapters 5 and 6 will examine in more detail the lasting effects that the digital revolution had on the work processes and knowledge regimes of the industrial worlds of Western Europe. This wide range of options offered by the technical revolution was exploited in very different ways by the industrial companies in the three countries we are using as examples here. In many cases, they were driven by a pragmatic 'trial and error' approach. There was also a wide variety in the use of technology within the different sectors, determined by various factors: the style and tradition of cooperation between the workforce and management; the market position of the company; the quality profile of the workforce; and sector-specific traditions of work organization. Any contemporary predictions about major trends and developments, therefore, proved to be correspondingly unreliable.

The effects of digital information technologies were clearer at the level of company organization. Many companies used the fact that it was now possible to combine greater flexibility in production with a better control of costs as a way of countering the problem of persistent losses or low profits. The ability to communicate and to share information more quickly in turn facilitated the outsourcing of entire departments or stages of production. The introduction of computer technology put both the vertical hierarchies in companies and their horizontal functional divisions to the test. In practice, the use of IT facilitated the process of outsourcing outlined above as well as the transfer of profit expectations to individual plants or parts of the company. This is a particularly clear illustration of how closely expectations of capital return by equity owners on the financial markets are connected with the technological capacity to link entire 'value chains' across national borders.

Pressures of competition and prices forced all Western European industrial sectors to outsource certain stages of production and to purchase intermediate products and services. This was of strategic importance for the further development of their own product range and production processes and was significantly influenced by the use of information technology. The development was particularly spectacular in the automobile industry, where it is also very well documented. By the early 2000s, for example, 93 per cent of the auto industry was already using electronic data interchange, especially for handling orders between suppliers and manufacturers. This meant that the major suppliers were able to shorten their delivery times for the required parts and the manufacturers were able to further reduce their own warehouse stocks.[43] Whereas at the beginning of the 1970s the large car manufacturers still created about 60 per cent of their value added in-house, at the beginning of the new century this figure had sunk to between 20 and 30 per cent. As a result, the component industry became more important. In the process, it was divided hierarchically into companies that supplied the automobile companies directly and those in the second tier that mainly worked for one or more of the component companies that had direct access to the automobile manufacturers.[44]

In summary, the trend towards medium-sized industrial enterprises is closely related to the revolution in information and communication technologies. It has enabled the emergence of the kind of corporate hierarchies, corporate networks and corporate clusters found in the automobile industry, all of which work closely together in the process of manufacturing complex industrial products. This led to the companies making increasing mutual demands on product quality, delivery punctuality and financial solvency, as well as on reliability and quality control.

Monetary stability, industrial subsidies and privatization

From the mid-1970s onwards, technological change together with the crises in the established industrial sectors and large companies created a variety of problems. The most serious was the persistently high rate of unemployment. All three countries had to react to this at the level of their national and regional economic policies, since regulations at the European level by no means replaced the need for national or local action. In any case, the necessary regulatory competencies were not assigned to the European Commission until the creation of the common European Economic Area in the 1990s.[45] From the outset, governments were faced with the dilemma of finding a balance between the long- and medium-term aims of their economic policy, the short-term need for stable industrial policies and the short- and medium-term need for intervention in social policy. These conflicting goals already explain why the three countries repeatedly sought pragmatic solutions. In practice, however, the economic policies of the Western European governments were incorporated in the reorientation and adjustments they were making to their programmes in the hope that they would help overcome the structural problems of the 'great inflation' of the long 1970s, comprising high inflation, the recessions of 1973–4 and 1980–2, rising unemployment and growing national debt.[46]

In all three countries, there were changes of government during the years of recession from 1980 to 1982, and at the time they were also perceived as a change of course in economic and industrial policies. In Britain, the Tory election victory in May 1979 marked the beginning of a long period of Conservative government (until 1997) which brought about a radical and lasting change in economic policy, especially in the Thatcher era (until 1990). In her programme, the new prime minister promised a break with previous practices in economic and monetary policy by declaring that inflation would no longer be fought by wage agreements and price controls, but by a policy of making money scarce and more expensive. Margaret Thatcher and her cabinet took further steps to make it quite clear that they were serious about change when their government refused any further government assistance for industrial companies during the crisis and announced mass privatization of the public sector.

In France, there was a change of political power just under two years after Britain. In spring 1981, the socialist François Mitterrand was elected president of France and in the subsequent parliamentary elections the left-wing parties won the majority. A change of economic system, which had been repeatedly anticipated since 1968, seemed imminent. While the British government was announcing the privatization of its state-owned enterprises, numerous large companies in France were being nationalized, with the effect that 20 per cent of industrial workers were now directly or indirectly employed by the state. This change, however, coincided with the worldwide economic slump of 1980–2, which hit France's industry and economy extremely hard. Companies went bankrupt, plants closed and production declined, all of which led to mass layoffs and catapulted the official unemployment figures to more than 2 million (as of December 1982).[47] At the same time, the situation on the foreign commercial markets deteriorated dramatically, the franc had to be devalued three times and the French foreign trade deficit doubled within a year.[48] What happened during this crisis explains to a certain extent why the economic and social policy of the early 'leftist' years remained nothing more than a brief episode in many respects, and why at the end of March 1983 it was quickly revised and redirected towards a policy of strict austerity and the stabilization of the French franc. However, this meant that the basis for any expansive industrial policy was destroyed and, even more than before, the recent nationalizations had the same effect as preservation subsidies.

Germany experienced its change of government in 1982 when the FDP (Free Democrats) left the then social–liberal coalition government and entered into a new coalition with the CDU/CSU (Christian Democrats), who, much like the British Tory government, were to remain in power for a long time (until 1998). However, the change of chancellor from Helmut Schmidt to Helmut Kohl had already been preceded by a prolonged dispute within the social–liberal coalition over the priorities of economic and social policy, which had led to cuts in the welfare budget and shifts in industrial policy.

For all three of these new governments, the monetary framework for their industrial policy changed. With the high inflation that began in the late 1960s, the system of fixed exchange rates with the US dollar as the reserve currency had collapsed. The German Bundesbank and several other central banks enforced the primacy of monetary stability as early as 1974, joined by the US Federal Reserve in 1979, and thus halted a long period of inflation. Annual inflation rates had reached double figures in France and Britain and had become the most pressing problem for economic and monetary policy.[49] Rising interest rates and high exchange rates for the US dollar had been massively affecting the profit margins of industrial companies since the early 1980s, with a variety of consequences. Both the extent and the impact of the first surge of deindustrialization that took place from the late 1970s to the mid-1980s were influenced significantly by differences in the three countries' monetary and economic policy frameworks.

Until the introduction of the euro in 1999 and its entry into circulation in 2002, the competitive strength of British, French and German industrial enterprises remained dependent on the exchange rate of their national currencies and thus on the monetary policy of their governments and national central banks. Between 1979 and 1983, in particular, changes in monetary policy had a considerable impact on the ability of industrial enterprises to compete on international and European markets. The position of British companies in the 1980–2 recession, for example, was exacerbated by the strict anti-inflationary course pursued by the Bank of England since the Thatcher government came to power. It increased their borrowing costs and made British industrial products more expensive on the export markets because of the rising value of sterling. Between 1981 and 1983, France, in complete contrast, pursued a Keynesian policy of stimulating demand, combining it with widespread nationalization, costly social reforms and multiple devaluations of the franc. This policy was, however, unsuccessful due to the economic crisis and hostile monetary policies of its neighbours, especially the German and Swiss federal banks. The French version of 'Keynesianism in one country' failed and with it the attempt at an ambitious industrial and technological policy led by nationalized industries. After barely two years, the socialist government was forced to radically change its own monetary policy.

West German industry was heavily export-oriented and survived the recession of 1980–2 better than its French and British competitors. This was against the background of a much calmer monetary policy environment as the German Bundesbank had been sustaining a policy of currency stability since the mid-1970s. This brought with it the pressure to adjust. The monetary policy conditions had to be complied with by all industrial enterprises – they were forced to adjust their cost structures to the new stricter credit conditions and at the same time offer competitive prices. 'Quality production' and 'high-tech' became the mantras of industrial management under these new conditions – with varying success, as we have seen.

What kind of success did these changes of government in the three countries lead to around industrial policy? Any comparison first has to consider the different conditions on which the respective economic policy interventions were founded. In France and Britain in the mid-1970s, sizeable sections of industrial production were publicly owned. In France, this was mainly the mining industry, which had been nationalized in 1945, and Renault (cars), SNECMA and Aérospatiale (both aerospace). On the other side of the Channel, it was also the mining industry that was nationalized, but in the industrial crises of the 1960s and 1970s other sectors were added, including most of British steel production (since 1967), part of the shipbuilding industry and, in the end, Rolls-Royce and British Leyland, the choicest companies in the national aerospace and automobile industries. In Germany, on the other hand, the share of state-owned industrial enterprises was very small: only the steel group Salzgitter AG, the energy concern VEBA and public shares in VW. The state-owned companies in Britain managed to incur increasing losses, so that objectives set by industrial policy repeatedly came up against the limits set by fiscal policy requirements. This also became a problem in France after the second wave of nationalization initiated by the Mauroy government. The nationalization of large corporations in the electrical, chemical and steel industries was linked to far-reaching industrial policy aims united under the slogan *redéploiment industriel*. This followed Gaullist industrial policy and was intended to create large companies that would be technological innovators and international leaders.[50]

In fact, in all three countries during this period, the main government subsidies went to the industries in crisis – steel, mining, shipbuilding and (in Britain) vehicle construction – either as direct investment in the nationalized companies or, as in Germany, as financial assistance for private corporations. In the first instance, these preservation subsidies were used to realize socially acceptable strategies for plant closures and mass redundancies, and only rarely did they serve their industrial policy aim of achieving long-term stability. This situation prepared the ground for the state to withdraw from its industrial

41

enterprises. Once again, the Thatcher government led the way. It had been advocating privatization since 1979 and was the first to adopt it as a policy. This created completely new perspectives for the future of the state-owned industries – British Steel, the National Coal Board and British Leyland – and the replacement of the directors of these companies was designed to make this clear. At the end of December 1980, the Scot Ian MacGregor was recruited from the US private sector to be appointed head of British Steel by the industry secretary, Keith Joseph. MacGregor introduced a rigorous restructuring programme which resulted in the loss of 55,000 jobs within a year but led to the successful privatization of the remaining plants. He was subsequently appointed head of the national coal industry (National Coal Board) in 1983 to prepare it for privatization, a process that was not completed until 1994.[51] Given the high level of demand on the investment markets, other companies were privatized in the 1980s in quick succession: British Aerospace (1981), the publicly owned shipyards (1985), Rolls-Royce (1987) and British Steel (1988).[52] The privatization of state-owned enterprises then also became the focus of 'modern' economic policy in France and Germany. State-owned companies were floated on the stock exchange or shares were put up for sale. In Germany, a corresponding law was passed in 1985 and by the end of the decade had led to the sale of federal shares in VW and Salzgitter AG and the privatization of the VIAG Group.[53] In France, the privatization wave began a year later and continued until the end of the 1990s. It affected Saint-Gobain (privatized in 1987), Rhône-Poulenc (1993), Thomson-Brandt (1998/2000), Usinor-Sacilor (1995) and Renault (partial privatization in 1999). Whereas in 1985 about 20 per cent of French industrial workers were employed in public companies, fifteen years later the figure was only 2 per cent. The change of course was striking and lasting – the state withdrew from any direct entrepreneurial role in industry. Again, Britain led the way, with government spending on industry-related research and direct investment in the 1980s and 1990s falling below the levels in Germany and France,[54] where the political authorities at national and regional level continued their policies of subsidizing industry and investing in technology. Finally, in all three countries, European regional and technology support entered the scene in the 1990s as an important new actor in industrial policy, replacing or complementing national and/or regional aid programmes.

This brief overview makes it clear that the British, French and German governments initially applied their economic policies in very different ways to pursue their own objectives, until from the mid-1980s onwards commonalities again prevailed in the shape of privatization and the abandonment of industry-focussed investment programmes. In Britain, the Conservative government's neoliberal shock therapy between 1979 and 1982 led to a market shakeout that left gaps in the national industrial structure. These were not filled by domestic industry but by imports from abroad. In short, deindustrialization in Britain was largely the result of the strategic decisions of an economic policy that saw the country's future in services, especially in the field of international finance. By the end of the 1990s, the birthplace of the industrial revolution was considered a model of a post-industrial national economy with spectacular growth rates, falling unemployment and a 'modern' industrial structure. In France and Germany, in contrast, the deindustrialization process in central sectors of the national economy was initially slowed down by the governments' policy of channelling substantial subsidies into the affected industries. This was originally a purely defensive strategy against plant closures and mass redundancies and was often only effective in the short or medium term. After its costly failure, national economic interests persuaded both countries to invest considerable sums in the promotion and support of industrial technology projects and so-called future technologies. In summary, it can be said that on close scrutiny 'deindustrialization' at this time was by no means a uniform trend leading each of the three countries in question in a direct and straightforward process towards a post-industrial service society. Rather, it was a process that at least partially reinforced the national differences between the British, French and German economies.

The path to financial market capitalism

The above comparison of economic macro-developments in Britain, France and Germany has already shown that during our investigation period their industries were affected not only by national economic and monetary policies, but also by widespread radical change which forced practically all aspects of entrepreneurial activity to adjust. Deindustrialization was part of a historic period of upheaval in which the rules of capitalism changed worldwide. Economists and economic historians agree in interpreting the 1970s as a phase in which the order established at international and national levels after World War II was in crisis.[55] Although descriptions may vary in their emphasis, there is a broad consensus that this crisis influenced not only monetary and trade policy regulations on the international level but also basic patterns of labour relations, business organization and the political representation of interests on the national level. What emerged was a new variety of capitalism which, following the demise of the socialist economies and the rise of the industrialized Asian nations, was established on a much broader international scale than its predecessor.

Historians are inherently sceptical of attempts to divide the history of capitalism into neatly separate phases. But there is much to be said for distinguishing contemporary capitalism and its formative decades from its earlier cousins, simply because the fundamental rules for investing capital and generating profit are no longer the same. The new system, which is pivotal to capital accumulation, has been given different names, but in the following I will draw on ideas explored in my book *Nach dem Boom* (*After the Boom*),[56] co-authored with Anselm Doering-Manteuffel, and adopt the concept 'digital financial market capitalism', developed by authors such as Paul Windolf, Christoph Deutschmann and Jürgen Beyer.[57] This new form of capitalism began to emerge in the 1980s, first in the US and then in Britain, before it reached other Western European countries, but it only slowly began to become part of the European and international context in the course of the 1990s and was not fully established until the beginning of the twenty-first century.[58] New players such as investment funds, analysts and business consulting firms began to promote the interests of capital owners, or more specifically shareholders, who wanted to maximize returns on their capital, enjoy greater transparency and tighten controls on large companies on the stock exchange. A prominent role in the implementation of this model was played by the so-called institutional investors on the international capital markets. These were the managers of private capital, on the one hand, and public capital investments, for example from the oil returns of the OPEC countries or from American pension funds, on the other. The establishment of the enlightened shareholder value principle as the main pillar of entrepreneurial action had far-reaching consequences. This was because business success now depended on the exposure and dismantling of opaque mutually dependent structures built up between large companies or individual companies and their house banks and main shareholders. Success also depended on business branches making their profitability, or lack of it, transparent, but above all it depended on the elevation of the share price to become the gold standard of corporate philosophy. From now on, companies had to compete on the 'stage of creditworthiness'.[59]

44

Markets emerged on which entire companies were traded, and listed companies in particular began to align themselves with the new standards of the international financial market, above all by forecasting anticipated rates of return for their shareholders. Even the large industrial companies gradually had to adapt to the capital markets, where long-term profit expectations based on previous successes alone were no longer sufficient to satisfy capital investors and shareholders. Projected rates of return in the short and medium term – that is, the principle of profit maximization – increased in importance across all industries, with a direct impact on their own financing options. The risk of hostile takeovers and the division of companies into profitable and non-profitable components became a potent weapon of this financial market capitalism, whose very existence was enough to push many into adapting to its rules – sweetened by exorbitant rises in executive salaries and bonus payments (see figure 1.3).

Such a shareholder value economy needed a framework of monetary and economic policy conditions to enable the necessary masses of capital to be mobilized. Growing prosperity in the Western world and in oil-exporting countries had stimulated the flow of capital since the 1970s, and by the 1980s the investment capital of so-called institutional investors in the US had already quadrupled.[60] The market model gained momentum properly in the 1990s and caused listed investment assets to swell twenty-two-fold. It took three decades for financial markets to become fully internationalized and above all for the controls and barriers faced by cross-border capital investments to be dismantled, and it required political approval. At the same time, the established structures of industrial capitalism encountered by the pioneers and advocates of this new economic system had strikingly distinctive national characteristics, at least in the countries studied here. They also included old-school business types, such as the 'captains of industry', who could not all be replaced overnight by a new generation of managers completely versed in financial market capitalism.[61]

Both the extent to which this globally expanding financial market capitalism changed the existing national differences within capitalist economies and the direction of this change are highly disputed by academic experts in political economics. Representatives of the *variety-of-capitalism* approach postulate that even at the end of the period of upheaval examined here, there were still nationally specific types of capitalism somewhere along the scale between the two ideal-typical poles of liberal and coordinated market economies.

Figure 1.3 Josef Ackermann, CEO of Deutsche Bank, making the victory sign in 2004.

On the fringes of the Mannesmann trial, which took place in 2004, two of the accused, Josef Ackermann, CEO of Deutsche Bank AG, and Klaus Esser, CEO of Mannesmann AG, met. Grinning, the banker Ackermann made the victory sign. The accusation was that illegal bonus payments had been made in the course of the hostile takeover of the former industrial group Mannesmann by the British mobile phone company Vodafone. The photograph quickly became an iconic image for the financial market capitalism of the 2000s, at least in Germany.

They emphasize the different ways in which markets, businesses, the state and society were linked at the national level. Britain and the US were seen as the model countries of a primarily market-oriented liberal model, while France, Germany and Japan were still associated with coordinated capitalism. Others, by contrast, believe that at least since the beginning of the twenty-first century, it was financial market capitalism itself that made this typology redundant and helped the liberal market model to gain the upper hand.[62] Representatives of regulation theory, however, rightly point out, first, that the dichotomy of liberal versus coordinated market capitalism does not capture the diversity of types of capitalist economic regimes but also, second, that international financial market capitalism has not become the new global model.[63] This is particularly true for industrial production, whose transformation in this period led to very different forms of cooperation between the main actors – state, society and business – all of whom had to react to the changing markets. This regulation theory approach emphasizes the importance of historically evolved institutions and attitudes and is, as such, still the most compatible with the socio-historical perspective I am developing here.

The country that came closest to the new 'spirit of financial market capitalism' was Britain. Traditionally, links between British industrial companies and the banks were quite weak and capital was not connected between large companies, capital owners and banks across industries, a crucial feature in France and Germany ('*Deutschland AG*') until the mid-1990s. What is decisive for my study is that from the end of the 1980s the new financial market economy took hold of industrial companies with increasing strength and speed and in Germany as in France initially weakened the above-mentioned structures connecting large companies and banks at the national level before finally dissolving them completely. For France and Germany, various studies have identified the years 1995 to 2005 as a phase of concentrated upheaval.[64] In both countries, old-style industrial capitalism was replaced by international capital arrangements in which – as described above – institutional investors often assumed a key role as guardians of investor interests. A major factor for the business strategies of industrial multinationals was the loss of importance of national and European borders. After 1990, it propelled their expansion in international markets and created the demand for investment capital necessary for takeovers or mergers with competitors.

Hostile takeovers are in general an indicator of the spread of the new financial market economy with its strict competition rules.

In Germany, the 1990s marked the beginning of this era. They saw the takeover of Hoesch by Krupp in 1991, the attempted takeover of Krupp by Thyssen in 1997, their eventual merger to form ThyssenKrupp in 1999, and the buyout and break-up of the Mannesmann Group by Vodafone in 1998 (see figure 1.3), to name only the most striking examples. Breaking large companies up and selling lucrative lines of business on the financial markets are also typical symptoms of the new competitive model. In Britain, this strategy was pursued by groups such as ICI, which sold off the profitable pharmaceutical business as a new company, Zeneca, in 1990, and Courtaulds, which separated the production of chemical fibre and textiles also in 1990, and were thus fully in line with the new trend, separating the most profitable or promising divisions from huge conglomerates and marketing them successfully.

This naturally led to the original companies shrinking and in many cases they themselves then became victims of hostile takeovers or were integrated into larger international corporations. This was the case with ICI, which was bought by Akzo Nobel in 2007.[65] However, as we have seen above and empirical studies show, at least for Germany, not everything was swept away by the new rush of money. In the management of industrial groups, there was still room for independent and stubborn business strategies. This is illustrated by the three large West German chemical multinationals Hoechst, Bayer and BASF. Between 1994 and 2001 and in the light of the new conditions, their management boards took very different paths into the future. Hoechst's management decided early on to make a radical break with its own corporate tradition, divided the company into individual divisions and finally created a completely new major international company focussing on pharmaceuticals and food chemistry. Bayer, on the other hand, held on to the concept of an integrated group, but transferred the group management to an independent holding company with six subsidiaries, while BASF in turn concentrated on its core business of chemicals and sold its pharmaceuticals division. All three companies found the necessary capital providers for these transformations.[66]

The findings of sociological studies of the effects of the new shareholder value economy on German companies show that despite the spread of capital market-oriented concepts, there was still room for longer-term innovation-oriented corporate strategies as well as for cooperative labour relations and co-determination. This was the case even if the short-term orientation towards rising returns increased competitive pressure on companies (management as well as workers) and thus further intensified the competition between sites.[67] Technological upheavals and new market situations also increased the entrepreneurial risks, but in return created a need for company cooperation, which in its turn set limits to the exclusive orientation towards short-term profit expectations.[68] In general, managing the tension between the two imperatives of short-term profit maximization and orientation towards longer-term innovation became a primary task of industrial management in the age of digital financial market capitalism. For a social history of industrial work, this basic tension is important in many respects and we will encounter it repeatedly in the following chapters, especially in chapter 7. And not least because of this, it seems to me to be much more appropriate to speak of a phase of technological innovation, strategic reorientation and experimentation in the field of industrial production in Western Europe between 1970 and 2000, which went hand in hand with the establishment of international financial market capitalism.[69] We will see that the established rules of conduct on which industrial capitalism was based in the three countries changed to very differing degrees.

Workers in times of deindustrialization

To conclude this chapter, I would like to take a first look at those who were probably most affected by the developments described so far, namely the workers who were employed in the industrial sector between 1970 and 2000. Even before the recession of 1973–4, jobs had been lost in industries such as coal mining, shipbuilding and the textile industry. But these losses were initially balanced by the creation of new employment opportunities, mostly still in the industrial sector. The loss of industrial jobs after the economic boom, on the other hand, generated mass unemployment, as new jobs were not created at the same pace either in the public sector or in the private service sector. All three countries have carried the spectre of imminent or real mass unemployment with them into the twenty-first century as a legacy of this period of upheaval.

In the decades after World War II, the industrial societies of Western Europe had experienced the 'end of proletarianism'.[70] The industrial labour force, as the largest group of employees in industry, had caught up with the middle classes' standards of social and labour law protection. Thanks to the power of their trade unions, they had fought successfully for higher wages and secured a growing share of the national income. At the beginning of the 1970s, the main elements of this initial position were continuity of employment, a growing share in social consumption and improved access to higher education for their own children, although this developed much more slowly and inconsistently. A minority benefited from the opportunities of upward mobility available during the boom. The conclusion that there was an end of 'proletarianism' referred primarily to the male workforce and their households. It applied to migrant workers, a group that grew rapidly in the decade between 1965 and 1975, and to single mothers in basic industrial jobs only to a much lesser extent. Their wages were still significantly lower than those of middle- or even higher-income groups, they had to put up with high employment risks and had few opportunities for promotion in the workplace. But in most cases these were situations only of relative poverty, as industrial workers had moved further and further away from the zones of absolute poverty.

At the beginning of the 1970s, the 'integration' or 'inclusion' of the industrial workforce was still one of the new fundamental realities of the social, political and economic order in Western Europe. Three decades later, the findings were more complicated and quite different in our three countries. In 2000, many industrial workers, especially skilled workers, still had incomes that ensured them a modest level of prosperity, which meant they tended to be in the middle- rather than the lower-income brackets. The situation for unskilled and semi-skilled workers, however, was very different. Their wage levels stagnated and in 2000 a growing minority were working in precarious or temporary employment, often in unfamiliar new service jobs for which they had no training. The only way for children from blue- and white-collar families with a migration background in particular to find secure jobs with future prospects was along circuitous paths with long periods of marking time. In view of the proliferation of such social situations, the new term that spread across France was *précarité* (precarity). It mainly referred to living situations on the unstable threshold between the shrinking world of industrial jobs and the growing but unreliable world of new services.[71]

In general, after 1973, concerns about jobs, securing living standards and social security returned to a more central position in the everyday lives of a growing number of industrial workers, in which conditions in specific regions and sectors played a decisive role. Where official unemployment statistics climbed to more than 15 or even over 20 per cent, conditions and expectations changed noticeably in the lives of blue- and ordinary white-collar workers. We will examine in more detail in chapter 8 how the social geography of the three countries was profoundly changed by deindustrialization. Regions of outright poverty and areas of urban crisis emerged, where there was an accumulation of unemployment, low wages, poverty and exclusion.

Ultimately, however, there were four categories of workers who were particularly affected by redundancies in all three countries: unskilled manual and white-collar workers, older workers, young people and women, with the former forming the largest group of those made redundant in all three countries. The proportion of unemployed in these groups climbed to a permanent level of well over 10 per cent. Most importantly, many of these workers had to adjust to longer phases of less stable employment and living conditions and to a constant back and forth between temporary employment and unemployment, without the chance of permanent employment, or, if so, only after many years. Unstable employment histories were and are synonymous with risks of exclusion (lower retirement pensions, poorer health care, low-standard housing conditions, and so on), which has increasingly confronted these categories of workers since the 1970s.

Deindustrialization also meant that an entire age cohort, namely male industrial workers over 50, left the labour market prematurely. Since the late 1970s, they had been among the first to be assigned to the new socio-statistical category of the long-term unemployed, even though many of them were soon able to lead more sheltered existences on disability or early retirement pensions. Exclusion from the labour market was final for many of these older industrial workers, especially if they were not skilled workers. The average values of the German Socio-Economic Panel studies speak for themselves: between 1985 and 1995, the proportion of workers (of all levels of qualification) in the over-60 age group who were no longer employed increased from just under 40 per cent to just under 64 per cent, and in the 56 to 60 age group from 14 to 32 per cent.[72] However, being driven out of the labour market did not necessarily lead to poverty or exclusion from other social relations. On the contrary, the 'farewell to the industrial labourer' took place surprisingly quietly in Britain as well as in France and Germany due to the considerable social transfer payments. This is all the more surprising since in all three countries the fight to salvage these classic industrial jobs was waged with considerable effort and public support. I will explore this political protest in chapter 3. However, these defensive battles, which were generally only marginally successful, if at all, were then followed by a retreat, especially among older workers, characterized by resignation, but also partial satisfaction with their material compensation. Early retirement schemes for older workers became an integral part of the social plans agreed between trade unions and management and co-financed by subsidies from public welfare funds. In Germany in particular, these early retirement schemes were often generous,[73] whereas the situation of older workers in Britain was often more precarious. The decline in the employment level of those close to retirement was therefore correspondingly more pronounced in Germany.[74]

The situation was much worse for the third main group of those affected, namely young people in industrial regions. The rapid spread of youth unemployment since the mid-1970s had already aroused the passions of contemporaries.[75] Children from working-class families and migrants were particularly affected, and even higher school-leaving qualifications initially only led many young people into unemployment or into one of the many job creation schemes or training schemes with which governments in all three countries tried to curb youth unemployment in the 1980s and 1990s. The development in Britain was particularly dramatic. At the end of the 1980s, half of 16- to 18-year-olds in Britain were unemployed or in youth training schemes.[76] There was more success in Germany, where the dual vocational training system was able to integrate a much higher number of entrants into the labour market than any measures in Britain or France. The official unemployment rate for young people in Britain and France in the 1980s was regularly above 20 per cent, partly because entry-level jobs in local industries that had been anticipated in the family disappeared with no alternative. In the case of Britain, deindustrialization in numerous regions was accompanied by an extreme decline in or even total loss of industrial training opportunities.

Moving on to the fourth main group, female industrial workers, we have first to note that in all three countries many industrial jobs for women disappeared. The silence around the loss of jobs in all three countries for semi-skilled female textile workers in particular, but also for female workers in the furniture or food industries, is striking. It sheds a harsh light on the continuing discrimination against women in the industrial working worlds of Western Europe, a factor which must be counted as one of its long-term legacies. As a result, the shrinking industrial work environments remained predominantly male. The proportion of women in employment actually decreased: in Britain from 29.75 per cent in 1972 to 27.7 per cent in 2002, in

Germany from 31.3 per cent in 1976 to 29.5 per cent in 2002, and in France from 31 per cent in 1972 also to 29.5 per cent in 2002.[77]

In the absence of industrial employment opportunities, it was and still is above all the new jobs in the private service sector that offered lower-paid work, to unskilled workers in particular, but also to women. Many wives and daughters and of course sons of industrial workers accepted these poorly paid full- or part-time jobs in retail, personal services, call centres and the care sector. In all three countries, industrial worker redundancies were in inverse proportion to the increase of jobs offered in the low-wage sector. This was also partly because industrial companies outsourced any appropriate services from their core plants, which meant that those workers moving to the service sector were subject to worse conditions in terms of labour law and wage agreements. The image of a category of female workers and ordinary employees whose circumstances were decidedly precarious is therefore a central aspect of the socio-political findings of the 1990s in the old industrial regions of the three countries and is part of the overall process of transformation.

The so-called low-wage sector became established in all three countries, first in Britain, only somewhat later in France and last and most belatedly in Germany, which had to wait for the labour market reforms of the first Red (SPD)–Green coalition government to clear the way for it and were thus able to reduce unemployment figures in the long term. When considering this period of upheaval, we have to remember that at the same time numerous new jobs were created at the upper end of the salary scale. Qualified jobs in the service sector, more or less demanding jobs in the IT sector and freelance openings all increased and frequently generated above-average increases in income. Since the spectrum of opportunities was widening and the overall wealth of society was increasing, the new debates about poverty and precarity were essentially debates about the distribution of income, wealth and job opportunities.

The trajectories of professional careers and labour biographies became more confusing overall and for younger people especially, and more precarious than they had been for their parents. After the major expansion phase of public administration in the 1970s had ended, even a socially coveted move into public service with its secure conditions of employment and income became increasingly less of a possibility for many workers and employees in the industrial and private service sectors. At the same time, advancement into the wealth and profit zones of the upper echelons of society proved increasingly elusive for most members of the *classes populaires* or working classes. Social inequality continued to grow in all three countries, while social mobility stagnated or declined.[78] In chapters 6 and 8, I will look in more detail at the consequences this had for the life courses and career paths of industrial workers.

The cumulative dynamics of economic structural change

Taken together, the changes described in this chapter paint a picture of dramatic structural upheaval with far-reaching social consequences. While this upheaval was part of the longer-term shifts in employment and value added in the economies of Western Europe, it was at the same time also closely linked to the rise of financial market capitalism and the technological revolutions of digitalization.

(1) In all three countries, the decline of traditional industries triggered a labour crisis, whose consequences could be felt particularly in the old industrial centres for more than three decades and the burdens of which were borne above all by industrial workers. The socio-spatial, collective-biographical and political-cultural consequences of this 'farewell to the industrial labourer' will be dealt with in more detail in the following chapters. All the evidence suggests that all three countries abandoned this model of society when it came adrift, having lost the stabilizing force of labour relations and social ties in these industries.

(2) In this phase, the deindustrialization of Western Europe was closely linked to a dynamic redistribution of industrial production worldwide. In an increasingly competitive international economy, most industrial sectors had to struggle to maintain or recover their position at the European and international level. Growing competitive pressure was the driving force behind rationalization and the implementation of technology that led to fundamental changes in the organization of Western European industrial businesses in the 1980s and 1990s. These changes in the structure of industrial production also affected the division of labour within companies while at the same time producing new forms of cooperation and competition between them. As a result, industrial labour changed in a process of continuous restructuring, pragmatic adaptation and experimental innovation that was difficult for contemporaries to grasp. These developments are so diverse and open that it is impossible to identify clear trends at the macro level. Instead, we have to look more closely at the forms of division of labour and knowledge organization that became established in the companies and examine the concrete effects

of the restructuring of production on the opportunities for employees to participate. These issues will be explored in chapters 5 and 7.

(3) The rise of financial market capitalism as a new form of capitalism reached the Western European world of industrial business relatively late. Britain had been its pioneer since the late 1980s and there the new rules of financialization also had a deeper and more lasting effect than in France and Germany. Contrary to what contemporaries initially suspected, the new methods of capital procurement, corporate governance and profit planning did not fundamentally change the regimes of industrial production that had been developed and tested since the 1980s. In all three countries, it is more apt to speak of mutual adjustment processes. There was still scope for different types of business organization and long-term business strategies, and trade unions and works councils were still able to assert workers' claims and demands, albeit under more difficult conditions. To determine the concrete effects of this complex situation, however, we need a more precise analysis of the changes in social and labour law which were connected with the two main instruments of change: deindustrialization and financial market capitalism. This is what we will do in chapter 4.

(4) The role of the state changed profoundly. The recessions in 1973–4 and 1980–2 were a severe test of the established routines of state industrial policy. Neither subsidies nor nationalization programmes and economic stimulus packages were able to halt the dynamic of deindustrialization. The early 1980s ushered in a retreat of the state from the industrial sector. The privatization of state- or publicly owned industries, the abandonment of economic stimulus programmes and the orientation of monetary policy towards monetary stability as its primary goal narrowed the scope for state intervention in the industrial sector considerably. What remained were state subsidies for some politically sensitive sectors (armaments, aviation, the nuclear industry) and also some at the regional level. The aim of these regional subsidies was to cushion the social impact of deindustrialization in the former industrial regions. This policy of using public money to help finance companies' social plans and more or less veiled regional social subsidies remained the most important area of state industrial policy in all three countries until the end of the period under study.

(5) The cumulative dynamics of both structural fractures and incremental change triggered a chain of conflicting reactions among those affected and their contemporaries. The combination of seemingly inescapable decline, dynamic technological innovation and growing

international interdependence inspired visions of the future, provoked social protest and produced fierce political and ideological conflict. While remaining aware of long-term processes and their conse-quences, it is important not to lose sight of this level of interpretive struggle and social conflict. It is here that contemporaries argued about the direction in which the dynamics of upheaval should be steered and what opportunities should be used for shaping them. This is the subject of the next chapter.

—— Chapter 2 ——

FAREWELL TO CLASS STRUGGLE AND FIXED SOCIAL STRUCTURES

What we consider to be social reality is to a great extent representation or the product of representation, in all senses of the term.

(Bourdieu)[1]

The numerous upheavals and changes of the period after the
economic boom were inextricably linked to the struggles to interpret
them. Some called for more and faster changes; others criticized or
legitimized their social effects. A social history of industrial working
environments in this period cannot be written without taking a
close look at these struggles to find interpretations. Especially if
this history is to be approached from the experiences of those who
were, if inadvertently, at the centre of these upheavals, particular
attention has to be paid to the interpretive schemes that made mass
redundancies, technical innovation, company relocations and new
management concepts plausible and acceptable.

The spectrum of political language, metaphor and *topoi* used in
this process is broad, with nothing to suggest that there was any
consensus or coherence within the three countries studied here
when naming the social world and changes in it. The social and
economic changes of the time were accompanied by a cacophony
of opinions, world views and arguments, in which a great number
of very different professional groups participated. Five influential
groups of experts had sufficient media coverage, political power
or scientific authority at their disposal to gain support for their
arguments through mass media presence, political influence or
scientific credibility. These were politicians both in government and
opposition; managers and trade unionists; journalists; economists;
and social scientists. However, it is also important to consider

the interpretations of those who were less close to power, such as those writing in the arts and culture sections of newspapers. The official, published interpretations of politicians, journalists and social scientists were often criticized by writers, filmmakers, artists and intellectuals, whose counter-interpretations were most effective when they were incorporated into the arguments of powerful actors with a media presence. In the three democratically constituted economies studied here, all these groups had privileged access to published opinion and their interpretations contributed significantly to popularizing and legitimizing economic interests and political goals. Three groups of actors who are closely connected to our topic, namely trade unionists, politicians and businesspeople, had a considerable influence on the economic and social processes outlined in chapter 1. Finally, we have to mention all those who appeared more as passive consumers of these many different interpretations but depended on their own sense of 'social orientation' (Bourdieu) to integrate changes and novelties into their world of work and everyday lives and to react to them.

Upheavals – a knowledge history

It is not easy to grasp the close links between the production of ideas and the development of society in all its facets. It is all the more difficult because the established methods and theories are notoriously complex and controversial. Studies in conceptual history, discourse analysis and numerous works on political ideas and ideologies offer promising openings but there is no single approach that would even begin to do justice to the complexity of this particular question. One major handicap is that in the history of knowledge and ideas long-term effects are very difficult to capture methodologically, although their impact can hardly be overestimated. A particular problem is that of unverified popular 'knowledge'. This occupies an intermediate space where interpretations, concepts and ideas about the social world which underpin spontaneous explanations in everyday life, in the media and in politics are repeated without recourse to elaborate or verifiable knowledge. This popularly accepted but unverified 'knowledge' is composed of unchallenged notions of social order. I call this kind of unverified popular 'knowledge' *doxa*, following Bourdieu.[2] It usually has a long evolution and lifespan, leaving its traces in metaphors, images and patterns of argumentation characteristically free of context and constantly revised.

A further difficulty is that during the period under study the volume of cultural and scientific production in Britain, France and Germany increased massively. There were more media products, more products of historical and social scientific knowledge, more social data and more political ideas in these three societies than ever before. It would be a hopeless task to try to map the history of ideas in this jungle, which is as fast-moving as it is diverse, and I am not even going to begin to attempt it here. Instead I will concentrate on a comparative analysis of that knowledge and opinion which was directly related to the fundamental structures of the industrial societies studied here and of those new and old notions of order which gave a name to the changes reshaping this industrial world in the last three decades of the twentieth century.

I have identified four principal areas in which social knowledge and opinion are produced. The first to be examined are the contemporary perceptions of social trends that were circulating at the time and so represented something like the *doxa* of the upheavals after the boom. Then I look at specific ideas about the structure and cohesion of 'society'. Such configurative patterns define the space within which political and social actors and their discourses operate. Of particular interest here are the official categories of social statistics in the three countries: that is, the socio-statistical classification into groups according to occupation, income and status. They defined the basic formats in which 'social data' were published. Third, I examine the language of mobilization used primarily by those organizations which represented industrial workers, the 'working class', *les classes populaires*. Fourth and finally, I turn to the cultural production of public images and self-images used to depict both male and female industrial workers in the media. These last two points also serve to make good my intention to put the primary focus of this social history on their experiences and expectations.

Neoliberal discourses of crisis and interpretations of trends

The decades between 1990 and 2008 have quite rightly been labelled the golden age of neoliberalism and as such have been enthusiastically celebrated or harshly criticized.[3] In Britain, France and reunified Germany a cross-party regulatory consensus was based on liberal principles: the privatization of public companies, supply-oriented economic and financial policies, the dismantling of state controls in the financial sector and cost reduction in social and welfare services.

The joint manifesto drawn up by the social democratic party leaders Tony Blair and Gerhard Schröder in 1998 spelt out important principles of this ideological consensus among left-wing parties (see figure 2.1).

This manifesto was attractive at the time because it promised to combine a flexible model of basic welfare support with economic policies that supported the new international financial market capitalism. However, the political consensus of the economic and political elites in Western Europe was deceptive in so far as it disregarded the problems of this model of radical market liberalization and left no room for alternative political models of shaping and interpreting society. There is, therefore, much to be said for heeding the warning of the American historian Daniel T. Rodgers that it is unwise to see the triumph or hegemony of only one ideology where conflicting interpretive patterns are at work and influential contemporary *topoi* may be charged with very different ideologies. Due caution is called for in the search for overarching commonalities and trends. Rodgers finds them for the US society of the long 1980s in the way society and its problems were represented. The use of stable categories such as 'structure', 'institution' or 'history' decreased and instead terms like 'negotiation', 'network' and 'potential' came into fashion.[4] According to Rodgers, society and its structures were replaced in political, media and social science interpretations by individuals and their choices.

Like so many trends from the US, this one made it across the Atlantic and spread to Western Europe. Whether in Britain, France or Germany, the old liberal truism that 'everyone is the architect of their own fortune' made a come-back in the three decades under discussion. Meritocratic interpretive schemes were used more broadly and emphatically than ever to legitimize or excuse both social discrimination and new privileges. Numerous political and cultural idioms confirmed this trend towards a 'liquefaction'[5] and 'subjectification'[6] of the social. It was nourished by orthodox liberal convictions, but also by libertarian tendencies, left-wing socialist criticism of the affluent society and the organized culture of consensus, as well as 'green' and 'alternative' ideas of life and economic activity.

Many of these ideas had been formulated and published long before 1970 but had gained little support. What was decisive for their success, however, was the presence of a diffuse crisis discourse, which became an underlying social motif in the three countries studied here. After the 1970s, a sprawling, omnipresent semantics of crisis unfolded with increasingly blurred contours and diverse fields

Figure 2.1 Bodo Hombach and Peter Mandelson (signing his book *The Blair Revolution*) in the restaurant Pont de La Tour in London, 22 November 1998.

On 8 June 1999, a few days before the European elections, Gerhard Schröder and Tony Blair presented a strategy document in London, 'Europe: The Third Way' (German: 'The Way Forward for Europe's Social Democrats'), written by Bodo Hombach and Peter Mandelson. Known as the Schröder–Blair paper, it contributed significantly to the programmatic realignment of the traditional labour parties. The Labour Party and the SPD now also spoke of cutting state spending and taxes, of flexibility and personal responsibility. This reorientation is also illustrated by a photograph taken a few months earlier showing Bodo Hombach and Peter Mandelson in a London restaurant. Apart from the word 'Labour' on the cover of the book Mandelson is holding, nothing is reminiscent of the labour movement. Instead, the wine rack in the background and the expensive suits reference the new priority of the 'Third Way': 'building a prosperous middle class'.

of application. There was a crisis boom. As well as the 'major crises', such as the crisis of late capitalism or the less frequently lamented 'spiritual crisis' of the current epoch, there was above all an increase in specific social crises: there was a 'crisis in urban development', a 'housing crisis', a 'crisis of the welfare state', a 'transport crisis', an 'education crisis', an 'environmental crisis'. Closely connected to this was a rise in 'crisis managers' and 'crisis experts', some self-appointed, some in high demand. After the beginning of the 1980s, personal topics such as life and mid-life crises were also discussed increasingly in the media. 'Crisis' also became a concept in personal lifestyle and life management. All this culminated in book titles such as *Facing the Crisis*. In France, a 1984 television documentary was even entitled *Vive la crise!*[7] Politicians, economists, social scientists, journalists and intellectuals used the word 'crisis' to lend urgency and pointedness to their messages. After the recession of 1980–2, however, its effect began to wear off and crisis discourses became an increasingly blunt weapon in the war of interpretations.

The confusion spread by the crisis discourses of the time also left its mark on the social sciences. It was not clear either what the 'norm' was from which current conditions could be identified as negative deviations, or what the causes of these regrettable crises were, let alone what could be learnt from them for the future in terms of expectations or guidelines for action. To the same extent that the concept of progress became detached from the concept of crisis as its optimistic companion and lost its overall appeal, the connection between criticism and crisis also disintegrated. In other words, the idea of using political tools or even political planning to find productive, innovative solutions to crisis-like conditions faded or was completely stifled.

It was only in Britain that the rhetoric of crisis endured and became the influential language of political mobilization. The term 'decline' came to mean the forced withdrawal from the British Empire and the continuing contraction of the share of British industrial products on the export and ultimately also the domestic market. But it also had socio-moral connotations when referring to the loss of old virtues and convictions. Much more clearly than in France and Germany, deindustrialization in Britain was therefore also linked to a political narrative that drew its persuasive power from this discourse of decline. It sought and found a way out of the crisis in a return to 'old values', new market freedoms and entirely new economic sectors.[8] It inspired a cross-party consensus in the 1990s that a return to the pre-1979 era in Britain must be avoided at all costs.

Faced with the upheavals described in chapter 1, this discourse of crisis was not in itself able to make any concrete contribution towards shaping economic policy or corporate strategies anywhere in Europe. Instead, some leading ideas were able to assign meaning and significance to concrete economic and social policy decisions. One idea was the 'modernization of the national economy',[9] which comprised concentrating on technical innovation in order to increase productivity by means of rationalization. After 1975, this technology-based argument was closely linked in our three countries to the implementation and rapid advancement of new computer technology in all its forms. This meant that technology was the clearly defined core of the future, even if its specific fields of application and business models were anything but uncontroversial. In all three countries, this interpretive scheme based on modernization theory also outlived the older consensus on progress that had led to the establishment of an industry-based model of the future. Faith in progress had already begun to weaken in the 1970s, but it was now subject to harsh criticism particularly from environmentalists. After 1975, it was increasingly replaced by two historical narratives. The first was based on the above-mentioned model of economic development from Allen Fisher, Colin Clark and Jean Fourastié.[10] It predicted the end of industrial society and its linear transition into a new service society. In the media of all three countries, this narrative was supported by the spread of the three-sector model (agriculture and mining – primary; manufacturing – secondary; service industries – tertiary) in economic statistics and data presentations. This older interpretation was supplemented by a second contemporary narrative, that of globalization, which had been spreading in all three countries since the 1980s and was becoming increasingly significant as a point of reference for controversial socio-political debates.[11] Although there was disagreement about the causalities, facets and consequences of this new far-reaching international development, everyone involved was convinced of its pervasive power. The fact that national societies and their economies were changed by the increasing power of cross-border markets and external influences can be seen as the lowest common denominator of this vague notion of globalization.

Three national perspectives on democratic class conflict

It is remarkable that the range of *doxa* described above can be observed in one way or another in all three countries, although they entered this accelerated period of structural social and economic transformation from extremely different starting points. They were, of course, all industrial societies in which capitalism had been regulated by socio-political measures and state intervention in the economy. These structural similarities, however, obscure the considerable differences in the way these three societies defined themselves. There was a very different approach on the part of the French, British and Germans towards the fact that industrial labour had become one of the central benchmarks of their social order, with the conflict of interest between capital and labour as its most salient feature. Over the previous 150 years, all three countries had developed their own language and vocabulary to express the political economy of capital and labour within the framework of their individual national patterns of order.

In Britain, industrialization had provided a model for the powerful interpretive patterns of industrial revolution, liberal capitalism and class struggle and so had also helped shape key concepts of political language in other countries. It is striking that the emerging British working classes, in contrast, developed their own political idiom to refer to the distinct specificities of their country.[12] Electoral reforms, the recognition of the trade unions and free collective bargaining were milestones in the development of the British labour movement, but they were at the same time significant enough experiences to shape the political language of the British nation as a whole. The existence of class struggle in their country was accepted, if grudgingly, even by liberals and conservatives, who solicited the support and votes of the growing number of industrial workers who were members of trade unions. The pragmatic representation of the interests of labour in parliament lent a highly idiosyncratic form of organization to a scheme of interpretation and order which is still effective today. In the twentieth century, the nationwide mobilization of industrial workers in the two victorious world wars helped to entrench this liberal model of the British nation as a political community with a society shaped by notions of class belonging and class origin. It was for this reason that 'class' remained an ambiguous but unchallenged reference point for the most diverse political languages, official statistics, social scientific studies and everyday sociological self-categorization.[13]

In West Germany, in contrast, both political and social terminology as well as official classification tried to neutralize differences in class and especially class conflict as far as they could.[14] The linguistic strategies of euphemism and harmonization were adopted in reaction to the ideological charge and the radicalization of the language of the conflict of interests in industry used during the *Kaiserreich* (German Empire 1871 to 1918) and the Weimar Republic. The German *Reich* had been turned into a battleground of conflicting interpretations of the social world and of quasi-religious world views in which industrial workers were assigned a key role in the fate of the nation's political and social order. Given the power of a labour movement whose political language was orthodox Marxist, the workers' question in the German *Reich* was far more than a socio-political problem. Rather, it was closely connected to the question of the legitimacy of class struggle and class antagonisms within the political order. This was a basic tension which was not resolved by the German defeat in World War I, nor by the 'socio-patriotic' integration of the SPD and trade unions during the war, and became more ideologically radicalized again in the following decades. The National Socialist movement and its dictatorship were a radical response to this ideological conflict. The new *völkisch* reinterpretation of the *Volksgemeinschaft* (national or people's community), already invoked in the Weimar Republic, lent an enhanced symbolic value to the working classes, which were at the same time excluded from power.[15] This enforced national and political integration was inherited by both parts of divided Germany, who were at great pains not to revive the opposition between (working) class and nation. In West Germany, the ideological confrontations of the Cold War enforced strict limits on any kind of socialist rhetoric involving class conflict, fuelling the deradicalization of the many nationalist and socially conservative patterns of interpreting the industrial world. In the postwar period, the prevailing attitudes were in support of free enterprise, business and management, thereby creating a climate of opinion in which the new model of a 'social market economy' initially took on a distinctly socially conservative character. It was not until social democracy abandoned its tradition of Marxist rhetoric with the Godesberg Programme of 1959 that the way was open to a social-liberal interpretation of this pattern of order. It stipulated that organized and legally regulated conflicts of interest between capital and labour were an integral part of West German democracy. From then onwards, the image of the class-conscious industrial worker that had been part of the political imagination before 1945 began to be replaced by that of the self-confident industrial citizen.[16]

In France, the development of socio-political interpretive schemes had less to do with the social reality of the new industrial society and more to do with the political and social confrontations originating in the French Revolution. Thanks to a broad class of peasant farmer landowners and the dominance of small-scale artisan industries well into the twentieth century, it was not until the interwar period that, in spite of their decidedly socialist traditions, industrial workers and their class conflict became a central concept in political discourse. Far more attention and respect were paid to the 'common people' of radical or republican leanings, the *peuple*, than to the workers, the *ouvriers*.[17] The notion of the *classes populaires* was dominant for more than 100 years and has remained in existence as a scheme of interpretation until the present day, underpinning a variety of political ideas. The impact of the Popular Front government (*front populaire*) that came to power in 1936, the founding of the authoritarian Vichy regime in 1940 following the defeat of Republican France, and the liberation of France in 1944 were to change the ways the industrial world of labour was interpreted for more than three decades until the 1970s. It was only after 1945 that the labour movement's rhetoric of class conflict found a wider echo and it was only then that the social problems in industry, which was still dominated by the regions, found their way into the general political consciousness. As a result, the industrial labour force became firmly integrated into the prevailing idea of France as a democratic nation. The socio-political and symbolic integration of this rapidly expanding group of new industrial workers soon became a central point of reference in the many reform programmes required for a social refounding of the democratic republic. This new social order was initially supported by Gaullists, Christian Democrats, socialists and communists after World War II, but with different interpretations. A precarious compromise emerged between the semantics of the left, which were firmly oriented to class conflict, and the conflicting ideas of the 'bourgeois' parties oriented towards social harmony and the middle classes.[18]

Social classification in official statistics

In Britain, France and Germany, the national patterns of order discussed above were both integrated in and supported by their official statistics. From 1970 to 2000, they all used specifically national systems of classification, although the official statistics of the European Union began to be more influential towards the end of the period. Official social data provide the essential components for all interpretive patterns of the social world that claim to be reliable and fact-based. For this reason, any changes in their categories and parameters must be seen as a realigning of patterns of social order and the result of silent but significant interpretive struggles over the definition of the social world.[19]

The political reforms that were introduced in France after its liberation at the end of World War II, and the significant increase in the power of the Communist Party, which styled itself clearly as the party of the working class and of all workers (*travailleurs*), led to the recognition of social class structures in political language and in official statistics. In 1946, the categories of social and labour law relating to profession and status were redrafted (*Les grilles Parodi-Croizat*); in 1954, the category of *classes socio-professionelles* was introduced into the census and official statistics and updated in 1981. Since then, official French statistics have been providing the country with descriptions and social data (*les données sociales*) that routinely separate French society into five different groups, each with their own subgroups: *cadres* (executives/higher civil servants), *professions intermédiaires* (medium-level employees/civil servants), *employés* (ordinary employees and skilled labourers), *ouvriers* (workers and unskilled labourers) and *agricultures/artisans/indépendants* (farmers, craftspeople, self-employed).[20] This concept of large socio-professional groups differentiated by income, qualification, wealth and housing became increasingly entrenched in the interpretive model of the social world of the late 1950s that circulated in France. It was developed by politicians, economists, social scientists and intellectuals as a way of explaining social problems and suggesting solutions to them. This led to a close and undisputed relationship between sociology and official statistics. As a result, the social positioning of individuals within French class society was much clearer than it was, for example, in Germany. At the same time, social differences and the effects of inequality were also made more visible than they were east of the Rhine.[21] In this respect, French society was much closer to its British counterpart than it was to (West) German society.

In Britain, a classification of the entire population according to occupation and social criteria had been carried out for the census of 1911, and revised and finalized in the 1921 census. Its aim was to represent the social classes of urban industrial society as adequately as possible. From 1911 to 1991, the Registrar General's Social Class Scheme registered five occupational groups: professional occupations (managers and managerial staff, higher grade civil servants and the self-employed), intermediate occupations (middle and lower management, technicians, middle-grade posts in administration and business), skilled occupations (with the differentiation between manual and non-manual introduced in 1971), partly skilled occupations and unskilled occupations.

In 2001, this primarily occupation-based classification was revised and refined using the structural functionalist model of the British sociologists John H. Goldthorpe and Keith Hope.[22] Differences in the labour markets and labour hierarchies were incorporated as further variables into the new model, resulting in a total of eight categories. They were then combined into either five or three classes according to the National Statistics Socio-Economic Classification (NS-SEC).[23] This shows that official statistics in Britain also elevated industrial labour and its divisions to the status of a framework for a class or stratification model. In this way, indirectly and politically quite unintentionally, those demarcation lines which existed between the various classes in everyday perception and cultural self-representation were reinforced. This is why, in spite of the fact that both Tory and Labour politicians such as Margaret Thatcher, John Major, Tony Blair and Gordon Brown were fond of propagating it as a new model of British society, the idea of the 'classless society' found less favour amongst the British public than had been expected from the efforts made in the media in its favour.[24]

In Germany, there was a completely different approach to compiling official statistics from that of Britain and France. Since the end of the *Kaiserreich*, three main categories had developed out of the social insurance laws of Bismarck's social reforms at the end of the nineteenth century, namely blue-collar workers, white-collar workers and civil servants. This meant that the only criterion used to distinguish between the official social categories was their different status in labour law and national social insurance. Additional official data on occupations were recorded solely for the purpose of economic statistics. There was never a combination of criteria according to sociological aspects as there was in French and British statistics. As a result, official German statistics presented a notoriously oversimplified picture of German society.[25]

This official reluctance to introduce and thus also to make official any other categories of socio-economic status relating to occupations and work beyond those defined by social and labour law was reflected in the conventions of political language in West Germany. It quite consciously avoided using classification to accentuate the existence of class antagonisms and social inequality. Instead it appealed to the political unity and ethnic homogeneity of the national population. There is certainly an echo of the Nazis' attempts to enforce homogeneity by means of their propaganda for the *Volksgemeinschaft* here. However, this strategy of misconstruction or denial was also supported by the new constellation of political parties after 1949, when two large parties, the CDU/CSU (Christian Democrats) and the SPD (Social Democrats), with otherwise very different programmes, established and marketed themselves as parties of the people across all social classes. The struggle for political majorities did not run primarily along socio-economic dividing lines but consistently emphasized what the voters of different social strata had in common and what united them. This attitude was also assisted by the social sciences. They portrayed a model of society beyond the old dividing lines of class and especially beyond the old class antagonisms as a social reality. This explains the resounding long-term success of Helmut Schelsky's concept of a 'levelled middle-class society', which was formulated in 1953 and was then promoted as the unofficial social model of the 'economic miracle'.[26] The tendency to ignore the class realities of both the middle classes and the working classes in postwar German society developed into a kind of cross-party socio-political consensus. This position went unchallenged except by left-wing intellectuals and academic neo-Marxists, whose criticism found a very limited public echo beyond a few specialist departments and lecture theatres in the social sciences.[27]

In the official statistics and mainstream sociology of Britain and France, sociological differences, whether large or small, were not concealed in the same way. This means that the 'theory effect' we are dealing with here is a unique feature and one that left its mark on West German society in the long term. It has, for example, led to the fact that the categorization of the self and others within society and the classification of socio-economic differences and inequalities has remained much more diffuse and unstable than in the two neighbouring countries. Because of this lack of official categorization, any sense of social orientation was and still is far more dependent on the changing ideas produced in the media and on opinion pages, as discussed above.

New boundaries

It comes as no surprise therefore that, of our three countries, Germany was particularly receptive to those schemes of interpretation which saw the decline of industrial labour structures as equivalent to the end of class structures and other similarly rough differentiations in the melange of income, education, occupation and ways of life, and that it incorporated this approach into its political language. West German sociology, for example, experienced only a brief neo-Marxist intermezzo, and by the 1980s at the latest, interpretations resurfaced that identified the disintegration of previously compact socio-economic positions of class or strata as the main trend of the transformation phase. These theories were linked to further claims about the structural transformation of society. Three such claims stand out: first, that vertical inequality was receding in favour of stronger horizontal inequality; second, that leisure and consumption were gaining in significance for the creation of socio-cultural milieus and groups; and, third, that an important role was played overall by the fact that ways of life were becoming increasingly individualized (see figure 2.2). However, this did not lead to a common interpretive scheme of social reality in the social sciences. On the contrary, as both dividing and connecting social facts became more diverse, so did their interpretations. For the German case, observers have spoken of a cacophony of interpretive paradigms.[28] Indeed, many sociological ideas competed with each other: the 'experience society' (Schulze), 'risk society' (Beck), 'information society' (Bell) and many others. They also occasionally competed more for media attention than they did for empirical verifiability.[29]

Margaret Thatcher's infamous statement that 'there is no such thing as society' may have initially found favour only with economists and psychologists. However, some social science experts and intellectuals who were cultural critics were in fact also approaching this radical position in one way or another. In doing so, they were undermining the scientific dignity and legitimacy of older approaches and languages of mobilization that worked with categories of socio-structural inequality and contrasts between larger social groups.

In France and Britain, this new trend of expertise in the social sciences was particularly affected by the knowledge and import of American interpretive paradigms. Since the 1960s, they had interpreted the growing level of consumption, the decline of inequality in income and education and the increase in social mobility as indications that a new type of society was taking the place of the old industrial class societies. Here the boundaries between the interpretation of empirical findings, the diagnosis of social trends and the forecast of new social patterns of order also remained fluid. To summarize: in all three countries, social scientists emphasized the trends towards individualization, towards the diversification of socio-economic situations and especially towards cross-border structural effects of globalization, particularly those that were cultural and

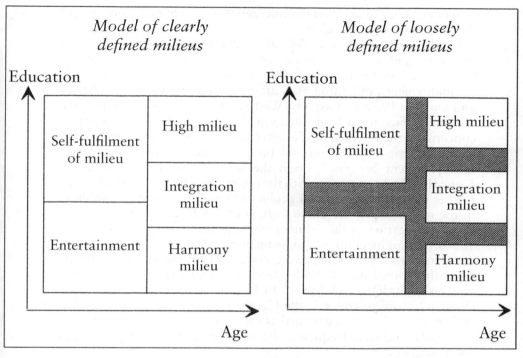

Figure 2.2 On the constellations of contemporary milieus.

Diagram from Gerhard Schulze, *Die Erlebnisgesellschaft. Kultursoziologie der Gegenwart* [*The Experience Society*], Frankfurt/M., 1992, p. 384.

In 1992, Gerhard Schulze published his diagnosis of the times, *Die Erlebnisgesellschaft. Kultursoziologie der Gegenwart* (an English translation, *The Experience Society*, appeared in 2005). It clearly portrayed the new self-image of West German society. The diagram above illustrates Schulze's approach. He uses lifestyle and leisure activities as a basis to differentiate between various social milieus and positions along the axes of education and age respectively. In spite of all the theoretical distinctions, work and income are no longer relevant. Social inequality has vanished behind the sociology of culture. The development in France ran in the opposite direction. Just one year after the publication of *The Experience Society* in 1992, a comprehensive cooperative study appeared under the direction of Pierre Bourdieu: *La misère du monde* (published in English as *The Weight of the World: Social Suffering in Contemporary Society*).

71

economic. They underlined the emergence of new lines of conflict and divisions within each society.

At the same time, the critical media focused on acute social problems and a small number of problem groups. In Germany, three topics predominated, namely unemployment (especially youth unemployment), migration and, after the mid-1990s, the differences and tensions between East and West Germany. The issue of poverty did not surface for a long time. On the other hand, it was a major concern in the French media after the 1980s. It was interpreted as an element of exclusion and precarity and led to the reform of unemployment benefits.[30] From the start, the issue of poverty in France had had to compete with the migration issue and also with two further closely related 'social problems' which were often combined in the media for effect. These were youth violence and the growing social segregation in the suburbs and outskirts of the large cities. In 1980s Britain, by contrast, 'mass unemployment' and 'poverty' were the dominant issues. They were combined by the media to reveal what they called a new 'underclass' of unemployed, 'work-averse', 'work-shy' welfare recipients.[31] In Britain, as in France, the youth riots and problem zones in the big cities played a major role. Race and ethnic background emerged as the most significant categories for the media, and were frequently discussed in follow-up studies in the social sciences.

Remarkably enough, the old and new worlds of labour began to disappear almost completely from any reporting on social problems. It is true that there were serious strikes, factory occupations and mass protests in the first ten years after 1974–5. But by the time it came to the wave of redundancies and closures after the second recession of 1980–2, they were no longer met by a series of social protests, but by just a few (albeit particularly spectacular) major events like the British miners' strike, the mass protests in Rheinhausen and the strike for the 35-hour week in the South German metal industry. Industrial working environments rarely found the media spotlight after this final uprising. In Germany, even the collapse of the industrial structures of the former GDR took place with very little media attention or attempt to analyse the problem, apart from coverage of the brief flurry of protests in spring 1991.[32] The media remained focused on unemployment and especially on its psychological and social consequences.

It is not difficult to see that this selective view of social problems follows the logic of the media in its orientation towards events. In all three countries, the boundaries of the perception of social reality were

72

regulated by the popular press and later primarily by commercial television. By showing violent images of attacks on asylum seekers' shelters and of street battles between the police and young people, and by regularly announcing figures for unemployment and apprenticeships, attention was drawn to these 'social problems', defined as such by the media. The stories were often processed and exploited by the media to show families with unusual fates, or the lives of welfare claimants, petty criminals and drug addicts, which in turn made them more visible. The result of this was that in all three countries an image arose of a society that had lost control over its social margins and borders and whose attempts at (social as well as systemic) integration had succeeded in including at best two-thirds of the population. On the one hand, the seductive images created by this language became increasingly popular and raised the status of a whole chain of corresponding categories, such as exclusion and precarity. On the other hand, they raised awareness of the phenomena accompanying the increasing religious and cultural diversity that had been celebrated in the context of globalization and the digital revolution. After the 1980s, racism, xenophobia, migration and religious and cultural differences became increasingly significant as political dividing lines in the representation and the reality of society.

Scepticism was growing among social scientists and intellectuals as to whether, in the new post-industrial dynamic of an increasingly globalized Europe, there still was such a thing as a 'close-knit' social structure that defined collective groups. It is striking that in all three countries this scepticism was accompanied by a growing attention to new (and many old) demarcation lines and lines of conflict in society. Cultural and religious differences were increasingly discussed in the context of characteristics such as ethnic origin, skin colour, citizenship and gender. Predictions that societies would be made up of increasingly flexible world citizens, expressed by the likes of Ulrich Beck and Zygmunt Bauman, suggested that subtle distinctions in, say, individual lifestyle and cultural background were of inordinate relevance. They assumed that personal and circumstantial choices would widely replace the earlier influences of socio-economic inequality, class culture and ethnic background. However, this assumption that there would be greater flexibility and mobility was disputed by an interpretive paradigm that raised these 'subtle distinctions' to the status of identity markers and paved the way for an essentialist interpretation of social conflict along the lines of customary symbols of exclusion such as race, religion and nation. These new interpretations of society thus

73

circumvented the entrenched pattern of right versus left that had dominated the established interpretive paradigms in postwar industrial societies.

As a consequence, social realities, conflicts and problems that were rooted in and caused by the widespread working conditions became increasingly marginalized. Although working-class societies in Britain, France and Germany were still influenced by industry, the images of society produced in the media focused more on generalities such as 'those up there' and 'those down here' and on 'them' and 'us'. In the case of France, sociologists have spoken of the fact that since the 1980s industrial workers and their living and working conditions have become 'invisible'.[33] A new and stable social distance had developed between journalists, media experts and social scientists, on the one hand, and the living conditions of ordinary industrial workers, on the other.

New political languages of mobilization

The question of whether and how the problems of industrial workers and labour conflicts were addressed by political parties, trade unions and other interest groups is one that a comparative social history of industrial labour cannot ignore, although responding to it would fill volumes. In chapter 3, I will examine several significant events that were directly linked with the fact that work experiences and labour conflicts became more politicized. These flashes of political mobilization and social protest, however, can be likened to isolated eruptions that briefly and generally only locally broke through the hardened crust of established political languages and routine courses of action. For this reason, I see them as seismographic indicators pointing to cracks and shifts in those interpretive schemes used by the established political and social representatives of the social groups to articulate conflicts and interests.

In the face of economic and social upheaval, and particularly in the wake of new forms of political mass communication in the media, the language and style of political mobilization in Britain, France and West Germany were transformed. In the last three decades of the twentieth century, television became the dominant and ultimately crucial medium of political communication, with political actors gradually adapting to it. This lent considerable weight to the those topics and images that were media-effective. But it also meant greater visibility for those schemes of interpretation and order that were reduced to the level of slogans and *doxa*, and for the political leaders representing them. The main political parties in all three countries adapted to these new media realities and allowed their individual ideological traditions to be replaced by slogans which were effective in this new media age. Party members and activists lost their influence as mediators between the political party leaders and the electorate. For the left-wing parties and trade unions, which had arisen out of the nineteenth-century labour movement, this had far-reaching consequences, because, from their beginnings right up until the 1970s, they had perpetuated the local traditions of fundamental counter-cultural opposition to the hegemony of middle-class representations of the social world.

In the long struggle for political and social visibility and recognition, the political representatives of the industrial labour force had learnt to mobilize a number of typical resources. One of these was the experience that although they were unable to obtain approval of their views and positions in the established media, they could depend on the support of the grassroots: that is, of their own supporters and those who belonged to the same social class or shared the same socio-moral background. This was expressed in the different 'class languages' used by British, French and German trade unionists, communists, socialists and left-wing Catholics to hold their own in the struggle for the interpretation of social reality.[34] Reasons of space prohibit me here from tracing the development of these different languages and their emergence and transformation up until the 1970s.[35] What is far more important for my analysis is the fact that when there were favourable conditions for industrial action in the 1960s and 1970s and it was backed by political uprisings and cultural revolts propagated by (bourgeois) cultural influencers, class languages experienced a renaissance. It was this '1968 effect' that strengthened radical ideas of revolt and protest. These ideas rivalled mainstream representations of social order and were often met with a more popular response both among sections of the workforce and among the new generation of young party members with a middle-class background and university education than were their liberal or conservative equivalents. These radical positions were sceptical of the socially harmonious interpretations of society that had been adopted by the established political left. But their success was short-lived and they did not survive the early 1980s. This was particularly true for Britain and France, since traditional support for the labour movement was much stronger there than in West Germany and was deliberately reactivated for the purposes of political mobilization.

In both national movements, this was above all the contribution of militant forces.[36]

A clear demonstration of this is the case of the two keepers of the holy grail of revolutionary class rhetoric in France: the Confédération Générale du Travail (CGT) and the Parti Communiste Français (PCF).[37] In their everyday representation of interests, they were realistically and consistently oriented towards reform and compromise. In spite of this, they clung to concepts in their programmes that were the antithesis of bourgeois interpretations of the social world. Both organizations gave a voice to social protest and resistance. They saw themselves as reaching out beyond the routine rhetoric of class struggle and providing an instrument and opportunity for the expression of the voice of the workers, particularly of those who opposed the demands of day-to-day conditions, however diffuse and emotional that opposition was. Especially in the 1970s, a similar role was played by the Confédération Française Démocratique du Travail (CFDT), the trade union confederation that competed with the CGT. In the same way as the CGT, the CFDT clung on to the key concepts of trade union militancy such as *lutte* (struggle), *classe* (class), *défense* (resistance) and *mobilisation* (mobilization) in all their variations and combinations.[38]

Interestingly enough, the *topoi* and stereotypes used by both major left-wing parties in France to mobilize their electorate until the mid-1980s came from the Marxist-socialist language of class struggle. This style of mobilization was undoubtedly at its peak in the election campaigns of the 1970s and early 1980s when the socialists and communists were successful. In this decade, more than 70 per cent of the *ouvriers* eligible to vote opted for one of the two left-wing parties. They promoted a number of policies based on anti-capitalism in the tradition of the class politics and oppositional rhetoric cultivated by the French left since 1945. This included extending the protection provided by the welfare state and committing in principle to a Keynesian-style interventionist economic policy with employment-creation schemes and nationalization as a means of taking political control of major French companies. So we see that in France in the initial post-boom years the mobilizing power of traditional class language was still huge. This was capitalized on particularly by the new socialist party, founded in 1970, the Parti Socialiste (PS), led by François Mitterrand. He went into the presidential elections of 1974 as the candidate of the left. As late as 1973, he maintained during the election campaign that: 'As envisaged in the manifesto of the Socialist Party, the real and complete destruction of all forms of exploitation of humans by humans presupposes the creation of an economic democracy whose starting point is the collective appropriation of the major resources of production, investment and trade.'[39]

The PS was initially able to use this political class language to its own advantage much more effectively than the Communist Party, the PCF. The credibility of the PCF had suffered in the eyes of many supporters and voters because of its close ties to Moscow and a phase of adherence to orthodox communist dogma, which had been supported only by its most loyal supporters.[40] As a result, the 'Tribunician mandate' (Georges Lavau) to represent the *classes populaires* that the PCF had successfully maintained in its political language after 1945 was effectively passed on to the PS (see figure 2.3). The PS was now by far the strongest party on the left, and its change of mobilization strategies and communication routines had a deep impact after 1984, when it turned its back on the left-wing Keynesian principles it had previously followed and sought ever stronger ties to the social democratic language of its northern and eastern sister parties. As it embarked on this 'course of modernization', the PS also adapted its political rhetoric. Now it propagated the virtues of technocratic pragmatism and pro-business efficiency and referred more and more frequently to the inherent necessity for a new policy of austerity. In effect it would align itself to the successful mainstream views on society circulating in the media in the same way as its sister party in West Germany, the SPD. In spite of critical voices from within, both the SPD and the PS now embraced those neoliberal currents which around 1980 they had still used as enemy stereotypes to create their profiles.

Within less than ten years, the PS was concentrating the focus of its communication strategies on middle-income swing voters and those falling into the categories of *cadres* and *professions intermédiaires*, particularly because, to a far greater extent than the SPD or the Labour Party, their party members came from a section of the middle class who did not work in industry, mostly public servants. At the same time, they neglected their traditional voters, the working classes. This gap in the mobilization languages could not and would not be filled by the PCF, with its strict maintenance of orthodox tradition. It managed to survive the demise of state socialism in Eastern Europe only as a minor party. As a result, a deep gulf opened up around 2000 between lower-income voters and the established left-wing political parties. Its clearest manifestation was the increase in the number of people from this group who did not vote at all. It was not without a certain degree of bitterness that the French working

Figure 2.3 'Let the workers have their say' (Security – Working Hours – Working Norms. Let the workers have their say.)

This 1978 poster from the 'business department' of the PS attempts to mobilize the three different categories of French workers (industrial workers, [male] middle management and [female] office workers) and bring them together under the common roof of their shared problems: safety at work, working hours and working norms. The changes in the working world can already be detected in the language of the images: large computers and office blocks are shown next to modern industrial plants; the workers are young. A socialist transformation of the working world (still) lies at the heart of the joint political programme of the French left-wing parties.

classes disassociated themselves from the two left-wing parties, the PS and the PCF.[41] After the turn of the millennium, the right-wing populist Front National (FN), which was founded in 1972 and whose main supporters had previously been the small-scale self-employed, became more attractive to industrial workers and low-level white-collar workers.

The development in Britain differed from that in France in many respects. There were many different languages of mobilization in British labour organizations and they were far less dominated by one single idiom.[42] 'Labourism' was an appeal to the traditions and solidarity of the same class or background as well as an appeal to trust the Labour Party and the trade union movement to look after the interests of the workers. In reality, however, it was associated with many different political terms and aims.[43] Because of the British electoral system, it was crucial that political languages were flexible enough to adapt to local conditions in the individual constituencies. Efforts at ideological unity within the Labour Party were, therefore, severely limited and led to very different strands of left-wing and socialist ideologies co-existing relatively peacefully within the party. However, this precarious alliance between different political currents collapsed under the impact of Labour's defeat in the general election in 1979 and the ongoing economic crisis in the industrial regions, and the party leadership fell into the hands of the left wing. When the Social Democratic Party (SDP) was founded in 1981, the moderate social-liberal wing of the labour movement was briefly marginalized. This was, however, only a brief interlude. Like its French and German counterparts, in the late 1980s and finally in the 1990s, the Labour Party transformed into a liberal market reform party. The last traces of class rhetoric, left-wing Keynesianism and socialism were removed and instead, as the example of the Blair–Schröder paper at the beginning of this chapter showed, liberal interpretive schemes of social and economic development were adopted.[44]

The pragmatic aspiration to better governance and the vague promise to cushion the social costs caused by the demand for greater flexibility from capital and labour became the key elements of a new type of social democratic language. It was practised above all by Tony Blair, with great success and to great media effect. From then on, interpretive struggles and inner party conflicts were divided explicitly between outdated and up-to-date views, between the tradi-tionalists and the modernists. It is striking, however, that at the local level New Labour still managed to win a large majority of traditional votes from the working class.[45]

The West German SPD developed in a similar direction. Its route was somewhat shorter and a little less circuitous, because the Godesberg Programme had already banned the last residues of left-wing class rhetoric from the language of the party in 1959. This meant that the ideological gap between the right and left wings of the party was far smaller than it was in the Labour Party. There was a return of explicitly Euro-Marxist positions within the SPD in the 1970s, but it was a brief and inconsequential interlude. Instead, the SPD membership moved closer towards the upper and middle ranks in society, in a similar way to its French sister party and earlier than its British counterpart. By the mid-1970s, a third of all party members worked in the public sector and were particularly overrepresented in the group of activists within the party. In the next two decades, their share continued to grow. In 1989, 26.4 per cent of working members were blue-collar workers, the proportion of white-collar workers was the same and nearly 11 per cent were civil servants.[46] Although industrial workers were still seen as the SPD's traditional core voters, increasingly less notice was taken of them in the party-political programme and its rhetoric. The SPD's image of itself as 'the party of the man on the street', however, only seriously lost its credibility and power to mobilize after 2004 and the socio-political U-turn of the red–green coalition government.

What is particularly interesting in the context of Germany is the way the language used by the German Trade Union Confederation (Deutscher Gewerkschaftsbund/DGB) and its individual trade unions developed in reaction to the upheavals following the postwar boom years.[47] Since the end of the war and as a reaction to the fiasco of left-wing class struggle rhetoric in the Weimar Republic, the West German trade union movement, which had been re-founded as a unified trade union system, had used the word 'employee' (*Arbeitnehmer*), originally a purely legal term. This was to emphasize that, as opposed to the communist use of the term 'workers' (*Werktätigen*), it represented the joint interests of all those employed in one sector. It was to distance itself from the German Union of Public Sector Workers (Deutsche Angestellten Gewerkschaft) and the German Association of Civil Servants (Deutscher Beamtenbund), which even after 1945 had defended the special status of these two minority groups of 'employees', the *Angestellte* and the *Beamte*. As long as workers did in fact make up a large or overwhelming majority of members in most of the DGB unions, this was absolutely no problem, since mobilization within plants and localities was more or less guaranteed to be within the social milieu of blue-collar workers.

However, it became different and more difficult when this group of 'employees' lost its power and influence within the DGB and began to demand to become a separate group within the confederation in order to gain more public attention for itself and its problems. The DGB did set up what it called 'workers' committees' and 'workers' conferences', but they became centres of conflict between the confederation and its individual trade unions, especially the public services and transport union (ÖTV) and the metalworkers' union (IG Metall). The result was that attempts by the DGB to put the problems of this status group onto the agenda and make them the subject of political and social debate by means of so-called federal workers' conferences (1981, 1985 and 1989) were largely unsuccessful for lack of support from within.

The unspecific concept of 'employee' (*Arbeitnehmer*) was still the benchmark for trade union mobilization rhetoric. This was particularly the case for the industrial trade unions, above all IG Metall, as their aim in both company negotiations and collective bargaining was to break down the existing barriers in social and labour law between blue- and white-collar workers. These efforts reached their conclusion in 2003 when after more than 100 years this official division was abolished and their parity was determined in social and labour law. This happened, however, at a time when differences in wages and the social and legal status of 'employees' (*Arbeitnehmer*), particularly in the new service industries, were increasing significantly and thus the socio-economic inequality between the various groups of employees was also growing again. This is one of the specific German phenomena that stems from the tradition discussed above of euphemizing interpretive patterns and uses of language when encountering aspects of social inequality. It also stems from the above-mentioned fact that official statistics were lacking in any binding or meaningful categories. When there was a conflict and workers' organizations and trade unions promoted their cause in public, the only counter-category they could use when attempting to mobilize the workforce was 'employee' (*Arbeitnehmer*) as a contrast to the official term 'member of staff' (*Mitarbeiter*) used by the management. In a similar way to France, the category of industrial labour also disappeared from the vocabulary of the trade unions in Germany and from public perception overall.

This changed typically in all three countries when increased inequality of income and wealth and of education and culture reappeared as problems and were increasingly identified as a threat to Western democracy. That only happened after the turn of the millennium and more intensively after the financial crisis that began in 2008.

Radical changes in the cultural representation of the world of industrial work

Needless to say, ideas, images and interpretations of societies were and are not only produced in the context of political parties and organizations or academic institutions. They are also produced in the sphere of culture, with its extremely diverse structure. Feature films and documentaries, museum exhibitions, television reports, autobiographies, novels and non-fiction books differ considerably in their reach and the scope of their impact. This is influenced significantly by the social spaces in which culture is produced and their respective roles and relative strengths. There is unfortunately very little cultural-historical research into the representation of industrial work after the postwar boom. The current state of research is, moreover, very different in the three countries of interest here. While numerous studies were devoted to this topic in France and Britain, particularly after the turn of the millennium, in Germany interest in cultural perceptions of industrial work and the people who carried it out has only recently revived.[48]

Around 1970, the cultural scene in all three countries turned its attention to the largely remote and alien world of industrial work. This occurred as intellectuals, writers and filmmakers moved towards the political left. It was their way of articulating their critical distance and independence from those wielding economic and political power. In a sense, Neo-Marxism wrote the basic code for a variety of films and books that were produced between 1965 and 1975. It was the aim of many of them to provide an antidote and counter-narrative both to the sleek versions of industry's promotional films and to the dominant representations of working classes supposedly having long become middle class. They did this by addressing the phenomenon of alienation in industrial mass production and the exploitation of the workers.[49] During this period, all three countries also began to experiment with including workers themselves in the artistic production process or organizing them as producers of cultural features. The results of these experiments, however, circulated almost exclusively in artistic avant-garde circles or amongst left-wing intellectuals. At best, they were adopted by the trade unions as an integral part of their mobilization and education programmes.[50] In Germany, a working group for literature of the working world (Werkkreis Literatur der Arbeitswelt) followed the socialist model and cultivated the traditional view of the exploitation of industrial workers under capitalism. It was successful during the 1970s, but the 1980s marked the beginning of its decline and the collapse of the GDR reduced its circle of influence to local working groups and networks.[51]

In France, it was mainly the interest of left-wing industrial sociologists that led to autobiographical texts of industrial workers being published and attracting interest. The greatest success was enjoyed by Robert Linhart's book about his experiences working on the production line in the Citroën factory at the Porte de Choisy in Paris.[52] He was one of the Maoist intellectuals who had gone to work in the factories in the early 1970s in order to precipitate the revolution. But Linhart's book is also a clear depiction of everyday life and social relations on the assembly line. This turned it into a literary classic that was at the same time the model for similar reports and autobiographies of industrial workers.[53] Generally speaking, however, it was rare for any of these books and films to succeed in reaching a wider public.

The themes and perspectives in the dedicated production of culture were shifted in the late 1970s and early 1980s by the surge of deindustrialization, factory closures and mass redundancies. A particularly striking example in this context is the local radio station Longwy-Cœur d'Acier financed by the CGT. During the strikes and protests against the proposed closure of the local steelworks in 1978–9, they also broadcast historical programmes as an independent pirate station. The two programmes *Le passé présent* (The Present Past) and *Histoire de quelqu'un* (Someone's Story) were particularly successful at representing a different kind of regional history. The stories they told were by 'people who lived in the region or who were visiting Longwy and came from different family, professional and political backgrounds, [...] about their origins, their childhood, family members, romantic relationships, material poverty, their work, strikes, the war, their political involvement and much more'.[54] This gave rise to something like a regional culture of remembrance, which focused both on regional labour struggles and on the German occupation and the *libération*. It also opened up points of reference which furthered a sense of collective belonging, especially for the European labour migrants who had made the region their home in the interwar period.[55] Although this culture of remembrance was initially born out of political conflict, it found its way into the various initiatives for the preservation of industrial monuments and the establishment of local and regional museums which were dedicated to the now-defunct industrial culture of Lorraine.[56] The example of Longwy is typical for the upsurge of everyday history and history workshops, which reached its peak at the same time as contemporary mobilization against factory closures and redundancies.[57] It was a harbinger of the accelerating trend towards turning the crisis-hit industrial regions into museum pieces and places of historical interest that continues to this day, especially in Britain and Germany.[58] It has led to numerous museums of technology being founded or redesigned and at the same time the aesthetic value of industrial buildings and derelict and decaying industrial ruins being rediscovered and re-evaluated.[59] It was typical that these regional museums, exhibitions and monuments created images of a whole epoch in which industrial labour had dominated and shaped the profile of the region and its population. The time span stretched from early evidence of industrialization to the machines and factories that had recently been closed. In Britain, where the demise of industrial production was rapid and transformed whole regions, there was a particularly powerful nostalgic view of this world that had disappeared in just the same way as the world of farming villages and small-town crafts.

As the consequences of deindustrialization became increasingly apparent, the various legacies of the decaying 'world of industrial labour and labourers', from classic industrial buildings to traces of workers' memories, became both subjects and objects of cultural recollection.[60] A self-historicization of industrial society quickly set in, which saw it as a concluded 'phase' of Western European 'modernism'. Culturally, this amounted to a retrospective re-evaluation of aspects of everyday industrial culture and its many heroes, both men and women, who had previously been neglected. But it also emphasized industry's image of being outdated and behind the times in its view of the present and future of Western European societies. This meant that when it came to 'industrial culture', 'working people's lives' and 'industrial heritage' in all three countries, nostalgic and social romantic tendencies grew. In Britain, a 'sociology of deindustrialization' developed and industrial monuments, museums and adventure parks mushroomed. They focused on the immediate or recent past of their own industrial development. In the public perception, a kind of golden haze often hung over the industrial world of work at precisely the same time as it was in the process of adapting to completely new conditions of a changing capitalism, whose actors were increasingly closely networked internationally and working on a global scale.

What stood out most amongst the cultural products engaging directly with the consequences of deindustrialization from the 1980s onwards were television programmes and films, not least because they often reached a nationwide audience. British productions in the style of social drama in particular focussed on the drawbacks of the structural transformation. In doing so, they contributed to the angry and accusatory tone of the crisis discourses of the time. In Britain, the BBC series *Boys from the Blackstuff* was a huge success. It portrayed the attempts of a group of redundant workers from Liverpool to find work again or to come to terms with their fate as unemployed and superfluous to society. The series was broadcast twice within nine weeks (in October/November 1982 and January/February 1983) and is said to have been watched by more than 30 million viewers in Britain.[61] Its realistic portrayal of the social and economic conditions of redundant road construction workers, their families and neighbourhoods painted a pessimistic picture of the consequences of deindustrialization in Liverpool. But it was also very funny and showed a wholly unsentimental picture of the protagonists' will to maintain their self-esteem. The realism of their portrayal made it easy to identify with them. As one of the many positive reviewers said, 'Never before have I seen my family, my friends and acquaintances, my class, the people I know and live among and often despair of, portrayed on the screen with such realism, sensitivity and affection: our hopes, our aspirations, our frailties and contradictions.'[62]

The feature films of British film director Ken Loach were not quite so successful, but met with a good deal of acclaim both in Britain and beyond, winning a number of awards. Loach began as a filmmaker in the 1960s and has remained loyal to the genre of British social drama and the living conditions and concerns of the working classes ever since. His films, such as *Riffraff* (1991) and *Bread and Roses* (2000), were designed explicitly to be critical interventions opposing politically intended upheavals.

Starting in the mid-1990s, a distinct genre of representation of the recent past was created by British comedies. Their dramatic yet amusing plots focused on the consequences of deindustrialization in the traditional mining villages of Yorkshire and Wales. Films like *The Full Monty* (1997), *Brassed Off* (1996) and *Billy Elliot* (2000) were full of sympathy for the collapse of the working world and the loss of the security that came with it for those who were affected (mostly men). In their own way, they showed how these men and their families radically yet successfully reorganized their lives (see figure 2.4). The solidarity and dignity of those suffering loss was one of the

Figure 2.4 'Inside every one of us is a special talent waiting to come out.'
Billy Elliot – I Will Dance (GB, 2000; director: Stephen Daldry).

The film *Billy Elliot* was released in 2000 and won numerous awards. It took the audience back to the time of the British miners' strikes in 1984–5. The deprivation and the violence of the industrial conflict are told from the perspective of an 11-year-old boy, Billy Elliot, who is growing up in a mining family. His future seems to be mapped out. But instead of boxing, which his father has enrolled him for, Billy is fascinated by dancing and has secret ballet lessons. Although his father, Jackie, is fiercely opposed to the idea, Billy gets his way and Jackie soon changes his mind. While the strike ends in a bitter defeat, with the help of his father, Billy manages to get to the Royal Ballet School in London and becomes a professional ballet dancer. The future does not belong to physical labour and collective solidarity but to artistic creativity and individual talent. The advertising slogan for the film makes this clear: 'Inside every one of us is a special talent waiting to come out. The trick is finding it.'

main subplots in these commercially successful films in the same way as in the workers' films of the early 1970s. They were also major box office successes in Germany. With a few exceptions, however (such as Werner Schroeter's *Palermo oder Wolfsburg*, 1980), German film and television producers showed practically no interest in the drama of deindustrialization or the new realities of the world of work.

In France and Germany in the 1980s and 1990s, film and television largely steered clear of traditional working-class environments and workers' living conditions. The 'normal life' they depicted was found outside the factories and very rarely amongst those families and households for whom industrial work was the main source of income. Far more attention and imagination was devoted to the social problems arising from long-term unemployment, living off benefits and migration. In 1986, for example, Günter Wallraff's undercover report *Ganz unten* (translated as *Lowest of the Low*) became a hit, selling millions of copies. The book vividly describes the everyday discrimination and different forms of racism to which Turks in Germany were subjected.[63] The response to this book was huge, indignation over the abuse it described was widespread and in the same year a documentary with the same title supplemented the reports with documentary footage and restaged interviews.[64]

The bleak settings of the new urban underclass became more significant as the antithesis of the social context of the rich and beautiful that had always been extensively projected in the media. While in the eponymous German TV crime series, the fictional inspector Derrick carried out his investigations in the posh districts of Munich, wearing a tailor-made suit and speaking High German, in the popular series *Tatort*, the homicide detective Schimanski roamed through the industrial wastelands of Duisburg, cursing and swearing. The two social environments that captured the imagination of viewers and cinemagoers in the 1980s and 1990s, apart from the usual criminal milieu, were the worlds of glamour and of the slums. The traditional boundaries within culturally still divided (industrial) societies became glaringly apparent.

Lack of voice and lack of visibility: society's blurred perceptions of industrial realities

To end this chapter, I would like to consolidate my findings and identify once more the conclusions that can be drawn from them for a social history of industrial labour.

First, in all three countries the voices that had previously procured a collective existence for the various groups of industrial workers as a represented class or socio-professional unit gradually faltered and were finally scarcely audible. This was also the result of left-wing social scientists and cultural producers distancing themselves more and more not only from established patterns of interpretation but also from their own criticism of the existing social and political situation on behalf of a supposedly underprivileged working class. They increasingly directed the focus of their artistic and cultural representation as advocates towards other groups. 'Artistic and social criticism'[65] addressed new aspects of social discrimination and inequality. In all three countries, the major topics of critical cultural production and intellectual interventions that emerged most strongly and urgently were the belated criticism of racism and xenophobia, feminist criticism of the continuing disadvantages and imbalance of power between the sexes and the protection of the freedoms of sexual minorities. This diminished the opportunities for average workers to make themselves heard in the media as a group participating in the political process and public debate about social problems and experiences of fairness and inequality. Instead, they became objects of cultural criticism and satire and to a certain extent replaced the figure of the 'petit bourgeois' in the imagined social world of cultural producers.[66]

Second, it is evident that in all three countries there was a disintegration of the means of representation which had given working people a place in the political arena in their own specific national form. This loss of representation corresponded to the growing distance between people from this socio-economic category and the organizations which claimed to represent them. This was true for trade unions as well as for political parties of all shades. For France, Louis Chauvel spoke of the *classes populaires* experiencing a 'sense of atomization': a class-specific variant of the process of subjectification that could be observed throughout society.[67] His colleagues Stéphane Beaud and Michel Pialoux talk about the 'end' of the *classe ouvrière*[68] and its 'becoming invisible'. By this they meant not only a class in the sense of social science analyses but also a concrete historical entity which had developed out of a process of political representation, group-specific solidarity and shared experiences and values. It had also comprised a clear and even self-confident rejection of 'bourgeois' schemes of interpretation and representatives of the established order. The French *classe ouvrière* was a class in the same sense as the English working class, whose 'making' E.P. Thompson described.[69] It disappeared during the dual process of the transformation of cultural representation and socio-economic upheaval. In West Germany, the balance of representation also shifted towards a lower profile and a widening gap, but there was a notable difference. West German workers had already lost this form of close-knit class existence long before 1989, namely in the 1930s. After 1945, they had become the subject and object of quite different political and trade union representation processes, and after 1975 their social and socio-economic situation was disrupted once again by recessions, crises in certain branches of industry and the third industrial revolution. Just as in France, the affiliation between German workers and the major political parties, especially the SPD, weakened. However, the level of trade union commitment remained high and the representation of workers' collective interests at company level even increased, as we will see. The British situation is somewhere between that of France and West Germany. Some sections of the working classes were dealt a massive material blow by deindustrialization, leading to the collapse of regional centres of traditional working-class culture in particular. The political crisis in the Labour Party and the trade unions in the 1980s and early 1990s aggravated this process and was responsible for the political representation of the working classes in Britain becoming even weaker or completely disappearing.

In all three countries, however, it took until the millennium for this trend to have any noticeable consequences for the left-wing parties. They were dramatic in France in the presidential elections of 2002 when the run-off was between the bourgeois candidate Jacques Chirac and the extreme right-wing populist Jean-Marie Le Pen and have been equally dramatic for the SPD in Germany since 2005. As a result, working-class voters were open to other political options and currents. This trend was also reinforced by the fact that jobseekers and the unemployed from the dwindling world of industry and first-time workers, particularly women, poured into the vacancies for ordinary service jobs. This was a working environment largely without tradition and working cultures, which allowed dominant interpretive schemes and *doxa* to advance unchallenged.

A third finding is connected to this. Empirical studies on the 'social sense' (*sens social*) of blue- and white-collar workers at the end of the 1990s have repeatedly confirmed that social inequality was still not perceived as a kaleidoscope of subtle distinctions as suggested by *doxa* in the media but rather seen to reflect traditional inequality in the structure of society. Interviewees in all three countries positioned themselves within the conventional pair of opposites 'us and them' and as 'working class' within the established paradigm of a three-tier social space (working class/middle class/upper class). Even in West Germany, where we have seen that the perception of social inequality was imprecise and lacked the support of official categories, those belonging to the lower-income group saw themselves as an independent section of society at a clear distance from 'them up there' and from mid-level workers and managers, and especially from the alien world of those in secure higher-level employment in the public sector.[70] If we take these results seriously, there is a strong argument against denying the existence of the socio-economic category 'the working class'. Rather, it makes more sense to locate it at the level of regional and local social spaces, in which both solidarity at the workplace and a more general solidarity, usually within trade unions, continued to exist and be articulated. It would then occur as particularly tangible and effective where this struggle for representation and mobilization continued to be important. Even during the early period of industrialization, the working classes were already a collection of diverse regional and local groups, owing their collective existence mainly to the struggle for political representation on a national level by members of the social democratic and socialist parties. In this respect, a social history of the late twentieth century needs to follow on from that of the nineteenth century but with one significant difference. In the case of the late twentieth century, we are dealing with a process of 'un-making', in which a significant role is played by the transformation of political forms of representation and political languages.

— Chapter 3 —

POLITICAL HISTORY FROM BELOW
Labour conflict and new social movements

'The history of all hitherto existing society is the history of class struggles.'[1] This statement from the *Communist Manifesto* of 1848 was the source of inspiration for a history of society which based its narrative of historical progress on labour conflicts and political conflicts between labour and capital. It developed in critical contrast to a 'grand' political history of powerful states and the biographical narratives of great statesmen, as a history of events, of strikes and of 'labour politics'. Its aim was to expose both fundamental conflicts in society and structural changes in capitalism. This tradition of a 'heroic' and activist understanding of history was still strong in the labour movements of Britain, France and West Germany in the 1970s, as we have just seen. The languages of mobilization of social democratic, socialist and communist groups were guided by these grand narratives in very different ways. That has long since changed, and the close but simple interconnection of economic, political and social progress with the history of emancipatory movements is no longer a major issue. However, social movements and social protests are still the focus of historical research, which increasingly adopts international and comparative perspectives and examines longer-term processes. This was how research in social science and history reacted to the worldwide spread of social movements after the 1960s.

New actors (students, schoolchildren, women, gay people, etc.) developed new forms of action and new movements, while at the same time drawing from the resources of the labour movement. In Western democracies, mass demonstrations, protest marches and the illegal occupation of buildings have become a more or less accepted part of the repertoire of action used in the arena of political conflict across the political spectrum. They were a crucial element

91

in the democratic revolutions of 1989–90 in Eastern and Central Europe, and their spread was promoted by the new information technologies and media.[2] It is interesting to see that their links to labour conflict and the social protests of industrial workers were never broken. On the contrary, in many countries they even became closer as a result of the global processes of industrialization. For this reason, a history of society in the deindustrialization period must also include a political history of events pertaining to labour conflict and social protests. Before I examine this more closely in this chapter, I would like briefly to outline the contribution that this makes to the history of society this book is attempting to narrate.

First, it shows how limited the opportunities for political participation in times of growing social inequality and economic crisis were (and still are). We must not forget that industrial workers are people whose position in society and politics did not normally allow them direct access to any means of influencing business and economic policy during the deindustrialization process. Only rarely did they articulate their demands directly. They were (and are) rarely able to participate in the political process in 'normal' times, since they were hampered by legal barriers (e.g. in the workplace), a feeling of social inferiority, lack of education and the established structures of delegation within political parties and trade unions. In the parliaments of the three countries studied in this book, industrial workers were increasingly seen as an 'exotic species'. Even among the officials in the left-wing parties and trade unions, who referred to the workers as 'their' bedrock, the proportion of those who had previously worked in industry sank. Since the 1990s, Britain, France and Germany have recorded a decline in voter turnout for democratic elections. This, together with the remarkably high support for right-wing populist parties, has meant that at least since the economic crisis of 2008–9, the question of the participation of the *classes populaires* or lower and working classes in democracy has returned to the agenda. As a result, the older issue of the distance between these classes and established forms of parliamentary democracy – 'them up there' – has re-emerged. It seemed to have been forgotten for decades, not only in politics but also in the academic world, because the established forms of representing the interests of industrial workers through trade unions and left-wing parties had become one of the basic features of all three democracies after 1945. What interests me most in all this, however, is the means that were used and the demands that were made when workers introduced the issues of social hardship, economic conditions and company decisions into political disputes.

As will be shown, their 'politics from below' challenged the established ways of delegating political decision-making power to political parties, parliaments and governments.

Second, a political history of events relating to labour conflict and social protests can examine the connection between specific political interventions and the concrete forms and surrounding circumstances of deindustrialization. In chapter 1, I analysed decisions taken by businesses, capital owners, government politicians and experts in international organizations, whereby industrial workers were mainly regarded as the affected party. Now it is time to examine this more closely and to discover whether social protests and social movements had any lasting effects on social and economic policy in these three countries. A further focus is the persistence and resistance demonstrated by those directly affected by mass redundancies, factory closures and company bankruptcies.

Third, a political history of events relating to social protests and the mobilization of workers since the late 1960s is to a large extent a history of the way they were presented and communicated by the media. It was only through their media presentation that social protests could become 'events'.[3] In the perception not only of the actors, but also of television and radio audiences and newspaper readers, they became trials of strength and veritable dramas with the potential to influence the future of politics, the economy and society. It was a question of moral recognition and the establishment of specific types of social order. Topics such as protests, mass rallies and strikes were typically addressed and evaluated using the military language of victory or defeat. The strike for the 35-hour working week in the German metal industry in 1984 was one of these dramas. So was the British miners' strike that began in the same year but lasted until March 1985. Although the consequences of these two events were very different, they did have one thing in common which makes them interesting for my history of society. Both of them were of enormous practical everyday significance, not only for those who were directly involved, whether on strike, locked out or as police officers, but also in the medium term for those who were not directly involved, so for other workers, businesses and social groups, and also for governments and parliaments.

In the following, therefore, I will focus exclusively on those occurrences which were 'events'. Events in this case are conflicts which were visible in the media, which proved in retrospect to be historical landmarks with long-term effects and which can be seen as exemplary in so far as they are structurally similar to other events in the same period. They are also symptomatic in character because they exposed changes and developments particularly clearly.

Social protests and labour conflicts: the frameworks and conditions specific to each nation

In chapter 2, I outlined the various perspectives from which the democratic class conflict in Britain, France and Germany was seen and evaluated. These perspectives were specific to each country and the major opportunities they offered for protest campaigns and social movements were very different. This is clearly illustrated by the legal regulation of strike action. In Britain, since the Trades Dispute Act of 1906, collective labour relations had developed into a purely politically managed sphere of democratic class conflict outside the reach of individual labour law. Its rules were negotiated between the two collective parties, the trade unions and businesses, in the 'free play of forces', and in a space that was regulated largely without recourse to the law but through convention and agreement. This left those involved a great deal of scope for interpretation and action. In Germany, by contrast, even after free collective bargaining and the right to strike had been reintroduced in 1945, strikes and labour conflicts were subject to tight legal restrictions. Strikes that were purely political and had no direct connection to wage bargaining conflicts – sympathy strikes and wildcat strikes – were considered here to be overstepping the mark. In British labour disputes, however, almost anything short of the direct use of violence was legal. France's position was somewhere in between. Although in contrast to Britain the right to strike was legally regulated, the scope for political strikes was much wider than in Germany. Strikes were used regularly by French trade unions and left-wing parties as a legitimate means of intervention in the political arena. The CGT with its socialist and communist leanings was at the forefront of developing a tradition of regular national token strikes to articulate political demands and mobilize its own supporters.[4] The trade union confederations in Britain and Germany, in contrast, the Trades Union Congress (TUC) and the German Trade Union Confederation (DGB), kept a much lower profile and made greater use of their close connections to the Labour Party and the SPD respectively to exert political influence.

The first point that becomes apparent when examining the relationship between the British, French and German labour organizations and the government or state is that in all three countries the left-wing parties saw themselves as the main representatives of workers' interests. This meant they cultivated friendly and even close relations with industrial unions. Trade unions and socialist and communist workers' parties were important actors in the realization of the far-reaching socio-political and economic reforms after the end of World War II and in the reconstruction phase. These reforms created the basis for the forms of so-called democratic capitalism specific to each country which moulded the social order in all three countries during the economic boom: that is, from 1948 to 1973.[5] Important achievements in this reform phase included the expansion of the welfare state, widespread nationalization in Britain and France and the right to union representation at factory and company level. In all three countries, workers who were (re-)politicized and mobilized, especially in the immediate postwar period, focussed on defending and/or extending these fundamental achievements during the subsequent two decades.

The brief immediate postwar period when left-wing parties exerted strong political influence and effective power in the shaping of social and labour policy was followed by the years of the economic boom, in which they were frequently in opposition. This spell was shortest in Britain, where the Labour Party returned to government in 1964 after thirteen years (1951) and remained in power with a brief interlude (1970–4) until 1979. In Germany, the SPD was not part of the government at the federal level until 1966, but led coalition governments from 1969 until 1982. In France during the Fourth Republic (1945–58), the socialists (and until 1947 the communists) had frequently been part of the government, but in 1958 a long period of Gaullist dominance began, lasting until 1981. This resulted in a major difference which is important for our topic here. During the long periods of opposition, extra-parliamentary protest and political strike action became established on the left as legitimate forms of political practice. But by the mid-1960s in Britain and Germany, they were already beginning to be regarded with some scepticism within the ranks of traditional organizations in the labour movement. They were in favour of moderating such protests and demands because they were banking on moving closer to the government and so being able to influence policies in a more discreet way.

In the end, styles of politicizing specific to the respective countries developed within the working populations in Britain, France and Germany. They focused particularly on the social experience and self-image of male industrial workers. In the period immediately after the war, it was miners, steelworkers and metalworkers who were endorsed as the leading figures in trade union representation and left-wing (social democratic or communist) politics in all three countries. This was helped by the fact that for industrial workers left-wing politics was based on a multi-level delegation model of political participation. It began within households and families, where men were responsible for politics. In the factories, the task of representing interests and articulating opinions was delegated to older skilled workers, and at the regional and national level, a largely uncontrolled mandate of representation and leadership was assigned to party and trade union functionaries, who were regularly re-elected and came from their own ranks. This delegation model was implicitly authoritarian but saw itself at the same time as an egalitarian and democratic power that could counteract established hierarchies in factories, businesses and bourgeois conservative government majorities. In this question of political style, the British, French and West German traditions of labour politics were surprisingly similar.

The traditional dichotomy between militancy and cooperation could also be found in all three countries, with the result that the delegation model described above combined two different styles of politics when mobilizing ordinary grassroots members. Activating them by means of mass rallies and strikes was considered by left-wing groups in these three countries to be best practice, because at the same time as advancing material interests, it promoted and strengthened political class consciousness. This approach contrasted with the more moderate wing, who were convinced that sufficient membership and money to support strikes would secure the power of the organizations and guarantee a conflict-oriented policy of cooperation with businesses and governments. For the representatives of this style of politics, mobilizing the grassroots was an exception to the rule to be carefully calculated. Both models, militancy and cooperation, found supporters in all three countries, and it was mainly political and institutional frameworks and economic developments that determined the fluctuation in the balance of power between them in the various organizations. The difference was most highly politically charged in France, since there the different political and ideological traditions behind these models were determined by rival trade unions and political parties. Militancy was strongly favoured by the communist-dominated CGT, while the cooperation model was represented by the other (much smaller) trade union groups: the Force Ouvrière (FO) and the Confédération Française des Travailleurs Chrétiens (CFTC), which was 'secularized' in 1964 to become the Confédération Française Democratique des Travailleurs (CFDT). In Britain, both directions were spread across the whole spectrum of industrial trade unions, with skilled workers' organizations tending more towards the cooperation model and those organizations which represented unskilled or semi-skilled workers often preferring the more militant model. In West Germany, the ideological neutrality of the unified trade unions after 1945 and their anti-communism ensured that the more militant wing only survived the boom years as a minority movement in a very few cases such as IG Druck und Papier and IG Metall. The more moderate wing, which was sceptical of political mobilization, had a far greater influence here than in Britain and France.

During the period of imperial expansion, national mobilization and two world wars, the internationalism which had been initially rooted in the labour organizations of the three countries was transformed into a strong national or even at times nationalist consciousness. It was evident in the way they distanced themselves to a greater or lesser extent from the traditions and customs of neighbouring labour cultures which they felt were inferior. Much more important in practical political terms was the passive acceptance or even blatant cultivation of ethnocentric and racist attitudes towards migrant workers.[6] All three labour movements initially either were critical of fellow workers who came into the factories from Asia, the Caribbean or Mediterranean countries after the 1950s or were openly hostile towards them. It has to be said that these attitudes were vigorously opposed by the most politicized members of the labour organizations in all three countries and never became part of their official philosophy. However, they still remained an underlying tendency and had considerable implications especially at company and local levels.

Militancy and new social movements (1968–79)

The recession in 1973–4 did not lead to a hiatus in the history of social protest movements in Britain, France or Germany. To find the beginning of an international cycle of strikes, labour conflicts and social protest, we have to go back to the second half of the 1960s. For the three countries in this study, we can take 1968 as its symbolic beginning. Let us first look at France. When student protests and local strikes developed into a general strike on 13 May and then rapidly escalated, with local factories being occupied and company managers detained, for fourteen days social and political protests took on proportions that had not been seen since the occupation

97

of the factories in 1936 after the election victory of the Popular Front. In terms of its militancy, the extent to which it mobilized people and its forms of action, the wave of strikes far exceeded the fears and expectations of the political establishment.[7] Businesses in rural and small town areas which had never or hardly ever been involved in any union action or labour conflict before became the scene of protest meetings and factory occupations and in many places there was close contact and cooperation between striking workers and protesting students. Trade unions and left-wing political parties found themselves challenged by new militant actors. The delegation model was criticized and in many places the wave of strikes resembled a broad protest movement against the established hierarchies in factories and the status quo in society. This radical break with the social order combined the forms of action in the factories with those of the student unrest in May 1968 (see figure 3.1). In actual fact, for a short period of time they made up just one single social movement. Its political potential was steered by the establishment in the labour movement, above all the CGT and PCF, towards the single goal of winning votes in the election called by Charles de Gaulle. The explosive potential of its labour policies was also defused by the trade unions' successful collective bargaining and wage agreements in the central negotiations for the Grenelle Agreement (see figure 4.1).[8]

The strikes in May and June 1968 triggered a cycle of labour conflicts and social protests that were not to finish until long after the economic crisis of 1973–4, in fact only after strikes and occupations, protests and the march of the steelworkers from Denain and Longwy to Paris in March 1979. Xavier Vigna once called this ten-year phase one of *insubordination ouvrière*, workers' 'defiance', 'rebellion' or 'refusal to be submissive'.[9] What was characteristic was that the labour conflicts often spread in the surrounding regions and that the strikers tried to mobilize their direct surroundings or at least found support there in other social settings and political groups. Especially when it came to factory occupations, many local inhabitants sided with the workers. At the same time, the activists attracted the attention of the national media by deliberately breaking rules and committing spectacular acts of violence. In the case of such 'active' occupations, public debates were organized, the strikers themselves made contact with journalists and were at pains to present their strikes to the public as a form of broad democratic participation. Overall, the radius of action and the repertoire of strike forms expanded considerably during these ten years and typically many of the protests and actions systematically overstepped the boundaries

Figure 3.1 'It's right to lock up the bosses.' Still from *Tout Va Bien* (France, 1972; director: Jean-Luc Godard).

Jean-Luc Godard's film *Tout Va Bien* was released in 1972. It concerns an American journalist, played by Jane Fonda, and her French husband, played by Yves Montand, who witness the occupation of a sausage factory. The film shows the relevance of the labour struggles after May 1968 to the whole of society. By using the occupied administration building as a backdrop, Godard makes it possible to see inside the factory. It seems for a moment that the barrier between the workers, on the one hand, and students and intellectuals, on the other, can be overcome. At the same time, it calls into question the very existence of the hierarchies within factories. This is made clear by the bloodstained overalls in the clean offices as well as the slogans on the banner. They read 'unlimited strike' and 'it's right to lock up the bosses'.

of legality. The circle of participants also expanded. The groups of labour migrants, unskilled women and young people that had first emerged in May 1968 continued to be active in the following years. Their mobilization undermined the established hierarchies in the representation of workers' interests and so altered the catalogue of demands of the trade unions, who found themselves forced to take more notice of hitherto neglected interests (such as those of low-paid workers) and issues (such as job design and job security). In many companies, the militancy of ordinary workers was closely linked to their rebellion against poor working conditions and the lack of social and political recognition in the large Taylorized factories. A new generation of strike leaders and spokespeople for labour protests became established in and alongside the trade unions. Some of them came from radical left-wing groups that had made their way into the factories after 1968, but most of them only became politicized during the strikes and protests of 1968 and afterwards took over the trade union representation of interests in many companies. Between 1968 and 1979, some of the new militant activists were welcomed into the ranks of the CGT and especially the CFDT, which was moving increasingly towards the left. As a result, the CFDT was able to establish itself as the alternative to the CGT, which was fiercely criticized by the left in May 1968 because of its strictly reform-oriented course. What was also typical for this cycle of strikes was their close association with issues that were already prominently represented by other social movements. This included the right to freedom of political expression and the protection of individual personal rights as well as the demand for education and professional qualifications.

An event that can exemplify this phase is the strike and occupation of LIP, a watch factory in Besançon. The 'LIP affair' began in April 1973 and lasted for more than three years. The conflict was triggered when the business was taken over by its Swiss minority shareholder and the workers discovered secret plans for redundancies and closures. They reacted by going on strike and occupying the factory, where they continued to produce and distribute watches unofficially and illegally. The conflict came to a head when the police evicted the strikers in August 1973, which led to sympathy strikes and violent clashes between workers and security forces in Besançon. The LIP workers' struggle was popularized throughout France, becoming a media event with the slogan 'C'est possible: on fabrique, on vend, on paie!' (It's possible: we make them, we sell them, we get paid). The protest march through the city on 19 September 1973 with more than 100,000 participants from all over France became a first turning point, since in the face of the broad wave of sympathy the Gaullist government and the business federation declared they were prepared to consent to self-management as a solution and agreed to negotiate with the strikers. On 29 January 1974, a contract was signed by a delegation of the workforce and government representatives agreeing to restart the company under the name of Compagnie europeénne d'horlogerie. The whole workforce was reinstated and production and sales were made legal again. However, this self-management experiment was brought down again within a few months. During the economic crisis of 1974–5, the new government under the presidency of Valéry Giscard d'Estaing, which rejected the concessions made by the previous government, withdrew the promise of financial support. In addition, creditors from the old company demanded payment in arrears and a major order from the state-owned company Renault was cancelled. The self-managed company had to go into liquidation in 1977, but the workforce continued some sections of production in seven separate production cooperatives for several years. While the first phase of the 'LIP affair' from 1973 to 1974 was still a political media event at the national level, the subsequent conflict over the continuation of the company was fought out as a conflict of interests behind the scenes. Its context was only exposed four decades later by research and debate around a documentary film.[10]

The struggle for LIP became a symbol and test for the demand for *autogestion* (self-management) which had become popular during the protests of May 1968.[11] The non-communist left and the CFDT union turned the factory occupation into an experiment for worker self-management to which many other factory occupiers referred as an alternative to the closure of factories. It was frequently imitated, especially in small and medium-sized companies. Between 1974 and 1984, between forty and 100 factories were occupied per year.[12] Other forms of action during these factory occupations included the hostage-taking or 'dismissal' of the employers (see figure 3.1) and the continuation of production (*grèves productives*, or 'productive strikes', was the definition given by one group of strikers).[13]

The 'LIP affair' was at the same time also representative of the basic conflicts underlying the wave of social mobilization. First, the factory regime established in France during the boom years – the Taylorist organization of work, authoritarian rules of conduct and patriarchal management style – was challenged and gradually robbed of its political and moral justification. The exclusion of labour from this distribution of power in the factories was disputed loudly and audibly. Second, both employers and the state, when confronted with this radical delegitimization of the factory order, were prepared to introduce only limited reforms. While they largely submitted to the trade unions and striking workforces in the case of wage demands, not least because of rising inflation, innovations such as in the area of union representation in the factories or as regards transparency within the companies failed due to resistance from conservative forces in parliament and industry.[14] The state, on the other hand, was prepared to make some concessions. These included raising and restructuring the legal minimum wage, initial agreements about early retirement in the steel industry, the legal introduction of a monthly wage and other socio-political measures following the 'Grenelle Agreement' that had ended the wave of strikes in 1968.

In Britain, the frequency and militancy of labour struggles also increased between 1964 and 1979. As shown in table 3.1, the years between 1968 and 1971 marked an initial peak, with the number of days of work lost in this period soaring from 2.5 million to more than 9 million per year. Both the rate of worker participation in strikes and their frequency were to remain at this high level until the end of the decade. The British cycle of militant labour conflicts came to a head in the winter of discontent of 1978–9.

This high frequency of strikes in Britain was linked to the increasing influence of a mostly younger generation of shop stewards: that is, union representatives within factories or departments. They tripled in number during the 1970s (to approximately 300,000 by the end of the decade) with the result that they were present in 74 per cent of all companies with more than fifty employees.[15] Much more than in France, the main focus of these labour struggles in Britain was on issues of pay and workplace organization as well as in-company conflicts. There were very few links to wider political topics or to other

Table 3.1 Frequency of strikes in Britain, 1964–79

Period	Number of participants per year (on average)	Lost labour days per year (on average)
1964–7	758,750	2,596,750
1968–71	1,725,500	9,016,750
1972–5	1,424,250	12,967,000
1976–9	1,871,000	13,076,250

Source: My calculations from John McIlroy and Alan Campbell, 'The High Tide of Trade Unionism: Mapping Industrial Politics, 1964–79', in John McIlroy et al. (eds), *The High Tide of British Trade Unionism: Trade Unions and Industrial Politics, 1964–79*, Monmouth, 2007, pp. 93–130, here p. 122; ibid., p. 100.

social groups or environments, since the spark from the universities and colleges and their circles did not spread to the industrial workers in the same way as it did in France. The social distance between them was too great. Instead, the unrest at the universities strengthened the socialist New Left and its various groupings in terms of people and ideas, and especially the Trotskyists, who were traditionally strong in Britain and in France. As a result, the small militant wing of the British labour movement, which had until then consisted mainly of traditional communist trade union cadres, gained new and younger supporters. They brought in fresh ideas and creative forms of action and were prepared to form alliances with other social groups.[16]

In Britain, too, it was the government and parliament that were the prime targets of this new militancy. As in France, it aimed beyond businesses and sectors of industry towards achieving structural changes in the political balance of power. The first opportunity for this kind of mobilization was provided by the Industrial Relations Act passed by the Conservative government in 1971. For the first time since 1906, this law attempted to place legal strictures on industrial relations, with the declared aim of curing the so-called British disease. Its symptoms were seen as frequent, often short-lived strikes involving only a limited group of workers, and a lack of negotiation procedures. The law was opposed by the trade unions without exception. Their supporters (and the Labour Party, which was dominated by their block votes) were mobilized against it. Their umbrella organization, the TUC, called for protest strikes and rallies on 1 March 1971 under the slogan 'Kill the Bill'. According to contemporary estimates, up to 1.5 million people participated in the protests nationwide. A second battle for power between the Conservative government and the trade unions and the labour movement was the miners' strike of 1972.[17] The adversaries in this strike, which was ostensibly about wage increases, were the National Coal Board, the management body of the nationalized coal industry, and the National Union of Mineworkers (NUM). The National Coal Board, however, was backed by the Conservative government, which had a vested interest in the failure of this strike as a means of promoting their own trade union policies and the anti-inflation policies they had recently introduced. The trade unions also soon saw the strike as a confrontation with the government.

The fact that the government was ultimately defeated and had to give in to the demands of the miners' union was mainly thanks to the aggressive strike tactics of a young trade union secretary from Yorkshire, Arthur Scargill. The focal point of the dispute was the battle between striking miners and the police over deliveries of coke from the Saltley depot near Birmingham. During the first few days of the siege of the depot, Scargill brought pickets into Birmingham from 'his' area of Yorkshire, but with only moderate success. When he managed to persuade local trade unions and businesses to take part in the protest, however, the floodgates opened. The sight of factory workers streaming in from all over Birmingham, singing and waving their banners, and the local police locking the gates of the coke depot became a national media event whose effect was not lost on the government.[18]

Scargill himself described this as a historic 'battle', which is also how it was treated in the media. Just like many young French activists in this decade of political movements, he and his supporters saw themselves as part of a heroic tradition of labour disputes on the path towards socialism, or at least towards more equality and democracy. For their political opponent, the government, the miners' strike of 1972 was also historic in the sense that it was a major blunder which should 'never again' be repeated. After Prime Minister Edward Heath's tactics for breaking the miners' strike in 1974 also proved unsuccessful, Conservative hard-liners drew up an internal strategy paper in 1978 so as to be better prepared for another round of strikes. These plans were drawn on by the Thatcher government in 1982 to prepare the framework for dealing with a fully anticipated future miners' strike in such a way that a government defeat would be impossible.[19]

Before this strategy was implemented in 1984, the return of the Labour government from 1974 to 1979 under first Harold Wilson and then James Callaghan led to the repeal of the Industrial Relations Act. But in no way did it lead to a change in the social climate. As in France, inflation and the threat of job losses further fuelled the willingness to take strike action. What followed was the so-called winter of discontent of 1978–9. It has gone down in British history as a socio-political lowpoint and watershed and has been interpreted by both conservatives and social democrats since the 1980s as the climax of the British disease. Official statistics registered 4.6 million workers on strike during this time – an peak unrivalled even in the turbulent 1970s.[20] There are, however, other features that clearly distinguish this accumulation of events from the miners' strikes of 1970 to 1974 and also from the 'LIP affair'. First, it was a series of uncoordinated strikes in specific occupations and branches of industry, focussing primarily on adjusting wages to spiralling inflation. At the same time, it was a social protest on the part of many different groups of workers against their working and living conditions, which had lagged behind the general increase of prosperity over the decade.[21] Various groups of workers now attempted to achieve what the miners had already achieved in 1972 and 1974 with their spectacular wage gains. However, while each group was fuelled by the success of others, they failed to specifically coordinate their efforts. What developed was outright wage militancy that included some features of social protest, for example when National Health Service workers went on strike against their low pay without compromise or consideration of the sick. In this context, Andy Beckett has spoken of a 'peasants' revolt', pointing out that this explosion of dissatisfaction more or less escaped the control of the trade unions and also that the proportion of militant left-wing activists was relatively small.[22] Once again, the media images – such as of mountains of rubbish (see figure 3.2), patients left unattended in hospitals and streets blockaded by lorries – were extremely important. They suggested a state of chaos close to anarchy. It was thus foreseeable, even during the final phase of the strike wave, that the Conservative policy of setting up the trade unions as a scapegoat responsible for the 'British decline' began to seem increasingly plausible, not only in the eyes of a wider public but also to some sections of the social sciences. By 1979, the result in political terms of the cycle of mobilization in Britain was mainly negative, before the next economic crisis at the beginning of the 1980s robbed it of its foundation in many sectors of industry.

In summary, it can be said that in Britain, as in France, social protests gained significance between 1968 and 1979. More people than ever went out onto the streets to protest and demonstrate, and they were striking not only in support of their own interests but also in support of workers in other types of jobs and factories. However, it is a characteristic of the British situation that alliances at the local, let alone national, level between trade unions and the new social movements were quite rare. The concerns and demands of the various groups of actors were very different and networking was practically non-existent. The trade unions and the Labour Party in particular were anxious to ensure that pragmatic short-term goals and traditional orientations continued to be dominant and that a fundamental politicization, for example with a view to working conditions and company hierarchies, did not take place.[23] The socio-cultural distance between the various groups of actors also turned out to be considerably more entrenched than, for example, in France. This meant that the socio-structural differences, which were already very pronounced in Britain, and their accompanying mechanisms of

105

Figure 3.2   Piles of rubbish in Leicester Square, London, 1979.

In the winter of 1978–9, the 'winter of discontent', strike action paralysed British public services. The mountains of rubbish collecting on the pavements became a symbol of the endless strikes that had got out of hand. Photos of London's Leicester Square were particularly popular. This was probably because of the large statue of Shakespeare in the park at the centre of the square ('winter of discontent' is a quotation from Shakespeare's *Richard III*), and also because of other statues of famous figures in British history in the park, including William Hogarth and Isaac Newton, whose head can be seen sticking out over the pile of rubbish in this picture. This is a meeting of the glorious past with the present ostensibly on the road to ruin.

106

cultural and ethnic exclusion, were far less seriously challenged by the social movements than they were across the Channel.

One exception was the Grunwick dispute. This involved the struggle for union recognition by the mostly female workers in their small film processing company in West London. It was a long local strike that lasted for nearly a year from August 1976 to July 1977, exciting a good deal of media attention. It also mobilized both the left-wing and right-wing political camps, each leaping to actively support one or other side in the struggle: either the mainly Asian female strikers or the company owner George Ward, himself the son of Anglo-Indian parents. The strike was over the trade union rights of notoriously poorly paid female workers from former British colonies in Southern Asia and Africa. While left-wing activists from various London groupings crowded the picket lines outside the company to prevent the developed photos being delivered to customers, George Ward found solid support for his rigid rejection of trade unions from an organization on the right-wing libertarian fringe of the conservative camp, the National Association for Freedom (NAFF). NAFF organized a clandestine distribution network to supply Ward's customers and so thwarted the actions of the unionized post office workers, who, in a show of solidarity, were trying to prevent the delivery of the company's products. This was another case of a conflict becoming politicized and widening the gap between the right wing of the Conservative Party and the 'trade unions', which had now come to symbolize support for the various social demands and social protests from below.

The picture of West Germany that presents itself to us at the end of this section differs significantly from that of Britain and France. Although the number of strikes increased, it remained very low by international standards. During this long decade from 1968 to 1979, West Germany participated in the cycle of militant labour conflicts only in a considerably weaker and more moderate form. In 1967–8, most German workers were sceptical or hostile towards the student protests, and the participation of the German Trade Union Confederation (Deutscher Gewerkschaftsbund/DGB) in the protest against the emergency laws (*Notstandsgesetze*) was no more than a brief episode of limited cooperation with the extra-parliamentary opposition (Außer Parlamentarische Opposition/APO). It ended in May 1968 when the emergency laws were passed by the German parliament. Nevertheless, the radical student protests did have a belated effect on German industrial workers after 1969 in a similar way to that in France and Britain. The 'September strikes' in 1969, the strikes at the Ford works in Cologne in 1973 and finally growing criticism from younger trade unionists of the pro-government and pro-business course of some of the industrial trade unions, especially the chemical workers' (IG Chemie) and the miners'/energy workers' unions (IG Bergbau und Energie), can all be seen within the wider context of the protest movements of 1968 in a similar way to the labour disputes and workplace conflicts in France and Britain.[24] However, as we have seen above, the frequency and scope of the strikes remained low in comparison to the other two countries. The official strike statistics for 1970–4 show that 1.24 million working days were lost to strikes, which is around one-tenth of the figure for Britain.[25] The industrial trade unions succeeded in swiftly containing the dissatisfaction and revolt of their rank and file and translating them into corresponding wage demands. In West Germany, the unions also profited from the wave of mobilization, gaining new members and replacing their own leaders and shop stewards in the factories.[26] The trade union representative bodies of the large companies began to include more foreign workers. The metal-workers' union (IG Metall) in particular tried its best to make up for lost time after 1969. Between 1969 and 1973, it registered 300,000 new members annually and its membership increased from 2.024 million in 1969 to 2.685 million in 1979.[27]

At the same time, the governing social–liberal coalition extended the legal scope for furthering the interests of factory workers by amending the law regulating industrial constitutions (*Betriebsverfassungsgesetz*) in 1972 and extending worker participation at company level in 1976. The motto of Willy Brandt's first government programme was 'Let's take a chance with more democracy' (*Mehr Demokratie wagen*). Unlike in France, it led to concrete reforms which the unions in turn felt obliged to support. The new social democratic government heralded a period of close corporatist links between the government and the unions. In the case of West Germany, the delegation model described at the beginning of this section was still combined with a political style on the part of the trade unions that relied on their bargaining power but tended to distrust militancy and the mobilization of their members. For this reason, this 'conflict partnership'[28] – that is, the readiness to compromise between the unions and employers – was able to survive even beyond the first oil crisis of 1973–4, in spite of the organizational strength of the unions and a strong tendency to militancy in the factories.

In contrast to Britain and France, the anti-nuclear movement, environmental groups and the new women's movement in Germany often developed their image by radically rejecting the trade unions and confronting their interest-based policies. This confrontation was particularly pronounced in the case of the anti-nuclear movement. Pictures in the media reinforced this impression and resulted in a clear and distinct line of demarcation being drawn between the 'old' labour movement and the 'new' social movements. This meant, for example, that when the new political party 'die Grünen' (the Greens) was founded in 1980 with its vision of itself as a political rallying point for the new social movements, it largely excluded industrial workers. Many green activists saw the 'workers' as typical representatives of an economic order that threatened the future and the environment because they supported the 'old' short-sighted interest-driven politics and profited from 'calcified' power structures.

The only movement that was able to gain at least a limited amount of support from the trade unions and in workers' circles and gain a foothold there was the peace movement. It gained momentum in 1979 with the so-called NATO 'double-track' decision, concerning the deployment of missiles in Europe, and by autumn 1983 had mushroomed into the biggest protest movement in the history of the Bonn Republic.[29] Especially in large companies, it led to the creation of 'company peace initiatives', whose numbers managed to reach triple figures at their peak in 1983. However, the 'companies' day of action' in the same year was a failure. In general, the German trade union movement frequently expressed reservations about the kinds of acts of civil disobedience practised and propagated by the social movements because they were against the law and had legal consequences. This reveals a strict legalism that was completely foreign to the British and French trade unionists.

Mobilization and protest in crisis (1979–90)

In chapter 1, we saw that industrial decline and restructuring in all three countries accelerated during the 1980s and 1990s. More and more jobs were lost as innovations in organization and technology increasingly shaped the world of work. The characteristics of the long 1970s, with both the beginning of the employment crisis and a peak period of strikes fuelling social protests as well as demands for greater participation, can no longer be seen as central to the following two decades. Again as we saw in chapter 1, the role of the state began to change. The aggressive promotion of industry and technology in those companies directly controlled by the state and job creation

109

schemes as a means of stimulating the economy were replaced by strict monetarist policies accompanied by the privatization of nationalized industries. This reorientation of policy was still highly politically controversial in the early 1980s and pragmatic alternatives to it were offered by the protest movements. This is why this period is particularly important for a political history of deindustrialization.

During the first half of the 1980s, the new governments in Britain, France and West Germany tried to set the course for a different type of industrial and labour policy. They did this in very different ways, as we have seen. They all found themselves faced with socio-political demands from trade unions and those whose jobs were directly threatened. At the same time, they had to defend their new course against other industrial policies which favoured an offensive industrial policy, state investment in threatened branches of industry and public control of business strategies. Nationalization, for example, was a topic that played a prominent role for the steelworkers' unions in all three countries, especially for their rank-and-file members. 'The call for nationalization is something like a call for hope. It is the hope that a nationalized industry or an industry influenced by the state will finally take some notice of the conditions formulated by the workers.'[30] This remark was made by Rudolf Judith, executive member of the metalworkers' union IG Metall and director of the branch office for iron and steel, at the union's congress in 1983, and shows why the demand for nationalization was so popular. But it also points to the disappointment that was felt as soon as it became clear that governments were no longer either able or willing to continue to finance the current losses in the metal industry or to secure sites in the long term. The situation was particularly complicated in France because its socialist government initially attempted to apply this alternative strategy at least partially between 1981 and 1983 before it switched to British and German austerity policies with the aim of financial stability and privatization. Table 3.2 provides an overview of how social protests and social mobilization developed under these new conditions.

The official figures on which this table is based, however, should be viewed with caution and are only used here to illustrate a general trend in rough quantitative dimensions. Labour disputes were and are a notorious problem in labour statistics, data collection varies from country to country and short strikes and work stoppages were often not recorded.[31] Nevertheless, in spite of their shortcomings, these figures demonstrate a Europe-wide trend, as can be seen from the comparative figures for Sweden and Italy.[32] At the beginning of

Table 3.2   Industrial disputes in the manufacturing sector: working days lost to strikes per thousand employees

	1981–2003	1981–5	1986–90	1991–5	1996–2000	2001–3
Germany	33	114	5	22	3	15
France	97	177	87	70	63	n.d.
Britain	269	1027	167	21	15	11
Sweden	60	18	204	47	1	12
Italy	442	1177	398	262	143	96

Source: Hagen Lesch, 'Arbeitskämpfe und Strukturwandel im internationalen Vergleich', in *IW-Trends – Vierteljahresschrift zur empirischen Wirtschaftsforschung aus dem Institut der deutschen Wirtschaft Köln* 32 (2005), no. 2, pp. 1–17, here table 1, p. 4.

the twenty-first century, all three of the countries studied here were situated in the lower range of officially measured strike activities.

In general, it can be said that the emergence of mass unemployment led to a marked drop in the frequency of strikes and to a sudden and rapid decrease in militant strike action across all sectors of industry. As a contrast to the many strikes in the 1970s, this trend was particularly perceptible in France and even more so in Britain. This makes the spectacular strikes and mass rallies that took place between 1977 and 1985 in the old industrial centres even more striking. The 'farewell to the industrial labourer' became a highly emotional and demanding local or regional struggle against the closure of local factories and for the preservation of jobs in areas that were dominated by a single industry. The local dimension is particularly striking. The places where local protest movements were able to attract considerable public attention were shipbuilding areas (Hamburg, Kiel, Bremerhaven, Emden, Glasgow, La Ciotat, Newcastle), areas with steelworks (Nord-Pas-de-Calais, Lorraine, Wales, South Yorkshire, Glasgow, the Ruhr, Saarland and Oberpfalz) and the British mining areas in Wales, Yorkshire and Scotland. Timing was also significant. At the end of the 1970s, just before the outbreak of the second oil crisis, those involved had greater room for manoeuvre and higher expectations and the return to the industrial 'normality' of the economic boom phase still seemed within the realm of possibility. By the beginning of the 1980s, the prospects for the preservation of local industrial sites were diminishing, so that often the only choice left was between a last-ditch stand and silent resignation. Table 3.2 illustrates that 1985 was something of a watershed for the labour conflicts of Western European industries. In the years immediately afterwards, the trend swiftly reversed and industrial strikes became an exception; the figures for industrial disputes in Britain and France reached the comparatively low level for Germany surprisingly quickly.

I have chosen five spectacular events to examine the specifics of 'politics from below' in this first critical phase of deindustrialization: the steelworkers' strike in Longwy/Denain in 1978–9, the British miners' strike in 1984–5 and the walkout and strike in Rheinhausen in 1987–8 as examples of forms of social protest in the old industrial areas that attracted mass media coverage; then the strike for the 35-hour week in 1984 and the anti-poll tax campaign in 1989–90 as examples of social movements whose objectives were relevant to society as a whole.

First to France. In 1978–9, strikes, factory occupations and protests effectively caused a state of emergency for several months in the two French steel towns of Denain in the *département* Nord/Pas de Calais and Longwy in Meurthe-et-Moselle. They came first in a whole series of mass protests against factory closures in regions of France, Britain and Germany that were mostly dependent on a single industry. The protests were triggered by the 'rescue plan' with which the French government wanted to realize its share in the European steel crisis policy. In France, as in Britain, the steel industry was initially nationalized de facto and then after 1981 de jure. The workers in both Denain and Longwy, two small industrial cities, were mostly employed in the factories that were threatened with closure or worked in their supplier companies. At the end of the 1970s in Longwy, this amounted to 14,000 people.[33] When plans for closure were announced in both regions, action committees were formed, factories were occupied and there were mass rallies. On 19 December 1978 in Longwy, 20,000 people participated (the equivalent of approximately a fifth of the population), and on 12 January 1979, there were 60,000 participants in Metz. Their actions soon became more violent and targeted symbols of both business and state power. Roads were blocked; police stations and security officers were attacked (in Denain, for example, seven police officers were injured by shots on 7 and 8 May). The two trade union groups that were strongest locally, the CGT and the CFDT, relied on a broad mobilization of the rank and file. In the first phase of the conflict, they tried to organize a broadly regional movement of solidarity to keep both steelworks open, while not forgetting to maintain their competitive relationship.[34]

To do this, they developed new forms of action. To avoid being dependent on national and local media and to counter widespread dissatisfaction with their reporting of events, the local unions set up their own illegal strike radio stations that broadcast regionally and created an alternative account to the reports in the mainstream media. In the previous chapter, we mentioned the CGT radio station Lorraine Cœur d'Acier (LCA), which was the more powerful station and run independently by two professional journalists. The key to its success was that it provided not only different groups of activists but also the wider public with a platform for uncensored information and direct communication. The two journalists ran it as a 'public access' radio station where everyone could have their say. This offer was widely used. Telephone contributions were broadcast without censorship and open discussion was the station's policy.

The LCA broadcast for eighteen months from March 1979 to July 1980 but was increasingly attacked by the CGT and the Communist Party, which felt that the diversity of opinion and internal criticism went too far and were afraid that their own political course might be weakened. At the same time, the illegal broadcasts, which were enormously popular amongst the locals, were subjected repeatedly to massive disruption by the government using helicopter operations. When the independent journalists were dismissed in June 1980 and the programmes placed under the direct control of the union, the audience and contributors lost interest. The project was effectively over.[35] It is worth noting that the demand for the democratization of media communication that had been formulated repeatedly since May 1968 was spectacularly implemented in this experimental strike radio initiative in the remote Lorraine steel town of Longwy, making media history.[36] The LCA programmes dealt not only with current issues from the point of view of different groups in the population, but also, as mentioned in the previous chapter, the programme called Le passé présent (The Present Past) created a regional history 'from below'. It allowed the industrial workforce, including a large proportion of immigrants from Belgium, Poland and Italy, to be reminded of their shared past, albeit effectively excluding the numerous North African labour migrants in the region, whose history was no less conflicted but doubly controversial in French and Algerian national memory.[37]

The two trade unions CFDT and CGT attempted to redirect the region's militant mood towards political goals, and the CGT, the strongest local union, mobilized a mass demonstration of the affected steelworkers in the capital to this purpose. More than 250,000 people took part in this 'March on Paris', although it was confined to demonstrations along the boulevards of the east of the city. The media response was ambivalent. Since there were once again violent clashes

113

between police and demonstrators on the fringes of the event, the media images of violent militancy resurfaced. They were reinforced in the following weeks by the violence of smaller groups in Denain and Longwy towards the police and local institutions (the so-called *coups de points*: 'punches'). The CGT's strategy was to force a fundamental revision of the French share of the European 'steel plan' by extending the strike to other steelworks in Fos-Sur-Mer and Dunkirk. However, this failed due to insufficient support from the workers. On 8 May 1979, the strike in Longwy was also called off and work resumed after the other side offered to postpone the closure of the steelworks in Denain for a year, to cut the number of redundancies in Longwy by 25 per cent and not to halt its production of coke. The social plan for the whole of the French steel industry, which was endorsed in July by all the unions except the CGT, provided for 12,000 employees to be offered early retirement, 3,000 workers to be transferred to other sites with financial compensation and a redundancy payment of 50,000 French francs for 6,100 workers. By summer 1979, more than 2,000 workers in the two steelworks, including many of the younger strikers, had already accepted this severance pay. It was steelworkers from North Africa in particular who saw no future for themselves in the two steelworks and in the affected regions.

The miners' strike in most British coalfields,[38] lasting for a year from March 1984 to March 1985, was an even more grimly fought battle. This is my second example of a spectacular event of 'politics from below' during this phase of deindustrialization. From its onset, the government in London defined the strike as a decisive battle whose outcome could be only either victory or defeat. In the course of events, the miners' union, the NUM, also adopted this interpretation of the conflict.[39] On both sides, it was seen as a repeat of the 1972 and 1974 strikes, whose outcome, as we have seen above, was favourable to the union. In the end, both the government and the miners' union were trapped in their own militant rhetoric and attitudes. To a certain extent, the bitterness of the strike also became proof to the protagonists of the high stakes. Its aim was nothing less than the success or failure of the entire economic policy of Margaret Thatcher's Conservative government. The declared aim of this policy was to get rid of the old industries and with them the traditions and methods of the old trade unions. This was why the leader of the majority militant wing of the miners' union, Arthur Scargill, and his supporters linked their fight to retain their jobs with an alternative economic programme, also supported at this time by sections of the Labour Party.

There were some similarities between the industrial disputes of 1972 and 1974 and the 1984 miners' strike in the way events unfolded and it was fought out.[40] Once again, it was the strikers' aim to force their opponents to defeat by creating a shortage of energy reserves. At the same time, the tactic of using flying pickets – that is, bringing pickets in from power stations, coal depots and oil ports that were not on strike – openly challenged the new strike laws introduced in the meantime by the Conservative government. The fact that Scargill refused to allow the members of the NUM a national strike ballot was a challenge to his political opponents but also proof of his own weakness (he had lost two votes in 1980 and 1983). It proved to be a grave tactical error. A split between miners from different regions had resulted from the reintroduction of wage policies awarding bonuses for productivity in specific regions in 1978. Since then, miners working in modern pits with more productive coal seams received higher rates of pay and were at the same time under less threat from ongoing closures than their colleagues in older pits and less productive regions.[41] This regional and sometimes local confrontation between opponents and supporters of the strike weakened the union and increased internal pressure for solidarity. It also led to unconditional commitment amongst the strikers, which they thought would help them to win a moral victory over the government. In the eyes of some of the British public, they were successful. The longer the strike lasted, the more entrenched both lines of confrontation became. One line ran between the pickets and the police at the vital coal delivery points and the other ran between strikers and those willing to work or the strike-breakers in the villages and outside the pits. The fights were bitter on both fronts. The government used all available methods to break the strike, only stopping short of direct military action, and endorsed heavy-handed police tactics to restore law and order. The willingness of both the British police and their opponents to use violence increased significantly in the 1980s (see figure 3.3). As social historian Arthur Marwick put it: 'Britain in the 1980s [...] was a country of confrontation, of demonstrations and riots.'[42]

The longer the strike lasted, the more the striking miners and their families had to depend on donations from the wider public as strike funds were exhausted or blocked and they were denied welfare payments. In essence, the country was divided into two halves: supporters and opponents of the miners. The miners' efforts at mobilization were largely successful, particularly in creating partnerships between local supporters' groups and mining communities. The supporting campaigns managed to reach groups that had not

Figure 3.3 Police arresting Arthur Scargill during the British miners' strike in 1984.

In May 1984, two police officers arrested the British union leader Arthur Scargill near a coke processing plant in Orgreave, Yorkshire. One of the police officers is carrying the megaphone which Scargill had wanted to use to address the crowd. A few weeks later, this was the scene of one of the most serious battles in the British miners' strike: 5,000 pickets and 6,000 police clashed on the streets and several people were injured, including Scargill himself. The hardened fronts between the Conservative government under Thatcher and the NUM under Scargill made it impossible to negotiate an agreement. A year later, the strike ended in total defeat for the miners. It cost the lives of ten people, more than 3,000 were injured and around 12,000 were arrested, at least temporarily.

been close to the unions in the 1970s, such as the feminist and gay movements.[43] On the other hand, there was little significant support from other unions. The dock workers' strike at the beginning of September 1984 was soon over and none of the local actions of other trade unions had any significant impact. The NUM never in fact managed to involve the trade union movement as a whole in its supposedly final battle. In retrospect, it is clear that by autumn 1984 at the latest the aims of the strike were no longer achievable. But as I suggested above, the strikers and particularly their leaders had become prisoners of their own self-image and their perception of society. Hopes of an about-turn, a sudden collapse of state resistance, were boosted by the strike experiences of 1972 and 1974 and nourished a kind of collective wishful thinking. The activists held out to the bitter end, refusing to be shaken by the constantly rising numbers of strike-breakers, who were considered traitors and social outlaws, or to recognize that the battle was lost. They were comforted by the conviction that they were defending their own honour and dignity and by their perception of having participated honourably in a historic battle in the class struggle. In some respects, the last few months of the strike resembled a social drama portraying the heroic demise of the old British labour movement. Both from the miners' point of view and from the point of view of outsiders, this expressive quality of the strike rescued them from disappearing without trace and ensured them a permanent place in British history. Paradoxically, this was precisely what the Conservative government wanted: a historic victory and the banishment of this type of wildcat strike to the broom cupboard of the Ancien Régime of British labour relations. By the time the NUM's strike committee voted with a narrow majority for an unconditional return to work in March 1985, it was already clear who had won. A repeat of the winter of discontent would not be tolerated; this was the clear signal from the Conservative government to the trade unions. However, the wave of mass redundancies, works closures and company bankruptcies since 1980 had already prepared the ground for a moderate realism, and this was how the British trade union movement reacted to the decline in membership, the restriction of rights to strike and the abolition of older privileges such as the principle of the closed shop.[44] After its all-out victory, the government was not prepared to make any kind of concessions. Within eight years, 80 per cent of the remaining miners would be made redundant, while the productivity of those pits that were still open was increased, thus preparing the way for the privatization of British coal production.[45]

117

The protests against the closure of the Krupp steelworks in Duisburg-Rheinhausen in Germany in the winter of 1987–8 came at the end of this cycle of strikes and social protests against closures and mass redundancies in the 'old' industries. As we saw in chapter 1, deindustrialization continued and accelerated in the 1980s in the three countries we are studying. By this time, it had become clear that both old and new methods of protest had not been successful in maintaining production, even if they had achieved some success in cushioning the social consequences of restructuring and works closures. What happened at the Rheinhausen steelworks came at the end of a long line of local protests at various locations throughout West Germany that were threatened with closure. The first protests took place as early as 1980 (such as in Dortmund on 27 November 1980), and reached a first peak with the 'March on Bonn' on 29 September 1983 with around 130,000 participants. When it became clear that the brief upswing in the steel industry after the crisis in 1980–2 would not last and the comparatively moderate plans for closures and redundancies agreed during this phase with the relevant social actors would not be realized, there was a third wave of social action. In 1987, the trade union IG Metall organized so-called steel days of action. The first of these took place on 16 January with over 70,000 participants at twenty-four different steelworks threatened with closure and the second was two months later in Hattingen and Oberhausen with 30,000 participants. Nevertheless, the ongoing political negotiations between the German government, the steel companies and the union were unable to produce a comprehensive framework for saving jobs. These negotiations were accompanied by two further days of action and brief walkouts organized by IG Metall.[46] The announcement on 26 November 1987 by the company Krupp-Stahl AG that they would close the steelworks in Rheinhausen by the end of 1988 triggered protest actions by the workers there. They no longer kept to the union regulations but instead, like the steelworkers in Lorraine eight years earlier, blocked motorway exits and other nearby roads, briefly occupied one of the bridges over the Rhine (figure 3.4) and finally stormed meetings of the Krupp-Stahl AG board of directors in Essen and Bochum. On IG Metall's fifth 'day of strike action' on 10 December 1987, there were also brief strikes. The press spoke of 'barricades on the Ruhr' (*Die Tageszeitung*, 12 December 1987) and made headlines with 'the wheels have stopped turning in the works' (*Frankfurter Rundschau*, 11 December 1987).[47]

To understand the militancy of these actions better, we need to look at two factors. First, by 1986, 70 per cent of those agreeing to

Figure 3.4 'Jobs not unemployment': occupation of the Rhine bridge between Rheinhausen and Hochfeld on 10 December 1987.

Several thousand workers occupied a Rhine bridge at the end of 1987 to protest against the closure of the Krupp steelworks in Duisburg-Rheinhausen. Many of them wore hard hats. On banners they demanded 'Jobs Not Unemployment'. Migrant workers also took part in the occupation, as the banners in Turkish made clear. Despite a great deal of support from the population, the industrial action ended in an only partial victory. In 1993, the steelworks closed its doors for ever. Today, the 'Bridge of Solidarity' is an important local place of remembrance.

redundancy packages in the West German steel industry had taken early retirement. That meant that the majority of older workers had already left the works, so now it was younger workers who saw their future threatened. Second, the announcement that the works was to close came unexpectedly and was met with great disappointment by the workforce, whose representatives had only just agreed to shed 2,000 jobs. It was seen as a huge breach of trust, particularly in a business that had agreed to the Coal, Iron and Steel Industry Co-determination Act (*Montanmitbestimmung*).[48]

The next step imitated the forms of action used by the peace movement. On 23 February 1988, a human chain was formed from Gate 1 of the works in Rheinhausen to Gate 11 of the Westphalia works in Dortmund under the motto '1,000 fires on the Ruhr'. This was a major event which attracted media coverage and was emotionally moving for all involved, including the local population. Not only did it correct the hitherto overwhelming impression that campaigns were militant, it also effectively exerted political pressure on the government of the state of North Rhine-Westphalia. All along, its interior minister, Herbert Schnoor, had ensured maximum restraint on the part of the police and followed a deliberate de-escalation strategy, which now paid off. The Düsseldorf Agreement of May 1988 postponed the closure of the Rheinhausen plant by two years. KruppStahl AG also agreed to retain 1,500 jobs in Rheinhausen. The state on its part committed to building a further training centre for those still employed. In actual fact, the steelworks was not closed until 15 August 1993. Nevertheless, in 1988 the actors returned to their workplace having achieved a partial victory: they had not only staged their departure publicly but had in reality secured two extra years of work.[49]

One form of social mobilization against the consequences of the crisis that was not seen either in Britain or in France was the strikes led by IG Metall in West Germany demanding a 35-hour week. The long-term significance of this strike for the strategies of West German industrial companies, management and works councils is much more visible when seen in an internationally comparative perspective than when focussing on a single nation, which only contrasts the expectations of the protagonists with later consequences or results.

The decision by the trade unions to make a reduction of working hours a central demand stemmed from earlier experiences with rationalization and job losses in core sectors of West German industry. The question of what should have priority – a reduction of annual working hours or weekly working hours – was hotly disputed between and within the unions. There were supporters of both options especially within IG Metall, whereas the leaders of the miners' and energy workers' union IG Bergbau/Energie and the chemical workers' union IG Chemie clearly favoured an extension of annual leave. This was less attractive in the sense of creating new jobs but extremely popular with their members and the workforce in these branches of industry. The leadership of IG Metall supported the demand for a 35-hour week initially in order to secure jobs in the steel industry, which in 1978–9 was already in crisis and threatened with massive redundancies. However, in spite of wide support and successful mobilization of their members for the strike, they were not able to achieve a breakthrough – not least because the employers firmly rejected their demand.[50]

The second attempt in the round of collective bargaining in 1984 was prepared in advance by IG Metall in a publicity campaign the previous year. To begin with, however, it was overshadowed by the large campaigns and media-effective activities of the peace movement which came to a head in autumn 1983. In the face of growing unemployment (the official figure in September 1983 was 2.134 million),[51] the chief focus of the public and the media was the question of how many jobs could be gained by a 35-hour week. The looming pay dispute was made more political by the fact that the government under Helmut Kohl took clear sides. In December 1983, Kohl called the unions' demands 'absurd, stupid and foolhardy'.[52] In the German parliament (*Bundestag*), the liberal minister of the economy, Otto Graf Lambsdorff, said cynically: 'The 35-hour week with full pay will certainly create jobs. But I've just come from the place where the jobs will be created – East Asia.'[53] The result was that the wage disputes of 1984 in the metal industries of North Württemberg/North Baden and Hessen turned into a political dispute over the introduction of the 35-hour week in West Germany. In the end, however, it was fought out not between the unions and the government, but between IG Metall and the employers' federation of the metal industry, Gesamtmetall, in a manner that was highly media-effective (see figure 3.5).

In spring 1984, IG Metall began to mobilize its members and the workforce in the two regional districts involved in this wage bargaining. There was determined opposition both from the employers' federations, which continued to consider any kind of negotiation of the 40-hour week taboo, as well as from the government. This made the mobilization of union members and public support particularly important. The strike itself lasted from 17 May until 27 July 1984.

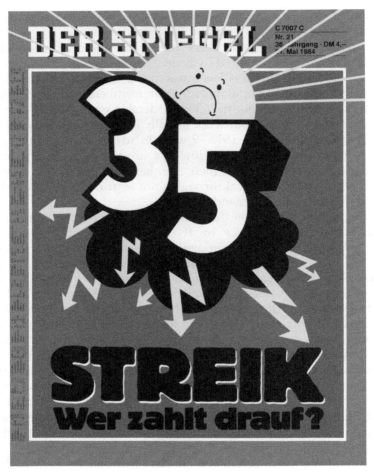

Figure 3.5   Cover of *Der Spiegel* on the strike for the 35-hour week.

In May 1984, the weekly magazine *Der Spiegel* turned its attention to the strike for the 35-hour week. Its cover references IG Metall's smiling sun with the number 35, to this day the most effective symbol of German trade unions. Its contemporary design is combined with a clear reference to the tradition of the labour movement ('Brothers, to the sun, to freedom' – *Brüder, zur Sonne, zur Freiheit*). The fact that this symbol made it to the front cover indicates that IG Metall still had the power to shape society as a whole. At the same time, its modification (the sun is sad not smiling; there is lightning) combined with the text 'Strike –who's paying for it?' foreshadows the imminent defeat of the unions and their incipient loss of importance.

122

The tactics employed by IG Metall were designed to have a maximum impact on the whole of the metal industry by going on strike in selected works. In response, the employers locked out as many workers as they could (union estimates put the figure at 450,000) in order to put as much pressure as possible on the union strike funds. This 'callous' lockout politicized the conflict still further since the use of lockouts as a weapon was explicitly forbidden in the constitution of the federal state of Hesse. A further sign of politicization was the decision taken by Heinrich Franke, a member of the Social Christian Union (CSU, part of the government coalition), not to pay any benefits from the Federal Labour Office, of which he was the president, to those only indirectly affected by the strike. This led to a full-scale showdown with protest actions and temporary walkouts by members of other unions. It also led to a further 'March on Bonn' on 28 May 1984 with 250,000 participants and to partial legal breakthroughs for the union related to the Federal Labour Office's refusals to pay unemployment benefit for being on short-time. After three weeks, the employers were prepared to negotiate the reduction of weekly working hours and both sides accepted 'special arbitration' proceedings. They also accepted their outcome: a 38.5-hour week with full pay, pay rises for all workers and early retirement pay of 65 per cent or 70 per cent of final gross income. It was a considerable success for the employers, however, that weekly working hours could be varied according to individual company agreements, since the new regulatory working hours were no longer reckoned per week but over two months.[54]

Although this compromise broke the taboo of the 40-hour week, it was a far cry from a breakthrough to the 35-hour week. In fact, the emphasis of the negotiations shifted to implementation at the company level and it was not clear what the effects of the strike would be on employment policy. This was the central focus of public debate, although the side effects of the strike in the medium term were more important. The organization of shorter but more flexible working hours became an increasingly important part of wage and company negotiations in Germany. Corresponding collective agreements were made for different industries. For metalworkers, the 35-hour week became reality as a result of a wage agreement in 1995. The more general political significance of this labour conflict can be seen in terms of what it signalled and how it changed orientation. It was a turning point in so far as the shorter working week forced German businesses to commit to the development of ever-increasing productivity and technological innovation.

I have one final example of a spectacular event which is a paradigmatic illustration of the strategies and forms of 'politics from below' at the height of deindustrialization. It is the anti-poll tax campaign, which caused a furore in Britain from 1989 to 1991.[55] It was directed against a new system of local taxation introduced by the Conservative majority government, first in Scotland in 1989 and then in England and Wales in 1990. This tax reform stipulated that instead of paying a property tax relative to the rental value of the property lived in, known as 'rates', a uniform annual sum was to be paid for by each adult resident in the council area. This local tax soon proved unpopular. Much of the population, especially those on low incomes, considered it unfair and an election gift from the Tories to higher earners and property owners. Opposition and social protests began in Scotland but soon spread to other parts of Britain. The anti-poll tax campaign was organized in local neighbourhood-based anti-poll-tax unions, comprising some 20 million people. This social movement was also coordinated by a national umbrella organization, the All Britain Anti-Poll Tax Federation. In contrast to the British and West German peace movements, for example, many industrial workers became involved in public protests, as did all their traditional organizations and local trade union associations. The movement's first achievement was to replace the government term 'community charge' with their own more media-effective 'poll tax'.[56] The campaign was also seen as revenge for more than ten years of 'class politics from above' which many British workers felt was being pursued by the Thatcher government. The climax of the campaign was once again a mass demonstration on 31 March 1990 in London with an estimated 200,000 to 250,000 participants from all over the country. Trafalgar Square had been initially registered as the meeting point for 60,000 people. When it became apparent that it was too small, the authorities refused to allow permission for them to collect in Hyde Park. This resulted in direct confrontation between the police and demonstrators since the demonstrators found themselves pushed up against a large contingent of mounted riot police. Scuffles escalated to become outright street battles between the police and demonstrators which culminated in shops in the West End being plundered and destroyed, cars set alight and more than 400 people arrested.[57] The mass demonstration had become a riot. The fact that some miners were among the protesters was interpreted by the press as an act of revenge for their defeat in the major strike of 1984–5. The government and the organizers initially blamed 'anarchists and provocateurs', but an official inquiry a year later was forced

124

to admit that this theory of the involvement of agents was false. A number of different factors had evidently combined to cause the violence to escalate: the aggressive, even hostile police presence, the emotional confrontations between the government and supporters of the campaign as well as the unsuitability of the location, which was too cramped and unmanageable for a demonstration of this size.[58]

The reaction of the public to what happened in London was divided. However, the anti-poll tax campaign continued to win support and by mid-1990 it was clear that a large majority of the electorate supported its aims (polls showed approval rates of 78 per cent). The overthrow of Thatcher in November 1990 was undoubtedly a side effect of this campaign. Nevertheless, its aim was not finally achieved until 1992 when the newly elected Conservative prime minister, John Major, fulfilled his election promise and replaced the poll tax with a new council tax, based once again on property values.

Return to rebellion (1990–2005)

I have already argued above that the mid-1980s was something of a watershed in the labour conflicts of Western European industries. Until then, social protests, demonstrations and strikes had been an integral part of the political debates over social and economic policies in Britain, France and Germany. Workers and their trade unions had always played an important and independent role in this process as direct participants. This 'politics from below' had a particular influence on the socio-political solutions developed by these three countries in the years between 1975 and 1983 when faced with the wave of deindustrialization. Their aim was to limit public protests against redundancies or even avoid them by finding timely compromises through consensus. The early retirement deals which found their way into the social plans of many industries hit by crisis show how these mobilizing events could have direct and practical effects. The sometimes lavish severance packages (such as those offered in Longwy and Denain) would also have been inconceivable had it not been for the mass demonstrations and regional action. Offers of this kind of financial compensation, often relying on state subsidies, were a frequently successful strategy employed by the opposing side, with the underlying aim of depriving the hard-core of the militant activists of its support. The metaphor of 'buying time',[59] used by Wolfgang Streeck to characterize the debt policies of Western European governments in our period, can also be applied to the appeasement strategies

125

that France and Germany pursued. In buying at least a temporary return to normality, they were able to avoid protracted and violent labour disputes and social protests that damaged the reputation of the politicians responsible. What typically escaped the attention of the politically aware public were the tangible difficulties that ensued: unemployment when payments ran out, people moving away to other regions and migrant workers returning to their home countries. They descended into a huge if individualized mass of fates to which little attention was paid in the three countries at the time, in spite of the social statistical observation routines that existed and were applied. Only gradually did social scientists develop specialized fields dedicated to the relevant topics: from (long-term) unemployment through migration to the 'problem neighbourhoods' in decaying industrial cities.

There are many reasons why social protests declined significantly after 1985. First, procedures for mass dismissal became routine. Second, in many cases, those affected were no longer confident that spectacular actions would mobilize the political public for their cause. When Thatcher ruthlessly referred to the nationalized British steel industry as one of 'yesterday's industries',[60] this was merely a particularly early and openly expressed conviction shared by most government ministers with economic portfolios. Deindustrialization was made to seem simply banal, with the sheer number of plant closures always happening according to the same pattern, which demoralized the workers involved. The conviction grew widely that resistance was futile.

A further reason is connected with the interpretive schemes discussed in the previous chapter, which spread at this time and placed increasing responsibility on individuals for their employment situation. Each individual was seen as 'the architect of their own fortune'. Public institutions were made available in the shape of employment offices (renamed 'job centres') and social welfare offices that broke collective outcomes down into single individual cases and treated them as such. This is a socio-psychological factor that should not be ignored if the relatively small number of events in the 1990s is to be adequately understood from a socio-historical point of view. This new format in the media and administration bolstered subjectification and had an increasing influence on the patterns of perception of those affected.

The reasons for social protest also changed and with them the groups of actors. In the defensive labour struggles of the late 1970s and early 1980s, younger workers had already been more frequently on the front line. They were also the ones who were more prepared to take illegal action and use violence. This was particularly the case in France and Britain, both countries in which strikes and political protest had always been accompanied with a certain level of militancy. In most cases, the massive deployment of security forces contributed significantly to the escalation of violence, as we have seen in the example of London in the anti-poll tax campaign or the decisive battle in the British miners' strike. In Germany, actions and campaigns related to the working world were rarely accompanied by similar confrontations between demonstrators and the police, whereas in the 1980s they played a central role in the local squatters' scenes in Hamburg and Berlin, in the dispute over the building of the new West runway (*Startbahn West*) at Frankfurt Airport or the nuclear reprocessing plant in Wackersdorf (Bavaria).

The campaign against the new 'community charge' in Britain shows how two different forms and traditions of social protests could overlap during a single mass event such as the London demonstration in March 1990. It also shows how 'riots', the official term favoured by the media, became re-established as a more or less regular accompaniment or form of expression in 'street politics' alongside other peaceful and legal forms of social and political protest. These riots and *émeutes* were particularly rife in major cities and urban neighbourhoods in Britain and France, where it was mainly jobless youth who were involved. The loss of industrial jobs with nothing to replace them and the growth of youth unemployment both locally and regionally destabilized many households and families. Segregation of suburban areas, fuelled by the privatization of the housing market, transformed many of the social housing developments once praised as progressive into 'problem zones' and 'social hotspots'.[61] Drugs and crime became the media-enhanced trademarks of these neighbourhoods. The presence of ethnic minorities also meant they became known as 'foreigners' districts' and favoured targets for racist emotions and stigmatization. The chain of social causes, as long and complex as it may have been in many cases, always leads back to the phenomena of the deindustrialization crisis.[62]

For this reason, it is hardly surprising that urban riots increased in the 1980s and 1990s. Before the 1970s, events like the 1958 Notting Hill riots were still a rare exception in Britain. In the 1970s, there were only three larger events classified as riots, whereas in the 1980s the total rose to eleven. In the 1990s, there were seven such events until they became less frequent (five) in the 2000s following the economic boom and a drop in unemployment. However, then came the summer of 2011, bringing a sudden outbreak of new unrest. Images of people killed and seriously injured, of houses and cars on fire and looted shops in London, Liverpool, Manchester and Birmingham, but also in smaller English cities, shocked the general public. In France, the 1980s was still comparatively calm ('only' four larger major clashes with the police), but in the 1990s the situation escalated and there was regular unrest in the suburbs of Lyons, Rouen, Paris and Toulouse as well as in smaller cities such as Melun. The riots in the *banlieues* that shook France in 2005, 2007 and 2010 as the climax of this development have not been forgotten.[63] The social neglect of entire cities and neighbourhoods certainly created a breeding ground for violence which seemed to erupt suddenly and unexpectedly, triggered by local circumstances. This unrest usually led to violent clashes with the police and the destruction and looting of shops and public facilities. The enormous interest they attracted in the media has also helped to ensure that they had a lasting effect on the public image of 'problem neighbourhoods' but also created an awareness of the social problems resulting from deindustrialization.

The vast majority of young people who took part in the 'riots' after the 1980s came from working- or lower-class families. Particularly in the early British riots (Toxteth/Liverpool 1981,[64] London neighbourhoods in 1981 and 1985), they often had very close personal connections to the world of industrial work. These connections became weaker as jobs were lost and factories closed or moved away until the only future for work in many of these places seemed to consist solely of (precarious) service sector jobs. However, the media and consequently the wider public increasingly and repeatedly focused on the presence of ethnic minorities and were inclined to label the unrest as 'race riots'. The young activists, on the other hand, were more likely to emphasize their common local identity and defend it symbolically during the riots.

The complex connections between urban violence and the crisis of industrial labour have been studied by sociologists Stéphane Beaud and Michel Pialoux for the industrial city of Montbéliard in eastern France, which is located in the immediate vicinity of the large Peugeot factory in Sochaux and within its social recruitment area.[65] They see a direct connection between the 'culture of provocation' that had been taking root amongst young people of mostly North African origin in the social housing blocks of the new housing estates since the 1990s and the disappointed career hopes and education expectations of these young people. They also find a connection to the widespread discrimination they experienced as 'minorities' as well as to the disappointments of their fathers, who had lost their jobs or gone into early retirement, having spent their working lives in unskilled production jobs, often with no hope of promotion. In this way, they became secret accomplices of their violent sons. As trade union activist H. put it in an interview with the two sociologists:

> In their efforts to avenge their fathers they destroy everything. By keeping silent, their fathers join their sons down the wrong route! [...] They have no respect for anyone apart from their fathers. [...] [They despise] even the other North Africans working for Peugeot: they're like animals, they don't speak out, they're cowards! [...] They've adopted all the expressions that we [the CGT] use when we insult the other unions. They [the young people] say to us: it's because of you, you agreed to work under inhuman conditions![66]

In this interview, H. described with great bitterness the loss of authority of the older generation, the gap between the generations and the overall feeling of powerlessness and (self-)hatred that profoundly shaped the social world of the suburbs' younger residents. The slogans of left-wing trade union activists, whose intention was originally political, were now used to justify various kinds of social violence and criminality that had very little in common with the progressive orientation of the 'politics from below' described above. Instead, anger and disillusionment dictated the riots, which involved fighting between young people and the security forces and the destruction of public buildings, particularly schools, and private cars and homes. Both in France and in Britain, separate cultures of violence developed which became a positive reference point for the social identity of an active minority. These young people may have been dismissed out of hand in media reports as immoral perpetrators of violence and members of criminal gangs, but, needless to say, there were also political and moral motives behind these events. The perpetrators used these acts of violence to express their protest against the way they were treated by the police and schools, the two main targets of their attacks, and they demanded that society afforded them the right to the 'relational equality' and 'equality of opportunity' denied to them.[67] Social scientific analyses agree that these urban protests were based on a diffuse, apolitical sense of injustice, a lack of opportunity for political participation and denied educational opportunities. This was in the face of increasing social inequality coupled with a strong feeling of political powerlessness as well as a pronounced dislike of

129

the representatives of public order and overall of 'the powers that be/ them up there'.[68]

The disappearance of industrial workers from the political arena

Riots had been thought to be a phenomenon from the distant past or from uncivilized regions of the world. Their return reflects the continuing decline of social movements directly connected with the working class or *classes populaires*. These riots should be read as symptoms of a change in circumstances for the remaining (industrial) labour force in the field of politics, which was characteristic for all three countries dealt with here. The cycle of labour disputes between 1968 and 1985 had been defined by a combination of social protest, political demands and economic interests, but in the 1990s this had more or less dissolved. Large numbers of industrial workers had gradually withdrawn from the type of political activities and forms of direct participation that we have been studying in this chapter. It was to be some time before their political attitudes and emotions resurfaced as social protest and political action. It is certainly difficult to understand the current growing support of workers for right-wing populist parties and politicians without considering this background.[69]

There are a number of explanations for this withdrawal from politics, this disappearance of industrial workers from the political arena. The first, which is repeatedly referenced in this context, is the disciplining effect of mass unemployment. Unemployment accompanied deindustrialization and effectively weakened industrial workers' negotiating power, particularly those who were poorly qualified. Their willingness to accept poor working conditions, overtime and even wage cuts without protest has been well documented. It can be found in numerous studies in contemporary industrial sociology, in interviews with those affected and reports from trade unions and employment lawyers. However, as an explanation, this notion of the silent force of circumstances is insufficient.

A second explanation is the fact that also, and particularly in the eyes of the workforce, the future of many companies in times of globalization and financial market capitalism appeared endangered. This meant that labour disputes and especially any kind of politicization visible to the public were seen as risky undertakings that could also threaten the future of their own company. In these circumstances, 'conflict partnerships', based on the reputation of West

German unions for focussing on negotiations and being prepared to compromise, became an alternative strategy for industrial trade unions in all three countries. It seemed clearly more attractive than militancy and politicization.[70] This also means that collective spheres of experience and ways of organizing the expression of collective interests continued to exist beneath the political level and far from any politicization. These need to be more closely studied. The 'politics from below' that I have been examining in this chapter is by no means the only level that can provide information about political participation and the social recognition of workers. I will be returning to this topic in chapter 7.

The third explanation has to do with the state. It had increasingly withdrawn from taking direct responsibility for industry and become less and less credible as the addressee for popular demands for investment or even nationalization. The left-wing parties, which in the 1980s were still potential champions of an interventionist state industrial policy, gradually turned their backs on such programmes in the course of the decade and began to move towards the new economic political consensus. The opening up of the markets, the reduction of the deficit, privatization and currency stability were declared the cornerstones of what was seen as realistic politics with no alternative. The left-wing Keynesian reform socialism which was the secret partner of radical verbal militancy receded into the past. Some remnants of politicization did, however, remain in the years up to the turn of the millennium (and beyond), namely the defence of social rights and welfare benefits achieved in earlier times and – new to Germany and Britain – the introduction of a state minimum wage as a protection against the spread of low wages.

Fourth, as we saw in chapter 2, the parameters of economic and social debate had shifted. For one thing, the aura of the collective singular 'class', *classe* or *Klasse* (in German more frequently 'workforce' – *Arbeiterschaft*), which had previously been part of the mobilization rhetoric of social protests, had been destroyed. For another, organizations that exerted considerable group pressure, such as trade unions, fell increasingly out of favour. A growing section of the public, not only in Britain, whether conservative, liberal or even politically sceptical, considered them to be a relic of a past era. At the same time, other categories found a secure place in the media. Ethnicity and gender became more or less naturally accepted social categories to which common characteristics and social roles were attributed and became the preferred objects of political mobilization. These shifts in popular opinion and media visibility have also been documented in social scientific and historical research. They have led to labour-related conflicts and protests being increasingly ascribed to a specific group, such as migrants or *immigrés*, even when the actors themselves identify as an integral part of a company workforce or even the working class.[71] In these decades after 1980, national and nationalist framings – the nation, *le peuple*, *das Volk* – won renewed media appeal as well as higher political, social and emotional credibility, at the same time as the European single market was being developed. One only has to think of the wars waged in the name of the nation in Britain (the Falklands War in 1982, the Gulf War in 1990 and the Iraq War in 2003) or the reunification of Germany (1989–90).

The fact that the cycle of politicized labour conflicts reconstructed in this chapter has come to an end and belongs to the past does not mean that this type of politicization has disappeared once and for all. In fact, the opposite tendency can be observed in all three countries since the turn of the millennium. The number of labour conflicts visible in the media and condensed into protest events, usually triggered by the announcement of factory closures, increased again slightly. One national media event, for example, was the occupation of the Cellatex factory, which produced viscose fibres in the French *département* of the Ardennes. In summer 2000, when the female textile workers were threatened with redundancy and the closure of the factory, they started to divert highly toxic chemicals from the factory into local water. In this way, they forced both their employers and the state representatives to make substantial concessions in the form of a social plan.[72] This type of illegal action against the loss of further jobs was normally part of a long-term conflict between the unions, the owners of the factories – often international capital investors who justified the closure plans on the grounds that their sales returns were unsatisfactory – and the workforce, whose local and regional networks were frequently very strong and who also fought their battle for jobs as a battle against the regional employment crisis.

It is impossible to say whether there is a new cycle or even a continuation of the old one. However, this and other sporadic protest events and the responses evoked show that there was scope for the politicization of labour conflicts even after the turn of the millennium and the restructuring of industry and society associated with deindustrialization. They also show that 'politics from below' could arouse the interest of critical social scientists, producers of culture and the media, who have all kept it alive in the political public sphere.[73]

— Chapter 4 —

INDUSTRIAL CITIZENS AND WAGE EARNERS
Labour relations, social benefits and wages

In 1996, the European Commission asked a group of academics to draw up a report on the transformation of work and the future of labour law in Europe. It was published in 1999.[1] The report and its recommendations for further developing the legal framework of labour relations in the European Union addressed the far-reaching changes that had taken place in the world of work since the European Coal and Steel Community was founded in 1951 as one of the forerunners of the EU, and also since the European Commission launched its first initiative for the expansion of workers' social rights in 1974. The chair of this working group, the French labour lawyer Alain Supiot, clearly defined its starting position as follows:

> In labour law, the notion underlying labour relations is both hierarchical and collective. The employment contract is basically defined here by the bond of subordination it establishes between the worker and the party to whom his services are delivered. [...] However, the core feature of this model [...] is the crucial importance of standard full-time non-temporary wage contracts (particularly for adult men), centring on the trade-off between high levels of subordination and disciplinary control on the part of the employer and high levels of stability and welfare/insurance compensations and guarantees for the employee [...]. It is hardly a novelty today to point out that these standardized patterns of social and economic regulation are fast losing ground.[2]

This broad definition of labour relations provides an ideal starting point for this chapter, which will examine the consequences of the post-1975 economic upheavals for labour and economic law in Western Europe. I will focus once again on how industrial labour has

133

changed – especially from the perspective of the labourers themselves – in times of job cuts and mass unemployment but also of new jobs and types of employment outside the established norms. Specifically, labour relations were regulated by a collection of laws and contractual agreements that went far beyond individual employment contracts. They included above all social benefits, health and safety at work and specific sectoral and collective bargaining norms. The authors of the 1999 report made this quite clear when they introduced the concept of 'social citizenship' (*citoyenneté social*) to define appropriate targets for developing European labour and economic law:

> The advantage it [the concept of social citizenship] has to offer is that it is extensive (it covers many social rights, not just social security); it links up social rights to the notion of social integration, and not just to the notion of work. Above all, it enshrines the idea of participation. Indeed, citizenship assumes the participation of the people concerned in the definition and implementation of their rights.[3]

I will use this key idea of European social citizenship within social and labour law to help analyse the developments in labour that could be observed between 1970 and 2000 in France, Britain and Germany and to evaluate their social consequences. In chapter 3, I described the withdrawal of the industrial workforce and of the working classes/ *classes populaires* from politics in general. This withdrawal created space for the transformation of employment relationships. New principles of 'good work' spread in the media and led to increased pressure to modify the established rules of labour and pay. At the same time, not least because of rising national debt and ever-increasing costs for companies and businesses, the social benefits and access to them linked with employment contracts were put to the test. The spread of sustained mass unemployment in all three countries at the beginning of the 1980s, if not before, led to an unravelling of the package of legal protection, statutory social benefits and entitlements that were still connected to permanent employment contracts. The interesting question to ask is what was still contained in this package by the turn of the century that could earn the agreeable label of social citizenship.

Industrial wage labour and social security in the early 1970s

In chapter 1, we saw that at the end of the long postwar period of growth the economic and social relevance of the industrial sector in our three West European countries had reached a peak rarely seen before in peacetime. The same is true for the influence of the industrial workforce. Its power at that time was based on different factors. In Britain and Germany, it was the power of the trade unions to negotiate and organize industrial relations and their influence on the Labour Party and SPD respectively. In France, it was the power of the trade unions to mobilize support in labour conflicts and social protests. This increase in power had a similar social effect in all three countries: it transformed the status of wage labour so that it was now comprehensively protected by social and labour law. It also gave the 'affluent worker' of contemporary industrial sociology what T.H. Marshall called 'industrial citizenship'.[4] He was referring to the outcome of a good hundred years of labour disputes and trade union representation in Britain. In the democratic tradition of social policy, the expansion of public services and welfare was closely linked to the task of making unequal wage labour relations more equal by means of union power and was secured by autonomous collective bargaining and the right to strike. As shown in the previous chapter, the regulation of labour law and collective bargaining was much tighter in France and Germany than it was in Britain, where the majority of these guarantees of status were based on contracts and agreements between the two autonomous partners in collective bargaining, the unions and employers. Nevertheless, different routes still led all three countries to the creation of a 'package' of guarantees and securities legally regulating labour, collective bargaining and welfare. In retrospect, what is particularly striking is the link between individual protection rights, trade union bargaining power and democratic rights of participation. They were all components of the social package surrounding individual employment contracts. The concrete effects for industrial workers were as follows:

1 Collective and legally supported safeguarding of wages, work processes and working hours by means of collective bargaining based on trade union rights such as the right to strike and free collective bargaining.
2 Various degrees of the right to worker participation and access to company information.
3 The existence of bodies responsible for enforcing and safeguarding these rights: that is, industrial and arbitration tribunals, shop stewards and/or elected representatives of company workforces.
4 The regulation of a minimum wage either by collective bargaining or by law. There was no statutory minimum wage in Britain or

Germany, but in Britain there were collective agreements relating to particular branches of industry or jobs and in West Germany regional collective agreements which amounted to the same as a minimum wage and in most areas were equivalent to the standards set by the inflation-indexed statutory minimum wage in France.

5 Individual protection rights which strictly regulated employment contracts, especially on the part of the employer. Most importantly, they included protection from dismissal and the prohibition of discrimination on the grounds of gender or race. But they also comprised health and safety regulations which aimed to avoid accidents and sickness at work and also provided for compensation and rehabilitation measures in the case of work-related illnesses and industrial accidents.

6 Work-based entitlement to welfare benefits such as unemployment benefit, disability and retirement pensions and medical care in the case of illness.

These six components were naturally developed to very different degrees in the three countries we are studying. Important sections of this work-based social package did not become widespread until the 1960s and early 1970s when legislators improved legal employment protection, raised the level of statutory retirement pensions, tightened health and safety regulations and extended statutory work inspections in the private sector. However, the general trend of reforms in industrial and social law in this final phase of the postwar boom shows that protective rights and social benefits for blue-collar wage earners in industrial enterprises became increasingly comparable to those that had been enjoyed for decades by salaried white-collar workers in private companies and the public sector. In addition to the benefits mentioned above, they included monthly wage payments, paid leave and additional company retirement pensions. The fact that these privileges, which had previously been vigorously defended by those entitled to them, were now extended in an egalitarian spirit to industrial workers and other wage earners was the conclusion of a development which began in all three countries in the political and social upheavals of the immediate postwar period.[5]

Social scientists frequently attribute the specific regulations of industrial relations and wage policies directly to the consequences of 'Fordist' industrial production methods. However, this makes little sense from a socio-historical point of view. First, their political foundations were laid at a time when Fordist production was the exception rather than the rule. Second, their political and social motives and intentions are alien to Fordist industrial practices.[6] Third, in all three countries, these regulations applied to skilled workers, who were the main upholders and beneficiaries. Unskilled workers found their own way, so to speak, into this model, gradually profiting from it (in the case of labour migrants, as in France and West Germany, not until much later). Fourth, this generalized status of being a wage worker, or *statut salarial*, as Robert Castel called it,[7] was not a phenomenon that could be observed everywhere in the wake of the global spread of Fordist production methods. In essence, it was limited to Europe. In the US and Japan, for example, standards of legal labour protection and social security lagged well behind those of European nations. Guarantees of status by the company had much greater importance in these and many other countries and functioned as systems of privilege within employment relations that were more powerfully influenced by authoritarian traditions and the liberal heritage of the nineteenth century.

This idea of an egalitarian status model was further undermined by the unequal treatment of the sexes. Work-related social benefits in all three countries confirmed the gendered division of labour in family and job structures. In fact, the role model of the male breadwinner was actually strengthened by the enhancement of the wage-earning status and the growth of mostly male industrial jobs in the postwar economic boom. The egalitarian status model was, however, linked only in some respects to this patriarchal order (see figure 4.1). In principle, it opened up the same labour-related and social rights for both sexes. The fact that work-related social citizenship reinforced 'traditional' role models resulted above all from the fact that around 1970 women were a long way from being granted equal access and equal opportunities on the labour market and within hierarchical job structures. At that time, the majority of industrial citizens were men. We will see in the following that in this respect deindustrialization worked as a catalyst for sweeping changes with highly ambivalent consequences.

The erosion of collective bargaining rights

Setting standards of pay and working conditions by means of collective agreements was one of the key elements of industrial citizenship. The most important actors in this arena were trade unions and the employers' organizations. After 1975, this collective bargaining framework was the first target of criticism when there

Figure 4.1   Negotiations in Grenelle, May 1968.

At the end of May 1968, French trade unions, employers' organizations and the French government successfully negotiated the Grenelle Agreement. Representatives of the CGT and the CFDT and those of the CNPF and the PME sat facing each other on opposite sides of a room in the Ministry of Labour in Paris. Members of the government took their seats, amongst them Prime Minister Georges Pompidou, at the head of the table connecting the two sides. The symmetrical layout of the tables emphasized the fact that these negotiations were between equals. However, they would never have taken place in this manner without the preceding general strike and factory occupations. At the same time, it is revealing to note who was not present at the table. There was no representation of women or migrants in the employers' organizations, the Gaullist government or the trade unions.

was an unexpected renaissance of earlier liberal reservations over the supposed 'monopolization' of labour as a commodity by trade unions with high membership and an ability to take strike action. Pay settlements restricted to certain industries or types of job and other agreements on work structures and working hours were also criticized. This attack was boosted by the economic argument that it was necessary to adapt to the growing pressure of international competition. A return to individual settlements or at best agreements at factory or company level on the regulation of pay and job structures became a constant topic of debate on labour policy in this transition period. Critics of collective bargaining often used 'ordoliberal' or neoliberal arguments; others were clearly guided by interest-based motives. In the 1980s, they were increasingly supported by social science 'experts' who saw trade unions as a relic of earlier social relations and failing industrial labour relations, leading inevitably to a crisis of union organization and representation of interests. Experts in new business forms and cultures, in particular, regarded the established forms of collective representation of interests with the mild indulgence of presumed victors. They saw a future for trade unions only if they adapted their role to become functional helpers in the new cooperative forms of information and communication connected to more flexible and more individualized work structures. From then on, the West German model of social partnership (*Sozialpartnerschaft*) became the battle cry of conservative and liberal reformers in France and Britain. *Partenariat social* and 'social partnership' were the watchwords for peaceful and business-friendly work structures – the crowning glory of 'modern' labour relations.[8] Table 3.2 showed the clear development of strike practice in this direction in all three countries. It is hardly surprising, therefore, to see that an undertaking to forgo strike action became a basic component of negotiated agreements based on 'social partnership' in Britain. It was the goal of Japanese companies, for example, in their British subsidiaries, if they were unable to avoid recognizing trade unions as negotiating partners.

Legislators faced with this (neo)liberal criticism of 'intransigent labour relations' in the European Economic Area reacted in very different ways. We have already seen that the British trade unions and the 'abuse' of their power to mobilize and to veto were at the heart of Conservative legislation between 1979 and 1997. This brought to an end a long phase (since 1906) in which, apart from a few positive regulations (against the use of force), there was a clearly defined area of legal immunity, which permitted collective industrial relations in Britain to develop into an area of common practices, situation-specific trials of strength and pragmatic adjustments to new conditions.[9] The parameters of this system shifted fundamentally between 1970 and 1993, mainly as a result of legalization of collective labour relations.[10] The main losers in the face of these legal regulations were the trade unions, whose scope for organization and action was deliberately restricted by the Conservative legislators. The main winners were the companies, whose freedom to organize and implement staff and wage policies was strengthened. It was the declared aim of Conservative labour legislation to increase the flexibility of labour markets in favour of a 'free and competitive market economy'.[11] The restrictions imposed on the unions' freedom to act stretched from the ban on 'closed shops' to regulations on the terms of democracy within the trade unions; in addition, the unions were to be made liable for the consequences of any illegal industrial action by their members. We have already seen the success of these post-1979 Thatcher government policies. Step by step, they broke the power of British trade unions, in particular their militant wing.

In France, on the other hand, throughout the period of regular seesawing between bourgeois and socialist government majorities, legislators strengthened the collective representation of workers' interests. They combined this with the declared aim of pushing unions and employers away from confrontation, which had been customary until then, and towards cooperation. The 1982 labour laws (*Lois Auroux*), in particular, strengthened the rights and the presence of trade unions in the workplace and extended workers' rights to collective participation. In addition to the *comités d'entreprise*, the French equivalent of the West German works councils, introduced in 1945, the trade union delegates (*délégués syndicaux* – since 1968) and the company-specific sections of the trade unions (*sections syndicales* – also since 1968), a fourth institutional pillar of collective representation of workers' interests in French companies was introduced in 1982: the committee for health and safety (*comité de sécurité et d'hygiène*).

In Germany, after the bitter conflict over the co-determination laws in the 1970s, legislators avoided any further interference in the established institutional structure of collective industrial relations. In contrast to Britain, the autonomy of the social partners – that is, the trade unions and the employers' associations – had been strictly regulated by existing laws and particularly by labour court rulings since the 1950s.[12] The conservative–liberal coalition government under Helmut Kohl stuck to this course until the late 1990s. At that time, employers and economists voiced substantial criticism of the 'rigidity' of the existing system of regional collective wage agreements and demanded the abolition of the unions' collective bargaining monopoly in favour of works councils. In line with British legislation in force since 1979, the aim of these initiatives was to widen the scope for management decisions and to achieve greater flexibility by collective employment contracts at factory or company level. These reform plans failed, however, as a result of united opposition from trade unions and labour law experts, who rejected them at the German Law Congress in 1996.[13]

If we compare the three countries, it is clear that there was no single (neo)liberal trend in Western Europe. Legislators in France and Germany stuck to the model of collective industrial relations whereas Britain began in the 1980s to move consistently towards liberating businesses from the restrictions of collective wage agreements and extending the scope for individual contracts between businesses and their workers in return for minimal standards and rights of protection. This legislative strategy also brought the Conservative government into serious conflict with the social and labour policy initiatives of the EC/EU in the late 1980s and 1990s.[14]

For a comparative analysis of the four first collective elements of industrial citizenship, we need to examine the development of the organizational strength of trade unions. In Britain, the findings are quite clear. As we saw in the previous chapter, the strength of British industrial trade unions was based on their wide membership and their presence in the factories. In many factories, it can be said that in the 1970s on issues of staff policy and work structures there was a tacitly agreed system of shared management between company executives and representatives of the unions and/or the workers.[15] The decisive factor was that manual workers had direct access to union representation in 44 per cent of industrial companies.[16] After 1979, very little of this organizational strength remained. With the closure of many factories and entire companies, many of the traditional sector-specific trade unions gradually lost their membership base. It was much more difficult for unions to recruit members and install shop stewards in newly established companies. In 2004, at the end of the long process of deindustrialization, the level of trade union organization in many branches of industry had shrunk to just over half its 1970s peak and averaged at only 34 per cent.[17] This was still a relatively high membership in comparison to other countries, but it could only rarely be transformed into trade union influence and wage-negotiating power. Surveys conducted in 2004 concluded that wage negotiations and wage agreements existed in only a third of industrial enterprises. Wages in most companies were now agreed individually or determined by the employer. After a good three decades of deindustrialization and government and business hostility to collective bargaining, there was no sign of a return to the confrontational practices of negotiating wages, bonuses and issues of work organization. By 2004, the idea of industrial citizenship, as defined by Marshall, had long disappeared in Britain or become a rare privilege.

Although government measures in respect of collective bargaining were completely different in France, we can still observe a similar crisis of trade union organization. Union membership declined significantly from the mid-1970s until the early 1990s. At the end of this period, the level of union organization had halved across the country and subsequently stagnated at this low level of between 8 and 9 per cent. In the private sector, it was even as low as 5 per cent.[18] The communist-led CGT, which was by far the strongest union in the industrial sector, but also amongst low- and mid-level workers in the public sector, experienced the most serious collapse of its membership. In 1993, at the end of the long crisis, of its 1.8 million members in 1974 it had retained only 480,000 and organized only 2.5 per cent of the workforce instead of nearly 11 per cent previously. Even its earlier strongholds in the industrial sector were affected by this collapse: only 2 per cent of metalworkers were CGT members. Only amongst the employees of the state-owned gas, water and electricity companies and amongst other workers in the public sector was the union still able to reach an organization level of more than 20 per cent.[19] The decline of the second largest trade union organization, the CFDT, was less dramatic but followed the same trend. This loss of real bargaining power was partly compensated in France by the legal expansion of the trade union right to participate in wage agreements specific to one factory or company and so shape the legal regulation of working hours reduction and employment policy.

The West German trade unions came through the crisis comparatively unscathed. The level of membership, especially among workers, in the industrial unions federated in the German Trade Union Confederation, DGB, was relatively high. It enabled them to weather the crisis more easily than in the other two countries and, following a peak of 47.3 per cent in 1980, membership even rose again to 48.4 per cent in 1990 after German reunification, before it started to shrink once more after the 1990s.[20] IG Metall alone had a continuous membership of more than 2.5 million in the 1980s and 1990s – more than all the French trade unions put together.[21] The industrial sector continued to be at the core of the organizational strength of the unions, while the service and public sectors had significantly lower levels of organization. Unlike their colleagues in Britain, the majority of German white-collar workers were not interested in becoming members of a union. Even after the 'fat' years of the 1970s, the level of union membership in this group was still only around 15–16 per cent.[22] The organizational strength of the trade unions in former West Germany was sufficient in practice to defend the established system of collective agreements for specific industries and regions against employers. From 1970 to 2000, the vast majority (more than 75 per cent of employees) belonged to companies bound by collective agreements.[23]

In former East Germany, however, the situation was very different. After initial success in gaining union members, their number declined rapidly in parallel with the slump in industrial employment after 1989. In addition, an increasing number of businesses left the employers' federations, thus avoiding regional agreements. This meant that the trend towards the 'liberation' of businesses from the 'shackles' of collective industrial relations already present in Britain reached reunified Germany, where at the beginning of the twenty-first-century the British and German models effectively existed side by side.[24] However, we have already seen that the West German model of collective bargaining was upheld by unions, employers' associations and employment law experts and that this system became stable again after the end of the 1990s.[25]

At the beginning of this chapter, we identified the right to information and consultation at the workplace as the second element of democratic social citizenship. In this case, the findings also differ widely from country to country. In Britain, the trade union crisis also led to the weakening of the collective representation of interests in companies, since only very few businesses had works councils with elected worker representatives. In the industrial sector, the proportion of companies that had functioning consultative committees sank between 1980 and 1998 from 30 to 23 per cent.[26] The flow of information and communication at the workplace increasingly became the sole responsibility of management.

In France, on the other hand, the representation of employees' interests at the workplace continued to develop institutionally in spite of the organizational weakness of the trade unions. Legal requirements led to the gradual introduction of the mandatory consultative committees mentioned above. While the trade unions managed to get their representatives elected to these committees in eight out of ten companies with more than 500 employees, in small and medium-sized companies there was a preponderance of non-union representatives.[27] Voter turnout, a good 70 per cent in 1977, sank between 1989 and 2004 to an average of 65 per cent.[28] These dense representation structures at company level meant that France became the pioneer of company-specific collective agreements while at the same time trade union bargaining power was weak. In the trade union camp, this policy was supported above all by the second largest group, the CFDT. In the 1980s, given the continuing crisis of the French trade union movement, it had turned away from its decidedly militant, confrontational course in favour of cooperation and compromise. Now it hoped to take advantage of the opportunities offered by the new legal options. This approach was backed by other smaller trade union groups such as the Force Ouvrière (FO), the Christian trade union Confédération Française des Travailleurs Chrétiens (CFTC) and the white-collar workers' union the Confédération Générale des Cadres (CGC). Even the CGT had to adapt to this new balance of power and began to engage increasingly in collective bargaining at company level without strike action.[29] This amounted to a silent French revolution of industrial relations. Above all, it turned the factory or the company into the central point of reference for the collective representation of interests.

In Germany, the starting point for all further developments was the improvement of worker participation in factories introduced by the Works Constitution Act (*Betriebsverfassungsgesetz*) of 1972.[30] From then on, the works councils had the right to participate in decisions on wage issues, the organization of working hours, appointments (recruitment, relocation, wage levels, dismissal) and company changes. In return for these rights, far-reaching in international comparison, they were obliged to cooperate with the management and initially had no collective bargaining powers. In-company deals could be concluded as long as the collective bargaining partners were in agreement. In 1976, this operational co-determination law was augmented by a new law concerning co-determination for large companies, the Company Co-Determination Law (*Mitbestimmungsgesetz*). As mentioned above, the conservative–liberal coalition government under Kohl did not use its long period in power to turn the clock back on co-determination. The employers' associations initially mobilized considerable political and legal opposition to an extension of co-determination rights, but they soon became accustomed to these new legal requirements, as did most company managers. Company co-determination became increasingly accepted and the number of works councils grew steadily. Even in small and medium-sized companies, where resistance to setting up this kind of representative body had been very strong well into the 1970s, the proportion of companies with company co-determination increased significantly. As working hours became more flexible and weekly working hours were reduced after the strike in 1984, company agreements in Germany became more important as a supplement to industry-specific and regional collective agreements, since they could determine details of working time and wage structures that deviated from or specified the framework agreements. As a result, by 1995, conditions of work and pay for more than 72 per cent of the workforce in West Germany were regulated by this kind of company-specific agreement.[31] Studies on works councils elections confirm that workers continued to show interest in these representative bodies and at the same time to trust in trade union members as suitable representatives of their interests at work. In the 1970s and 1980s, over 80 per cent of workers turned out to vote, and in reunified Germany the figure was between 75 and 77 per cent. This is a level equivalent to that of elections to the national parliament (*Bundestag*).[32] As these councils spread, so did the number of their elected representatives. In 1981, there were 19,900 members of works councils,[33] whereas by 2006, more than 33,000 representatives were elected, 14,095 of them in the industrial sector. In the 1970s and 1980s, an average of eight out of ten works councils chairpersons were also trade union members. Although this proportion sank notably after the 1990s (in 2006 it was only just over 57 per cent),[34] it can still be said that the idea of collective representation of interests in industry displayed remarkable continuity in Germany over the period we are studying.

At this point, we can draw an initial conclusion regarding the collective dimension of social citizenship, namely that in the course of this period of transition the differences between the three countries became more pronounced. Industrial workers in West Germany had much greater opportunities than their British counterparts to represent their interests collectively – indeed these were even legally guaranteed. The bargaining power of trade unions had only managed to survive in Germany and to a much lesser extent in France as a component of social citizenship. In Britain, by contrast, this tradition of bargaining was continued only in isolated companies or factories. In the case of in-company co-determination, a certain continuity can be seen in France and Germany at a high or very high level from the point of view of the workers, although in France this was increasingly without the participation of the unions. The situation in Britain, however, was much bleaker. There in-company co-determination collapsed at the same time as the bargaining power of the unions.

Significantly, there are many more similarities between the countries on the level of work practices and working conditions in the newly emerging private service sector. In all three countries, zones without any worker representation or trade union presence swiftly emerged. Sectors such as logistics, retail and wholesale, the hotel and catering industries and household-related services offering unskilled jobs were particularly barren ground for trade union organizers and promoters. In the absence of collective bargaining powers, they soon developed into flourishing landscapes of low-waged, part-time and temporary work. The power of this trend outside the core sectors of stable employment and professional qualifications is clearly illustrated by the fact that after France, which had a long tradition of statutory minimum wages in the face of a relatively weak trade union movement, Britain (late 1990s) and Germany (2014) also introduced a statutory minimum wage to provide basic worker protection.

Wages and payment systems in transition

Wages and payment systems are key issues in industrial relations. Since the 1980s at the latest, sections of management, and especially contemporary trend analysts and economic experts, had been dreaming of a revolution in this area, especially as payment practices initially resisted the contemporary trend towards individualization and flexibility. Let us look in detail at the changes which actually took place.

In the 1970s, piece rates negotiated by the trade unions were still standard practice in industry. They were gradually replaced, first by time rates in combination with a complex wage class system based on a value analysis of the workplace and later more often by team time rates or team piece rates – a change necessitated by the introduction of teamwork. The automobile industry is a typical example of this development towards group piecework or more complex wage calculation systems (incentive earnings) in which a basic wage calculated on being assigned to a certain wage category was combined with piece- or time work and bonuses.[35] Forever rising costs of production systems and means of production in industrial manufacturing meant that pay systems that used machine running time and productivity as an essential element of wage-setting became increasingly attractive. Pay systems that were furthest removed from the classic hourly wage were those that paid the collective labour force based on output and machine running time under the terms of group contracts drawn up between individual teams and the company.[36]

Since the negotiating power of the trade unions in Germany remained stable, the gap between negotiated/fixed levels of earnings and actual earnings, the so-called wage drift, remained under 2 per cent for a long period, from the early 1960s until the end of the twentieth century.[37] The differences in earnings between the various wage categories also remained constant in the three decades between 1970 and 2000 at an average of 15 per cent. A similar pattern of continuity in agreed wage levels is evident in regulations of incentive pay (piecework/bonus payments) that were laid down in detail, for example, in the automobile industry. Regulations for the protection of wages for older workers (protection of average earnings) or annual bonuses were also continued throughout the entire period of this study. The result is an overall picture of collective wage protection. As late as 1998, only a small minority of workers were subject to forms of company performance-related pay (between 9.6 and 16 per cent),[38] but individual performance was an element of most pay schemes. Depending on the industry, the proportion of workers who were time-rate workers but were paid a varying amount according to the assessment of their individual performance stood at around 75 per cent. The share of this varying amount fluctuated between 11 and 30 per cent.[39] Germany remained a high-wage area regulated by collective wage agreements which protected workers in the manufacturing industry but also other sectors of the economy, especially the expanding public sector. As we have seen, this edifice of collective wage and income regulations began to crumble after 1990, especially in businesses in former East Germany and in private service industries.

The situation was different in Britain, where the share of collectively agreed wages for whole branches of industry had always been lower than in West Germany and works- or company-based collective agreements had dominated as early as the 1970s. In the course of deindustrialization and the trade union crisis, the proportion of workers whose contracts were fixed by collective agreements shrank dramatically. In spite of the general trend towards individualized and flexible wages, however, some branches of industry, such as metalworking and printing, stuck to sector-specific wage agreements in which minimum wages, training standards and other matters were agreed on an industry-wide level. Industrial companies followed the general trend towards paying bonuses to their workers, albeit with some hesitation.[40] Bonuses were common, for example, in the auto industry, where they comprised up to 30 per cent or even 50 per cent of the basic wage.[41]

All in all, compared with Germany, wage structures in Britain were swifter to adapt to the liberal desire to take more account of the profit rate and a worker's individual performance. The result was a patchwork of company-specific regulations and an increasingly broad spread of wage structures and wage levels. This means that the average figures available for Britain are not as meaningful as those for Germany. This is also because in Britain overtime and long working weeks partly compensated for hourly wages being relatively low compared to Germany. Between 1980 and 1995, the hourly wage after adjustment for inflation rose in Britain by 22 per cent (i.e. an annual rise of just under 1.5 per cent). This was well below West German hourly wages, which were already higher in 1980 and had risen by a good 26 per cent (i.e. 1.7 per cent per year) by 1995.[42]

In France, industry-specific and company-specific wage agreements ensured that the majority of workers were employed in areas that applied collective wage agreements. In addition, the statutory minimum wage guaranteed a nationwide legally binding minimum wage level. Here, too, the proportion of output-related pay structures and variable performance-based components developed faster and more robustly than in Germany. The weaker position of the trade unions was also reflected in the fact that wage differences were greater than in the equivalent West German industries. However, we have to remember that before the technological innovations of the 1980s and 1990s, overtime and shift work was also common practice for a high percentage of industrial workers in many industries. In France, the average wage stagnated between 1978 and 1996 when adjusted for inflation, which meant that – depending on the industry and the company – the gap widened between wage levels in Germany and Britain.[43]

Individual protection rights and legalization

The combination of the negotiating powers of trade unions and frequent labour conflicts led to the expansion of protection rights in all three countries in the 1970s. From the end of the decade, when deindustrialization had created new parameters for labour market policies, calls to adjust individual labour law began to increase. A classic case for revision in the view of liberal economists was, for example, protection against dismissal. In Germany, the Employment

Protection Act (*Kündigungsschutzgesetz*) passed on 25 August 1969 had tightened the legal framework. The notice period for permanently employed workers was raised to six months, the statutory minimum sum for redundancy payments was increased and the burden of proof was placed on employers: from then on, they had to provide a valid reason for the termination of an employment contract.[44] When the right of works councils to have a say in dismissals was strengthened in the Works Constitution Act (*Mitbestimmungsgesetz*) of 1972, the legal position of employees improved considerably. In France, employment protection was tightened in 1973 and in 1975 a requirement was introduced that dismissals of more than twenty workers had to be authorized (by employment inspectors). This remained in place until 1986. Dismissal rights were also amended in Britain in 1971 when arbitration procedures and the fixing of a minimum level of redundancy payment in particular helped improve the position of employees. Since then, British labour law has also required valid reasons for dismissing workers (fair dismissal), but is less clear about its definition than German law. In Britain, however, an unfair dismissal claim could only be brought after at least one year of employment and the notice period was extended to a maximum of twelve weeks depending on the length of employment. Minimum and maximum levels of redundancy pay were also prescribed by law.

Comparing legal norms is notoriously difficult, especially when this includes their practical implementation. The French solution was (and still is) to limit the scope for action as far as possible by legal means. The system in Germany, and even more so in Britain, allowed more freedom to the collective bargaining parties, and then also to the arbitration bodies and finally to the courts. In practice, a major role was played by the fact that there were company committees representing the workers that had a power of veto and that could, therefore, potentially act in a protective capacity. After the 1980s, a gap grew in this respect between Britain and the other two countries. On the continent, company representation bodies remained intact, whereas in Britain, apart from in the public sector, they became considerably less relevant.

An analysis of the further development of employment protection shows that the basic rules in all three countries were maintained, meaning that the original differences in the extent and severity of the regulations and in the level of prevention continued to exist. In Britain, regulations were decidedly more liberal from the outset and permitted the employer more freedom and room to manoeuvre than was the case in France and Germany. These differences had consequences in legal practice. Cases of dismissal were brought before the German labour courts five times as frequently as in Britain.[45] In France during the structural and economic crises of the 1970s, employment protection regulations that demanded social plans and administrative approval in the case of business redundancies were of particularly direct practical relevance. The right of works councils to have a say in dismissals in Germany had a similar effect. In both countries, it became standard practice to draw up social plans when there were mass redundancies in the industrial sector. There was no equivalent legal obligation in Britain, which meant that it was only collective agreements in an individual company or site that led to the same kind of social plans. This was the case in the late 1970s, for example, in what was then the nationalized steel industry, where social plans were agreed on the closure of various steelworks. More recent studies comparing the legal situation conclude that in France and Germany regulations are more far-reaching and still have significant preventative effects whereas in Britain they are much weaker.[46]

A particularly revealing case of protection claims under labour law is the ban on discrimination. Whereas nineteenth-century labour law introduced positive rules of discrimination, such as to protect women and children from especially dangerous or hazardous jobs and occupations, anti-discrimination laws forbidding unequal pay for men and women on the grounds of race or ethnic background were not introduced until relatively late, namely in the 1960s. In Britain, equal pay legislation for both genders was introduced after female workers at the Ford car factory in Dagenham went on strike in 1968, demanding the same pay as their male colleagues. The strikers sought and won the support of the public and the Labour government after the reaction of their own union representatives to their demands was evasive and dismissive. The Equal Pay Act of 1970, which in fact did not come into force until 1975 and was supplemented by the Sex Discrimination Act in that year,[47] has still not outlived its purpose. It has helped to ensure that gender discrimination has become both illegal and a legitimate ground for complaint and thus belongs to one of the legal and cultural advances of this transition phase.[48] The British laws against race discrimination in 1968–76 were of similar epoch-making significance. Once again, two attempts were needed by the legislators to enforce the principle of equality, which, although politically uncontroversial, was frequently disregarded in real life. Social scientific panel data indicate that the laws against race discrimination gradually began to have an effect on the world of work in Britain. Regular surveys of British companies undertaken since 1980 show that by the end of the twentieth century, members of ethnic minorities and migrants were working in an increasing number of industries and occupations, demonstrating that the barriers which had existed in practice since the 1970s were falling.[49]

In France, the corresponding legislation (equal pay) was introduced in 1972 and reinforced in 1983. Several readjustments to the law were required here as well to close the loopholes allowing discriminatory practices against women and labour migrants from Africa in particular. However, studies of the difficulties faced particularly by young entrants to the labour market from migrant backgrounds in the 1990s and early 2000s revealed that they were still met with considerable reservations, which made it particularly difficult for this group to embark on a working life.[50]

A further individual right of protection concerns statutory regulation of daily, weekly and annual working time. The extent to which the parliaments of our three countries were actively involved in this issue varied until the mid-1970s. In France, following no action at all, various initiatives to limit and regulate working time were introduced after May 1968. Important legislation included the introduction of four weeks of regular paid leave in 1969, the statutory introduction of the 39-hour week and a fifth week of paid leave in 1982, followed by two laws in 1998 and 2002 introducing the 35-hour week.[51] The socialist governments used this framework legislation to pave the way for the reduction of weekly working hours, which was then implemented flexibly at sector and company level by means of collective agreements.

Legislators in Germany and Britain generally avoided involvement in the organization of working time. In West Germany, the standard working time of 48 hours per week passed by law in 1938 was formally valid until 1994. Weekly working hours and annual leave were regulated by sector-specific collective agreements. As we saw in the previous chapter, in 1984 in the metalworking industry, the working week lasted 40 hours. After the arbitration settlement at the end of the industrial dispute in 1984, this had dropped to 38.5 hours by the end of the 1980s and reached 35 hours in the second half of the 1990s. Until 1989, the average collectively agreed number of weekly working hours in all branches of industry followed this trend set by the metalworking industry but remained at 37.4 hours in former West Germany and 39.1 hours in former East Germany until the end of the 1990s.[52] In West Germany, the total period of annual leave rose by almost seven days between 1974 and 2000 from 23.7 days (1974) to 31.2 days (2004), thus exceeding the average of five

151

weeks in France.[53] The trend in Britain again deviated considerably from that of its continental neighbours as legislators refrained from regulating working time and annual leave. Average working hours before 1970 were already higher than in France and Germany, and this difference increased still further in the following decades.

Once again, average figures are misleading in some respects, since it was the aim of industries in all three countries to be able to deploy their production workers more flexibly: that is, in line with fluctuations of demand. This was helped, on the one hand, by the long-established practice of higher paid overtime, which was particularly widespread in Britain.[54] In Germany and France, there were legal restrictions on overtime, which meant that other means of managing working time had to be found in order to introduce the desired increase in flexibility in the deployment of labour and production. Comparative studies have concluded that in 1995 the average working time for men in Britain was just as long as in 1977, at just under 45 hours per week, and for women it had even increased slightly (from just under 40 to just under 41 hours per week), while in the same period in Germany it had dropped from 42 to 38.4 hours per week for men and from just under 40 to 37.2 hours per week for women.[55]

Another concern of legislators, and a matter for administrative control and for employers in their obligation to provide information, was health and safety at the workplace. Legal requirements were tightened in this area in all three countries[56] and more competent specialists were employed or trained (labour inspectors, safety engineers, company doctors). In 1989, a corresponding occupational health and safety directive came into force at the European level.[57] Yet if we examine how these inspection practices developed, in other words how they were complied with, the picture looks slightly different. In Britain in the 1980s, for example, the number of public health and safety inspectors was reduced, and in France the *inspecteurs du travail* were notoriously overworked, while for Germany the figures are better but by no means ideal. The main difference was, however, that in contrast to Britain, Germany and France had given legal powers of intervention to workers' representatives, which improved the chances of adherence to legal standards independently of routine inspections.

It becomes clear from this overview of the most important areas of individual protection rights for workers that there is in fact no question of a deliberate dismantling of these rights. We can say that the world of industrial work has been shaped by the protective functions of labour regulations right up to the present day. The fact that we can nevertheless speak of an erosion of protection rights is because since the late 1980s legislators have been increasingly less prepared to extend established protection rights to new and 'non-standard' jobs unconditionally. In the case of Britain, this was connected with the neoliberal conviction that reverting to individually negotiated employment contracts was the best guarantee of a swift return to full employment and that the existing protection regulations set hurdles so high that they prevented new and additional workers being employed and deployed. The result was that safety provisions in existing health and safety laws, for example, could be modified or overridden by ministerial decrees.

Finally, the spread of part-time work led to an increasing number of workers being unable to take advantage of statutory protection rights because these were still linked to permanent employment contracts and length of employment. This was and still is true, for example, for protection against dismissal but also, if not in law at least in fact, for anti-discrimination safeguards. These were usually not applicable in the case of fixed-term employment contracts and agency work: that is, for two categories of employment that could be found in all three countries in the industrial sector but were spreading rapidly above all in the new service sectors. In Britain in 2002, 7 per cent of all workers were employed on fixed-term contracts and 4 per cent were employed as agency workers. In France in the same period, the proportion was considerably more, namely 15 per cent who worked on fixed-term contracts, while the number of agency workers was lower, at 2.7 per cent. As a result of the then stricter legal regulations, the level of agency work in Germany was even lower, at 1.2 per cent, while the share of those employed on fixed-term contracts was 11 per cent.[58]

Farewell to the social package

Employment contracts for factory workers were directly and inseparably coupled to a package of social security benefits. In Germany and France, compulsory insurance payments to cover such classic risks as accident and invalidity, sickness, old age and unemployment were an integral part of 'normal' employment practices and were financed by both employers' and employees' contributions to the social insurance institutions.

In the case of Britain, the National Health Service was free and financed by taxes so this component of social insurance was absent.

In contrast to the other two countries we are comparing, retirement pensions in Britain were also not financed solely by contributions from employers and employees but also by taxes. This meant that the share of non-wage labour costs was considerably lower. The step towards employment practices which no longer automatically linked social benefits to the employment contract was correspondingly shorter. This was what the new liberal and social-liberal reformers had envisaged since the 1980s as a solution to the labour market crisis. The proportion in the wage contract allocated to social benefits in France and Germany was also higher than in Britain because all insurance benefits were calculated to safeguard the standard of living and social position if benefits were needed. This principle of 'securing the standard of living' was not applicable to the great majority of industrial workers until after the 1970s.[59] The levels of pension and unemployment benefits were calculated so that in the average case it would contribute towards social stability.

In Britain, the level of social security was much lower and there were far greater differences depending on the branch of industry or the company. This was mainly because the state retirement pension was designed only to protect from poverty in old age, so did not reach a level that secured a continuation of the social standard of living without an additional workplace pension. The Supplementary Benefits Act of 1976 raised supplementary pensions for people of retirement age but only to 25 per cent of the average income of a person's twenty years of highest contributions; a further 19 per cent came from the basic state pension.[60] Similarly, wage compensation payments from unemployment insurance covered only an average of 41 per cent of income, whereas in Germany this figure was 61 per cent and in France, depending on the social insurance fund responsible, it was between 60 and 70 per cent and for certain job categories even up to 90 per cent.[61]

The level of what was considered to be standard social security for wage earners was, therefore, quite different in all three countries by the mid-1970s. The dismantling of these social security networks in the 1980s and 1990s was by no means uncontested – politically it was a highly controversial process. Surveys in all three countries endorse the continued popularity of the old welfare standards.[62] The trade union confederations protested repeatedly against 'dismantling the welfare state'. For governing parties, restructuring social security systems and cutting social benefits remained a policy area that was as risky as it was delicate. To quote Wolfgang Streeck again: everyone 'was buying time' by initially accepting an increase in social transfer payments while at the same time initiating a long-term plan to dismantle wage-based social benefits. Once again it was Britain that led the way. Margaret Thatcher's Conservative government had already set the course for an erosion of social benefits as early as the 1980s. It began by decoupling state pensions from wage trends, shortening benefit periods and restricting the circle of those who were entitled to the jobseekers' allowance, and continued by cutting the supplementary state pension in favour of private insurance policies.[63]

In Germany, wage-related social benefits also began to be scaled down in the early 1980s, still under the social–liberal coalition government of Helmut Schmidt, and continued after that under Helmut Kohl's conservative government. First, the minimum period of employment to qualify for unemployment benefit was raised from two to three years. Then in 1984 the standard benefit for the unemployed without children was significantly reduced (from 68 per cent to 63 per cent for full unemployment benefit and 58 per cent to 56 per cent for unemployment assistance). The result was that these rates were no longer adequate for 13 per cent of the unemployed, who then had to claim welfare benefits.[64] The standard rates in France over the same period were similar (64.7 per cent in the first year of an unemployment benefit claim).[65]

Spectacular cracks in the model of social security provision began to appear when there was little sign of re-employment after layoffs and the phenomenon of so-called long-term employment began to spread. This was already visible in the early 1980s and attracted the attention of experts. It became a constant theme on the social policy agenda of our three countries, which all adopted early retirement schemes as a way out for older industrial workers, which, if nothing else, took the edge off the social protests of this time, as we saw in chapter 3 (see figure 4.2). It soon became evident, however, that those hardest hit by the strain on the labour market were young people beginning their working lives with poor qualifications as well as unskilled and low-skilled workers. For them, fixed-term contracts, part-time jobs, job creation schemes and illegal employment meant that their entitlement to social support and protection rights was much more limited.

The extent to which workers in the private sector were provided with social security by the various types of employment and employment contracts became increasingly unclear in the early decades of the twenty-first century and became far more difficult to calculate than for their parents' generation. The most important consequence of this period of upheaval was not linear cuts but the

Figure 4.2 No work or no pension? Cartoon accompanying an article entitled 'Those Without Work Get Old Quicker', in *Der Spiegel* 43 (1983), pp. 76–92, here p. 92.

A cartoon published in *Der Spiegel* in 1983 shows the then employment Minister Norbert Blüm. He has just got out of his camper van to find a way that would lead between 'no work' and 'no pension'. In the 1980s politicians from both the Social Democrats and Christian Democrats saw early retirement as a promising solution to the pressing problem of mass unemployment, despite the high costs involved. The only person who seems not too happy about a longer period of his life being without work is the typical German, 'Michel', waiting on the passenger seat.

increase in insecurity and disparity: that is, the departure from largely uniform standards in the package of employment-related social security. The situation can best be described similarly for all three countries as an erosion of the wage-based social security system.

The older model was by its nature at its most vulnerable in those areas where it was not firmly established in labour and social law. This was the case only in Britain, where after 1979 widespread signs of the new economic and political climate appeared correspondingly swiftly. Means-tested welfare benefits came back into the lives of more and more workers. It also happened earlier and more frequently in France than in Germany, but the design and level of social welfare benefits from tax revenues became a permanent issue even in German social policy, at the latest after the wave of mass unemployment following reunification. The tone and arguments used in these debates were closely linked to the advance of neoliberal interpretations of unemployment and social benefits. The reform of pensions in 2001 and the so-called Hartz Laws I to IV in 2002 and 2003 brought Germany into line with Britain. From then on, Germany chose to combat unemployment and poverty by relying on flexible labour markets and low wages if need be, rather than on benefits that secured social status.[66]

This deterioration in legal social status had far-reaching consequences for the way the workers themselves perceived and judged social reality. Eroding social standards at work were experienced first-hand by far more workers than the aggregate data suggest. Many working households experienced the reappearance of the basic risks of wage labour, and this began to restrict the horizon of their collective expectations. But we have to be wary since at this point generalizations on the macro level are misleading. Rather, we need to look carefully at career trajectories, employment histories and household constellations in order to grasp the precise extent of these changes. What can be seen is that the erosion of social benefits is less sharply defined as soon as we look at the households themselves as the smallest social unit. Many low-wage earners or 'non-typical' employees profited as spouses, children or other family members from the continuation of secure employment. This was because fully employed male industrial workers or female employees in the public sector were responsible for mitigating the social consequences of this process of erosion in an increasing number of working-class/classes populaires households. This will be my topic in chapter 6.

Crisis of social citizenship

The promise of secure social status and social equality, which had only been expanded to all workers, male and female, as a result of the reforms and extensions of benefits in the 1970s, was, however, gradually dismantled in the experience of very many people. The erosion of work-related social protection reinforced the tendency of workers to withdraw from the social and political arena, as described in the previous chapters. One of the causes of the erosion of democratic equality, which was identified fifteen years ago as one of the key problems in the current crisis of capitalist democracies, lies in the crisis of social citizenship, which again is inextricably linked to the process of deindustrialization.

Triggered by deindustrialization, the employment crisis first undermined the social package that had provided wage labour with a secure job and life perspective. Whereas in the 1970s demands for participation and promises of security had driven the model of social citizenship, from the 1980s onwards opposing economic, social and political forces became stronger. This led to the legal regulation of labour, social benefits and wages becoming correspondingly insignificant as possible forces of stability and continuity in this long phase of deindustrialization.

Although labour market policies varied in the three countries, they ultimately created legal frameworks for more flexible employment regulations. This happened earlier and more decisively in Britain than in Germany and France, which followed more hesitantly and where the legal basis for the old model stayed intact. When this process of adapting labour policy came to an end, it resulted in slowly decreasing unemployment figures but also in increasing numbers of workers on fixed-term contracts and in part-time or temporary work. The model of social citizenship, originating as it did from industry, was considered no longer suited to the new service sector and came under pressure everywhere.

However, this model was not based solely on social benefits and rights but also comprised a genuine political dimension. It embodied the representation of collective interests towards capital and within the company. We saw above how and why powerful trade unions were still the main representatives of these collective interests at the end of the 1970s. By the beginning of the twenty-first century, however, there was practically nothing left of this trade union power, especially in France and Britain. In Germany, the industrial unions found themselves on the defensive but had succeeded in stabilizing their organization at a much higher level than their Western counterparts.

In Britain, the established model of industrial citizenship collapsed during deindustrialization, partly due to pressure from the clearly anti-union legislation of the Conservative government. But even there there were some factories and companies where shop stewards could still exercise their co-determination rights and still had the power to veto management decisions. In France and Germany, as described above, the interest groups within companies had profited from greater legal backing and their connection to the trade unions remained overall so strong that they gradually became important negotiating partners within the company and played a significant role in managing various transformations in the organization of industrial production at company level. The size and scope of this in-company participation were again dependent on many factors and the way it was organized was of direct economic significance in the face of increasing competition and technological transformation.

According to Wolfgang Schroeder, at the end of the transition period studied here, so around 2000, a distinction can be made between three different worlds of work in all three countries.[67] In the first, the social citizenship model determined the statutory conditions of labour, social bargaining and social security which applied to most workers. It still included mainly large industrial concerns, but also medium-sized industrial companies oriented towards export. Trade unions and shop stewards/*Betriebsräte*/*comités d'entreprise* continued to be influential and effective. This was the dominant pattern in most industrial sectors in former West Germany, whereas in France it was already much more restricted to larger companies and in Britain only small pockets remained. The second world of work represents a zone in which some components of the social citizenship model were still valid but above all collective representations of interests were suppressed. In such companies, it was typical for there to be an increase in employment contracts which no longer included full protective rights. This transition zone comprised small and medium-sized companies in particular, but also new branches of US and Japanese companies in France and Britain. The third world of work was made up of those companies and businesses in which all aspects of the social citizenship model had either been terminated by law or in practice or were as good as ignored. This comprised mainly small manufacturing companies. But what became far more important in statistical terms in all three countries was the employment relationship in the private service sector. This third world of work was far removed from the standards of social citizenship, but was again in itself disparate in terms of employment contracts, wage forms and working conditions. It is to this world of work that we now turn.

— Chapter 5 —

SKILLED WORK, PRODUCTION KNOWLEDGE AND EDUCATIONAL CAPITAL
Conflicts of interpretation and readjustments

For a long time, hard physical work and monotonous routine tasks were considered the epitome of industrial labour. Factory work did not require any manual or technical skills; 'common sense' and 'common skills' were sufficient. This image of industrial labour became increasingly less valid after the 1970s. As we saw in chapter 1, during the third industrial revolution, numerous production processes were mechanized and automized. This resulted, among other things, in the disappearance of many jobs that required no specialist qualifications and only short periods of training. The new technological framework significantly altered the conditions for machine operators and production workers. Certain job routines and skills became redundant (such as typesetting in the printing industry) and new knowledge (IT, programming) and new skills (controlling, evaluation) were now required.

In this chapter, I will examine how the much-cited 'transition from an industrial society to a knowledge society'[1] took place in Britain, France and Germany in these three transformational decades. Again, I will take the perspective of industrial labour. In all three countries, contemporaries reacted with acute awareness to these changes. Knowledge and education were suddenly evoked everywhere as the main resources with which to secure the future viability of society. A topic that was also hotly debated amongst industrial sociologists at the beginning of the transformation phase in the mid-1970s was whether the practical and often experience-based knowledge of industrial labourers would have an important part to play in this future. There was also serious disagreement over the significance of this transition. Neo-Marxist sceptics were afraid that manual work would be even further devalued, while liberal optimists painted a picture of a brave new world in which interesting, knowledge-based work would be the norm. For a long time, there was no clear evidence to show which way things would develop. However, what did soon become clear was that the automated factory, which had been the subject of broad debate in the 1960s, would still remain nothing more than a utopian dream in the digital age. Although industrial robots did appear on the factory floor and industrial production was dominated to an ever-growing extent by computer-controlled machines and processes, human labour remained indispensable.[2] The crucial question to emerge was rather how tasks and competencies were actually allocated and distributed and how this affected education and remuneration systems, on the one hand, and professional codes for industrial workers, on the other.

Before we look at these developments in detail, it must be said that the interconnection of the various operational processes in manufacturing also increased demands on linguistic and communicative competence, and more generally on the ability to cooperate with others. The 'isolation' from social life which Maurice Halbwachs highlighted as the central characteristic of industrial workers – what he saw as a typical lack of exchange with others and fixation on machines and apparatus[3] – faded more and more into the background.

The longue durée of production knowledge and educational capital

It is clear, therefore, that the third industrial revolution required a readjustment of knowledge and competencies, tested established hierarchies of knowledge and inspired reforms to the general education and vocational training systems. The knowledge systems and educational hierarchies encountered by these plans for reform were, however, firmly and institutionally anchored in the three societies studied here. The view of manual work as less valuable than intellectual activity and aristocratic leisure has a long history and the social structures that determined this attitude had not been destroyed by the first industrial revolution. On the contrary, it had plunged the crafts and trade regulations, which attempted to protect the professional skills and knowledge of skilled craftspeople from 'unfair competition', into a serious crisis. The result was that for manual workers in industry the value of specialist skills and knowledge seriously deteriorated, as already clearly indicated by Marx.

162

Every kind of capitalist production, in so far as it is not only a labour-process, but also a process of creating surplus-value, has this in common, that it is not the workman that employs the instruments of labour, but the instruments of labour that employ the workman. But it is only in the factory system that this inversion for the first time acquires technical and palpable reality. By means of its conversion into an automaton, the instrument of labour confronts the labourer, during the labour-process, in the shape of capital, of dead labour, that dominates, and pumps dry, living labour-power. The separation of the intellectual powers of production from the manual labour, and the conversion of those powers into the might of capital over labour, is, as we have already shown, finally completed by modern industry erected on the foundation of machinery. The special skill of each individual insignificant factory operative vanishes as an infinitesimal quantity before the science, the gigantic physical forces, and the mass of labour that are embodied in the factory mechanism and, together with that mechanism, constitute the power of the 'master'.[4]

The separation of the knowledge at large in society from individual manual labour, of 'the factory mechanism' from 'the mass of labour', was taken to extremes in capitalist factory work. The actual concrete task of industrial labourers was reduced to maintaining a knowledge-based production system. For Marx, the appropriation of knowledge and competence based solely on private property was, therefore, one of capitalist industrial production's central structural features and areas of tension. Factory regulations and workplace organization were used to subsume the traditional hierarchies of knowledge and skills to the rule of capital. The appropriation and devaluation of knowledge and skills as well as the battle over the availability and the price of production knowledge have remained central issues in the conflict between trade unions and employers, between capital, labour and the state. It was still highly contested, for example, whether the skills necessary for industrial labour processes became part of socially controlled occupational rules and whether the protection of job titles and professional training standards negotiated by collective bargaining replaced the old craft and trade regulations from the guilds, which had been abolished in the course of liberal trade reforms.

The separation of production knowledge and manual industrial labour analysed by Marx led to industrial production knowledge being strictly divided into three job categories based on status, income and agency. First, representatives of capital – that is, factory owners and their managers; second, technical experts – that is, engineers, scientists and technicians, who were responsible for planning and controlling production; third, male and female workers who were active in production.

This perspective on production knowledge emphasizing the antagonism between capital and labour must, however, be complemented by a second perspective focussing on cooperative aspects. It contends that in the development and application of specific industrial production technologies, workers, engineers and scientists collaborate and contribute their various skills and experience to them. This means that these shared work processes and the resulting products incorporate various types of knowledge of different origins and sources: applied science and technology as well as knowledge from operational experience and professional skills. This gives rise to something like a common industrial professionalism or production competence. The knowledge of a particular job or task in this sense involves the quality of the product as well as cooperation between people with very different skills.

Technical know-how, professional cooperation and the subjection of production knowledge to the power of capital have all contributed to the creation of specific hierarchies of knowledge in industrial production since the eighteenth century. The beginnings of industrial production were still closely tied to workers' manual skills and knowledge. In the nineteenth century, they developed into specific forms of highly specialized skilled work. This was in stark contrast to and with a clear social and economic disassociation from common labourers and unskilled workers with no knowledge or education, the 'mass of labour' Marx speaks of in the above quotation.[5] The large industrial factories created a new category of semi-skilled production workers, whose technical and theoretical knowledge may have been limited but who had concrete experiential knowledge related to their particular job, such as knowledge of complex technical processes and machines, which made them indispensable.

The importance of vocational training and qualifications for industrial workers in all three countries increased with the development of industrial production. Recognition of their knowledge and skills was closely linked to recognition of their trade unions and political parties as the collective representatives of their political and economic interests.[6]

Those who benefited from this institutional security in all three countries were the skilled workers, *ouvriers professionels* or *Facharbeiter*. Their knowledge and skills were defined as belonging to a more inferior category than that of engineers and technicians but complementary to them. The hierarchy of knowledge and decision-making power this entailed remained stable for a surprisingly long time and adapted more or less effortlessly to the constant techno-logical innovations that had been driving industrial production since the end of the nineteenth century. Even the rise of the 'mass labourer' on the Fordist production line as it increased in importance between 1920 and 1970 did not change this regime fundamentally. In all three countries, workers normally acquired skilled knowledge by means of in-company apprenticeships. The proportion of skilled workers trained in this way in Britain, however, was at most a third of the total industrial workforce. This had to do among other things with the control exerted by the specialist trade unions over the apprenticeships. In France and West Germany, the proportion was noticeably higher. In the censuses of 1954 and 1975 in France they made up 46 per cent and just under 45 per cent of all workers (*ouvriers*) respectively.[7] The fact that this proportion did not increase further in the 1960s and early 1970s was due above all to the inflow of mainly unskilled labour migrants from the Mediterranean. There are no similarly precise data for Germany but the overall picture corresponds to the development in France. As we have seen, the influence of the trade unions increased during the final phase of the postwar economic boom. They used this influence, on the one hand, by cooperating with employers, the state and representatives of the public education system to shape vocational training institu-tions, and, on the other hand, by negotiating collective agreements concerning the employment of skilled and professionally qualified workers. It is fair to say that in this final phase of the boom trained skilled workers were the most prominent representatives of legitimate workers' interests in trade unions and workers' parties.

If we now look at Britain, France and Germany in more detail, we can first determine that their national frameworks for this basic pattern of the distribution and hierarchy of knowledge differed significantly. In Britain, a liberal pattern prevailed, which meant that the transmission of production knowledge was left to employers and employees. Specifications for job training in industry could be freely negotiated between capital and labour: that is, between the specialized trade unions and employers' organizations or individual companies. As a result, there was a dominance of local and sector-specific solutions and state regulations were largely absent.[8] In France, where the old craft guilds and training systems had been abolished during the 1789 revolution, the gap left by this revolutionary deregulation was only slowly filled by the state in the early twentieth century. First, an institutional framework was created by defining educational and vocational qualifications and establishing corresponding vocational training courses within the state secondary education system. Private initiatives were, on the other hand, plainly sidelined.[9] In Germany after World War I, a combination of the traditional craft apprenticeships and new industrial training opportunities produced the so-called dual vocational training system. In contrast to school-based education, which was regulated by the state, this vocational, in-company training was in the hands of employers and their organizations.[10]

Post-industrial education ideologies

At the beginning of the 1970s, it was not only the old industries that were plunged into crisis but also the knowledge systems described above. This was due to the value of production-related knowledge shifting as science-based technological innovations gained in importance. A few years earlier, analysts had already predicted that knowledge and technology would determine the future. 'Post-industrial society', they concluded, whether capitalist or socialist, would be an 'information' or 'knowledge' society.[11] This prophecy soon became generally accepted and part of the unverified 'knowledge' (*doxa*) about current trends and the near future. Everyone talked about the disappearance of manual and physical labour in general, about the increasing significance of abstract, school-based knowledge and higher (academic) education and about 'lifelong learning'. A core feature of all these diagnoses was the displacement of 'jobs', or less often 'professions', in favour of 'competence', or rather 'competencies' or 'competency profiles', which were understood as a coherent bundle of different knowledge and skills. The definition of 'competencies' and their empirical investigation from a comparative 'global' perspective became an important area of research in the social and educational sciences, promoted and advanced above all by large international institutions such as the Organization for Economic Cooperation and Development (OECD), the EU Commission and the International Labour Organization (ILO).The theory behind this trend was the connection between the third industrial revolution and knowledge as found in the concept of 'human capital' (see figure 5.1). In this concept, promoted by Gary Becker in the mid-1960s,[12] human capital refers to the individually

Figure 5.1 Gary S. Becker, *Human Capital*. Cover of the 1993 edition.

After the first and second editions in 1964 and 1975 respectively, the third edition of Gary Becker's *Human Capital: A Theoretical and Empirical Analysis with Special Reference to Education* was published in 1993. As a US economist, he had won the Nobel Prize the previous year because, so the prize committee declared, he had extended micro-economic theory to apply to broad areas of human behaviour. Becker became one of the most influential pioneers of a new direction in education, especially in Britain. It was now no longer in-company vocational training controlled by the trade unions that was considered to be important for the future, but individually acquired skills.

167

invested capital of skills, knowledge and health. Responsibility for its development and nurture rests with the individual, for it assumes, as Brigitta Bernet puts it, that 'an economic policy oriented towards productivity must begin with the individual, with their training, their economic nature and their pursuit of profit maximization'.[13] Nevertheless, it requires adjustments in society for it to be applied profitably

Looking at the situation in the US, Becker recommended combining public education opportunities with additional private investment in educational capital (to be made by individuals or their companies) and dispensing with any other regulations. This model won favour, even though empirical findings seemed to discredit it.[14] It reassembled the content and forms of work-related knowledge and was taken to its logical conclusion by the so-called modularization of competencies and knowledge. The aim here was to determine clearly defined key competencies and to distinguish them from specialized technical competencies or ad hoc skills so that they could then be taught as cheaply and flexibly as possible. The control and supervision of competence acquisition became an important part of new management strategies. As a consequence, companies were able to free themselves from job training monopolies controlled by the unions and from the rigid hierarchies of general educational qualifications.

In times of great uncertainty, human capital theory and the *doxa* generated from it provided businesses, governments and even strategically calculating parents with a framework on which to base their increasingly risky investments in education and qualifications. Human capital soon became something like the key to a compact educational ideology. It was used not only to diagnose ongoing changes but also to put the case for a specific educational model for a future post-industrial era. It did not fail to have a performative effect. Education policy-makers, educational scientists and finally international institutions like the OECD became advocates of this educational model with its clear aims. These were to extend general education in schools and particularly further education as a means of teaching key skills and to abolish strictly defined job profiles and vocational training in favour of an acquisition of broad competencies. This was accompanied by promotion of the meritocratic idea that individual educational achievements justified differences in income in later life. Lifelong learning of ever-new competencies related to specific jobs and areas of work was elevated to the ideal. Creative artists and visionary entrepreneurs as well as scientists involved in innovative research were held up as the role models of future-oriented knowledge. A kind of pragmatic version of this heroic ideal was embodied by professionals: that is, academically educated and highly qualified experts and specialists. The established and prestigious professions of doctors, lawyers and engineers became blueprints for a growing number of new academic professions. Computer scientists, financial experts and controllers also gained academic qualifications or held doctorates. In the radical version of this model, vocational training and apprenticeship systems were completely replaced by flexible skills-training schemes.

What stands out here is that not only the classic industrial jobs but also the many 'low-level'and 'mid-level' jobs in the service sector were more or less excluded from this vision. Their focus was increasingly seen as outdated, their knowledge basis as not sufficiently complex and the competencies associated with them as dispensable or no longer suited to the new technological challenges. The traditional virtues of industrial work were made to look old in every sense by the ideological stranglehold of social interpreters, educational reformers and management gurus.[15] However, it turned out that the established structures were far harder to shift and their defenders far more stubborn than the prophets of the new era had presumed.

In reality, the education systems in Britain, France and Germany in the early 1970s were still a good way from conforming to these future scenarios. That had to do with the fact that all three countries still had an extremely socially selective general education system inherited from the first half of the twentieth century. Its 'democratization' – that is, the effective opening of all secondary schools to the majority of the population – had only been at the top of the political agenda since the 1960s. 'Democratization' also meant opening academic qualifications to practical knowledge and especially to knowledge that was useful in industry and on the labour market. Although not all at the same time, the education systems in our three countries experienced notable expansion and growth. At the end of it, the majority of 16- to 24-year-olds were acquiring skills or higher education qualifications from state technical schools, technical colleges and universities with the overarching aim of achieving success on the labour market and so fulfilling the key criterion of employability. In all three countries, the traditional hierarchy of qualifications was preserved and the new jobs and training courses were integrated into the existing order.

Contrary to what some prophets of the knowledge society had expected or even hoped, the response to the constantly changing demands of the (post-industrial) world was not, therefore, a complete re-orientation of the educational hierarchy or even a devaluation of traditional educational qualifications in favour of lifelong acquisition of skills and knowledge. As mentioned above, the proportion of jobs and training courses that were organized according to the model of (academic) professions increased overall. Whether it was doctors, engineers, lawyers or pilots, their professional associations helped determine the standards of training and work, admission to the labour market and labour regulations.

France set the pace with the expansion and 'democratization' of its secondary and tertiary education system after the end of the 1960s. Germany managed to keep up with the changes in the 1970s and 1980s only with difficulty, whereas Britain did not open its tertiary education institutions to the majority of its young people until the New Labour era in the second half of the 1990s. However, in the course of this expansion and liberalization, the standing and power of industrial vocational training shifted in these three countries in very different ways.

The many lives of the German vocational education and training system

International comparisons of developments in Western industries show that the standing of the dual vocational training system in Germany experienced a surprising upsurge in the 1980s and 1990s. Economists and sociologists highlighted the close connection between flexible quality production and the presence of qualified skilled workers everywhere in West German companies. Yet at the beginning of the new millennium, the jury was still out over whether this vision of labour was flexible enough to react appropriately to the technological and organizational changes in industrial production.[16] In Germany itself, the system of vocational training had been under fire for some time and the voices of the sceptics and critics drowned out the softer arguments of those who defended it. By 1980, there seemed to be no future for occupations (in trades and industry) which required vocational training. In other areas of work, the technical requirements and practical fields of application had long since changed. In addition, the vocational training system was part of the selective tripartite school system and was suspected of reproducing class and educational barriers.[17]

One educational scientist pointed out that the West German vocational training system was surprisingly adaptable during this period and labelled this the 'modernity of the outmoded'.[18] It can be said to have started with a statutory revision of the vocational training system, introduced by the grand coalition of the CDU/CSU and the SPD in 1969.[19] This Vocational Training Act (*Berufsbildungsgesetz*) was still completely in the spirit of the boom and its purpose was primarily to consolidate and extend the wide range of available vocational qualifications that had mushroomed since the end of World War II. The mass of jobs requiring vocational training varied widely according to region and type and had grown to become the numerically largest branch of the public education system (even if society tended to dismiss and/or underrate it). Between 60 and 70 per cent of those born after 1930 had completed an apprenticeship and most of them had chosen to train in the technical or industrial sector (crafts or trade). But it was the Vocational Training Act of 1969 that first created the dual system with its four features: (a) it included all areas of the economy; (b) it was administered by professional associations; (c) jobs requiring vocational training were state-approved; and (d) trade unions, the federal states (*Länder*) and teachers at the vocational schools all had the right to influence the design of the courses.[20] The law thus strengthened the corporatist nature of vocational training. Over the next ten years, education reformers and trade unionists tried to modernize the system further, such as by increasing the share of school-based education and corresponding knowledge or reducing employers' influence on the design of the company-based course modules. All these attempts, however, were unsuccessful.

For the prophets of the knowledge society, this construct and its resistance to reform was by its very nature a relic of outdated ideas of knowledge and education.[21] Then in the mid-1970s a surprising thing happened. Those responsible for dual vocational training – that is, employer associations, trade unions and chambers of trade and commerce – began meeting in a variety of coalitions, lasting until the 1990s, with the aim of preventing the system from being radically overhauled. Also, when it became necessary to adapt job profiles and curricula to changes in the work environment, as happened at several points during this period, they cooperated in design committees. As a result, the reformed system was able to withstand the many attempts to erode it coming from society and business. The fact that it was able to survive was also a side effect of the permanent failure of youth policy between 1975 and 1991, when the lack of apprenticeship places for school leavers was particularly severe.[22] The weak economy happened to coincide with the baby boomer generation, who were hit by the shortage of training and job opportunities. In

171

this situation, the dual vocational system became the most important means of counteracting youth unemployment and therefore indispensable. Even education reformers saw it as the lesser evil. The struggle to provide sufficient apprenticeships became an annual ritual during the era of Helmut Kohl, in which all the actors in the political arena were happy to participate.[23]

Overall, these reforms merged the narrowly defined job profiles of traditional trades to become new overarching profiles for skilled workers in whole branches or production processes, but also led to the introduction of new jobs requiring training. As a result of a vital reform of metalworking jobs in 1987, for example, the number of jobs requiring training in the sector shrank from forty-five to sixteen.[24] The reforms of 1997 led to sixty-two new jobs requiring training being created between 1997 and 2006, particularly in the areas of health, tourism, service industries and IT, and 162 job profiles were modernized.[25] All these efforts were inspired particularly by the companies' reawakened interest in young skilled workers, whom they saw as the key to coping with restructuring production as it intensified in the 1980s (see figure 5.2).

In this assortment of different constellations of motives and actors, what is clear is that the standing of skilled workers' production knowledge and its significance for innovation and market adaptation strategies increased notably in many German companies. Retaining the three-year model of training for skilled workers (from 1987 it could be extended for a further six months) strengthened the system of wider wage agreements, whose central reference point was still the wages of skilled workers.

In actual fact, however, in the same period the balance between general education and the dual system shifted within the (West) German education system. Entry requirements for training courses were tightened and the number of pupils at the mid-level schools (*Realschulen*) and grammar schools (*Gymnasien*) rose. This meant that more and more school leavers with higher qualifications went into vocational training. As a result, the dual system opened up further towards technical colleges and other institutions in tertiary education, leading to the proportion of apprenticeships in the 16- to 19-year-old age group rising between 1970 and 1990 from 53 per cent to just below 75 per cent.[26] The main focus remained on occupations in industry and skilled trades. At the same time, it became much more difficult for those who had dropped out of school or for weaker students, especially from the lower-tier schools (*Hauptschulen*), to access vocational training. For many (eight out of ten), the only way

172

Figure 5.2   Apprentices at Daimler-Benz, 1997.

In view of the continuing shortage of apprenticeships, the magazine *Der Spiegel* interviewed the human resources manager at Daimler Benz, Heiner Tropitzsch. He made explicit reference to the advantages of the dual system with its combination of academic learning and practical training. The interview was published in *Der Spiegel* (edition 26/1997, p. 30) and illustrated with the above photo. It shows several apprentices in overalls bearing the company logo surrounding a robot they had built. The image represents the cooperation between traditional time-honoured craftsmanship and new computer technology that contributed significantly to the success of export-oriented quality production in Germany.

to do so was by the roundabout route of preparatory courses and publicly funded special youth measures. In 2002, the majority of school leavers (680,000) started their vocational training in this way, while only a minority (480,000) began apprenticeships directly.[27]

Skills acquisition, knowledge loss and de-qualification: the road to the knowledge society in Britain

Ever since the employment successes of the 1990s, social policy-makers and labour economists saw Britain as the prime example of an alternative to the comparatively conservative West German continuation of the dual system. Within a very short period, Britain had experienced two radical changes of course in state vocational education policy.

First, Labour governments in the 1960s tried to come to corporatist arrangements between trade unions, employer associations and the state to raise the number of specialists (engineers, technicians and skilled workers) in industry, which was low by international comparison. The Industrial Training Act of 1964 began a relatively short phase of fifteen years in which the previously dominant model of training standards in British industry regulated by the market or by collective bargaining was reshaped by state regulations in the form of decentralized Industrial Training Boards.[28] Remnants of the liberal model still existed at the beginning of this phase in the great variety of vocational qualifications and training patterns in the different regions, sectors and companies. The relatively elaborate model of traditional apprenticeships (lasting up to five years) survived as a means of qualification for a small number of first-time workers in industry, but even in its best years, the 1950s, it had only reached at most a third of industrial workers. The 1964 Act, however, failed to achieve its aim of improving the level of vocational qualifications in British industry. First, young people still preferred to take the direct route from school to industry. Second, small and medium-sized companies in particular shied away from investing in qualifications for their workers, not least because of the risk of subsequently losing well-trained workers to larger companies. Third, the specialized trade unions also defended their existing role of negotiating the scope and standards of skilled vocational training within companies or sectors. This enabled them to regulate and control access to the labour market and the work situation for their own members. Things changed when unemployment figures began to rise in the early 1970s

174

and short-term programmes to combat youth unemployment became more important.[29] In 1979 at the end of this phase, only 21.7 per cent of workers employed in manufacturing and construction reported having done an apprenticeship. Significantly, this share was 3 per cent higher amongst older workers (above 35) than for younger workers who had not started work until after 1964.[30]

This combination of the effects of the economic cycle with certain special interests made the 1964 Act less effective than had been expected. However, it was then completely undermined by the Conservative government's about-turn in education policy between 1979 and 1994, leading to the second radical change of course in state vocational education policy. With its declared aim of breaking the power of the trade unions across the board, the policy included ousting the trade unions from any co-determination on questions of training and returning full responsibility for the vocational qualifications of their workforce to employers. At the same time, youth unemployment, which had been rising since the late 1970s, was to be combated as quickly as possible and with the greatest available publicity. Whereas traditional apprenticeships were neglected, there was an increase in state support for preparatory vocational courses, so-called Youth Training Schemes, for school leavers, which often lasted only one or two years. This meant that the entry into a career or the path to unemployment was delayed by two years. It had a positive effect on the unemployment statistics and thus on the public image of the government but did very little to prepare the participants of these measures for future employment. Since the sector-based trade unions had designed and controlled many of the traditional skilled jobs, their decline was one further step towards narrowing opportunities for vocational qualifications.

The risks connected with this liberal deregulation of established vocational qualifications did not go unrecognized. Calls for a change of direction became increasingly vocal after the end of the 1980s. In 1994, they led to an official change of course and the rediscovery of the virtues of vocational training, now rebranded as 'modern apprenticeships'.[31] The new Labour government extended this state-supported programme but without notable success, since by then the tertiary education sector had been expanded as the new way to acquiring key qualifications and skills relevant to the labour market. The new apprenticeships thus ran counter to the idea behind the transformation of the polytechnics into universities in 1992. The aim of New Labour's education offensive was to create better-paid jobs for everyone and was linked to its ideal of meritocracy and to the Blair government's promise to create equality of opportunity in British society through education and to eliminate clear-cut class boundaries. Both aims remained no more than empty phrases and illusions.

As a result of its weak vocational training structures, Britain became the pioneer of the new modular concept of flexible 'job skills'. The actual acquisition of these skills was considered the responsibility of company management and thus left to employers' discretion. It was understood and propagated as the result of investment into further training and qualifications, perfectly in tune with the human capital approach. The process of delegating work-related qualifications and technical expertise to companies was thus further advanced. At the same time, it was translated into the new language of general skills and competencies which individuals were expected to accumulate but whose recognition as human capital was at the discretion of the employer or regulated by labour markets. Particularly in view of the dramatic restructuring of British industry in the Thatcher era, this competence-based training system created the flexibility without which a change of job or sector would have been even more difficult.

It was the aim of the various public support programmes for work-related training and continuing education to meet the overall growth in the knowledge required in the work environment. The extent to which the liberal market model was a success remains controversial. In relation to its relatively low level at the end of the 1970s, the level of qualifications improved throughout all sectors and occupations, but there were still considerable differences between skilled and unskilled jobs.[32] In the declining industrial sector, there was a clear trend towards higher qualifications. For example, in 2000 the proportion of those who reported having completed an apprenticeship had risen to 37 per cent (in 1979 it was 22 per cent). Of these, the proportion of younger workers (15- to 24-year-olds) at 28.5 per cent was still clearly below the level of the older workers (55- to 64-year-olds), which lay at 41 per cent.[33] Within the British employment system, the diminished industrial sector had become an area in which a greater amount of more demanding knowledge was required than in many other jobs in the new service industries, where in many cases practical skills took precedence over technical or other expertise.

One reason why the British case is so interesting is that it revealed long-lasting gender images and social orientations which reinforced the social inequality of education and knowledge. In the industrial centres, the school hierarchy was also a class hierarchy. Achieving a higher level of education could mean a person leaving their original social milieu and its solidarity structures. Studies such as that by Paul Willis have documented the existence of a decidedly anti-intellectual counter-culture of young British men from traditional working-class backgrounds in the early 1970s. Their natural career path after leaving school would have led to jobs in manufacturing and the acquisition of competencies within male working-class hierarchies.[34] Whereas the rejection of their former schools and any kind of schooling was also widespread amongst male apprentices in German industry,[35] the fact that learning in the German dual system took place at work was able to break down this antagonism in the majority of cases. In Britain, workers' alienation from education was to a certain extent perpetuated through institutional sanctioning. Areas and forms of recognized work-related knowledge typically emerged in sectors and companies where the trade unions had a significant influence on vocational training and where vocational qualifications could be obtained within the personal and work environment.

Traditional distance and new hierarchies: qualifications and production knowledge in France

At first glance and in the light of what we have documented so far, it would seem natural to assign France an intermediate position between the two extreme cases of job skills (Britain) and jobs requiring training or apprenticeships (Germany), particularly as liberal and interventionist traditions on the other side of the Channel and the river Rhine affected developments in France. A closer look, however, shows that France had its own distinct position. In this case, the framework for the further development of industrial knowledge systems was significantly determined by the general education system and its consistent and systematic extensions.[36] In effect, internal company hierarchies followed the strict classifications of state education qualifications. In contrast to Germany, though not to Britain, at the end of the boom a clear dividing line had developed in French industry between the majority of production workers, on the one hand, and the managers (*cadres*, including engineers) and technically trained workers, on the other. Skilled workers (*ouvriers professionnels*) made up only a minority of the workers. They normally held either a CAP (*certificat d'aptitude professionnelle*) or a BEP (*brevet d'études professionnelles*), two diplomas awarded by both state vocational schools and company training institutes. The level of knowledge taught in technology, the natural sciences and mathematics was often equal to that in West Germany and generally higher than that of comparable British training courses.[37]

What is significant for the development in France since the 1970s is the speed at which this traditional skilled workforce, its training methods and its standards of knowledge lost their importance. Unlike in Germany, the form and content of specialist vocational training courses and diplomas changed dramatically. They were now increasingly and more frequently taken at technical grammar schools (*lycées professionnels*) or at technical colleges (*instituts universitaires de technologie*) so that the younger generation of skilled industrial workers, now mostly known as operators (*opérateurs*), had little or nothing in common with the old-school *ouvriers professionnels*. In 1981, an expansion of the general school education system was advanced with the political aim of enabling 80 per cent of an age cohort to obtain the French grammar school leaving certificate, the *baccalauréat*, or *bac* for short. This caused a huge change in the profile of specialist vocational training courses (see figure 5.3).[38]

Although the French government's strategy was conceived as a long-term, systematic drive towards combating the threatening rise of youth unemployment, the opening up of the *lycées* and colleges caused a radical change in the vocational education system. The proliferation of vocational qualifications on offer in the general public education system widened the existing gap between the world of (industrial) work and the education system still further. A growing number of school leavers with the *bac* and graduates from colleges and universities were in fact qualified for future positions at the level of technicians or industrial supervisors but they were faced with labour markets where they could at best begin work as *opérateurs* or first had to gain professional experience as highly qualified temporary workers. Whereas in Germany the reform of the various training courses took place within a framework of continuity at school and at work, in France it became standard practice to break with the former training specifications.[39] Behind the category of *ouvrier professionnel* lay a radical shift in conditions of employment and the actual knowledge required to qualify for a skilled job.

This has been clearly demonstrated in the studies by Beaud, Pialoux and Hatzfeld for the automobile company Peugeot and its factory in Sochaux.[40] The vocational school belonging to the company was closed in 1970. Although its graduates had frequently worked in the factory as *ouvriers professionnels*, these old-school skilled workers became increasingly marginalized. Since the late 1980s, the company

Figure 5.3 'Everyone to leave school with the *bac*.' Front page of the newspaper *Libération* on 13 November 1985.

When the French education minister Jean-Pierre Chevènement announced in November 1985 that the number of high school graduates would be doubled by 2000, the daily *Libération* headlined with 'Tous Bacheliers', 'Everyone to leave school with the *bac*.' However, the vision of social advancement held in this promise proved to be deceptive. School leavers with the *bac* and students found it increasingly difficult to find suitable jobs. There was also a rise in the number of industrial workers who were overqualified.

had introduced technological innovations in its own production by falling back on young skilled workers who had been trained in various vocational high schools and technical colleges. Although they had a correspondingly higher level of specialist technical knowledge than their older colleagues, they were at a clear disadvantage in terms of practical work experience.

In accordance with their training profile and their self-perception, these new skilled industrial workers aspired to positions at the middle level of the job hierarchy, even if they were employed directly in production. The introduction of new technologies and production regimes at Peugeot and other French companies resulted in a generational rift between the older *ouvriers spéciaux* and *professionnels* and the younger *opérateurs*. These conflicts were particularly conspicuous where Taylorized work processes were being replaced by new forms of teamwork. Conflict also arose, however, where opportunities for in-company promotion were blocked for workers and technicians by the external recruitment of skilled workers with higher formal qualifications.[41] West German companies were naturally not free from these kinds of conflict between older and younger workers, skilled workers and technical employees, either. However, an essential difference between Germany and France was that in Germany the continuity of the training courses for skilled workers, in terms of both content and staff, permitted comparatively permeable status boundaries and facilitated integration.

Knowledge systems and new production regimes

The state education systems of Britain, France and Germany thus played an essential part in the re-evaluation of industrial skills and production knowledge on the labour market and of social status allocation that took place in the course of the third industrial revolution. Education was responsible to a considerable extent for managing the redistribution of knowledge required by technological and economic developments since 1970. Germany was the only country where the skilled occupations trained in its dual vocational education system survived the transformation of the industrial world between 1975 and 2000 surprisingly unscathed and where they still constituted an independent and widespread type of employment at the beginning of the twenty-first century. The main reasons why it was successful on the labour market were that these vocational courses and qualifications were recognized by the state, they were tied to collective wage agreements, and the skilled workers' diploma was safeguarded by the trade unions.[42] Neither the skilled workers in Britain nor the *ouvriers professionnels* in France were able to uphold their originally similarly strong position in the job arena to a comparable extent during the changes after the 1970s. The situation of the working classes and *classes populaires* in the fight for 'titles and jobs'[43] was seriously damaged by the proliferation of general diplomas in education without any specialization and by the definition of job-related skills without any legal safeguarding or wage agreements. This is one of the long-term paradoxes resulting from the liberalization of general education systems.

The effects of these training patterns can be illustrated by table 5.1, which shows the development of national vocational training systems in the period under study. In spite of all the problems of finding corresponding categories for an international comparison of diplomas specific to certain countries, these figures do reveal differences. Professional qualifications in British industry were less common overall than in France and Germany. However, the differences between the three countries are much slighter when it comes to more highly qualified scientists, engineers and technicians than they are in the much larger group of skilled workers.

Table 5.1 shows that in the middle of the transformations of the third industrial revolution, far fewer people in Britain had similar specialist knowledge (skilled worker diplomas/*Facharbeiterdiplom*) than in Germany and France. However, a direct comparison is based on the false assumption that apprenticeships in British industry are more or less equivalent to the skilled worker training in Germany and the CAP courses in France. This can only be said with a great deal of

Table 5.1 Vocational qualifications in industry and technology per hundred thousand employees in 1985

Qualifications	Britain	France	W. Germany
Doctorates	1.2	0.5	1.6
Masters and enhanced degrees	4	11	7
Bachelor degrees	25	27	34
Technicians	51	63	72
Craftspeople	62	167	197

Source: Extracted (without numbers for Japan) from Christel Lane, 'Vocational Training and New Production Concepts in Germany: Some Lessons for Britain', in *Industrial Relations Journal* 21 (1990), pp. 247–59, here p. 250.

reservation. While only a small share of the British training courses corresponded, for example, to the extent of specialized knowledge taught according to West German specifications, the British apprenticeships placed great emphasis, in some cases more emphasis, on the teaching of practical competencies and on job experience at the workplace.[44] Both the German and British models are very different from the French CAP or BEP, professional qualifications which were usually acquired away from the workplace. This meant that the share of specialized knowledge in France was similar to that in Germany or higher. In the mid-1980s, Hilary Steedman studied training standards in Britain and France in the two core industrial fields of electrics and mechanics. She concluded that the level of French training (CAP and BEP) was higher but that training in Britain (the more demanding City and Guilds Diplomas) was more practice-oriented. She came to the conclusion that because of the greater number of skilled workers and technicians trained in this way, French industry was better prepared to cope with new technologies in manufacturing and production.[45] These findings were confirmed by further comparative studies in the 1990s with regard to both France and Germany as competitors.[46]

A further aspect has to be taken into consideration when comparing these three training systems. The different qualifications were integrated into different company hierarchies. Corresponding studies from the early and mid-1970s show that under similar conditions there were many more levels of hierarchy in production in French companies. Workers had far less influence on planning and design and the gap between the individual status groups was far larger than in comparable West German companies. Where a French engineering company needed six levels of hierarchy, a West German company managed with four. French companies valued the experience of the *ouvriers professionnels* and even of the *ouvriers spéciaux* correspondingly less highly.[47] In Britain, the gap between the three status groups of engineers/managers, skilled manual workers and semi-skilled and unskilled workers was traditionally wide. Company hierarchy was therefore at the same time a hierarchy of knowledge whose order was cemented by diplomas and educational qualifications but also by different professional organizations. The French and British systems were at a considerable disadvantage when it came to dismantling hierarchies and creating flexible work processes in international competition. These national differences also affected business strategies in the face of the technological upheaval of the 1980s and 1990s.

In West German companies, personnel departments usually relied on the job profiles of their skilled workers as a basis for their strategy of exploiting surplus capacities and competencies. In-company training and further training programmes as well as opportunities to pursue further qualifications to become a technician or engineer as a 'mature student', known in Germany as the 'second educational pathway', were part of this strategy. Specialization and professionality were still the cornerstones of industrial production knowledge in West German capitalism, and the 'trade proficiency certificate' for skilled workers was no less recognized and appreciated in West German industry than an engineering diploma. Skilled workers became important targets of new management strategies aiming at increasing both productivity and quality by means of quality circles, work groups and so on. At the same time, the companies used the opportunities offered by the introduction of computer-based communication and manufacturing processes to control performance at work. The higher wage costs that resulted from the higher qualifications of their employees led to the introduction of new labour-saving machinery and corresponding gains in productivity.[48]

British industry was in rapid decline and followed the Conservative government's change of course in educational policy more or less willingly. It hoped above all that it would provide more flexibility in the deployment of labour, especially as a result of the dwindling influence of the trade unions, and so improve productivity and cost-effectiveness. Very few branches of industry continued to take advantage of the opportunities offered by the mandatory Industrial Training Boards to meet their needs for skilled labour: in 1981 only the clothing, construction, mechanical engineering and plastics industries did so.[49] By faithfully following the path defined by human capital theory, British industry exacerbated the skills deficit which they had to contend with when competing, for example, with other European producers.[50] The path towards flexible quality production was therefore steeper, and more often other forms of in-company labour organization had to be found. Companies tried to overcome the overall increase in the demand for skills by 'on-the-job training' and by sticking to the stricter and narrower division of labour inherent in Taylorist production.

This at least is the conclusion reached by a series of comparative studies carried out in the 1980s in various branches of industry by the National Institute of Economic and Social Research.[51] They found that for British vehicle component suppliers, their workforce's lack of qualifications led to an immediate competitive disadvantage since the quality, flexibility and productivity of their West German and French competitors was higher. Production workers in French and German companies were better qualified (40 per cent were skilled workers in Germany compared to 3 per cent in Britain), and they could be employed more flexibly on different machines but also to service and repair them. At the same time, they normally had more technicians and engineers with college or university qualifications at their disposal who were able to adapt their production range to the specific demands of various customers.[52]

French companies, for their part, took advantage of the surplus of career beginners with different types of higher diplomas to fill vacancies in production with these overqualified 'young workers'.[53] This often meant that there was a mismatch between the person in a job and the job itself in terms of knowledge, competencies and skills. In many industrial companies in France, a generation of disillusioned, academically overqualified first-time workers emerged who still expected in-company hierarchies to reproduce the hierarchies of qualifications from state education. The more rigid boundaries in France between technicians and skilled workers, however, made this much more difficult to achieve than, for example, in Germany.

French companies were, therefore, faced with an increasing discrepancy between academic qualifications and the ensuing job expectations of young workers and their own requirements for the competencies of their employees. They reacted with initiatives for in-service training and their own evaluation criteria for workplaces and employees so as to be less dependent on academic qualifications and the hierarchies they brought with them. Attempts to introduce new dual training pathways based on the German model were, however, largely unsuccessful because neither employers nor employees wanted to free themselves sufficiently from the gold standard of official state qualifications.[54] This meant the scope for dismantling knowledge hierarchies within companies was considerably diminished and restricted any exchange of specialist knowledge outside the employees' status groups. A successful way out was offered, as it was in Britain, by the move towards connecting knowledge systems and career options more tightly to individual companies – very much in accordance with the principles of human resource management.

French studies for the 1990s and the first decade of the new century came to very different conclusions about the qualification requirements for production workers, depending on the branch of industry. The proportion of unskilled workers decreased in those sectors where it used to be high (the textile and clothing industries, the wood and paper industry and chemistry and plastics) but it increased slightly (up to 20 per cent) in those sectors where it used to be lower (the automobile, electrical and printing industries and metalworking companies). There were two conflicting processes at work behind this: on the one hand, there was a rise in demand for professionally qualified workers who could be deployed more flexibly and, on the other hand, companies used the weak negotiating power of the unions to replace higher-qualified and better-paid jobs with new lower-level positions such as *opérateurs* and to fill them with overqualified staff. In the case of France as of Britain, by the end of the period under study, the effects of the erosion of collective bargaining standards and union negotiating power described in chapter 4 had become clearly visible.[55]

This comparison of countries shows that during the upheaval period the practically oriented transfer of up-to-date specialist knowledge proved to be a considerable advantage for realizing diverse business strategies. More flexible in-company hierarchies facilitated, for example, the reorganization of the flow of information and communication. Contemporary socio-industrial studies repeatedly show that in medium-sized as well as large companies the restructuring of production was frequently carried out in small steps, often cautiously and decidedly pragmatically. They also show that an important role in this was played both by the experience of the core workforce of skilled workers and by their willingness to cooperate.[56]

The companies that went particularly far were those that wanted to overcome the separation of planning and production in order to enhance cooperation between innovations in product development and their manufacture. This meant more attention was paid to skilled workers' knowledge of machines and their positive and negative experiences of concrete production processes. This strategy was particularly successful in the capital goods sector, especially in mechanical engineering and construction. It proved an increasingly strong competitive advantage for many companies, particularly in West Germany, to include skilled production workers in planning and to use this to improve customer service and connect it directly with product development and manufacture. This could even create jobs which disregarded the established division of labour between technicians, commercial employees, engineers and skilled workers. These jobs, however, remained the privilege of a minority of industrial workers. Nevertheless, these examples show that the scope for experimentation within companies was very wide in principle, but that it was heavily dependent on the availability of professional knowledge resources: that is, on national education and vocational training systems. In Britain certainly, and partially also in France, they set very tight limits on such new arrangements.

This verifies the theory put forward in 1988 by David Finegold and David Soskice that businesses in countries with high standards of vocational training tended towards export-oriented quality production, whereas businesses in countries whose vocational training standards tended to be lower maintained their international competitiveness primarily by cutting costs.[57]

Winners and losers

To conclude this chapter, I want to turn back to those who were directly affected by these changes: the industrial workers. What did they experience when applying old or new knowledge to production, and what strategies did they develop in the face of the growing demands on individual skills, professional competencies and technical know-how described above? My answer to these questions has seven parts.

(1) The increase in demand for technical know-how meant an increase in the importance of acquired knowledge in everyday work. This trend is illustrated for Germany by data from the Socio-Economic Panel (SOEP). The number of skilled workers employed in the job they trained for was already 63 per cent in 1985, and by 2000 it had risen by 12 per cent to 75 per cent. In addition, nine out of ten skilled workers stressed the fact that their vocational training was necessary for their current job (in 1985 it was only 65 per cent) and a clear majority stated that it was (fully or partially) true to say that they carried out their work independently. In 2000, this figure was 78.1 per cent, whereas in 1985 it had only been 69.8 per cent.[58]

(2) Further training and qualifications now became important aspects of the working lives of industrial workers. In Germany in 2000, a good 21 per cent of unskilled and semi-skilled workers, 38 per cent of skilled workers, 58 per cent of supervisors and 79 per cent of *Meister* (a special lower/middle management category) stated that during the last year they had taken part in work-relevant in-company programmes.[59] It remains unclear, however, to what extent it was company practice to include the different categories of workers systematically in this kind of further training. The data in corresponding company surveys reveal a wide spectrum of standard

practice, ranging from the complete absence of such offers and requirements to their systematic application.[60] A related study on the 1980s came to the conclusion that after ten years, approximately one-third of the industrial workers surveyed in companies in 1981 had moved to positions requiring further professional qualifications (technicians via technical schools and engineers via technical colleges or universities).[61] Many of these skilled workers used the opportunities for further qualification offered internally and moved up to a higher position within their own company, for example by taking a course to qualify as a *Meister*. The much-vaunted dynamics of the knowledge society are shown here to be fairly traditional, in the form of in-company further training or a 'second educational pathway'.

(3)Taking a historical angle on concrete work processes shows that in the 1970s the constant repetition of the same hand or body movement or of technical routines was still the main characteristic of industrial work for semi-skilled and unskilled workers but also for many skilled workers. Specialists in 'work studies' and 'time studies', experts from the REFA[62] and McKinsey and the masters of the Bedaux system had had a profound effect, at least in Germany and France. But after the boom, very few companies found their way out of the crisis by tightening the division of labour in order to make their workforce produce more in a shorter time with new or even old machines. On the contrary, most companies focussed on making work processes which had been intensified by means of technical improvements more flexible by expecting or even 'trusting' their production workers to work at various workstations on various processes and on various tasks. The question of skills resurfaced and this time the response was different. More and more work processes were organized so that semi-skilled and unskilled production workers could carry out more than one limited task and also take on more demanding tasks such as minor repairs and maintenance work. At the same time, skilled workers who had previously only been involved in provisioning and maintenance work were now more closely involved in product and production planning and distribution and customer service. Hermann Kotthoff and Josef Reindl observed an extreme case in a vehicle component factory in the German Saarland region in the mid-1990s. Here the production workers were 'on the move': that is, they had no permanent workstation but were deployed flexibly at various machines in the company so as to satisfy the demands of just-in-time production.[63] The authors report, however, that the flexibilization of the workforce was far less dramatic in most other companies in this sector. Frequently, three to five stages or tasks were

187

mentioned, which were carried out by the production workers either in regular rotation or according to demand. In many cases, these multi-tasking machine operators and assembly-line workers were part of the company's permanent workforce. Around them would be part-time workers and agency workers as well as those who were only temporarily employed at their respective individual workstations. Practical reports show that 'multi-skilling', one of the new buzzwords in the management literature, depended on the seniority and professional qualifications of the workers.[64] The British manager of a Hitachi plant in Wales highlighted the difference between vision and reality: 'Ideally, we like each operator to be able to do five jobs, but this is difficult to achieve because of labour turnover and in periods of production pressure. [But] 30 percent of operators have been with us five years plus, and these are very flexible people.'[65] Thus, under cover of the new terms 'multi-skilling' and 'job rotation' it was evidently also possible for workers to quietly return to their routine jobs when circumstances and supervisors permitted.[66] The tension between the new norms and the old practices demonstrates once again the significance attached to the workforce's level of qualification in these times of change.

(4) This kind of restructuring of the allocation of tasks signified a break with past routines, and it was by no means the case that all production workers accepted the challenge of working swiftly and confidently at several different tasks gladly or voluntarily. Here again, the devil lay in the detail: what incentives went with the new job profiles; were there wage increases or ergonomic improvements; was there a reduction in the workload?

(5) Saying 'farewell to the industrial labourer' also meant saying farewell to established knowledge and experience, since during the crisis-driven transformation in the 1970s, and especially the early 1980s, it was older and unskilled workers in particular who were made redundant or stopped working. This meant in essence that most of their practical knowledge was lost. Companies were happy to use the excuse of new production processes and the restructuring of the workplace to build up a younger workforce and to raise the technical knowledge level in the company. Whether this happened gradually or with generational breaks also depended, as we have seen, on education and training systems. We have also seen that there were clear differences here between the three countries. In general, however, the perception of the new workloads varied greatly according to the age and expectations of the workers. Younger workers at the Peugeot plant in Sochaux, for example, assessed the

reorganization of production there quite differently from their older colleagues. Whereas the younger workers saw the intensified routine in the new production hall more as a sporting challenge, the older workers, in spite of some lowering of physical demands, focussed more on the higher level of stress caused by the scrapping of breaks and individual space.[67]

(6) Knowledge redistribution brought with it new demands on concentration and discipline. 'Zero-defect manufacturing' – an uninterrupted production process with no downtimes or technical breakdowns – and the permanent improvement of production processes were propagated as realistic aims according to the Japanese model. The implementation of these 'lean production' programmes had a massive effect on workplace design. The opportunities offered by electronic data storage increased the level of control overall and meant that even those workers who did not necessarily have the quality of their products at heart felt compelled to comply with high standards. The number of unskilled and semi-skilled workers who complained about too much control and supervision and too little power and room for decision-making was correspondingly high. Skilled workers saw the relation between autonomy and control differently. For them, taking on more responsibility was to a certain extent part of their professional self-image. Participants in the SOEP were regularly asked about their experience at work. The answers presented in tables 5.2 and 5.3 highlight two aspects which together may be a key to a better understanding of the changes in the workplace for skilled workers. On the one hand, it becomes clear that working independently became part of their everyday work. On the other hand, it becomes equally clear that only a third of the skilled workers questioned were not tightly controlled. Stricter computer-based controls and greater creative freedom are two sides of the same coin, namely greater personal responsibility for the product and performance. Sociologists Wilfried Glißmann and Klaus Peters have aptly called this 'more pressure through more freedom'.[68]

(7) In the course of the deindustrialization process, the traditional gendered division of knowledge was endorsed. Neither the increase of school-based knowledge nor the increased significance of social and communicative competencies led to an increase in the proportion of women who were skilled workers, technicians, *Meister* or engineers. It could even be said that the introduction of computer-based machinery further cemented the marginal position of women in skilled industrial occupations. A study on the effects of new technologies in the food industry in Austria, Germany and Britain in

Table 5.2   Independent work design for skilled West German workers

Skilled workers in West Germany: answers concerning 'autonomous work' (in per cent)

	1985	2000
Agree	27.9	26.6
Partially agree	39.9	51.5
Disagree	32.3	21.9
Total	1,026	1,027
No answer	15.4	21.2

Source: These figures are from my database *Arbeiterhaushalte in Westdeutschland 1984–2001* based on the SOEP

Table 5.3   Performance control for skilled West German workers

Skilled workers in West Germany: answers concerning 'strictly controlled work' (in per cent)

	1985	2000
Agree	20.0	19.3
Partially agree	40.5	47.7
Disagree	39.5	33.0
Total	1,023	1,025
No answer	15.6	21.4

Source: As table 5.2.

the mid-1990s came to the conclusion that after the restructuring of production and a massive reduction of staff, female workers continued to be employed as unskilled workers. No higher knowledge skills were required of them and the opportunities for further in-company training were correspondingly scarce.[69] A critical factor in this was undoubtedly the school system, which directed boys and girls early on towards different areas of work and so predetermined the further steps in their careers (apprenticeships, factory employment). The continuation of this gender-specific dividing line is further emphasized by the unbroken dominance of male graduates in industrial training courses as well as in engineering degree courses and technical training courses. In all three countries, this is quite simply a fact, but with typical individual exceptions and sector-specific enclaves. This led in turn to far-reaching effects on the erosion of work-related social citizenship since the new and poorly paid part-time jobs which appeared in this phase of change, particularly in the private service sector, went mainly to women.

Last but not least, and in conclusion, we should recall an issue already discussed several times, namely the subjectivization of the evaluation of competencies and performance at work. Production workers were given more responsibility for production processes and product quality, and management felt bound to ensure their commitment and sense of responsibility not only with monetary incentives but also by means of consultation and inclusion. The trend away from atomizing work processes towards assigning individual workers more and different tasks points in a similar direction. The number of jobs that consisted in no more than the repetition of a precise hand movement and whose actors were mere cogs in the wheel of a Taylorist production process decreased during the period under study. At the beginning of the twenty-first-century, experts in labour studies and industrial sociologists all agreed that the application and evaluation of every single worker's individual knowledge had gained in significance. This meant that, whether they liked it or not, industrial workers had entered the world of human capital, but that in these three countries, as I have attempted to show in this chapter, they tended to have very different chances of transforming their concrete knowledge and skills into (relatively) secure positions at the workplace or on the labour market. As a result, the development of career paths, promotion prospects and income opportunities varied hugely according to age, gender and qualifications, but also depended on local circumstances such as the company, sector or region. More detailed information on this can only be obtained by leaving the macro level and examining work biographies in more detail and comparing them with each other. This is precisely what I will do in the next chapter, which opens the second part of this book.

— PART II —

CLOSE-UPS

Fields of experience and horizons of
expectation in times of upheaval

— Chapter 6 —

LIFE COURSES, WORK
AND UNEMPLOYMENT IN
TIMES OF UPHEAVAL

Biography may have long been re-established as a valuable genre in historiography, but it plays a very minor role in socio-historical studies in Germany.[1] The lives of 'ordinary people' rarely attract the attention of contemporary historians. Even the emergence of oral history has not changed much in this respect.[2] In this book, I have deliberately adopted a biographical perspective to gain insights into the social dynamics related to the structural fractures after the boom in Western Europe. Studying working lives and careers seems to be an ideal tool for looking beyond the momentary snapshots of social statisticians and the descriptions of wider trends for the decades between 1970 and 2000. Such studies also help us to discover continuities and fractures in the social situation of those people who were particularly strongly affected by the transformation caused by deindustrialization in Western European societies. Looking at employment histories and working careers of the working classes, *Arbeiterklasse* and *classes populaires*, promises to provide substantial evidence of relevant changes in the social spaces of Britain, France and Germany.

Working-life stories and life-course research

General interest in individual life stories has grown to the same extent as has 'subjectification' as the increasingly prevalent standard framework for describing oneself or others in Western European societies.[3] In the decades after 1970, growing social inequality came to be regarded as a legitimate consequence of the equality of opportunity inherent in a meritocracy and had an increasing effect

195

on society. It inspired many different forms of (self-)examination and (self-)evaluation by and of individuals which adopted a performance-oriented standpoint or a moral-political or moral-therapeutic perspective. This meant that for many people the 'biographical illusion' took on a greater significance.[4] The 'biographical illusion' is understood here as the need for individuals to construct a coherent narrative of themselves and their place in society. We have already examined this development in the context of the history of ideas in chapter 2.

During the decades of upheaval, contemporary social surveys were already carefully recording the many indications of the disintegration of close social environments and the end of traditional job profiles and working careers. They provide an insight into generational conflicts and emphasize the allegedly growing significance of ethnic differences within the industrial workforce.[5] Methods in the social sciences moved from describing and observing supposedly predetermined group contexts towards more individualized life situations. Social historians are well advised to engage with these changes. Before making any claims about whether the working-life courses of individuals and their social position necessarily translate into 'class positions' determining their lives, we need to search for underlying patterns in individual life courses: that is, for similarities and differences that allow the identification of types. In particular, we need to explore certain situational and structural risks, such as those arising from the transition from education into work and from work into retirement and those within specific labour markets.

In this chapter, I follow the principles of life-history and life-course research in the social sciences, whose approaches and empirical findings provide valuable stimulus for social historians.[6] Unfortunately, at least in (West) Germany, scholars have shown little interest in investigating class, or specific work contexts,[7] preferring to focus instead on the more obvious and traceable differences arising from age, education, gender and ethnicity. The orthodox comparative-quantitative approach of this line of research assumed that the development of 'modern industrial societies' with their institutional frameworks, from state schools to state-financed pensions, led to workers' lives becoming more standardized and thus more predictable. However, the radical changes that occurred during the period analysed here – that is, between 1970 and 2000 – give good cause to suggest that in addition to this view, which is based on the theory of modernization, there is room for other interpretations, such as those of contemporary sociologists, which place more focus on a shift towards the de-institutionalization, pluralization and individualization of life courses. While their interpretations were particularly fashionable in the 1980s and 1990s, their empirical findings are anything but definitive. This chapter can, therefore, also be read as a contribution to this debate from the perspective of a history of society.

It concentrates on four specific episodes or events in the lives of industrial workers: first, the transition from school or vocational training to working life; second, the point at which workers chose a partner and started a family; third, a change of job and/or type of work; and, fourth, the end of active working life and the beginning of retirement.

By tracing these four events, it is possible to analyse and compare the social logic of individual life courses, the emergence of specific clusters of life courses, and how they are linked to the career paths of industrial workers in the three countries concerned. To do this, historians can select from a range of different methods available. One is quantitative social surveys, which provide a range of statistical data that at each point of capture can be interpreted as 'objective opportunities'[8] within individual life courses. The collection of panel data is another method that can provide information about actual career paths and life courses. This method makes it possible to trace life-course patterns more precisely, which can then be used as a basis for establishing different life-course types. A third method is to reconstruct in detail individual life stories based on various types of ego-documents. From these, the different backgrounds, patterns of behaviour and logic of decision-making which contributed to the formation of these specific types of life courses can be more accurately reconstructed. A conscious effort is therefore made here to combine different methods and approaches for the purpose of socio-historical analysis. As a strategy, it seems all the more advisable since the data available for the three countries investigated here differ widely, at least for the period in question. There is, therefore, no single ideal method that could be applied to this kind of comparative study.[9]

Paths into industrial employment in the 1950s and 1960s

It is difficult to establish a clear-cut boundary between the period from 1948 to 1973, when economies were booming, and the years that followed. The postwar boom years appear at first glance to contrast with the later period as a time when life courses, social positions and group structures were decidedly more straightforward, more homogeneous and more standardized. We saw in chapter 4 that the development of labour and employment laws helped to establish minimum standards which in their turn enabled living circumstances and levels of income to realign at a much higher level than, for example, in 1945. However, it was the growth rates experienced in most branches of industry in these decades that generated an increase in mobility and also produced labour markets that offered opportunities for a great variety of life courses and career paths. This meant that in spite of social standardization by law, there were vast differences within the industrial labour force.[10]

So, for example, in all three countries, employment as unskilled, semi-skilled or even skilled workers in industry was a temporary episode for a good share of the workforce. Many were able to continue their careers in better-paid or higher-status jobs as clerical or administrative workers, state employees or managers. Given the constantly growing number of jobs in industry, services and administration, industrial work increasingly intersected with a variety of different career pathways. People who had fled from former East Germany, German people displaced after World War II and 'guest workers' from Mediterranean countries and the British Commonwealth frequently found work in industry as it expanded and flourished, whether as an initial option for want of alternatives or as permanent employment. Especially in the 1960s, many new labour migrants came to Western Europe within a relatively short period. They found jobs in industry and construction, often with fixed-term contracts and precarious living conditions. In France and West Germany, with the demise of traditional peasant agriculture, they were joined by the many sons of farmers who were forced to look for ways to earn their living in industry and the public sector. In 1970, approximately 25 per cent of the fathers of the male industrial workers of the cohort aged between 25 and 34 in France were farmers; for Germany, the figure was around 15 per cent.[11] This is in marked contrast to the situation in Britain, where the figures for workers with a migration or agricultural background are of little significance.[12]

World War II and its direct consequences, such as flight, expulsion and imprisonment, led to major changes for the age groups affected. For this reason, it seemed a good idea by way of simplification to examine the first postwar cohorts of industrial workers to discover if patterns could be found in their working careers and life courses. These are the people who were born in the second half of the 1930s and in the 1940s and so started their working lives in the first postwar decade. These age cohorts constitute the majority of industrial workers in the 1960s. This is already an indication that the industrial workforce in the boom period in all three countries was a relatively young section of the population. This stems not least from the fact that in all three countries the majority of young people left school at 14 or 15 and many of them immediately got an apprenticeship or a job in industry or a traditional trade. Since the general situation on the labour market was favourable for industrial workers in all three countries, an early phase of employment with frequent changes of jobs was the classic profile of many young workers who had completed vocational training. This was followed by a second phase of their working career, typically between the ages of 25 and 30, connected with marriage and starting a family. In this phase, a large proportion of skilled workers took on a longer-term commitment to a particular company and made use of its opportunities for in-company promotion and wage increases. This biographical pattern can be seen in the fast-growing large companies as well as in the numerous small and medium-sized factories which were expanding their workforce during these decades of continuous growth.[13]

These boom decades were golden years for skilled workers, *Facharbeiter* and *ouvriers professionnels*.[14] The opportunities for promotion or a change of job within a company or a branch of industry meant that this cohort of skilled workers experienced something close to a stable, preordained career path. The risks traditionally faced by industrial workers, such as declining (piece) wages due to their diminishing performance after years of work, receded into the background. The opportunity to move up in the internal hierarchy to become a supervisor, to take on jobs which were not on the production line, such as in maintenance and repairs, and to gain further qualifications and become a master technician (*Meister*) – all these options opened up new horizons for career paths and provided scope for individual ambitions. At the same time, openings for careers in the trade unions were available to those who were critical of the offers made by employers and were able to realize their own professional ideals and hopes of promotion at the same time as representing workers' interests.[15]

In the three countries analysed here, this group of skilled industrial workers amounted to between 30 and 40 per cent of the total industrial labour force. In France and Germany in particular, a smaller group of skilled workers among them had been trained as apprentices in a traditional trade outside industry, where they often spent their first working years. Their paths into the new world of industrial work were frequently less straightforward and more conflict-ridden than those of skilled workers trained in industry. Some of them moved into industry because of the significantly better pay and company social benefits, but began their industrial careers as semi-skilled production workers. Together with their unskilled colleagues who went straight into production work, for example from farming or from school, they make up a second group to which an occupational biographical pattern can be assigned.

The number of unskilled and semi-skilled workers rose significantly during these boom years of 1948 to 1973. In all three countries, they comprised the majority of the workers in large mass-producing companies. In reality, however, the career options open to them varied greatly depending on the branch of industry, the size of the company and its location. In this world of production, the steel and mining industries belonged to discrete areas with their own occupational patterns and career stages. They provided internal promotion paths for semi-skilled production workers, with specific career stages that not only accounted for the level of high physical strain but also generated a kind of structured career path within the company or sector.[16]

A different pattern was to be found in the consumer goods industry. Here, 30 to 40 per cent of unskilled workers, including a very large number of women and labour migrants, worked on the production lines and at Taylorist workplaces only temporarily. These jobs were particularly attractive for those younger men and women who had no vocational qualifications and started their working lives with only basic or low-status school leaving qualifications. The main attraction of these jobs was their high wages and the opportunity to earn more by doing shift work and overtime. Very often, the years spent working on the production lines of VW, Renault, British Leyland and Vauxhall or in the textile factories in all three countries were only a brief episode in these young people's working lives. They either progressed to a phase of domestic work, as was the case for many women after marrying and having their first child, or moved into a completely different sector and type of job. Especially in the swiftly expanding large companies, in the 1960s and 1970s these branches of industry also offered many semi-skilled workers opportunities for internal promotion. This meant that in a similar way to the steel and mining industries, a growing number of men, more rarely women, followed careers within a branch of industry that promised them a high level of pay, job security and promotion prospects. For a portion of labour migrants in West Germany and France in particular, this option developed into a biographical pattern which became more attractive, especially after their families were able to join them at the end of the 1970s, and at the latest after the recruitment of migrant workers was halted in 1973–4.

It is also important to remember the women who were employed more or less permanently as unskilled or semi-skilled industrial workers. They were particularly numerous in the textile and clothing industries and in the food industry, but in practice only very few of them had the option of following an actual career path. Since the qualified jobs were generally taken by men, women were left with very little chance of internal promotion. It was precisely during the years of plenty in the boom period that this pattern of industrial jobs without career paths or chances of promotion established itself, typically in small towns and rural areas, and hand in hand with the restructuring of rural agrarian societies. Women who had previously been helping the family became industrial workers, but the option of returning to the household or family business remained open to them.

All these career options depended on improved conditions for industrial wage labour which paved the way for the social citizenship described in chapter 4.[17] In all three countries, for unskilled workers in smaller and medium-sized companies especially, the chances of these promises of status actually being fulfilled were still tied to favourable conditions on the labour market and the strength and influence of the trade unions representing their interests. The following may serve as an illustration: in 1967, 540,000 labour migrants in Germany – that is, more than 50 per cent of their total – were in possession of 'work permits' that were tied to their jobs and had to be applied for again if they became unemployed.[18] Unskilled and semi-skilled migrant workers and female labourers did not enjoy improved rights until the waves of protests and strikes from 1968 to 1979 ensured the introduction of far-reaching labour and socio-political reforms (see chapter 4).

It can be claimed for Germany, and to a slightly lesser extent for Britain and France, that at the beginning of the 1970s, career prospects and life courses for skilled workers and some semi-skilled workers had moved into line with those for low- and mid-level administrative and clerical workers. At the same time, in all three countries, the persistence of traditional gender role models in the division of labour meant that as a result of marriage or civil partnerships the career prospects for (male) industrial workers and (female) administrative and clerical workers in working households began to converge. A further factor that is not insignificant in a dynamic study of career paths is that the relative rise in income for industrial workers led to the model of the sole male breadwinner becoming established in working families, in the same way as it had been before in the middle classes and bourgeoisie. The result was that among women born between 1935 and 1950 who had no further education, the number whose careers were interrupted by marriage and child-rearing and who then re-entered working life rose significantly. When they then re-entered working life, it was frequently in new administrative jobs or in part-time jobs.[19]

These trends galvanized social researchers during our period of study. They claimed that increasing job security, the spread of specific work careers and the rising proportion of skilled workers indicated the end of proletarianism. What was probably the most successful and influential British sociological study of the 1960s advanced the popular idea of the 'affluent worker'. In describing the new consumer needs and the growing individualism of car workers, John H. Goldthorpe and his colleagues thought they could discern a growing instrumentalist attitude to work and a trend towards the disintegration of traditional proletarian social milieus.[20]

In the cold light of day, it can be seen that in fact the incomes and consumer practices of all industrial workers remained quite modest in comparison to the rest of society, but they did increase steadily and were in sharp contrast to the scarcity and insecurity experienced in the first half of the century. The kind of poverty that had characterized proletarian existence since the beginning of industrialization was also declining for unskilled and semi-skilled workers. The division between the upper and lower working-class income groups, in terms of poverty and respectability, was certainly no longer as clear in 1970 as it had been thirty years before. However, at the lower end of the workforce in all three countries there was still a minority of workers whose life courses did not lead them out of relative poverty and whose lives were marked by poor living conditions, precarious employment and a lack of any financial reserves. It is true that female industrial workers in rural areas and all workers in the low-wage sectors, such as in the textile and food industries, enjoyed much greater job security in the 1960s and early 1970s than in the interwar period. But their household incomes were still modest and they lived on the brink of poverty unless their spouses and older children were also earning and could fill existing gaps in the family budget. In all three countries, labour migrants often began their working careers unmarried and in relative poverty. One of the reasons they accepted this was the comparison to the much more severe poverty in their home countries. This double standard has to be taken into account if the relentless persistence of poverty in Western European societies of this period is to be understood.

To conclude this necessarily simplified sketch of the situation at the beginning of the period under study, it is important to emphasize the disparities that had evolved by the beginning of the 1970s between Britain, on the one hand, and France and Germany, on the other. Owing to a much slower rate of industrial growth and a lower influx of migrant and agricultural workers into industry, the range of career paths for British workers was more homogeneous than in France and Germany. The differences that did exist stemmed from discrepancies between the various branches of industry and the regions (Scotland, Northern England and Wales, on the one hand, and the South-East, on the other).[21] Second, it was not unusual at that time for unskilled and semi-skilled workers in Britain, particularly in the traditional industrial regions of the North, to experience unemployment, whereas there was practically no unemployment on the other side of the Channel.[22]

As described above, the first serious economic crisis of 1973–4 marked the beginning of a longer period of slower economic growth and accelerating structural change in industrial production. This altered the situation in all three countries. In the next sections, I will examine the extent to which unemployment, crises in certain industrial sectors and new technologies affected the working lives and prospects of men and women working in industry. The lack of similarity between the data and sources available in each of the three countries makes it expedient to first present the results for each country individually.

Continuity and change: career paths and working lives in France after the boom

First, a brief summary of what we have learnt from the previous chapters about conditions for workers' career paths in France. Well over 1.5 million industrial sector jobs were lost between 1972 and 2002. Between 1975 and 1985, the annual rise in real wages for workers fell to around 1 per cent, dropping to more or less zero by 2005.[23] The relation of skilled workers (*ouvriers professionnels*) to unskilled or semi-skilled workers (*ouvriers spéciaux*) shifted in favour of skilled workers between 1975 and 1995, but more and more unskilled industrial jobs became available in the second half of the 1990s, so that by 1999 the proportion of skilled workers stood at 42 per cent of all workers, practically the same as in 1975.[24]

A further interesting statistic is the number of migrants in the French industrial workforce. The figure remained relatively stable, only shrinking marginally from 13 per cent in 1968 to 11 per cent in 1995, although in the subgroup of unskilled and semi-skilled workers it was slightly higher at 17 per cent.[25] What is striking, however, is a further shift in the gender hierarchy of industrial labour. The proportion of skilled women workers, which was already low before the crisis, sank further, from 17 per cent to 12 per cent between 1962 and 1995, while the proportion of unskilled women workers rose still further, from 26 per cent to 30 per cent. This shows that in times of mass unemployment and mass redundancies, the traditional gender hierarchy in the world of industrial labour intensified. A last point is that in France high youth unemployment was a constant accompaniment to deindustrialization. The rate of 15- to 24-year-olds who were registered unemployed rose continuously from around 5 per cent in the early 1970s until it reached a peak of 25 per cent in 1984, stabilizing at around 20 per cent in 1990.[26]

After the French *baccalauréat* was extended to become the standard secondary school leaving qualification in the 1980s, as described in chapter 5, the proportion of those who had a vocational qualification or the *baccalauréat* or even higher qualifications but were working in unskilled jobs rose to 44 per cent.[27] This meant that at the end of the period of this study nearly half of all those working in unskilled jobs had the kind of qualification which thirty years earlier would have enabled them to begin a career at the least as a skilled worker if not as a technician.

Lastly, long-term industrial decline reduced the chances of upward social mobility for every age group. Whereas approximately 30 per cent of industrial workers moved up into another professional group during the boom years, objectively speaking the chances of moving up into a higher-status group (skilled worker, supervisor, technician) stood at 5.4 per cent in the crisis year 1982 and at 7.7 per cent in 1998 (in a period of growth). That meant that only one out of twelve workers moved up into the group of mid-level employees; one in twenty became self-employed.[28]

What significance do these shifts in the socio-economic framework have for workers' career paths? One initial finding concerns age. Deindustrialization in France meant most notably that the age structure of the industrial workforce underwent a massive change. Factory work began much later in life and ended earlier. Consequently, the average length of working life for all those born after 1925 gradually decreased. During the 1980s and 1990s, the last of the industrial workers who had been 'labouring' for more than forty years, typically from the age of 15 to 60, retired from working life completely. After the mid-1980s, the new typical age for working life to begin was 20 or 25 and 50 or 55 to finish. When the statutory retirement age was lowered to 60 at the beginning of the 1980s, the 'third age' (*troisième âge*) soon became popular and, as with the period of youth, became an integral part of workers' lives. This was undoubtedly the greatest and – especially in connection with increasing life expectancy – most lasting change in the lives of French workers.

This was also true for workers in Germany and, to a lesser extent, in Britain. The transformation took place relatively quickly, the main phase occurring in the 1980s. Many companies solved the problem of reducing staff by offering early retirement and social plans that were financially supported by the state and social security systems. As a result, the age structure of the workforce shifted further in favour of the 30- to 50-year-olds. This can be illustrated by a few examples. In the car industry in 1975, 40 per cent of workers were still under 30 years old but by 1990 this figure was only 24 per cent. There were similar developments in the textile and clothing industries and in the electronics industry. The iron and steel industry made half of its workers 'redundant' between 1975 and 1982 and another 70 per cent between 1982 and 1990, with 40 per cent of those who left taking early retirement. It was only in those branches where there was no or hardly any reduction in jobs (the food industry, the plastics processing industry, printing and publishing) that younger people were more or less continuously joining the workforce and the proportion of young workers remained constant.[29]

At the same time, drastic reductions in the workforce of most French industries forced younger workers to change to a different career or a different branch of industry. From 1975 to 1990, between five and seven out of ten workers in any one branch of industry moved to a different sector, became unemployed or retired, often prematurely.[30] The risk of unemployment varied considerably, depending on age, qualifications and industrial sector. In the same period, for example, between 55 per cent and 59 per cent of women textile workers in France lost their jobs. Only 6 per cent found a new job in the textile industry, while about 30 per cent of them moved to a different branch of industry and 20 per cent were unemployed or withdrew from the world of gainful employment. It was clearly women's employment careers that suffered most from the decline of the textile and clothing industries – a frequently recurring pattern.

The move away from industry to another economic sector was sometimes accompanied by a change of legal status to become *employés*, or less often *techniciens*, but more frequently all that this move meant was that the person was now employed as an *ouvrier* in public administration or the health and transport sectors. The number of those employed as unskilled workers in France rose correspondingly after the mid-1990s, an increase that took place mainly in the service sector. In 1990, 37 per cent of the total category of 'workers' were already employed outside the industrial sector, and between 1982 and 2001 1.27 million new jobs were created for unskilled workers in the areas of health, social services, schools, trade, transport, logistics and security.

This trend towards enforced career mobility was at odds with the patterns of stable, uninterrupted career paths within a factory or company, which became particularly common amongst skilled workers. In 1995, more than 56 per cent of skilled workers had been working in the same company for more than ten years. However, persistently high unemployment and the fact that the economic situation in whole branches of industry was often precarious led to a change in the motives behind this strategy of continuity. Since opportunities for wage increases and promotion within the company were often disappearing, the main motivation for company loyalty now was that it would provide protection from the risk of unemployment. Company loyalty and professional routine had become the safest strategy, particularly for older skilled workers. The social logic of holding on to a job, even at the cost of poorer chances of promotion and lower wages, resulting, for example, from a lack of bonus payments or extra shifts, also applied to semi-skilled workers in large companies. The particular reason for this was that the chance of their being employed outside their own company sank dramatically after 1975, since the specific competencies they had acquired there, whether as production line workers or highly specialized steelworkers, were no longer in demand.

The consequences of this strategy of 'sitting tight' have been studied for the French automobile industry. Results show that older workers no longer had access to internal promotion and that, in contrast to the situation in the growth period, it was increasingly the older rather than the younger workers who were expected to carry out demanding work on the production line.[31] The price or the prize for their loyalty in these cases was early retirement. It should also be

206

noted that a certain proportion of labour migrants returned to their home countries and tried to continue their careers there.[32]

In addition to mobility and continuity, a third pattern developed, in which, again as a result of greater access to general education, younger workers entered working life by a much less clear-cut and direct route. An increasing number of young men in particular completed vocational training or further education courses, then spent time waiting for work while enrolled in job creation schemes or retraining courses for the young unemployed, until they finally started their careers as unqualified industrial workers on fixed-term contracts. Depending on the economic situation, this could develop into longer phases of temporary work interspersed with periods of unemployment. It is typical for France that in this group there was a relatively high proportion of contract workers (*intérimaires*). By 2001, the end of the period covered by this study, they comprised up to 10 per cent of unskilled French industrial workers, male and female.[33]

The behaviour of the older workers who clung to their jobs in a company, however low in status, contrasted therefore with the mobility and flexibility enforced on younger workers. This has been described and analysed for the French automobile industry in a powerful study of the Peugeot plant in Sochaux by Nicolas Hatzfeld, Stéphane Beaud and Michel Pialoux, which I have already mentioned.[34] They show that after the end of the 1980s, for the first time in a long time, younger workers started joining the company, initially by means of fixed-term contracts and employment agencies. They had vocational or other general qualifications and were counting on the organizational and technological restructuring of the companies to fulfil their ambitions, hoping for swift internal promotion. The majority of older production workers, on the other hand, who had started work with few or no qualifications and had 'sat out' the cuts in the workforce for several decades, were simply waiting for early retirement. As a result, they greeted any technical or organizational innovations in the company with scepticism and fiercely defended its established production system. As the sociologists' interviews show, the attitude of these two generations of workers towards each other was reserved, estranged, sometimes even hostile and mutually contemptuous.[35]

As an illustration of the situation of industrial workers in France during this period of transformation, two working-life stories are described here in more detail. The first is based on an individual personal account while the second has been reconstructed from a sociological interview.

Abdallah Jelidi, who worked in a Renault automobile plant from 1975 to 1991, published his autobiography in 2015.[36] In it, he describes the various phases of working life which were typical for many migrant workers who came to France during the years of the economic boom from the Maghreb states: Morocco, Algeria and Tunisia. Jelidi was the son of a day labourer from Gabès in Tunisia. In 1973 or 1974 (his narrative is unclear about this) at the age of 20, he arrived in Belfort in eastern France following a recruitment campaign by French companies. His working life began in the Peugeot automobile factory as an unskilled industrial worker in the aluminium smelter. This was both a dangerous and physically demanding job, but thanks to his sister and brother-in-law, who were already living in Paris, he was able to quit and find work as a temporary contract worker, first filling down sleeping bags in a textile factory and then on the major construction site of the Centre Pompidou. Next he became a contract worker in the Renault factory in Billancourt, where he finally found permanent employment. Before the factory was closed and he was made redundant in 1991, Jelidi was employed in the smelter again at first, but then after an industrial accident he spent twelve years as a semi-skilled worker fitting rear mirrors in the upholstery workshop. As both a representative of a trade union (the CGT) and an immigrant (*immigré*), he was unable to find a better job in another department. However, despite being an active trade union member, he still identified wholly with the world of Renault, with its reasonably priced, spacious company housing and other social benefits. In 1991, at the age of 38 and married since he was 24, Jelidi found himself unemployed for the first time in his life. A retraining programme allowed him quickly to find the job he was still doing when he wrote his autobiography in 2015, namely as a truck driver delivering goods from his company to supermarkets in and around Paris at night. Jelidi's full account of his working life shows clearly how limited the opportunities for promotion and professional advancement were for unskilled and semi-skilled migrants. It also shows how, in typical precarious transition phases, a good portion of luck was required to gain or regain stable employment. The price Jelidi had to pay for the loss of his job as an industrial worker was high: for the last twenty years of his working life, he worked nightshifts.[37]

An insight into the situation of the younger generation of workers is provided by an interview carried out by the research group 'Emploi salarié et conditions de vie'.[38] Monsieur G. was a skilled worker born in 1962 and married with two children.

He worked in the *département* of Vienne in the Ranger furniture factory as a computer programmer for the new computer-operated production machines, which at the time of the interview had been recently purchased by the company. He was a trained milling machine and lathe operator and had originally been employed in the metal industry near Clermont-Ferrand but used the opportunity of further vocational training to become a qualified programmer. In the new company, the management was happy to take advantage of his skills whenever they were needed to cope with shortages or crises. However, in the last ten years, the company had shed nearly 1,000 jobs and, even after having been taken over by a financial group, was still suffering a serious crisis. For Monsieur G. and his fellow employees (with an average age of 49), a future within the company was far from secure. He saw no chance of advancement as a skilled worker, and in the interview he bemoaned the fact that after its sale the number of managerial jobs in the company had risen from two to fifteen. It was the lack of trust and the inadequate financial reward for job skills and expertise that caused him bitter resentment as an (over)qualified skilled worker. However, his anger was directed not only at the authoritarian incompetence of the management, but also at the studied indifference of his mostly older colleagues, who fatalistically acquiesced in the demise of the company, hoping to escape into early retirement. This and other contemporary interviews clearly demonstrate the problems and risks that younger skilled workers had to face during their working lives. Studies by Serge Paugam and others show that in many companies, especially small and medium-sized ones, there was a growing disparity between individual career aspirations and companies' survival strategies.[39]

These developments in France can be summarized in a few points. First, mass unemployment cast a shadow over the career paths of workers of all ages. Typical evidence for the effects of this threat can be found in life stories of industrial workers describing a lack of job security, long waiting periods and circuitous paths into their careers for young first-time workers and the incorporation of periods of unemployment in workers' careers. Second, a pattern of early retirement soon became established as a response to high youth unemployment and mass redundancies, resulting in many industrial workers, both male and female, retiring before their sixtieth birthday. Third, as the industrial workforce overall grew older and the labour market more volatile, one widespread strategy that developed in the hope of securing a livelihood was to remain in service with a single company over many years or to demonstrate calculated loyalty to that company. Fourth, the discrepancy between qualifications gained and jobs on offer, especially for those born after 1965, widened and with it the gap between the expectations and the reality of career paths.

Britain: working lives between catastrophe and radical change

One of the most salient factors in the case of Britain is that in the three decades between 1970 and 2000 industry there lost even more jobs and even greater market shares than its French and West German competitors. Specifically, 2.3 million jobs were shed between 1972 and 1992, amounting to one in four jobs in the construction, mining and manufacturing industries. Another 544,000 jobs were lost between 1992 and 2002, representing a reduction of 13 per cent compared to the already dramatically low level of 1992.[40] The risk of losing your job as an industrial worker in Britain was nearly twice as high as it was in France and West Germany. In the 1980s, mass unemployment spread throughout many industrial regions in Britain. British workers, male and female, found themselves confronted with radical changes that were as unexpected as they were long-lasting, and whose immediate consequences were experienced by some of them in the shape of a fall in income, job loss and unemployment. As a result of the huge regional differences in wages and income, national averages in Britain are not very helpful. Depending on the method of calculation, the gross hourly wage paid to British industrial workers between 1972 and 1992 can be said to have stagnated in real terms or to have risen annually by a moderate 1.3 per cent.[41] But the era of increasing prosperity was clearly over for British industrial workers too, and in most cases they were simply concerned to try to maintain the status quo.

The standard reaction to this, as can be seen from these workers' lives, was reorientation. Many industrial workers moved across into the gradually expanding service industries. In Britain, it was again young people at the beginning of their careers and from working-class households who suffered initially from the fact that so many jobs in industry were cut and rarely replaced. The rate of youth unemployment was correspondingly high, exacerbated by the fact that access to general education was more restricted than in France and opportunities for retraining and obtaining further qualifications opened up much later. At the end of the 1980s, at the height of the employment crisis, half of 16- to 18-year-olds were either unemployed or enrolled in employment programmes for school leavers, known as Youth Training Schemes (see figure 6.1).[42]

In a pattern similar to France and, as we will see below, West Germany, plant closures and redundancies brought working lives to an end, especially those of a large number of older steelworkers and miners. For many over-fifties, their lives of 'labour' culminated in long-term sick leave, unemployment or early retirement. This path had been followed since 1977 by the British steel industry with its offer of redundancy packages.[43] In the mining industry, more than 175,000 people lost their jobs between 1985 and 2000. Half of them remained unemployed and became chronically ill or invalids or retired early. Others found part-time jobs, but only a minority found full-time work in the first ten years after the wave of redundancies.[44] Results of a study of mining areas in Yorkshire show that in the mid-1990s, 40 per cent of former miners under 65 were either unemployed, sick or in early retirement.[45] In a related interview, Terry Sargeant, a former miner and supporter of the strikes in 1984–5, commented on the situation, saying: 'But I will say this: Maggie Thatcher closed the pits, right enough, but I think she saved my life. I was fifty-one when I finished, and I would have been another fifteen years underground if they'd stayed open. But what would have become of me after another fifteen years underground?'[46]

The situation of the British miners may have been exceptional, but Sargeant's remark about the unexpected (and originally unwelcome) premature end to his working career illustrates the ambivalence that was felt about this 'farewell to industrial labour' in all three countries. Many of those born before 1940 never actually came into contact with the new industrial world that was developing with the advent of the computer age. This meant they soon seemed rather like wounded veterans from a past industrial culture. In some cases, they found a new role in their regions as representatives and witnesses of a bygone proletarian age and its values, such as solidarity and comradeship. But at best this only served to delay the inevitable process of dying a 'social death', in the sense that they were forced to withdraw not only from working life and their workmates but also from other social contacts.

It can be concluded so far, therefore, that the speed of British deindustrialization forced many industrial workers who were 40 or younger at the beginning of the 1980s to change jobs at a time when conditions on the labour market were particularly difficult.

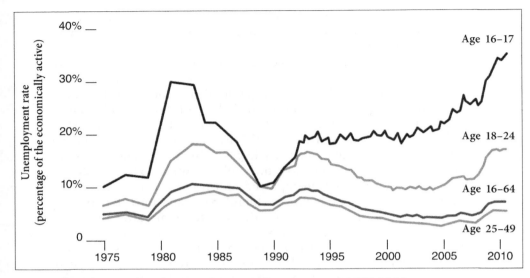

Figure 6.1 Unemployment in Britain by age group, 1975–2010.

Different perspectives are required to understand working-life courses in times of deindustrialization, including overviews. This graph visualizes highly aggregated statistical data on unemployment in Britain. From this angle, a deep fracture is visible. At the beginning of the 1980s, the number of unemployed in the 16- to 17-year-old age group soared. Nearly every third young person had no job. In contrast, the curve is much flatter for the 25- to 49-year-olds. In spite of all the changes, for them continuity predominated.

For some, there was no alternative to a change of course as far as their work and life plans were concerned, since the chances of finding work in the ailing industrial sector were shrinking fast. This change could lead to a reduction in income of 20 per cent and more, as shown, for example, by an analysis of the employment of former car workers after the closure of the Rover factory in Birmingham at the beginning of the millennium.[47] Figures from the Labour Force Survey (carried out regularly since 1975) provide further evidence of change. Although some members of the labour force were compelled to be more mobile and flexible as regards their work, the majority were able to secure long-term jobs in those industrial companies that survived. Once again, we find older workers adopting the strategy of sitting tight and remaining loyal to the company. In 1975, 63.1 per cent of 55-to 64-year-olds had been working for their current employer for more than twenty years. In 2000, this figure still stood at 58.2 per cent.[48] The difference between the generations is brought into sharp focus here, considering that, in the same period, there was a sharp drop in the length of time younger workers aged between 25 and 34 remained in any one company. In 1975, 50.5 per cent of these younger workers had been with the same employer for longer than five years, but by 2000 this figure had sunk to 37.5 per cent.

In Britain as in France, the gap widened between loyal core workers and those who, whether in the short or long term, had to look to the more mobile, less secure jobs in the service sector for their working future. In 1995 and 2005, the proportion of the total number of people employed who were so-called low-wage earners was over 20 per cent.[49] At 18 per cent, this figure was only slightly lower for skilled workers but rose to more than 50 per cent in the trade and service sectors. In the industrial sector, it was the food industry that developed into a distinctly low-wage sector. A good third of its employees earned low wages, women in particular.[50]

The wave of factory closures and mass redundancies in the 1980s was recorded in many interview series and, as a result, the career paths of British miners and steelworkers are relatively well documented.[51] One example is Lyn Bendle, a Welsh steelworker, and one of the numerous employees of the state-owned British Steel company who went into early retirement as a result of the widespread closures and redundancies that began in 1977. In 1991, when the interview was carried out, he was aged 60 and had retired in 1987 at the age of 57 after forty-three years of working life. Like most British industrial workers of his generation, he had started work as soon as he was

213

allowed to leave school at the age of 14, and in this case had gone straight into the steelworks. He had spent the whole of his working life there until the wave of redundancies after the major strike in 1980 and had gradually climbed the internal job ladder in his plant. In the last years of his working life, he left his Welsh homeland to work in a different British Steel plant, where he had to put up with a drop in wages and life in a hostel before he was able to take early retirement. For him, as for many others, the familiar world of work in the boom years lasted until his early retirement. By the time he was interviewed in 1991, nearly four years after he retired, he was able to look back dispassionately.

> Q: When you retired what were you doing, what was your position?
> *Lyn Bendle*: Same job as always, operator [on the caster]. I did 43 years in the steel industry, I have a good pension, [...] a good lump sum, so the youngsters are at the door, why not? [I] see the boys now on the caster, they are all about 45, no-one's older than that. You didn't get a second chance. [...] It's tight now, they can't get out now. We had the choice, we were lucky. And everybody over 54 went, I was 57, 57 and a half.[52]

In summary and in comparison, it can be said, first, that the decline of the industrial sector hit British industrial workers much harder than their French or, as we will see below, their West German counterparts. The extent of this dramatic change and its effect on the career paths of many industrial workers, male and female, is evident from the huge-scale return of precarious living conditions to working-class households and the sharp rise in benefit claims in the industrial heartlands of Northern England, Wales and Scotland in the 1980s. Second, British workers, especially older skilled workers, also developed the safeguarding strategy of remaining loyal to a company over a long period. Third, Britain was similar to France in that it was particularly difficult for young people entering the labour market to find a way into (industrial) working life, especially as traditional paths into skilled jobs such as apprenticeships became much less easily available.[53] This meant that in this period the career paths and living conditions for younger male and female workers in industry became increasingly insecure and were notably more precarious than during the boom years. Fourth, the spread of the low-wage sector and the rapid decline of the industrial sector caused British working-class households to adopt the dual-income model much earlier than their French and German counterparts.

Industrial labour in West Germany: between growth and precarious stability

Between 1972 and 2002, 1.9 million industrial jobs were lost in former West Germany, amounting to an average loss of 13 per cent every ten years. This was a development similar to that in France and meant that the need to change jobs or sectors was much less compelling than it was in Britain. The career patterns of industrial workers in the northern industrial areas of Britain were much closer in this respect to those of former East German workers after 1990, when in a comparatively short period and over a much greater area whole regions were deindustrialized. In former West Germany, the process of adaptation and transformation developed much more slowly and along partially different lines. Here, too, the rise in incomes was lower during the transition phase than in the boom years, but not dramatically so, as can be seen from the fact that from 1975 to 2000 the annual rise in net real income was 1.35 per cent.[54] This figure applies to the former West German regions, where the average earnings of both male and female industrial workers were higher than those of their British and French counterparts.

Data collected since 1984 by the German Socio-Economic Panel (SOEP) from more than 12,000 households, first in West then also in East Germany, allow a closer analysis of working life courses. The same people or the same members of the household were questioned in detail every year about their social and economic circumstances. As a result, we have access to information about the respondents over more than twenty years,[55] sometimes even for the whole of their lives up to 1984, so that in some fortuitous cases it is possible to reconstruct their entire working lives right up until their retirement. The following analysis is based on the biographical data of more than 3,000 people who could be classified as members of the industrial labour force in West Germany. Working-life stories from 630 households were selected from this sample. They provided detailed information about career paths over a period of at least fifteen years. In the first instance, quantitative analysis was carried out on key data concerning job situation, professional qualifications, age, gender and nationality. To this end, the respondents were divided into five different age cohorts to better observe generational effects.[56] Second, the biographies of the men (636) and women (405) were evaluated separately. Many of the women in the 630 households surveyed either did not go out to work at all or worked in other, non-industrial economic sectors. Those who were employed in the industrial sector like their husbands and partners were in the minority and it is only their career paths that are analysed in detail here.[57] Third, a distinction was made between German and non-German workers, and since there were only very few cases of other nationalities, only the largest group of foreign workers, those from Turkey, were selected.[58] Fourth, continuity of employment was included as a category. The criterion taken here was one included as a variable in the SOEP, namely how often the respondent changed jobs and/or industrial sector.[59] In the sample selected, workers' career paths were taken from all the major industrial sectors[60] in order to reconstruct different patterns of working-life courses. Their social logic could then be analysed more closely with reference to individual careers and with a view to discovering possible typical patterns.

The first example comes from the oldest age cohort: that is, those who in 1975 could look back on at least ten years of work and were in the middle of their working lives when their companies were hit by structural and economic turbulence. A typical case is the working life of A., a trained carpenter born in 1939 – so belonging to this first age cohort [1] – and living in a village not far from Bremen. After finishing his apprenticeship, he began work in 1957 and was employed as a skilled worker from then on without a break; from 1965, even in the same branch of the automobile industry. In the 1980s, he became a supervisor or head of a team but was made redundant in 1996 at the age of 57, presumably under a severance scheme. He was unemployed for twenty months until he went into early retirement. During the 1980s, his actual earnings rose more or less steadily but after 1989, so after his fiftieth birthday, they began to fall, and by 1996 had reached a level of 17 per cent below that of 1990.[61] His wife, who was born in 1948 (age cohort [2]), had also been employed since she left school, first as an unskilled worker on the shopfloor of a plastics company, then as a semi-skilled worker in a large company canteen. During the 1990s, her wage increases compensated for the losses suffered by her husband, nine years her senior. Neither of these working-life courses were seriously affected by the post-boom upheavals and they adhered to older patterns of working lives.

A more dramatic variant of the same working-life pattern is illustrated by a different biography, this time of an unskilled worker. M. was a Turkish metalworker who was born in 1941 (age cohort [1]) and had lived in Dortmund since the mid-1960s. He also worked for more than twenty years in the same place, a medium-sized

216

metalworking company, where he had started at 26 as an unskilled worker, operating various machines. He was made redundant in 1990 at the age of 49 and began a long period of unemployment (more than eighty-five months, a full seven years), until he went into early retirement at the age of 56. At the same time as his working life came to an end, his personal life also changed dramatically. In 1990, M. separated from his wife and two children, then aged 6 and 3, and from then on lived alone without a long-term partner. At the same time, his economic situation changed, since his income was reduced by over half.[62]

M.'s biography may seem to be an exception to the rule, but it may also be nothing more than an unusual twist in an otherwise standard case of a widespread working-life pattern in his age cohort. Older workers were frequently 'let go' in the wake of rationalization measures resulting from the constant pressure of technological change and international competition. The threat posed to previously stable relationships by unemployment and the ensuing socio-economic and psychological strain has been proven, for example in French studies by Serge Paugam in the 1990s. In the French case, the number of separations in the 35- to 50-year-old age group in particular rose to 50 per cent.[63]

An analysis of the figures from the samples here shows that of older workers in West German households (age cohort [1], born before 1946), 68 per cent ended their working lives before they were 60 years old; for Turkish workers, this figure was 81 per cent. The path leading from the end of work to the point at which they could draw a pension varied considerably and could entail longer periods of unemployment or invalidity benefits. Whereas most German workers managed to stay in work until they were 57 or 58 years old, 37 per cent of Turkish workers left work when they were between 50 and 55. Further detailed research would be necessary to discover the reasons for this marked difference in age between Germans and migrant workers. In this age cohort, a working life of often more than thirty years, generally begun at the age of 14 or 15, ended as a rule in early retirement.

The same is as true here as it was for British workers, namely that this premature end to their working life constituted a break in their lives that they viewed with ambivalence. On the one hand, it prevented further damage to their health and opened up new opportunities in their private lives. On the other hand, however, it usually brought an abrupt end to their integration into social networks and any other kinds of social contacts at work and could put a strain on their marriage and family life. During the interviews for the SOEP, the Turkish metalworker M. frequently emphasized that he was 'on good terms' with his work colleagues. It is important to remember that at the beginning of the 1970s M.'s life course was similar to that of other 'guest workers', in that it was by no means clearly mapped out in advance. As a rule, decisions about where to start a family, whether to buy a suitable flat or house and where the focal point of their lives should be still had to be taken and were frequently put off. By 1973 at the latest, however, the majority of first-generation Turkish migrant workers had decided, more or less of their own accord, to stay in Germany for good and to bring their families to join them, thus committing themselves to a long-term career in industry.[64] At this point, they also experienced a dramatic change in their job prospects. A premature end to their working life often brought with it the end of social contacts within the region to which they had migrated and meant that they had to fall back on their families or other migrants from their home country. There has been far too little consideration of the long-term effects of this working-life pattern in analyses of the integration, identity and experiences specific to certain generations of migrants in West Germany.

The working-life courses depicted above are examples of two different variants of a pattern that can be ascribed to the so-called core workforce of West German industrial workers. When they were between 35 and 40 years old, this age group survived the first wave of redundancies and subsequently profited from the economic growth of the 1980s. When they reached their fifties, however, they began to be affected by the imminent threat of early retirement or an interim period of long-term unemployment. It is important to realize that this was a pattern that had been established in industry in West Germany – as it had in France and Britain – since the late 1970s, and had been welcomed and promoted, not only by industry itself but also by the trade unions and the state. As we saw in chapter 5, the introduction of new manufacturing techniques and the constant reorganization of production had the same effect as the closure of older plants and the 'death' of certain branches of manufacturing. It brought about the end of traditional industrial employment, the 'farewell to the industrial labourer', which was often accomplished by sending long-serving workers into early retirement. But it was also part of a general trend in former West Germany: the employment rate of 60- to 64-year-olds sank from 70 per cent to 40 per cent between 1970 and 1983 and remained relatively stable between the late 1980s and the late 1990s at around 33 per cent.[65]

We turn now to the career paths of younger workers: that is, those who first started work after 1975, when there were already signs of restructuring and upheaval. Their careers differed from those of their older colleagues in that they were much more varied and the variation was on a much wider scale.[66] In the sample period between 1980 and 2000, workers in the age cohorts [2], [3] and [4] – that is, those born between 1946 and 1969 – frequently changed their jobs, moving into new companies and industrial sectors, with these changes more frequently accompanied by periods of unemployment than in the case of their older colleagues. This initially appears to suggest a pattern similar to that found in France, and also in Britain, although in Britain it was much more marked. However, closer analysis shows that despite some delay and uncertainty, many workers succeeded in securing stable employment, which then usually resulted in long-term service and loyalty to one company. These working-life stories are a clear indication of the opportunities available to young industrial workers as a result of the expansion and reform of the dual vocational training system we described in chapter 5 (see figure 6.2). It explains the fact that the career paths of younger skilled workers in Germany in this study were frequently characterized by in-company promotion and/or further professional qualifications.[67]

B., who was born in 1958 and lived in Duisburg in the 1980s and 1990s, began his working life there as an electrician in 1975, after nine years at school and a three-year apprenticeship. He was employed by the company that had trained him, probably the Thyssen steelworks in Duisburg, just fifteen minutes away from his home, and worked his way up within its ranks. After training as a master technician (*Industriemeister*) from 1990 to 1993, he became head of a team in 1993 at the age of 35. In 1996, he moved up into the category of higher-status employee (*Angestellter*) and became a supervisor. Throughout this period, his real wages rose steadily, and by 2002, when he was 45, after adjusting for inflation, he was earning three-and-a-half times his income of 1985.[68] In the SOEP interviews, he was regularly asked to rate his job satisfaction. In 1985, 1990 and 1992 (when he was studying for further professional qualifications), it was very high, but between 1992 and 1995, it fell dramatically from ten to only three points on the scale. The young man may well have been frustrated by the threat of a thwarted career, in the same way as his French counterpart in the Ranger furniture factory in the *département* of Vienne. In 1996, he finally gained the promotion within the company he had hoped for.[69] Internal promotion continued to be an essential element in the careers of skilled workers, especially when

Figure 6.2 Cover of *Mit 15 hat man noch Träume: Arbeiterjugend in der BRD* (At 15 We Still Dream: Working-Class Youth in West Germany), published by S. Fischer, 1975.

During the 1970s, many autobiographical texts by industrial workers were published (see chapter 2). For West Germany, the Werkkreis Literatur der Arbeitswelt (Working Group for Literature of the Working World) led the way by publishing several anthologies with the prestigious publishing house S. Fischer, including the one illustrated here. The cover shows a drawing of a nonchalant young man. His sunglasses reflect two contrasting perspectives of the future. Either he will be filling the coffers of the companies or he will be kicked out onto the street. Looming unemployment at the time heralded an uncertain future. But at the same time the boom period continued to have an effect. Working life still began at the age of 15.

the chances of moving to another company were diminishing, either because there were no local alternatives or because it would have meant moving to a different area.

However, even in these prosperous and stable zones, there were changes. Young industrial workers now went to school for ten or eleven years (much more frequently attending the middle school (*Realschule*) before they started an apprenticeship, meaning they began their working careers much later. Whether their careers will end as soon as those of their older colleagues remains to be seen, since those who were born in 1960 or later are only just reaching the stage of the over-55s. D., who was born in 1969, obtained his middle-school certificate (*Realschulabschluss*) before doing an apprenticeship as a painter and varnisher, and was 20 when he began to work in the trade in 1989. But he soon gave up his painting job, and after being unemployed for a month he began a new career as a production worker in a glass factory. From then on, both his working life and his private life were marked by continuity. He married in 1991 at the age of 22 and bought his own house or flat – the sources are unclear – in 1996. During the first ten years in his new company, his real income rose steadily.[70] In 2006, when he was 37, D. became a supervisor, but his real wages no longer rose and during the next ten years his monthly wage fluctuated between €1,700 and €2,300, depending on the incoming orders and productive output of the company.[71]

The working life of a young man of Turkish origin, however, who was born in 1966 and so was three years older than D., was completely different (see table 6.1). F. came to Germany as an adolescent of school age and lived first in Wuppertal, then in Düsseldorf. He failed to gain any German school leaving qualifications or complete any vocational training and his working life was initially very erratic. For more than twelve years, he was evidently in search of a good job, was made redundant four times, was unemployed and worked in various branches of industry. This phase of short-term solutions and experimentation came to an end in 1995 when, at the age of 29, he got a job in a steelworks, first as a forklift driver and later in its foundry. According to the most recent information available, in 2001 when he was 35, he was still working in the same job and had been with the same partner since 1992.[72]

The pattern so clearly described in this last life story is different, though not totally new, and had been spreading since 1975. It shows a clear initial phase of working life defined by precarious and short-term jobs, particularly in the case of unskilled workers. It

221

Table 6.1 Reconstruction of the working life of F.

Age	Employment	Year	Comments
14–17	Apprenticeship/training (2 years)	1982–3	No qualification
18	Technical school	1984	No qualification
19	Unskilled metalworker	1985	Redundant
19	**Unemployed**	**1986**	**8 months**
20–2	Warehouse worker	1986–8	Redundant
23	Unskilled process mechanic	1989	n/s
24	**Unemployed**	**1990**	**7 months**
25	Machine worker	1991	Redundant
26–9	**Unemployed**	**1992–5**	**46 months**
29–3	Lift truck driver	1995–9	Uninterrupted
33–5	Foundry mechanic	2000–1	employment

Note: The focus of this table is more detailed. It reconstructs the individual career path of a semi-skilled worker based on the statistical data of the SOEP. F. is of Turkish origin and was born in 1966. He lived first in Wuppertal and then in Düsseldorf. Over many years, his life alternated between short phases of unemployment and employment. It was not until he was 29 that he managed to find a permanent job. This typical worker's biography illustrates the fact that at the end of the boom period the smooth transition from school and apprenticeship into employment ended and periods of continuous employment became increasingly shorter.
Source: Based on data from the SOEP (PID 563 701).

was evidently not a pattern restricted to British and French workers but merely differed in frequency in Germany. It was often encountered among younger migrants who had moved to Germany while they were still at school or shortly afterwards. Compared to those of their fathers and older brothers and cousins who had arrived between 1965 and 1970, their careers clearly demonstrate the effects of deindustrialization and technological change. In the core industrial production areas, jobs for unskilled workers in Germany were being progressively cut, making it increasingly difficult to find a way into highly paid industrial jobs, especially without the added social capital of family contacts. Most of their working lives began in the building trade or in trades such as car repairs, and by no means all of them culminated in a stable job in industry. As a result, the period of unstable, precarious work for this cohort of unskilled workers in Germany extended, as it did in France, until they were about 30 years old. Evidence for the frequency of this kind of career path is provided by the quantitative evaluation of the sample of working-life stories. The results show that in the age cohorts [3] and [4] born between 1956 and 1969, 16.5 per cent of men entering the labour market were registered unemployed in more than two calendar years. On the other hand, the career paths of 72 per cent of this age cohort were fairly steady and even, demonstrated in the interviews by the fact that a change of job or branch of industry or a period of unemployment occurred no more than three times in fifteen years.

With regard to the women in these working-class households, it would appear initially that very little had changed for them compared to the boom period. Now, as in the period before 1975, only a minority (22 per cent) were in full-time work, and of those the majority were employed in unskilled or semi-skilled posts for five or at the most seven years. Their careers generally ended between the ages of 20 and 25 when they married or had their first child. Most of the cases analysed here can be defined as 'domestic' careers rather than employment careers. In other words, the type and extent of these women's employment were determined primarily by the needs and requirements of the household in which they were living as wives, mothers or daughters. Their working lives were evidently determined by the age and number of children and the job situation of their partners to a much greater extent than by any career options available at work. The model of part-time employment to bring in extra income that was so successful in the 1960s developed to an even greater extent in Germany in subsequent decades. In the households studied here, this kind of life course was widespread amongst migrant women and German-born women alike.[73] Although new, specifically female career patterns developed during this period, they were typically found either in the service sector or in the education and health sectors and there mainly amongst highly qualified women, particularly academics. These options are demonstrated by one group in the sample, those who returned to working life as widows or single mothers after a family crisis. This path was followed by around a quarter of women, but only a small minority (thirteen out of ninety-nine) had a career in industry.

The following is a final example. G. was born in 1966 of Turkish parents and, after being at school for nine years and completing a three-year apprenticeship in retail sales, she worked both full- and part-time before she got married at the age of 23 and became pregnant. Her working career in industry did not begin until ten years later, when at the age of 33 she moved to Augsburg with her child but without her husband and began employment as a semi-skilled worker in an electrical company, earning a modest income.[74] Eight years later, in 2007, the news was good: at the age of 41, G. had saved enough money to be able to afford to buy her own flat.[75]

Marriage, household and family solidarity

Working life curtailed after 55; circuitous paths into the working world; 'domestic' careers for working women – these phenomena have been observed from the perspective of the life stories of individual workers. Yet they all demonstrate that these life stories are embedded in personal relationships and family contexts. These social connections can be at least partially revealed to outsiders by looking at households. Economic and demographic data and information have been collected regularly from households since the 1980s and this makes it possible to investigate correlations between the life courses of age cohorts and generations around three significant events in their working lives, namely starting work, marrying or leaving home and retiring. Only a few examples can be shown here, and they are based solely on data from the SOEP, so refer only to West German households. For British or French households, there are no similar data that could be evaluated systematically and used for comparison. However, it is quite clear that there are many structural similarities between British, French and German working-class households during the decades covered by this study.

In all three countries, young men and women from families of manual workers or junior office workers tended to find their partners for life – or at least, given the high divorce rates, for the next phase of their lives – from their immediate or closely related social milieu. This choice, conservative from a social perspective, survived the social and economic turbulence of the 1980s and 1990s. The figures paint an unmistakable picture for all three countries. In the case of West Germany, Sonja Weber-Menges has observed that marrying into the same class, so-called class monogamy, which was evident as the preferred option in the 1970s, was still the norm in the 1990s. In the mid-1970s, two-thirds of male manual workers were married to daughters of manual workers. Twenty-five years later, in 1999, the data Weber-Menges collected from the manual and clerical workers she interviewed about their marriage and origin showed that half of skilled male workers were married to manual workers and the other half to clerical or office workers, of whom the latter were generally daughters of manual workers.[76] Similar marriage patterns can be found for British and French (male) manual workers and (female) office or administrative workers and the much smaller circle of female industrial workers. They show that social ties between the diminishing male world of industry and the expanding female world

224

of the service industry and part-time jobs were strengthening in all three countries in question here, while new family ties with people working in the managerial sector or in academic jobs, new or old, remained the exception.[77]

A look at the situations of families shows that in general during this transformational phase, many households with children between the ages of 16 and 25 found that the longer period of education and training and the difficulty of finding a way into the world of work made it necessary for them to provide their offspring with accommodation at home and support them financially. At the same time, younger members of the household were able to use their income to support their parents, when, for example, their father was out of work or forced to retire early. In 2000, at the end of the period in question, nearly a third of all the working-class households surveyed in Germany were in this kind of transitional state, so had adults and young people over 16 – or even more than two generations – living together. A further third were households with smaller children. The rest was made up of households without children (30 per cent) and single-parent households (4 per cent).[78]

The biographical data available for these households reveal a variety of different living situations, income levels and decisions about life. On the one hand, there are situations in which the expectation of job security has been to a certain extent handed down. This is particularly well illustrated by a life story from Accrington in Lancashire, the traditional heartland of British industry.[79] Marilyn Kenyon, the factory worker in question, was born in 1953 and was 50 at the time of her interview. She and her husband and her only son (born in 1975) worked at Holland's, a regionally and nationally renowned producer of pies that was established in 1851. She herself had worked there since she was 25 and her husband and son both joined the company in 1992. Throughout the turbulent period of deindustrialization after the mid-1970s, this company had, therefore, acted as an inter-generational anchor, providing stability for a working-class family with local roots. 'Family careers' of this kind were not uncommon in large companies in Germany and France either, and they point to a specific correlation between the social order in families and the social order in companies, which I will be examining in more detail in the next chapter.

More often, however, the younger generation continued their parents' modest rise in social status or took this as the starting position for planning their own lives or careers. An example would be the L. family household, which lived near Landshut between

1984 and 1994. The parents had no vocational training: the father (born in 1932) was employed as semi-skilled worker in industry in the production of pre-cast concrete elements and the mother (born in 1936) worked part-time as a cleaner, both remaining in the employment of the same company over a long period. Their only son (born in 1965), on the other hand, trained as a typesetter in a printing and publishing company in the early 1980s and continued to be employed there until the last interview in 2009. His parents suffered a period of insecurity and unemployment (thirteen months between 1984 and 1986 for his father, eleven months in 1992 and 1993 for his mother) before they were able to take early retirement, both at the age of 58. He, on the other hand, continued to live in his parents' household and was already earning considerably more than they had. In 1995, at the age of 30, he left his parental home and moved in with his partner, who was eight years his junior and not from a working-class background: her parents had the *Abitur*, the university entrance qualification, and her father was a civil servant. At that time, she was still training to become a higher-level administrative assistant. When it came to the key events in the life story of the L. family, namely entry into working life, marriage and retirement, their circumstances were characterized across the generations by a minor rise in social status and a modest level of financial security but also by disruption and insecurity at the end of their working lives.[80]

A much more complex social situation appears from the analysis of the strategies of larger family households, which often belonged to migrant workers in West Germany. These households were typically faced with risks on two different fronts. First, as we have seen above, there was the threat of the father prematurely losing his job. This happened to the first generation of unskilled and semi-skilled migrant workers far more frequently than to their German colleagues. Second, these households also had to cope more often with their younger members having to take a far longer and more tortuous path into working life. Both factors made it necessary to mobilize collective household strategies.

The case of the M. family can serve as an illustration of this kind of situation. Mr and Mrs M. were born in Turkey in 1945 and 1947 respectively and had three sons and two daughters. While Mr M. was employed as a semi-skilled worker in a West German metal-works from 1970, his wife originally stayed in Turkey with their four children. The fifth child was the only one to be born in Germany in 1979. They continued to be in touch with their home country over the years and their daughters-in-law were also Turkish. The period that is relevant here, involving the pivotal events in this family's life course, namely entry into working life, marriage/leaving home and retirement, stretches over a good fifteen years from 1986, when the interviews began, until 2001 (see table 6.2). During this time, the family lived in a small town near Düsseldorf and moved house twice, in 1987 and 1999. Mr M. was employed in the same metalworks until 2000, working shifts. During this period, his two eldest sons, born in Turkey in 1965 and 1968, married and had their own children, born in 1986, 1990 and two in 1993. After fairly unsuccessful school careers, the sons started work at the ages of 18 and 20 respectively in a large metal company, like their father. They were the breadwinners for their young families, as initially neither of their wives went out to work. It was not until 1996, when she was 34 years old, that the older daughter-in-law was employed for the first time. Even after they had married and the grandchildren were born, the young families lived in the parental household – until 1997 and 1999 respectively. It can be assumed that they provided financial support for their parents and three younger siblings, since their father was made redundant in 2000 at the age of 55. The eldest daughter, who was born in 1970 also in Turkey, left her parents' home at the relatively young age of 17, whereas, unlike his brothers, the third son, born in 1974, successfully completed an apprenticeship, and in 1993 married and also began employment in the metal industry as a skilled worker. However, in the 1990s, his life and career did not progress as smoothly as those of his elder brothers. He was made redundant twice between 1993 and 1996 and was unemployed for a total of thirty-five months. The youngest child, the second daughter, was born in Germany in 1979 and trained as a hairdresser. She moved in and out of part-time work until 2001, when she married and was the last to leave the parental household.

Between 1986 and 2001, this household had, therefore, comprised three generations and accommodated at times more than ten people. Of these, at least three adults were out of work, with this figure rising to five towards the end of the 1990s when the grandchildren were older. The total monthly income of this household stated in the interviews fluctuated considerably from year to year, but the reduction in income suffered by the three main breadwinners was at least partly compensated for between 1990 and 1998 by the additional earnings of younger and female family members. Between 1990 and 1996, their total disposable household income sank by approximately 20 per cent, until the two younger families moved out in 1997 and 1999 respectively, and their joint income in the separate households rose again significantly until 2004.

Table 6.2 The M. family: a multi-generational household, 1986–2001

Member of family	Year of birth	Professional qualification	Employment	Unemployment	Family status	Left home/ moved
Father	1945	None	Semi-skilled metal worker (1970-2000)	Since 2000/ Early retirement	Marriage in ? 5 children	1987, 1999
Mother	1947	None	Housewife, part-time jobs			
1st son	1965	None	Various jobs, semi-skilled metalworker	1984-86 (25 months)	Marriage 1987 3 children: born in 1986, 1991, 1993	1999
1st daughter-in-law	1962	None	Part-time, various	2001 (11 months)		
2nd son	1968	None	Semi-skilled metalworker	1988 (7 months)	Marriage 1990 child, born in 1993	1997
2nd daughter-in-law	1973	None	Housewife			
3rd daughter	1970	Apprenticeship	No further information			1987
4th son	1974	Apprenticeship	Skilled metalworker	1993 (2 months), 1996–8 (33 months)	Unmarried partnership (1999)	1999
5th daughter	1979	Apprenticeship	Hairdresser, part-time, various jobs	2001/2 (11 months)	Unmarried	2001

Greyshading: household member until 2001 ▇; until 1999 ▨; until 1997 ▢; until 1987 ☐.

Note: This close-up view shows the stabilizing effects of multi-generational support in a large family household as if through a magnifying glass. It enabled flexible responses to the vicissitudes of employment and personal lives. Working-class households were increasingly dependent on the incomes of all their members. The model of the male householder as the sole breadwinner became less and less common. Around 1995, the question of whether the earnings of male or female members of the household were highest was far more open than twenty years previously.

Source: Based on data from the SOEP (PID56510).

Looking back and looking ahead

Influenced not least by empirical data from the boom decades, life-course research in the social sciences tended to emphasize the significance of institutional frameworks (schooling, employment status, qualifications/vocational training, retirement age) for the formation of stable, long-term careers. These frameworks were then taken to create standard categories based on gender and age, which provided the foundation for so-called standard or normal life courses, focussing on employment and the household. Other, much less stable life-course patterns had existed before the recession in 1973–4, but they had for the most part been typical of groups excluded from mainstream society, most notably migrants. However, as shown above, the change in these life-course patterns in what was formerly the core sector of industrial labour was much slower in the three decades after the boom than was initially anticipated based on contemporary perceptions and preoccupations with long-term unemployment, youth unemployment and non-standard or atypical employment (part-time, temporary or contract work). The technological and organizational restructuring of industrial production also suggested more far-reaching and immediate consequences to contemporary observers than those that can actually be detected in retrospect. How can this be explained?

Precisely because the labour market was becoming more volatile and most people were confronted with an apparently more uncertain future, there was a growing desire in society for security and more precisely for stability in the field of employment. This may have been a coping strategy on the part of industrial workers, but it also suited the strategy of businesses. Complex technological advances, the pressure of increased competition and rapidly rising quality standards meant they were reliant on the competence and cooperation of their workforce. The extent to which this was the case varied in the three countries in question, but also between the various branches of industry. Other strategies were also implemented, such as stricter performance-related checks on fluctuating workforces, reductions in labour costs and the 'Taylorization' of production. The diverse patterns of working lives were, therefore, largely determined by the strategies adopted in reaction to the increasing globalization and Europeanization of the industrial production process. But they were also determined by the negotiating power of the works councils and trade unions when it came to job cuts and drawing up redundancy and severance schemes. A key factor here was the recognition and exploitation of the specialist knowledge and competence of skilled industrial workers.

The differences in vocational and skills qualifications were discussed in chapter 5. As well as the fact that fewer industrial jobs in total were shed in former West Germany than in France and Britain, these differences were the main reason why, even in the years of change after the boom, the working careers of most young skilled industrial workers in Germany followed the same pattern of internal promotion and continuous employment. This career pattern can also be encountered in some sectors in France and Britain, where it survived the rifts of the 1980s and 1990s caused by rationalization, changes of ownership and plant closures. In France, it was found primarily in the public sector and in nationalized industries. In both Britain and France, certain large-scale businesses used their human resources and training policies to encourage their core workforce to follow this kind of in-house career. These were, however, no more than small pockets of stable employment in a world of industrial work which was characterized to a much greater extent by precarity and the transition to the less stable employment patterns typical of the rapidly growing service sector. It is clear, therefore, that the extent to which this first element of stability was sustainable depended largely on the conditions in each of the individual nation-states.

Changes in the general economic climate and in competitive conditions brought the working lives of many older workers in former key industries to an abrupt and premature end. In response to the increasing demands of globalized competition, they were sent into early retirement. Within a surprisingly short space of time, the 'farewell to the industrial labourer' led to many steelworkers, miners, shipbuilders and other major groups of male industrial workers being forced to end their working lives while they were still in their fifties.

In Britain, France and Germany, a kind of general social consensus seemed to emerge that at this late stage of their careers the older generation of industrial labourers could not be expected to have to endure the job losses and permanent unemployment which they would have faced as a result of deindustrialization and rationalization. As a result, businesses, trade unions and the state united in setting up conditions under which it was possible to follow working-life patterns that avoided the demands of flexibility and the risks of a more precarious existence. The working-life stories show the significance of social citizenship for the older generation in concrete terms by providing not only them with security in old age, but also their households and families. Part-time work and more extensive and repeated phases of unemployment indicate that the incidence of precarious work began to spread and threaten the standards of social citizenship.

It has become clear that remaining loyal to the same company and in the same kind of job were strategies frequently adopted by workers in an attempt to secure their living. They were increasingly openly referred to as 'owning' a job and saw very little opportunity to change their job or risk retraining. The social cost of this safeguarding strategy was borne, on the one hand, by women, whose careers in the industrial sector remained virtually non-existent, with very few exceptions, and, on the other, by young workers at the start of their careers, especially in Britain and France. They often had to put up with unemployment, and precarious (fixed-term) and poorly paid jobs, in order to get a foot in the door of relatively stable industrial employment. As a result, the initial phase leading up to a career path as an industrial worker was stretched by a good ten years, meaning that the careers of an increasing number of young people did not start until they were between 25 and 30 years old. This, in turn, led to the actual active phase of employment in the lives of male industrial workers shrinking within a short space of time from forty years to between twenty-five and thirty years.

Labour-related migration was a particularly significant factor. In Germany and France, labour migrants played an important role as unskilled and semi-skilled workers in mass production when it was booming in the period up to 1975. The same was true for Britain, although the numbers there were far lower. Older migrant workers were often part of the group of those who took early retirement, whereas for those who had migrated later, and/or were younger or second-generation migrants, the consequences of belonging to an ethnic subgroup that had become established in many companies were far more apparent. It was much more difficult for this group to gain access to further qualifications and higher-status jobs. In all three countries, they made up a disproportionately high share of unskilled and semi-skilled workers, and as such, their working-life patterns frequently reveal erratic and/or interrupted career paths. This lack of security was a part of the class-specific and generation-specific background to the social protests staged by young people in the suburbs and *banlieues* of Britain and France analysed in chapter 3.

However, it would be mistaken to speak of a systematic exclusion of specific groups from better-paid and more secure industrial jobs. In the industrial world of all three countries, the gender-specific division of labour remained unchanged. The declining number of women working in industry were 'stuck' in unskilled and semi-skilled jobs and the option of a career in industry for them was unrealistic, except for a small minority of skilled workers. The proportion of part-time workers increased and, with it, the proportion of those who could be considered to have (unpaid) 'domestic' careers. However, the working lives of women began to play an ever-increasing role in the social and economic lives of the predominantly male industrial labour force. The short-lived bourgeois dream of the male 'pater-familias' and sole breadwinner was soon brought to an abrupt end by the change in socio-economic conditions. Whether the men were skilled or unskilled workers, they were often in a relationship with or married to women who were themselves employed in jobs in education, social work or administration, in the health sector, retail or any of the other numerous jobs in the rapidly growing service sector. As the threat of unemployment increased and wages stagnated or even fell, women's contributions to the household income became of increasing strategic importance. There is an urgent need for more research into the working lives of these women, particularly those employed in low- and mid-level jobs in the service industry, in order to discover more about the social realities of the working classes in Britain, France and Germany after the boom.[81]

Many important aspects have had to be neglected in this chapter. The socio-cultural contexts of these working-life stories have only occasionally surfaced, for example, as have the very different ways that they were embedded in the life plans and career expectations of their families and neighbours. It was also not possible to take into consideration any principles and concepts related to the particular time, nation or social class in question which may have influenced the different phases of life such as youth, child-raising, partnership and retirement. Nevertheless, the life-course patterns which have emerged here should be able to help researchers see beyond trends specific to individual countries and better recognize and interpret transnational similarities and differences in the world of industrial labour during a period of globalizing production systems. They allow us, for example, to propose a working hypothesis that the patterns of working lives in East Germany post-1989 were more similar to British career paths, where the relevant developments began ten years earlier, than to their West German counterparts. It is also true that the proportion of precarious or 'flexible' career paths in 'atypical' forms of German industrial employment increased steadily after the turn of the century. As Philipp Ther has pointed out, a trend emerged in

Europe towards a clear polarization of industrial working-life courses according to qualifications and/or social or ethnic background.[82]

Finally, it would also be important to clarify whether the discovery of early retirement as the least controversial and most 'socially acceptable' means of softening the effects of job losses was as widespread in other European countries. In the face of swiftly rising pension costs, it soon became one of the areas of tension in social relations between the generations. This was particularly the case in France, where lowering the retirement age was perceived as the ideal way to bring about a socially acceptable transformation of the economy and society.

In these times of upheaval, workers' careers depended more and more on the survival of their working sites and the management strategies or market chances of their companies. The biographies we have studied here were part of the larger histories of these companies, which will be addressed in the following chapter.

— Chapter 7 —

TRANSFORMATIONS IN
COMPANY REGIMES

Since the 1980s and in all three countries in this study, companies have gained huge public recognition and esteem as places teeming with creative colleagues, value-adding dynamism and innovative ideas for products. Dreams of comfortable social idylls faded and '*Die grenzenlose Unternehmung*' (The Unlimited Enterprise), to quote the programmatic title of a successful German business management textbook,[1] took the place of any clichéd criticism of capitalism. Notions of 'exploitation' by companies and 'alienation' at work lost their influence in public discourse and allowed the emergence of a much more positive view of companies dominated by terms such as 'creativity' and 'innovation' from the new vocabulary of self-fulfilment, and categories such as market orientation, customer focus, precision and flexibility. 'The new spirit of capitalism', as Luc Boltanski and Ève Chiapello called this *doxa*, hugely increased public esteem for business and enterprise.[2]

Given the shift in values in Western societies frequently cited in diverse handbooks, 'human resource management' evolved into a demanding task whose strategic significance was seen in terms of motivated workers and their 'strategically important competitive potential, difficult to replicate'.[3] The new management concepts all revolved around mobilizing employees for company goals. Company loyalty, employee qualifications and employee motivation as well as personal responsibility, team spirit and 'creative space' were terms used by the management of market-leading companies to characterize their own successful personnel policies.[4] The management doctrines of the 1980s and 1990s created largely idealized images of the working worlds of the future where 'company culture' and 'democratic' leadership replaced what was now termed 'macho'

234

management. This was no less than a vision of new social relations in a world of work in which the old hierarchies and oppositional interests were overcome and the promise of greater participation for employees was fulfilled.

The path to these new working worlds was, however, by no means smooth, especially for the large industrial companies, which had been relatively ill prepared for the turbulences after the boom. As seen in chapters 1 and 3, poor sales, falling profits and industrial disputes belonged to the bitter realities of the 1970s and early 1980s. As a consequence, companies were compelled to reinvent themselves simply to survive rather than out of any enthusiasm for innovative business concepts. The pressure to rationalize coupled with the new data-processing and communication technologies made it seem a tempting option for large bureaucratic organizations to restructure. Their main aim was to track down and eliminate the time loss and inefficiencies which had been intrinsic in the previous system due to the rigid division of labour amongst discrete function-based departments. The pressure in nearly all companies and branches of industry for production to be faster and cheaper and yet still improve the quality of the end product had lasting effects on French, British and West German companies. Yet improvements in productivity could not be achieved only by introducing new computer technologies. It soon became clear that organizational structures also had to be changed, and that work processes had not only to be restructured but, above all, to be differently distributed between the various departments and occupational groups within the companies. The time had come for new management concepts whose keywords were soon to determine the vocabulary of executive floors and management training centres. The result was a fundamental transformation of organizational structures, especially in large manufacturing companies.

One of the keywords that began to circulate at the beginning of the 1990s was 'lean management'. Within a short time, it had become firmly established in management handbooks and textbooks in all three countries. It owed its popularity to a study carried out by the Massachusetts Institute of Technology, whose aim was to show how the US automobile industry could regain or improve its competitiveness. It focussed on the organizational models of its Japanese rivals, particularly Toyota, which were stylized into the concept of 'lean manufacturing' and then propagated as a recipe for success regardless of culture or context.[5] German-speaking discourse adopted the principle as 'holistic production systems' (*ganzheitliche Produktionssysteme*).[6]

To get a better idea of what actually happened in factories, I would like to look at an example in France. In the 1990s, the French sociologist Serge Paugam carried out a series of factory studies to examine experiences and situations at work and discover their significance for the social integration of individual workers in French society.[7] Apart from such factors as job security, professional qualifications and the work itself, he turned his attention to the company. He discovered that both social relations among the workers and the relationship of the workers to the companies had changed significantly in France in the 1990s. This is illustrated by the following excerpt from an interview with a 55-year-old unskilled worker at Ranger, a furniture manufacturer in rural France (*département* of Vienne). At the time of the interview in 1998, he had been employed in the company for twenty-seven years. After a long period of dynamic growth led by the company's founder, between 1,200 and 1,300 people had been employed in the factory. After the founder's death in 1982, the company had changed hands several times and had finally become part of a larger business. There had already been a wave of redundancies in the 1980s, affecting about half the workforce. In 1998, the company employed only 370 workers, its order books were looking bleak and the future of the whole company was uncertain. As Paugam's interviewee put it:[8]

- The mood hasn't been the same since the two waves of redundancies and then you don't work as hard. It's not the same as it was, because before there was a lot to do but people helped each other. If one person was under pressure, well, if you were ahead a bit, you helped, but nowadays, no it's not the same atmosphere, not at all.
- Is that because people are dissatisfied with the company?
- [*Sighs*] I don't know. I know that there is a connection between that and ... maybe because two or three people have been made redundant, maybe that's had an effect, I don't know. Perhaps people are less motivated, perhaps they're bitter, I don't know ... and then the boss keeps changing. He's just been replaced, nobody knows where they stand. You hear rumours, nothing but rumours, so people are completely confused.
- How about you, do you do your work like you should?
- Yes, of course, but not like I used to. I don't know, but I used to enjoy going to work but now I tend to take it steady. And you're often ordered around by people who don't really know what they're talking about, that's the problem. So it's no wonder you're fed up.
- Do you speak your mind, argue sometimes?

– Yes, that's happened too, but now I just let it go, they tell me what to do and I do what they say; that's it, full stop. Otherwise you'd never get anywhere, you'd be at it every day.[9]

The ongoing sales crisis in the furniture industry had left its mark on the company: redundancies and frequent changes in management meant that the workers no longer trusted their bosses and expected the worst, namely the closure of the factory. At the same time, solidarity amongst the workers had disappeared, leaving everyone to fight for themselves, with each individual hoping somehow to survive unscathed. In other interviews by researchers in Paugam's team, workers complained of a lack of promotion prospects and investment. The picture was always the same: a factory run by its energetic and omnipresent founder with a tight, patriarchal management style had been booming until 1982 and then turned into a bleak and doomed 'workhouse' where people only worked because there was no other local alternative and mass unemployment deterred them from taking any risks. What was left was at best an instrumentalized relationship between the workers and the company and its management. The contrast to the idealized images of future working environments outlined above could hardly be greater.

This example illustrates the far-reaching socio-psychological consequences that typical crisis phenomena of deindustrialization could cause in companies. The decline of the Ranger factory led to what Paugam called a 'negative identity'.[10] The workers had withdrawn into their private lives, were suffering from the loss of in-company solidarity and had lost confidence in the management. The underlying attitude amongst the workers was resentful and fatalistic, but at the same time they were tied to the company. They had become precarious occupants of their jobs and had lost their professional identities and their emotional bonds with Ranger. However, Paugam sees this as an extreme case and contrasts it with examples of quite different experiences of work and companies. Of the 1,025 workers interviewed for his study, the majority were satisfied with their work. Even amongst semi-skilled and unskilled workers, more than 65 per cent were satisfied and nearly everyone (90 per cent) said relations with their fellow workers were good, although only 60 per cent described the climate in their company as good. The more stable the job situation, the greater the subjective job satisfaction and the more positive the assessment of the company.[11] The effects of these conditions on social cohesion have been critically analysed and debated, not only in France.

Both management ideology and the workers' dashed hopes reveal the role of companies as the focus of a sense of belonging and identification and their evidently growing importance during the period under study. A series of factors contributed to this boost in companies as the focal point of social ties. As we saw in the previous chapter, in view of the problems on the labour market, many workers stayed in the same jobs. The length of employment in manufacturing remained on the same high level of the boom years during the subsequent decades of upheaval, and in some sectors it even rose. In parallel, the reorganization of industrial production was accompanied by a greater involvement of all sections of the workforce in the quality assurance of tasks and products. The workers became more independent and were given more responsibility, but laid claim to more participation as individuals, teams or a collective workforce. At the same time, more refined control mechanisms were introduced in all sections of the company. In other words, during the period of upheaval, companies became increasingly important as places where contrasting models of participation and belonging were negotiated. I will subsume the different models of relationships between management and workforce within a company under the notion of 'company regime'.

Companies rely on the decision-making powers and directives of their owners or management, restricted in the best case by a statutory framework. Employment contracts and factory regulations create a space in which democratic procedures are not automatically provided for. Without the trade unions and their powers of opposition and veto, the social citizenship described in chapter 4 would not have developed and would be inconceivable. The statutory regulation of worker participation may have secured various compromises between democracy and capitalism, and therefore management and workforce, at the national and regional level, but their concrete realization depends on how these rules and rights are implemented by each individual company. Democracy as a way of life depends crucially on the extent to which it influences relations in the world of work and does not therefore stop outside the factory gates. The specific question is whether class relations at work – that is, the forms of power and the division of labour established there – produce a type of social inequality that is no longer compatible with the democratic principle of equality. Pierre Rosanvallon calls this basic principle of democratic societies 'relational equality'.[12] Without 'social recognition', 'relational equality' is meaningless. Translated into the reality of the workplace, this means management must respect the needs

238

and interests of the workforce and recognize their 'dignity' without discrimination or coercion.

Before I begin to examine the actual conditions of social citizenship in working life, and above all to explore the effect of the economic and organizational changes in industrial companies since the 1970s, I would first like to explain the theoretical perspective I am adopting.

The factory as a 'field of social action'

Anyone who deals with work relations in a company cannot avoid taking up a position in the long-running dispute over appropriate categories and theories of capitalist enterprise. In this case, approaches are helpful that combine two questions: how 'entrepreneurial authority'[13] is organized and what kind of relationships are established between capital and labour in the factory. In other words, it is a question of combining perspectives of organizational and labour sociology – a procedure that only began to be tested by researchers as a response to the processes studied here.

The perspective of organizational sociology on the issue of entrepreneurial authority builds on research examining questions: first, what actually sustains complex organizations like factories and businesses with their variety of functions; second, what constitutes the basis for the authority of management apart from the asymmetry of power based on private property and employment contracts; and, third, how do different status groups and occupational groups try to change the distributions of power and functions within the company in their favour? Particular attention has been paid to the 'micropolitics' beneath and beyond the formal rules of the 'bureaucratic' division of labour and decision-making monopolies. The 'debureaucratization' of companies has become a starting point for quite different directions in research which, however, generally concentrate on modelling the micro-effects of networks, communication patterns and dynamics within companies and operating units.[14] Either the effects of external factors such as labour markets or contemporary hierarchies in society and culture are ignored, or such frameworks are assumed to be 'natural' and so unchangeable. Game-theoretical approaches following models of rational choice find it particularly difficult to take into account the genuinely social basis of these micropolitics, namely consensual action and an enduring willingness to cooperate. In their functional analyses, they attach little or no significance to the emotional, affective aspects of company regimes and asymmetries of power between workers and management. Social ties and a development of a sense of community are either completely excluded or interpreted as minor side effects of the interest-based strategies of rational actors.[15]

In German-speaking labour and industrial sociology, however, the company as a production community (*Produktionsgemeinschaft*) plays a prominent role. Particularly in its beginnings, which stretch back into the nineteenth century, it saw the essence of company-oriented integration in the production-focussed consensus between management and workers. In this reading, company regimes are the result of this underlying consensus – they grow more or less naturally out of the experience of cooperation in everyday work.[16] There is an obvious affinity here to older paternalistic and social partnership arrangements in companies. Conflict is seen as a considerable and unnecessary breach of the social peace in a company. This kind of harmonistic perspective has been adopted in recent studies on human resource management, organizational psychology and business management in the applied social sciences in particular, but with a different aim. The goal here is not the voluntary subordination of the individual in an authoritarian company but the best possible coordination of individual capabilities with respect to the overall company goals.

Such approaches were and still are in direct contrast to the view of work processes and 'factory regimes' in Marxist criticism of capitalism.[17] The community-building aspects of factory work under capitalist conditions are seen as a relic of pre-capitalist modes of production, as remnants of craft occupations surviving in a modern factory or as the result of social techniques employed by management to conceal the basic conflict of interest between capital and labour and to extract from workers hidden resources in terms of performance and ability that they might otherwise withhold. This critical view thus sees stable company regimes as the result either of successful human resource management or of long-term compromise with the craft traditions of skilled workers. In both cases, however, their future is precarious, since the basic conflict of interests remains unsolved and continues to smoulder beneath the surface. In addition, there is a certain theoretical tension in this approach, since the social relationships within the workforce can be interpreted, on the one hand, as a seemingly natural result of class relations in the labour process and, on the other hand, as the result of political education on the part of trade union or political activists.[18] On the positive side, this industrial sociological perspective takes particular care to

240

record how far the devaluation of their professional competencies undermines the cohesion and oppositional strength of a company's production workers.[19]

A further problem with the Marxist tradition stems from the close connection it makes between company regimes and the prevailing capitalist 'production regime', which for its part is heavily influenced by politico-economic frameworks and conditions. It claims therefore that from the beginning of the 'post-Fordist' era in the mid-1970s, worker participation was strictly limited and more or less directly dependent on profit margins, qualification profiles and the state of the market.[20] This had, or, from the point of view of contemporary critics, would have, a direct and inevitable influence on work relations in the company. In short, the state of technology and the economy would not only determine a general direction, but would ultimately lead to only a single model of company regime surviving, namely the neoliberal model. That at least was the forecast – but it was wrong. The truth is, rather, that the organizational experiments of the 1980s and 1990s by no means led to company regimes of an exclusively neoliberal hue. Instead, a surprising range survived and, as indicated in chapter 1, they were not eradicated by the advance of financial market capitalist principles in business executives' boardrooms.[21]

In the following, I will not disregard the basic Marxist assumption that an asymmetry of power between capital and labour is an element that provides structure to company reality. At the same time, however, I will consider company regimes as a concrete expression of the conflict of interests and constraints on cooperation between management and workforce. In my view, approaches that rely solely on the rationality of *homo economicus* or *homo faber* do not do justice to the social relations which develop in a company. My interpretation of an industrial company is of a 'field of social action',[22] whose structures are neither exclusively the result of regulations, nor of the interest-based market and power strategies of businesses, nor of the counter-strategies of union representatives. Company regimes are a social and above all historical reality *sui generis*. As Hermann Kotthoff puts it: 'The idea of "social order" does not presume a certain form of coordination in action but assumes that in every company there is some form of coordination through which management and workforce are socially connected and consolidated.'[23] Accordingly, we need to examine the routines of social relations and the connections and mutual responsibilities that exist amongst the various actors in a company. My interest is in social practices that are defined and sometimes even eroded and turned into empty rhetoric by institutional regulations. My premise is that company regimes are influenced by the patterns of social and political order which the actors bring with them to the workplace.

This also means that company regimes are constantly contested and that they can be interpreted as outcomes of conflicts over participation on the shopfloor. If management succeeds in determining the corporate social structure unilaterally and can bring the workforce to accept and support this preordained order, we speak of a monocratic company regime. If, on the other hand, the workforce is mobilized or organized and is able to assert itself, two types of company regime are established: cooperative and consensus-oriented or confrontational and conflict-oriented. Either side can of course withdraw from the mutual respect and responsibilities not legally stipulated and instead insist on keeping to the formal order, particularly of employment contracts, or rely solely and unilaterally on their own abilities and vision. Then the result is contract-based company regimes with labour relations based solely on power and interests. All four of these basic types of regimes were widespread in Western Europe. Their concrete implementation came in many different forms and social researchers have given them a variety of different names. In the following, I will make as sparing use of them as possible and return to the four basic types (see table 7.1) so as to be better able to explain the most important tendencies.

One further preliminary remark is necessary. Battles for social recognition and relational equality are marked by social drama and emotionality. This divides them from routine and ritualized negotiations over pay, working hours, shift schedules and workplace design. These negotiations also take place within the company, but merely reproduce an existing and generally accepted or tolerated company regime.

Table 7.1 Types of company regime

	Monocratic	Pluralistic
Socially integrative	Paternalistic and patriarchal companies	Cooperative and consensus-oriented Confrontational and conflict-oriented
Contractual	'Workhouses'	'Market societies'

The company as an interface of solidarities and ties

I will now focus on specific countries and take a closer look at those social relationships within an industrial company that played a role in building up a company regime. At least four different types of these relationships can be distinguished.

The first type of relationship is based on a sense of solidarity and community building (*Vergemeinschaftung*) arising from having a particular skill or occupation. As members of their occupational groups, skilled workers, technicians and engineers retained their special status and shared identity over decades and defended it against management. They represented correspondingly closely knit status groups which in most companies had a pronounced sense of self-confidence and a clearly defined self-image, distinguishing them from the rest of the workforce. In previous chapters, we have seen that traditional divisions of labour and demarcations between occupational groups were affected by technological and organizational changes in production processes. Such changes were also reflected in the income, scope, authority and status of the various occupational groups and necessarily led to shifts in their relationships to each other within the company.

In many British factories, for example, when crisis hit the old industrial occupational hierarchies and divisions of labour, the internal social order was deeply shaken. Since management had largely left union-based workers to organize the details of the production process in the company themselves, specific privileges for certain occupational groups, which had often been defended with a zealous hostility towards the company, had become increasingly anachronistic. The status-based participatory model collapsed as the companies became less competitive. This left a gap in organization mainly filled since 1980 by corporate initiatives profiting from the anti-union course of the Conservative governments. Many companies established forms of labour and communication channels that aimed to strengthen ties between individuals and weaken solidarity between groups linked by trade unions or specific occupations.

In West Germany, the tradition of sector-specific trade unions meant that there was not a decidedly company-hostile tendency in occupational group relations. In many companies, it was engineers and skilled workers who formed the core groups cooperating between workforce and management. The institutional basis for this combination of a sense of identification both with the company and with

243

their status group came from company collective bargaining, in which skilled workers regularly took on key positions. The social basis for this model was provided by longer-term employment in one company and in-company promotion prospects.

I have deliberately overemphasized the contrast between the situation in Britain and West Germany to make it clear that traditions of community building within a company were not *per se* hostile to company-related offers of integration. Since the 1980s, company managers in all three countries increasingly used this situation in various ways to tie individual groups within the workforce more closely to the company. This applied, for example, to young skilled workers and technicians, who found that the technical changes resulting from digitalization at work could offer new prospects and career opportunities.[24]

Second, an important role in community building was played by relationships established by concrete work contexts within a company. Particularly in large companies, they were the most important concrete social unit to which company regimes were related and were significantly affected by the reorganization of work processes since the 1980s. Teamwork did not replace the strict and small-scale division of labour but rather existed alongside it. Methods of self-monitoring and self-regulating work teams were on the rise. Individualized work processes using new technologies were 're-Taylorized' and developed side-by-side with the team-related 'enrichment' and 'professionalization' of industrial work. This altered the conditions for the design of company regimes. These innovations in the organization of the production process in particular have attracted the attention of industrial sociologists, resulting in numerous studies of social relations in work teams.[25] Growing demands on quality with tight deadlines and pressures on budgets meant that company social citizenship with its demands on time and costs was seriously restricted. I will be examining what this meant in concrete terms in more detail later by looking at the working environment in the French, British and German automobile industries during this period of upheaval.

Factories, large and small, represent the third focus for community building within the workforce. Unsurprisingly, it is only in the small and medium-sized companies that the factory is a manageable and tangible social space. In larger companies with several production halls and departments and 1,000 or more employees, it is in contrast usually the management and/or the representatives of the workforce who ensure that the wider company can become the concrete object

244

of affiliation, obligation or commitment. Chapter 1 showed that since the 1970s in all three countries the proportion of workers in small and medium-sized factories increased significantly, resulting in the number of industrial workers in large factories with more than 1,000 employees in 1995 being just under 16 per cent in Britain and 31 per cent in Germany (see above, table 1.3).

This trend reversal was accompanied by a further decentralization of decision-making powers and partial responsibilities to individual production sites or departments in the company, so that as an abstract focus, the large factory lost its significance for industrial relations within the overall picture. At the same time, however, the concentration of capital continued to advance. Many small and medium-sized enterprises only survived as subsidiaries of large multi-national concerns or were the property of holding companies, and their management was by no means autonomous in its entrepreneurial strategies. This resulted in similar trends in company regimes. A very strange world of survival communities emerged within companies in which workforces fought for the continued existence of their factory and their jobs. In the process, they either trusted the management for competent leadership or felt that they had been 'betrayed and sold' by it, as was illustrated at the beginning of this chapter by the example of the externally controlled French furniture company Ranger. Direct dependence on markets (for their own products as well as for their own company) had an immediate influence on the social climate in many smaller and medium-sized companies.

The fourth type of relationship relevant for community building in a company is between the workforce and the company or corporate group, to be taken here for the sake of analysis as separate from the individual factory. As a rule, it was the corporate management that concerned itself with the development and maintenance of this relationship, and in many cases this was successful, as, for example, in the case of IBM, Krupp, Unilever and Renault. This kind of corporate philosophy or corporate culture is usually the product of a long and successful company history. Often prominent entre-preneurs or managers had initially forged these company regimes and introduced special social benefits when the company was estab-lished and expanding. They also ensured that the 'superiority of the masters' was legally prescribed and embedded in the corporate culture and presented in a form that was tolerated, if not accepted, by the workforce. This kind of socially integrative corporate tradition was generally expressed in active company policy in the form of substantial additional benefits for some or all of the workforce, from cheap company housing to holiday and leisure facilities and company pensions. Examples of this kind of company tradition can be found in all three countries. In Britain, for example, the food companies Rowntree (from 1969 Rowntree Macintosh) and Cadbury, founded and run by Quaker families, distinguished themselves with a pronounced socially integrative corporate philosophy. In Germany, the new electrical companies that had been expanding since the beginning of the twentieth century, such as Bosch, AEG and Siemens, had positive corporate social policies. In all these cases, the company executives considered their management style and these social policies an integral part of their corporate identity and a trademark of their eminent position as leaders in the market or industry. Traces of the socio-ethical motives of the company founders and owner families were also present in this model.

Significant changes to this kind of comprehensive corporate culture arose initially during the late 1970s and then in the 1990s. In the first decade of the transformation phase, the development and maintenance of such corporate affiliation had to keep up with the companies' Europeanization and internationalization. The next challenge then came with the takeovers and mergers of the 1990s, when it became evident that the symbolic and practical integration into new global corporations was successful only in particularly favourable circumstances even at management level. At the end of the 1990s, the automobile company Daimler-Benz had fifty-four different production sites, and even medium-sized companies were producing at several different sites, many of them abroad. The workforce at the individual sites either remained unaffected or were faced with new forms of internal competition between the different sites for lucrative contracts and production. This tended to increase local solidarity amongst the workforce rather than solidarity towards the central company. An institutional counterbalance, albeit a weak one, was created by the introduction of European works councils.[26]

The workforce of successful medium-sized industrial companies that managed to internationalize rapidly in the 1990s experienced an interesting development. The number of employees in the 1,356 'hidden champions' studied by Hermann Simon – that is, market-leading or market-dominating medium-sized companies – grew overall by 59 per cent between 1995 and 2005. A significantly greater number of these jobs were located abroad (+110 per cent) rather than in Germany (+28 per cent), so that the proportion of foreign workers but also of international work teams and cooperation within the company increased considerably.[27]

246

A comparison of institutional frameworks and long-term effects in the three countries

In Germany, there is a long tradition of company-based and company-centred cooperation between capital and labour.[28] From the end of World War I, statutory regulation of worker participation in companies was variously and repeatedly renewed and ensured institutional commitment to cooperation between capital and labour in pursuit of the overall goal of production as a public asset. This is even true of the twelve years of the Nazi dictatorship. Although the overall guiding principles of a company community were unilaterally dictated in favour of its management by the authoritarian Nazi regime, the idea of mutual obligation was still firmly established and extended.[29] The basic institutional difference that emerged in West Germany and also constitutes the demarcation line between monocratic and pluralistic company regimes in Germany can be summed up as 'company regimes with or without works councils'. In the case of small companies, however, the demarcation line is blurred because comparable company regimes can be found with and without works councils.[30] The long tradition of the representation of interests at the workplace, unique in this form in Europe, led in turn to the development of a particularly broad range of different forms of company-based cooperation between union representatives on works councils and corporate management.

The situation in Britain was quite different. There, works councils or similar means of representing the workforce remained the exception rather than the rule and the design of company regimes was legally a matter for collective bargaining or a private affair between the company and its workforce. According to the industrial sociologist T.H. Marshall, the British trade union movement lacked any willingness to accept mutual obligations for the sake of the company.[31] An additional factor was that, as we saw above, after the economic and political defeats of the militant trade union movement in the strikes of the late 1970s and 1980s, the balance of power between management, workforce and trade unions in many companies changed so rapidly and profoundly that new company regimes often appeared without any collective representation of the interests of the workforce. This meant that the change of company regimes after the boom took place in Britain largely unhindered by any institutional restrictions and was left to situation-specific, informal negotiations between the actors in the company. It is,

247

however, revealing that after the rapid decline of joint consultative committees in the 1980s (from 32 per cent to 21 per cent of the companies studied between 1981 and 1990), their number rose slightly in the 1990s and had stabilized at 24 per cent by 1998. A section of the management also decided to concede more participation rights to their own workforce, in line with the principles of human resource management.[32]

In France in the 1970s, the legislature supported actors and measures that backed social partnerships in companies, but only with limited success. Given the dominance of monocratic company regimes with authoritarian tendencies, the labour struggles since 1968 had in many companies taken on the character of a workforce revolt against dictates and control 'from above'. By means of confrontational powers of veto and protest, they triggered the first wave of revision of these authoritarian, paternalistic traditions. Economic crises and deindustrialization, however, soon left these trade union strategies very little room for manoeuvre within the companies. This meant that when the militancy and mobilization of the trade unions began to decline, the statutory representation of workers' interests introduced earlier was something of a lifeline safeguarding worker participation at company level. Most of the large state-owned companies, on the other hand, went down their own path of liberal-pluralistic company regimes, as they had already included a major role for trade union co-determination rights since 1945, particularly in staff policy and the administration of their mostly well-developed social institutions and special benefits.

It is clear that the sector of industry to which a company belongs is central to its corporate climate and company regime. We have only to consider the different industrial work environments such as breweries, textile factories, canning factories, shipyards and glassworks, or the fact that major sectors such as the automobile, chemical and electrical industries had completely different production processes and subsections and had developed correspondingly diverse social regimes at company level. So it also seems clear that a comparison of three countries focussing on similarities, differences and general trends can in this respect at most offer a cursory overview. It can, however, provide at least an idea of the range of different situations specific to the particular industrial sector.

The old world of the 'industrial labourer' in the coal, iron and steel industries had created company regimes in all three countries that had a surprising number of common features, in spite of numerous distinctive traditions specific to the respective country.

Until the 1970s, steel production and coal mining were still characterized by hard physical labour carried out at a considerable risk to health. At the core of company regimes was essentially the so-called 'crew' system of hierarchically organized work teams, consisting mainly of unskilled and semi-skilled workers and structured internally according to experience, expertise and seniority.[33] At the same time, the workforces of the coal, iron and steel industries were decidedly company-oriented and so developed a strong affiliation to their own production site. Their own steelworks or their own colliery became the typical focus of group-specific community-building processes. These were always accompanied by a stubborn, though not necessarily ideologically antagonistic, self-assertion towards the local management. Authoritarian paternalistic models were dominant in the steelworks and collieries and their companies until well into the twentieth century. Participatory rights were then granted to the workforces and cooperative company regimes developed as a result of political upheavals such as nationalization (of the coal industry and parts of the steel industry in France and Britain), the introduction of company collective bargaining and workers' co-determination (*Montanmitbestimmung*) (in West Germany) and the general shift to the political left in the immediate postwar period. The company regimes based on the hierarchical 'crew' system increasingly lost significance as the technology in coal and steel production was revolutionized. This led to a paradigm shift in work organization, particularly in the steel industry in the wake of the steel crisis at the end of the 1970s. As a result, the work of skilled individuals at large technically sophisticated machines became the new focus for cooperative company regimes, which in some respects began to resemble those in the mechanical engineering industries.[34]

In the mechanical engineering industries in all three countries, strong professional traditions influenced in-company relationships, both for the dominant group of skilled workers and for technicians and engineers.[35] After World War II, many companies in this sector were able to establish technical, production-centred cooperation models on a pluralistic basis because management often found it necessary to make concessions to its technically competent, unionized workers in matters of co-determination and internal structuring. As a result, cooperative company regimes with widely differing institutional bases prevailed in this sector.

The situation was very different in many food and textile companies. Work was organized on the basis of a clear distinction between skilled workers (in maintenance and repairs) and unskilled or semi-skilled production workers. In many cases, this also meant a division between men and women as well as between local workers and migrant workers. Under these circumstances, particularly in small and medium-sized companies, patriarchal-paternalistic models remained intact. They persisted in the many firms that were founded during the postwar boom period and were far more widespread in all three countries at the beginning of the 1970s than would have been expected given the anti-authoritarian climate of public opinion dominant after the end of the previous decade. Kotthoff sums this up incisively when he describes workers in these autocratic-paternalistic models as 'children' who have to be cared for but also guided, punished and rewarded. The reality of these company regimes described above was by nature far removed from the model of industrial citizenship. The question of whether more 'pluralistic' or more 'contractual' models developed during our period of study depended on how both sides processed the conflict that led to the end of this kind of paternalistic company regime. Frequently, a disappointed management withdrew the provision of social benefits for its intransigent workers, requiring no more than their labour and performance, and both sides agreed on a minimalist model of a purely instrumental company regime. The unions then ensured that fair rules were kept and appropriate wages paid.

A further factor that had an influence on the structure of company regimes was the location of a factory and the local and regional work cultures that were the basis and focus of its internal organ-ization and social relations. These regional nuances have generally been ignored in comparative social science research since they are socio-cultural factors that tend to have long-term effects and as such are not easy to record. Yet it was hardly possible for small and medium-sized companies in particular to avoid the influence of local and regional customs and expectations. On the contrary, the social relationship patterns in these companies were largely based on the involvement and assertion of established local and regional traditions. There is no precise map of these varying regional work cultures over a large area for any of the three countries studied here, which means that fine regional differences cannot be meaning-fully addressed. I have to confine myself to overarching trends and will do so using case studies of just one branch of industry, which nevertheless played and still plays a significant role in all three economies.[36]

Company regimes in the automobile industry, 1970–2000

Since the 1970s, the automobile industry has become the most studied field of industrial sociological research, and, above all, there is fortunately no lack of international comparative studies.[37] This may be related to the fact that it was one of the key industries in Britain, France and Germany. The company regimes described in this section concerned 1.649 million workers in the three countries (see above, table 1.2).

The numerous company upheavals in this sector were triggered by a serious crisis in sales, production and profits in the Western European automobile industry in the 1970s. As we saw in chapter 3, the traditional Fordist assembly-line production came under pressure. Neither cooperative industrial relations nor autocratic-paternalistic company regimes were able to prevent strikes on the production line and trade unions demanding higher wages and/or more humane working conditions. In their diagnosis of the crisis, the management side frequently cited a high turnover rate in the workforce, high levels of sickness and declining discipline at the workplace. The turnover rate at the main Peugeot plant in Sochaux, for example, was 12 per cent at the beginning of the 1970s and the level of absence due to sickness 9 per cent. The gaps this caused were filled primarily by foreign workers, whose proportion of the workforce rapidly grew to 40 per cent.[38] The crisis on the assembly line, especially in British and French automobile companies, led to confrontational industrial relations – management and production workers distrusted each other.

Trade union demands to make assembly-line work more humane were taken seriously, for example, by Renault, VW and Daimler-Benz, which followed the example of the Swedish company Volvo in their aim to improve both productivity and the social situation, particularly in their assembly workshops.[39] In 1974, the Volvo works in Kalmar collaborated with trade unions to introduce a counter-model to the Taylorist organization of work. The assembly was carried out by teams who elected their own representatives and had a say in their work processes and organization. Individual assembly-line workers were assigned to different workstations and could vary their work processes.[40] The alternative to this 'social democratic path' was the introduction of robots and automatization. This was also chosen, particularly in the 1980s, but, as it soon turned out, with relatively modest results since only

251

a small proportion of production could be made more cost-effective in this way.[41]

A further factor was that after the recession in 1973–4, if not before, the global advance of Asian, particularly Japanese, competitors could no longer be ignored. They were rapidly conquering first North America but then also the markets in Europe. 'Toyotism' or 'lean production' inevitably became the reference point for the restructuring plans of British, French and German companies as well as their US competitors such as Ford and General Motors with European production sites and subsidiaries.[42] What is crucial for my topic is that not only did Japanese automobile production entail changes in the technical processes of manufacture but also its productivity advantages were based to a considerable extent on different company regimes. The common denominator was the active participation of production workers in the ongoing task of effecting lasting improvements to production processes, securing quality standards and making working hours and work processes more flexible. At Toyota, for example, there was a company regime which created a sense of community belonging. It offset extremely high demands on performance and identification with the company against lifelong employment, high wages, company social benefits, in-company promotion prospects (including for assembly-line workers) and business-friendly in-house trade unions.[43] This model also functioned because Toyota had a commanding position over suppliers whose dominant company regimes were autocratic-patriarchal, meaning that work was carried out under worse conditions and productivity was lower. They offered an alternative to any production workers who did not meet the performance requirements of the Toyota system.

Interestingly enough, specific historical and socio-cultural conditions did not permit Toyota's company regime to be simply imported. European car manufacturers adopted eye-catching elements of their system (such as quality control, just-in-time production and so on), but beyond this their main focus was on the cost reduction achieved by their Japanese competitors, mainly by cutting back warehousing and outsourcing sections of their production. In all three Western European countries. automobile manufacturers followed the Japanese and contracted out a large share of their production. As a result, an international market for the production of vehicle components developed between 1985 and 2000 and the large vehicle factories were surrounded by a whole new network of suppliers and subsidiaries working in direct cooperation with the large companies and directly controlled by them.[44] In this way, the automobile companies externalized some of the cost pressure and constraints of greater flexibility forced on them by the rise in competition. They also gained or retained enough scope for developing new company regimes in their own factories.

Three factors were particularly important for such new company regimes: the restructuring of the deployment of labour by introducing work groups and teams; a massive reduction in the workforce; and the increased flexibility of working hours. They affected all areas of vehicle manufacturing. Contemporary studies on forms of team and group work specific to particular companies or factories show that the individual factories dealt with them quite differently.[45] However, in the majority of European companies, the legacy of Fordist organization of labour, the central planning of production processes and the 'science-based organization of work' remained extremely influential.[46] What did disappear more or less without trace was the authoritarian management style in the factory workshops. In the politicized strikes of the late 1960s and 1970s, as we saw in chapter 3, the focus was also on social recognition of the unskilled and semi-skilled assembly-line workers, especially when they were migrant workers or women.

This transformation of manufacturing processes took place at approximately the same pace as the constant increase in international competition in the automobile sector. In the recession of 1980–2, if not before, vehicle manufacturers were at increasing risk of losing sections of their production to other factories or suppliers and their workforces were constantly faced with the threat of being 'wound up'. This meant that securing the survival of their own factory became a central issue for workers' representatives and again strengthened orientation towards the specific local factory that already existed in the automobile industry. In all three countries, the dominance of company-based collective bargaining also contributed to the development of strong company loyalties. In this situation, both management and trade union representatives discovered they had a joint interest in cooperative company regimes, even where strikes and confrontational solutions of everyday conflicts had previously dominated.

The General Motors factory in Ellesmere Port near Liverpool is a good example of this. At the end of the 1990s, it employed 4,500 people. Between 1975 and 1979, industrial relations there had reached an all-time low and culminated in a three-month-long conflict triggered by an announcement by the management that it wished to re-establish control of production. In 1989, after

253

redundancies and outsourcing of production, the management and the trade union (here the main union in the factory, the Transport and General Workers' Union – TGWU) agreed on a programme of rationalization and modernization (the V6 agreement). It included a mutually agreed restructuring of production, the introduction of permanent quality enhancement systems, means of increasing productivity and improving health and safety at work, the protection of 'workers' dignity' and a commitment to teamwork and mutual trust and cooperation. Joint committees of management and union delegates were responsible for the implementation of this agreement, which itself then became the basis for further investment by General Motors in Ellesmere Port in the 1990s.[47]

The confrontational industrial relations that had dominated British and French automobile factories since the early 1970s, and had in turn developed since the 1960s from a variety of different partly authoritarian-monocratic, partly liberal-pluralistic company regimes, disappeared from the scene practically without trace. They were remembered by the management as a menacing past when production processes were threatened by strikes and by the older generation of trade union members as a heroic past when opposition was successful, but their influence on company social relations diminished after the 1980s.[48] This was true both at the level of the shopfloor, where the power of the trade union countervailing model and its protagonists (shop stewards and trade union delegates) was based, but also at the level of the individual factory or even company. Large companies such as Renault, Peugeot, Rover and Ford succeeded in using the wave of rationalization in the 1980s and 1990s to establish new social relations in their factories. Trade unions were now tolerated in all companies and accepted as partners in negotiations on company level. At the same time, the section of the trade union movement oriented to class conflict and opposition was deliberately marginalized and systematically delegitimized.[49] A major contribution to this was made by the new management ideologies. Inspired by the international discourse of human resource management, they formulated company-specific ideals of participation and community. This was the basis for the development of a type of company regime that depended on tolerating the participation of elected delegates but making more targeted and intensive use than before of methods of involving individual workers directly in the company. Taking Peugeot as an example, observers have spoken of a modern form of paternalistic company regime.[50] Trade unions and workers' representatives were still important if not indispensable as negotiating partners for company agreements on more flexible working hours and the deployment of labour and as a peacekeeping authority in the case of conflicts. Thus there were also simple economic reasons for this kind of limited, liberal-pluralistic cooperation model becoming predominant.[51]

In the Japanese factories set up in France and Britain during the 1980s and 1990s (Toyota in Valenciennes, Nissan in Sunderland, Honda in Swindon), management also sought to establish cooperative industrial relations and brought with them a complete programme of offers of integration to help build a sense of community. In all these cases, the management profited from the fact that the factories were founded at a time when the effects of the crisis of the old company regimes in the British automobile industry were still being felt and the introduction of company-related cooperative industrial relations met with little resistance from the new workforces. The opening of the new factory in Sunderland, for example, allowed management to keep a variety of sector-specific trade unions out of the factory and to accept only one union as its negotiating partner. At the same time, the model of 'social partnership from above' was unilaterally institutionalized as a binding operational framework (see figure 7.1).[52] This did not necessarily mean that the Japanese-style company community was incorporated into everyday working life in British automobile factories, but elements of paternalistic company involvement, which had previously been negligible in Britain, increased significantly.

However, the example of the new Toyota factory in Valenciennes, in the industrial north of France, which began production in 2001, shows that programmes to impose the idea of a company community from above according to the Japanese model were not necessarily successful. The management in Valenciennes was unable to tie the newly recruited young workforce to the company in the long term. This was because low wages and limited promotion prospects led not only to frequent resignations and a high staff turnover, but also to an increase in conflict between production workers and middle management, who then used repressive measures against supporters and members of the confrontational CGT union. This culminated in an eighteen-day strike in 2009, the first in a Toyota factory since 1950 (see figure 7.2).[53]

In British factories, workforce participation was restricted to quality control procedures, the distribution of time and tasks within individual units and the involvement of delegates from the workforce and the trade unions. It was not extended to concrete planning of production or decisions about investment. In Germany, the situation

Figure 7.1   100,000 Bluebirds: employees at the Nissan works in Sunderland, 1989.

In 1989, the 100,000th 'British Bluebird' drove off the assembly line. Workers from all departments and levels joined the management round the Bluebird and one of many similar photos of this new British industry was taken. In this presentation of the company community, two participants are particularly noteworthy: the worker in the foreground in the overalls who is holding the car keys in his right hand and resting his left arm on 'his' car and the Japanese manager who is standing on the right next to the car and wearing overalls over his suit.

Figure 7.2 Toyota workers on strike in Valenciennes, 2009.

In 2001, Toyota began production at a new factory close to the city of Valenciennes in northern France. Here again a Japanese automobile manufacturer settled in a region affected by the decline of traditional industries. But unlike the development in Sunderland in Britain, the militant attitude of the industrial workforce had survived the economic upheaval. Over the years, tensions between the workforce and management continued to grow. Eventually, barricades outside the French factory were set alight in 2009.

was different. West German works councils had gained significantly more participation rights within the institutional framework of co-determination, so that among other things they negotiated decisions about investment and production planning. A distinctly corporatist co-management system developed especially in the works councils at VW and was secured by corresponding company agreements. When the West German automobile industry experienced a major sales crisis in 1993–4 and a further round of rationalization was introduced in companies and factories, these cooperative agreements were still honoured on both sides.[54] All the important decisions about the future at VW between 1975 and 2000 were based on company agreements, important aspects of which the IG Metall union and the works councils had helped to shape. The agreements of 1998 were spectacular. By agreeing on major reductions in working hours, they prevented large-scale redundancies. The reduction of working hours with partial pay cuts but with job guarantees was a compromise which was supported by a substantial majority of the workforce and was due to the fact that the culture of co-determination had become established as a successful factor in crisis management (see figure 7.3). At VW, those aspects of industrial relations that were based on social recognition and relational equality were evidently consolidated. At Daimler, BMW, Opel and Ford, the corporatist characteristics of their company regimes were also further consolidated when they were faced with tougher competition in the 1980s and 1990s. The management of West German automobile factories was typically more prepared to give its workforce more autonomy when it came, for example, to the introduction of teamwork than was the case in France or Britain.[55] In the 1980s, economic studies already came to the conclusion that West German production models that were based on co-determination gave them an advantage in productivity over their competitors. Although the significance of such snapshots should not be overestimated, they do illustrate the economic background to the continuity that was typical of social relations in most automobile factories in West Germany during this period of upheaval.[56]

In the supplier factories in the three countries, however, the situation was often completely different from that in the workshops of the large companies. If they did not have a dominant position in their own market segment and therefore sufficient negotiating power over the price specifications and oversight requirements of their major customers, the individual companies and their factories were exposed to considerable pressure from the market. Last-minute orders and deliveries, quality controls in their factories by their major

Figure 7.3   Cover of the business magazine *Die Wirtschaftswoche* of 5 November 1993 on the four-day week at Volkswagen.

At the beginning of November 1993, the cover of one of the magazines that was compulsory reading for the Frankfurt stock exchange, *Die Wirtschaftswoche*, showed a brightly shining sun in front of a red background. It was triggered by the agreement reached between the VW management and the trade union IG Metall on a four-day week. The fact that the cover picture of this business-friendly magazine could refer to the strikes for the 35-hour week in 1984 proves that the trade unions continued to be influential. Yet repeated economic crises and continuing mass unemployment had led to a notable shift in the balance of power within society as a whole. In order to prevent further mass redundancies, IG Metall was prepared to accept considerable reductions in wages and special agreements outside those reached by sector-wide collective bargaining.

customers, cost pressures and planning insecurity were the adverse conditions against which the companies, especially those in the third and fourth ranks, had to struggle.[57]

In order to illustrate how company regimes developed under these circumstances, and how the frequently described 'marketization tendencies' affected company relations, I will refer to an example from a study of rationalization measures in the late 1990s. It examined a variety of different companies in the locally dense car manufacturing sector in the Saarland area in Germany. Of the 40,000 workers employed in this sector in the region, only 6,000 worked directly for Ford, so for one of the large automobile companies; 20,000 worked for companies that only supplied automobile companies and a further 10,000 for subcontractors. These 'amputated companies'[58] were production sites belonging solely to outside, non-local companies and were linked by an 'immense acceleration of the pace of rationalization'.[59] The working atmosphere and labour relations in some of these companies, though by no means all, were determined by high demands on flexibility from the automobile companies, short-term supply contracts and a commitment to reduce prices. In one particular factory, the pressure of reducing costs led to an adaptation strategy that attempted to combine the introduction of more technology and automation with more intensive Taylorist control over all work processes and the fully flexible deployment of production workers to all workstations. Labour relations were based on mutual distrust between management and workers and in the end the factory functioned as a mere 'workhouse', held together by cost pressures, control and piecework. In the words of two sociological observers of this authoritarian 'Taylorism': 'The idealized notions of the new management philosophy seem out of place in the straitjacket of just-in-time production. The benevolent pathos of self-responsibility, self-regulation and social competence does not fit into a reality determined by time constraints, work pressure, the constant struggle to survive and social coldness.'[60]

Another company had also hugely increased its productivity but relied on the self-motivation of its workforce through teamwork and job rotation as well as transparent wage incentives. Faced with production costs that threatened the existence of the company, management and workforce, represented by the works council, reorganized the whole system of work and wages. Teamwork and productivity-oriented wages transformed the factory into a 'cooperative market society' in which management and workforce had negotiated a transparent market deal on their share of productivity gains. The key to this system was that individual production groups were offered maximum wage premiums if they agreed at the same time to raise the levels of standard performance for their team piece rate. With its 1,000 employees, this company had 120 semi-autonomous teams whose members were all trained technically and socially for the new work processes and whose right to self-direction had been clearly established. The intensity of work and increase in performance were 'safeguarded' by a company regime that was negotiated by the works council in return for supplementary benefits such as for lower-performing workers. The workforce considered this an improvement because it promised higher wages for more qualified work and more recognition and independence for the majority of production workers.[61] The establishment of this 'cooperative market society' was a race against time, since it was unclear whether it would succeed in maintaining the pace of productivity increases and quality improvements that had guaranteed its success during its initial transition years.

A third case study concerns the Bosch factory in the Saarland. The pressure to rationalize did not enter the factory gates during the 1990s, while within the factory a modern form of paternalistic factory regime was in practice. It ensured that work on the Taylorist production line of this price-determining market leader ran like clockwork, that the women working on the assembly line were paid by the hour, that there were employment opportunities for people with serious disabilities and that fixed teams strengthened the social ties and cohesion among the production workers, most of whom were unskilled women.[62] The company's previous rigid, authoritarian management style had adapted to the principles of contemporary management philosophy, but the introduction of teamwork hardly changed the routines of the work processes and had even less impact on the 'unbroken paternalist social order'.[63]

These three regional snapshots from the West German supply sector show that even under difficult economic conditions and tightened external controls, company actors still had room for manoeuvre. They also show, however, the factors that these company solutions had to contend with in order to be successful: the pressure to rationalize, the qualification structure of the workforce and, not least, local labour markets and workers' cultures.

A telling example of the weight of regional factors is given by a company study from 1991 that examined a supplier in South Wales in more detail. The factory was founded in the late 1960s, and after it had changed hands four times it was bought by one of the large multinational component companies. Its main customers were Volvo, Nissan, Rover and Honda.[64] Of the total workforce of 225, 180 were industrial workers and of these 80 per cent were women, all of whom worked on the shopfloor, while the management and skilled workers were all men. The company regime was that of an improvised market society that found itself constantly struggling to maintain its quality standards and to react flexibly so as to cope with the demands of its overpowerful major customers. The company also paid slightly under the local average wage but most of the men and women employed there saw no realistic alternative on the local labour market, which was suffering from high long-term unemployment following the closure of the pits and the steelworks. The trade union representatives were cooperative and accepted by the management as legitimate representatives of the workers' interests and as mediators and arbitrators. The continuing existence of the factory relied essentially on the fact that management errors and structural weaknesses could be ironed out by means of improvisation that went beyond the newly established regulations of 'just-in-time' and 'total quality' management, and pragmatic compromises were reached between management and workers' representatives. In many ways, it was the typical strengths of British industrial culture that were brought to bear in the labour relations of this small branch of a multinational company in Wales. However, it also became clear in the study that the survival of this community was not secure in the long term and was precarious. The average length of service was four years, and so most workers had very few ties to the company. Nevertheless, they supported its struggle for survival daily through their tireless efforts at production improvisation.[65]

Several company studies carried out in 1996 in French component factories paint a similar picture. In many of the thirty-six companies studied, the work conditions that were described met the category of 'workhouse' or 'market society' in terms of their company regime. Many of the companies had a particularly young workforce who were recruited by means of elaborate testing and selection procedures and were initially employed on fixed contracts before they were offered a permanent contract.[66] Fluctuations in production, frequently only predictable at short notice, were offset by agency workers or part-time workers, for example for special late shifts. This kind of arrangement in the company inevitably tied only some types of workers to the company in the long term. On the one hand, these were young, hard-working and capable workers who did their job while dreaming of being able to move to a company that would be altogether more attractive, for example the nearby car manufacturer. The other workers tied to the factory were those whose prospects on the labour market were poor because they were insufficiently or inappropriately qualified or because of their age and/or their background.[67] If these kinds of relations developed in companies that had previously been managed under more favourable market conditions and in a more autocratic-patriarchal style under different owners or directors, injuries and absences of older workers were particularly prevalent. To a certain extent, the soul had been taken out of these market societies. Solidarities and ties were sacrificed on the altar of efficiency, flexibility and profit – with correspondingly negative consequences for the corporate climate. The risk of losing the support of the workforce in difficult times was high, and it was this loss in particular, not only the lack of social recognition, which made these companies susceptible to conflicts when business slumped.

The above studies also show that medium-sized French suppliers occupying market niches as specialists and employing mainly skilled workers tended to organize their factory regimes differently. In some cases, close cooperative relations continued between management and representatives of the workforce active in the trade unions. This was true, for example, of a supplier with 250 workers that specialized in 'coldworking' metal parts. One of the main reasons for its excellent position in the market was that it encouraged cooperative relations with workers' representatives from the trade unions, reflected in the rejection of agency work and fixed-term contracts and leading to wage levels above those collectively agreed for the sector.[68] A different variant of this kind of 'production community' was practised in another highly specialized medium-sized metalworking company with approximately 100 employees, whose workforce was made up almost exclusively of skilled workers. The ideology followed here was classic and patriarchal, perpetuating a family tradition whose principles were good, 'humane' social relations in the factory as well as above-average wages and high-quality products. In a similar way to the above example of Bosch, the continuation of this socially integrative business philosophy was based on the company being a market leader and independent of the automobile companies and major companies in the supply sector.[69]

In summary, it can be said that in the factories of the surviving automobile companies and the large suppliers in all three countries there was a trend towards cooperative labour relations. However, social partnership was interpreted differently. In Britain and France, it was implemented by companies such as Peugeot, Toyota, Nissan and Ford to tie their workforce more closely to them, preferably without the involvement of the trade unions. Companies located in West Germany, however, used the tradition of trade union cooperation and the mechanisms of co-determination to negotiate rationalization and increases in productivity with IG Metall and the works councils in a socially acceptable and consensual manner. The kind of co-management practised at VW represented the most far-reaching variety of cooperative social order.

On the other hand, the ever-increasing world of suppliers remained an area in which socially integrative patterns played a role only in a very small number of companies. Most of the company regimes in this sector of the automobile industry developed under harsh market conditions towards the models of rationalized 'market societies' or repressive 'workhouses' in which performance pressure, Taylorized work processes and comparatively lower wages were at best contained by in-company controls, but where little was done to develop a company identity or forms of industrial citizenship. Between these two extremes, individual companies can be found in which the workforce and management had at least selectively agreed on improvised 'alliances for work' (*Bündnisse für Arbeit*) with the aim of securing the survival of the company. Overall, however, it is noticeable that, especially in larger companies, pluralistic factory regimes became established which depended in one way or another on the cooperation of the workforce, represented by elected delegates, usually from the trade unions, with the management. This finding belies contemporary expectations that Japanese factory communities would also belong to the future in Europe and that the visions of brave new worlds in Western European automobile manufacturing sketched out in the relevant handbooks and manuals would sooner or later become reality.

Exceptional normality: after the breakdown of company regimes

At the end of this chapter, I would like to take a step back and by way of conclusion identify three paradigmatic constellations of problems which confronted the corporate actors in these three countries and to give examples of solutions. What were the exceptionally normal situations and conflicts in West European companies between 1975 and 2000, and what was the response to them?

First, we can cite the acute crises which arose when the survival of the factory or company was at stake, for instance because the economic climate shifted to their disadvantage. In Germany, for example, in the context of the recession of 1992–3, 'alliances for work' were created in some companies. These were company agreements or wage settlements whose aim was to protect jobs but which included concessions from the workforce in return. These kinds of corporate pacts were also concluded in large companies,[70] but they were particularly widespread in small and medium-sized firms, where they developed further into production communities and partnerships of convenience made up of industrial citizens. We have already come across early variants of this type in the context of the factory occupations in the 1970s. The continuation of production by the workers of the watch-maker LIP, which I analysed in detail in chapter 3, was embraced as an alternative to the threat of closure or company bankruptcy, particularly in France. Here, the framework for these company regimes was provided by the anti-capitalist programme of *autogestion* (workers' self-management). They were generally oriented internally towards the alternative cooperative models of production which had quietly accompanied the triumph of capitalist enterprise since the nineteenth century.

In the 1990s, partnerships of convenience between owners and workers frequently evolved which resembled 'alliances for work'. In effect, shop stewards slipped into the role of co-managers and mobilized their workforces to support sweeping changes in production and the organization of the company – all in close cooperation and formally agreed with the company management. Such situations have been illustrated in reports from the 1990s on West German shop stewards and their work. They show shop stewards taking over tasks in their company that were otherwise allocated to management or consultancy firms: drawing up plans to raise productivity and participating in the development of products and the restructuring of the organization. In every case, the aim was to rescue the company and to protect jobs, or at least to make any necessary redundancies socially acceptable.[71] The programmes included reducing wages, undercutting limits agreed in collective wage agreements by introducing flexible working hours and offering opportunities for further qualification and retraining. This kind of production community was, however, to be found not only in crisis-ridden companies but also in flourishing businesses, for example in mechanical engineering, where a change of generation and/or ownership led to the end of monocratic regimes. Examples can be found in studies of small and medium-sized West

German companies at the end of the 1980s.[72] They demonstrate that even in those companies which were previously organized on a hierarchical basis with an autocratic-patriarchal management style, the significance of production-oriented community building increased substantially.[73]

These 'democratic production communities' are not simply exceptional cases. They are, in fact, an indicator of the basic structural change in the nature of industrial work evident in many work processes and working environments in all three countries. As Western European industrial companies were increasingly forced to reinvent themselves in order to be able to sell new products with new machines in new organizational structures to new customers, it became evident that the experience-based competence of skilled workers, technicians and engineers was indispensable. The general trend towards marketization described in chapter 1, however, also meant that workforces were now forced to become involved in business evaluation procedures, cost calculations and profit-level expectations if they wanted to secure their jobs. Conversely, company management realized that it could significantly increase its chances of success if it was able and willing to initiate a 'social partnership revolution' in its companies. The 'production community' model was a response to this situation. However, it could only be successfully introduced in those companies that employed a majority of workers who already had or were willing to acquire skills and qualifications relevant to the innovations required by this transition.

The second typical constellation of problems concerns the establishment of pluralistic company regimes or the 'arduous exodus from small-scale patriarchy'.[74] As described above, in many companies, monocratic management styles were replaced by a regime based on negotiation and cooperation, in which management accepted elected workers' representatives as independent actors. In the follow-up study on company co-determination in West German companies carried out by Kotthoff and others in 1990, as many as two-thirds of the companies that had still had an autocratic-patriarchal structure in 1975 had undergone this kind of change of status, mostly accompanied by dramatic emotional conflict before the new *modus vivendi* could be established. The struggle for social recognition in these companies was usually led by a small group of protagonists or sometimes individual prominent spokespeople who did not shy away from personal conflict with the boss or bosses and in this way boosted the collective solidarity of the workforce against the status quo. They practically transported the demands for democratic participation articulated in all three countries in the 1970s into their companies and forced industrial citizenship to be recognized both socially and morally.

This can be illustrated by the case of a medium-sized West German metalworking company with several hundred employees. A test of strength in the form of a one-day strike in 1984 was won by the new chair of the works council. He successfully opposed the chief executive, who was still head of management but only owned a 50 per cent share of the company. When the company was taken over in 1987 by a larger concern which had already had shares in the organization, the new management switched over to the revised policy of pluralistic cooperation without batting an eyelid.[75]

The third constellation of problems concerns the upheaval caused when firms whose social relations were firmly anchored in company tradition and local work cultures entered the critical phase of deindustrialization and were suddenly faced with a sales crisis, rationalization and a change of ownership. This happened to two traditional companies in Britain, more precisely in Willenhall in the West Midlands, the centre of British key and lock manufacturing since the early nineteenth century. Both of these major firms had cultivated a paternalistic company culture until the 1980s, continuing a long tradition of the originally family-run businesses. Their company culture was closely linked to the local work culture by typical elements such as sports clubs, social clubs, family affiliations over several generations and in-company promotion prospects.[76] The representation of workers' interests by the local professional or sector-specific trade unions was also part of this traditional social order. At the same time, it preserved a strict division of labour between men and women in the factories. Before the upheavals of the late 1980s and early 1990s, two-thirds of the workers were female. They worked on the assembly line or in the packaging department while the more highly qualified jobs in maintenance, repair and development were reserved for men. This traditional gender-specific division of labour following Taylorist principles was reinforced by the fact that frequently whole families or kinship networks were employed in the two companies.[77]

In 1988, the regimes in these companies came under pressure when the whole of the British lock and key industry became a desirable asset for financial investors whose business model was to buy up unprofitable companies with attractive brand names at low prices and merge and restructure them so that either the large, newly amalgamated corporation could be placed successfully on the stock market or individual segments could be sold on. After a short spell in US ownership, the two companies (Chubb and Yale Locks) ended up in the hands of a British industrial holding company, Williams. Williams Holdings was created by financial experts Nigel Rudd and Brian McGovern in 1982 and by the end of the decade had grown into a flourishing company on the British stock exchange with both a high turnover and high returns. When their business strategy failed in the security industry, Chubb and Yale went through a series of mergers, divisions and resales between 1997 and 2000 and finally ended up as the property of the Swedish multinational Assa Abloy.

This is a particularly stark example of innovative business models from the pioneering days[78] of financial market capitalism, whose core elements included dispatching 'modern' management teams to restructure 'old' companies. However, in this particular case of Chubb and Yale Locks in Willenhall, the modernization task proved difficult since the proposed restructuring of the whole of their production process according to the new principles of human resource management ran anything but smoothly. After the workforce in both factories had been reduced to less than a third, from 1,500 to 450 altogether, the remaining workers were profoundly and persistently distrustful towards the introduction of teamwork, the reorganization of the wage system to incorporate team bonuses and the new forms of direct communication between management and workforce. The managers, who were outsiders and aloof, were unable to free the potential for productivity which had remained underexploited in the established Taylorist system. On the contrary, the restructuring, which was aligned to the 'cooperative market society' model, made the remaining workers feel insecure. Cooperation had been established previously between members of a manufacturing team in spite of individual piece wages, but it did not work as well as before under the formal requirements of group work and group piecework wages. At the same time, the withdrawal of the new management from local involvement entrenched the classic 'us and them' divide between management and production workers handed down in traditional worker culture together with the paternalistic company regime. In a similar way to their West German colleagues, but under much more difficult circumstances, the shop stewards were faced with the problem of encouraging the workforce to support rationalization and modernization in order to rescue the company.[79]

When it was sold on to Assa Abloy in 2000, this business, created from two traditional companies, found itself in a social crisis. At its heart was the clash between two worlds stemming from two seemingly different eras. The traditional but still lively work culture of an internationally successful company collided head-on with managers intent on restructuring, who saw their own futures in the light of financial market-oriented corporate management and profit expectations. The sociological reports and documents on this encounter between two different interpretations and worldviews clearly demonstrate the limitations that confronted short-term, voluntaristic restructuring plans of company regimes even in times of crisis.[80] Social recognition, relational equality and industrial citizenship could be easily integrated into the democratically compatible rhetoric of a brave new working world, but their concrete realization within historically developed local company cultures was altogether a more difficult undertaking. This may be an extreme example, but again it shows in all clarity that company regimes could not be changed without social drama and fierce feelings and emotions. This field of action, the company, was in these cases far removed from the rational-choice models of organizational sociology and management consultants.

The industrial company as a safe refuge

The purpose of my journey through a number of industrial companies in this chapter has been to investigate how the industrial citizenship and demands for participation whose legal and political outlines we analysed in chapter 4 were enacted in social terms. At the beginning of this chapter, I emphasized social recognition and relational equality as crucial to the social dimension of company industrial relations. What conclusions can we draw at the end of this journey?

First, deindustrialization naturally plays an important role as an overall framework, since in most companies jobs were rationalized, reorganized and redesigned. Factories whose workforce expanded in the period studied here were clearly in the minority. As a result, the value of a job in a functioning or successful factory or company increased for all employees. The significance of the corporate climate, in practice the prospects of the company, for integration and a feeling of loyalty to it can hardly be overestimated. Since company regimes always react particularly sensitively to the withdrawal of trust and to uncertainty, the sector-specific corporate climate and the lifespan of companies are good indicators of the probable distribution of company regimes. Well-integrated social partnerships and firmly established, socially benevolent patriarchs also weathered economic downturns and sales slumps only if they succeeded in overcoming such economic crises. For this reason, survival communities and 'production communities' were solutions that could develop mobilizing effects, particularly in the context of these specific upheavals and crises, and function successfully as 'alliances for work'. On the other hand, they were constantly under pressure to prove their economic profitability, and this could only be secured or regained in many companies during the period under study by sweeping organizational restructuring and the introduction of technical innovation. It was not least computerized 'market-centred control mechanisms'[81] that gained significance as a counterweight to participatory industrial relations and the decentralization of decision-making opportunities. The interview at the beginning of this chapter, however, shows the precarious and socially deficient nature of labour relations developed in the shadow of sales crises, partial redundancies and the threat of the company being sold, for example, to foreign capital investors. Declining prospects and negative experiences with workers' own management but also growing competition amongst colleagues led to the erosion of production societies and communities, whether they were based on older paternalistic structures or on collective citizenship. What was left in these cases was 'soulless workhouses'.

During the period studied here, shifts in opportunities for social recognition and relational equality in industrial companies came in phases. In the 1970s, labour struggles and social protests resulted not only in economic improvements, but also in improvements in symbolic recognition and equality, particularly for previously discriminated groups such as labour migrants and semi-skilled women workers. The dismantling of authoritarian structures observed throughout Western Europe also found its way into the factories. Co-determination and reforms of labour law created institutional frameworks which in France and Germany encouraged a shift in company regimes from monocratic to liberal-pluralistic models. This was not, however, the case for Britain. There, legislators tended to restrict trade union positions and provided far greater opportunities for new company regimes to be developed from above in keeping with the new management concepts for the 'unlimited company'.

Further shifts were linked to the economic crises of 1980–2 and 1992–4. Unlike in the 1970s, in this phase, company and/or trade union activities that supported socially integrative and pluralistic social orders had to manage without broad public support. The media debate on globalization propagated the principles of a new and people-friendly management and a participatory business culture

270

to a wider public. In the light of this interpretation, the struggles for social recognition and participation at work resembled an after-effect of old class struggles and antiquated collective bargaining rules. Nevertheless, findings from very different sectors attest to opportunities for decision-making within factories in these crisis situations that were in this sense genuine opportunities, as was often emphasized in contemporary crisis jargon.

Contrary to the expectations of contemporary diagnoses, especially Marxist-oriented ones, there was no clear pressure to change company regimes ensuing from the rise of financial market capitalism after the 1980s and more intensively in the 1990s.[82] Evaluations and analyses of expected returns may have changed after the 1990s – they were projected to accrue more quickly and be higher – but their effect on the shaping of company regimes remained vague. The surge of internationalization of industrial capital observed in all three countries since the 1990s was by no means matched by a shift towards internationally dominant American- or Japanese-style company models. Even foreign capital owners found it necessary to take national or regional or sometimes even local specifics of industrial relations into account and to share decision-making powers with workers' representatives and trade unions. Co-determination was by no means immediately recognized as a competitive advantage. It was accepted reluctantly by neoliberal ideologues but followed pragmatically by investors and managers. It can therefore be argued that the convergence of European markets and the emergence of pan-European businesses and companies contributed towards the spread of the minimum standards of (tolerated) liberal-pluralistic company regimes beyond nationally specific, institutional and ideological differences. Although European works councils were not introduced until the end of the transition period under study, their establishment marks an important institutional stage in this trend.

The development of company regimes was also not pushed in any particular direction by technical changes in work processes. On the contrary, all the essentially technology-based forecasts proved to be wrong or of little significance during this period. Approaches which emphasize the interdependence between company regimes and opportunities for developing new technologies are more convincing. Cooperative company regimes strengthened entrepreneurial investment decisions whose aim was to produce goods and services of a higher quality in order to generate profits on international markets, which would then secure the 'expensive' production sites in Western Europe. In this context, it is instructive to consider the

271

solutions that were developed successfully in German companies in response to the major economic crisis at the beginning of the 1990s. In many cases, they seem to have been based on the fact that the socially integrative models of cooperation between workforce and management were not abolished, but adapted and modernized. This kind of 'alliance for work' company model was effective beyond the 'great recession' of the late 2000s. Some companies in Britain and France also adopted this pattern and were successful. In their evaluation of a company study which was carried out in France every five years after 1992–3, the sociologists Thomas Amossé and Thomas Coutrot came to the conclusion that in approximately a third of the representative samples, socio-productive models of the Toyota type were in practice. The study used this label for company regimes which combined high participation rates at work meetings, greater scope for organizing work, low levels of concern about losing jobs, good working conditions, social recognition and low rates of conflict.[83] It also became apparent that consequences of this kind did not only emerge in high-tech companies and sectors that were hugely innovative. Socially integrative regimes that were adapted and developed in old-fashioned Taylorist companies are also cases of the 'coevolution' we are concerned with here.

The case studies on the automobile industry have provided us with numerous examples of this latter variant. Many company studies suggest that cooperative industrial relations were backed by workforce and management when it came to changing work processes and reorganizing the companies. In British and French companies in particular, this signifies a shift away from the model of trade union confrontation and militancy. Especially in Britain, the foreign, multinational companies ensured that explicit 'social partnership' contracts were drawn up which recognized only one trade union as their negotiating partner and that at the same time management followed socially integrative pacification and mobilization strategies, with varying success.

In nearly all companies, the old instruments of company social policy, mostly established in the interwar period, were undermined at this time by competitive pressure and the pursuit of production cost-cutting. Company housing became rarer, company sports, leisure and holiday facilities were reduced or abolished and credit offers for workers were limited. There is, however, no single unified picture in the fractured world of company social welfare. Whereas special benefits used to be the domain of large corporations and branch leaders, during the period studied here they became more evenly distributed: that is, they were withdrawn by large companies but they were more likely to be retained by medium-sized companies.

Social diagnosticians have emphasized the trend towards individualization or 'subjectivization' of workers during this period of transition. In this, they see a paradigmatic change in the relations between the company and its employees taking place parallel to deindustrialization.[84] However, in this context, there is again no direct and certainly no clear path to new company regimes. Professional individuals in industrial production (whether skilled workers, technicians or engineers) proved to be committed team workers and group contributors who valued recognition within the social structures of the department and company just as highly as recognition of their own individual performance. Forecasts of the triumph of individualistic work ethics and instrumentalized company regimes proved to be irrelevant, at least in the light of the results of company case studies. If group cohesion at the workplace broke down, those affected tended to react with bitterness and resentment. In 2000, company regimes based on recognition of the work collectives that made up the total workforce were still a more stable basis for industrial production units than performance-oriented individuals gathered under one roof, a phenomenon which, incidentally, was also in evidence long before the upheavals of the third industrial revolution.

Darker areas with deteriorating company regimes emerged not only where sales crises, mismanagement or permanent conflict led to the decline of the company or the factory. Economically successful rationalization strategies which resulted in a company functioning more as a monocratically organized 'workhouse', with management whose sole aim was to extract maximum performance from the workforce, also led to situations where labour and capital distrusted each other and where there was little potential for successful medium-term competitive strategies. The entrepreneurial flexibility gained was often at the expense of a high workforce turnover and the introduction of agency workers, fixed-term contracts and part-time work. Thus it reinforced the tendencies that simultaneously led to the erosion of social citizenship in many companies in the private service sector.

Overall, in the course of the many and diverse upheavals, the relative importance of the cooperative company regime increased, whether as a reality or as a threatened norm. For middle-aged workers in particular, a 'good' industrial company regime became more valuable, not least because of the comparatively worse situation in the new service sectors and the high risk of becoming unemployed.

Possibly one of the most surprising finds of this study is that the industrial company was a haven of stability, providing an alternative world to the remoteness and powerlessness experienced in society and politics. A good twenty years after the end of the period of my study, industrial sociologists defined this as identification with the 'narrow world of work', to illustrate that for many workers this was an expression of the withdrawal from politics and social involvement described in chapters 2 and 3.[85] This world, however, deserves attention as an experiential space of democratic participation, as it provides a firm foothold for democracy in all three countries studied here.

— Chapter 8 —

INDUSTRIAL DISTRICTS, SOCIAL SPACES, 'PROBLEM NEIGHBOURHOODS' AND OWNER-OCCUPIER AREAS
Social spaces and deindustrialization

'In space we read time.' This is the title of a book by the historian Karl Schlögel[1] and is a succinct expression of the way the British, French and Germans perceive their industrial past today. This past is preserved in industrial monuments and in derelict industrial sites, wastelands and spoil heaps on the edge of residential areas, between settlements or in the middle of parks smartened up to attract tourists. Since the late 1980s, the areas where imposing ruins were left in the landscape by the industrial past have been converted and regenerated. These ruins have been incorporated into new urban architecture and the past has been systematically exploited to enhance the value of new residential neighbourhoods, tourist and cultural attractions and office landscapes. In Britain, the 'heritage industry' became an important element of the urban regeneration of docks, factories and warehouses. The dockland areas close to the centres of Hamburg, Glasgow and Liverpool thus became the cornerstone of urban regeneration after the industrial decline of these cities in the 1970s and 1980s (see figure 8.1).[2]

Romantic industrial sites of remembrance are a reminder not only of the heyday of old industrial capitalism but also of the painful process of deindustrialization which has reshaped the spatial structures of our three countries since the 1970s. This is the case even though the withdrawal of capital from industry and manufacturing in Western Europe rarely left such devastating traces of destruction as, for example, in the US rustbelt.[3] But even beyond these visible reminders of the industrial past, now highly valued as sites of collective memory and promoted as new centres of high culture, the upheavals of deindustrialization have permanently transformed the socio-spatial structures of all three countries. It is the purpose of this

275

Figure 8.1 The Clyde Waterfront, Glasgow, 2013.

Glasgow on the river Clyde in Scotland was one of the most important industrial cities in north-west Europe until the 1960s. It was defined by its huge shipyards, steelworks, engineering factories and dockyards. Among its industrial facilities was the giant Finnieston Crane, which was used for loading steam locomotives onto merchant ships. Today, Glasgow is transformed. Most industrial facilities have disappeared from the city and instead its economy is dominated by financial services, the media and entertainment industry and tourism. Spectacular cultural buildings such as The Clyde Auditorium, illuminated in this picture, are visible signs of structural change. Of the old industrial buildings, only the Finnieston Crane remains – as a monument to Glasgow's industrial past.

last chapter to examine these transformations in more detail. I will approach this with a method similar, as it were, to Google Earth, beginning with a satellite picture of entire regions of Western Europe, progressing to views of large conurbations, then to specific urban districts and finally to individual residential areas. It can already be said at this point that each of these steps will reveal different effects of deindustrialization.

New regional disparities

At the beginning of this book, I described the specific national pathways towards deindustrialization and pointed out that this process changed the economic geography of all three countries to varying degrees. The change was particularly stark in Britain. There, the decline of industry introduced a new dimension to the old disparity between the North of the country, which depended on the coal, steel and textile industries, and the South, shaped by the new consumer goods and service industries. With the loss of traditional industries, the North also lost its economic substance and entered into a long phase of crisis-ridden structural change. On the other hand, the South, or more precisely the South-East of England around Greater London, developed into a booming centre of new growth industries led by the financial services industry.

First signs of this twofold development were visible by the early 1970s, but the divide between North and South widened dramatically as a result of the recession of 1980–2 as well as the neoliberal economic policies of the Conservative governments between 1979 and 1997. In the 1980s, unemployment figures in nearly all the major regions of the North of Britain rose to levels above 13 per cent. At the same time, the number of people in poverty and receiving benefits also rose and more and more people left the industrial crisis regions of Scotland, Lancashire, the Midlands and Yorkshire. The peak of this regional crisis came in 1985–6 when official unemployment figures rose to their highest ever: 15.7 per cent in the North (Cumbria, Northumberland, Durham) and 14.2 per cent in the North-West and in Wales. In the South-East, on the other hand, the loss of industrial jobs had already been partly offset by the creation of new jobs in the service sectors and unemployment stood at 8.6 per cent in 1986, well below the official figures for the northern industrial areas. Although unemployment sank overall, this North–South divide was to remain crucial over the next two decades. Lower wages and hidden unemployment meant that people continued to migrate from the northern regions of the country. Between 1980 and 2000, the total population in the North-East and North-West shrank by 2.2 and 0.7 per cent respectively, whereas in England as a whole the population grew by 6.8 per cent.[4]

The industrial regions of the North, therefore, were exposed to a process of overall decline but with clear regional differences. Regions with coal mines, steelworks and shipyards were particularly hard hit. The deepest fractures in economic and social structures occurred in areas with a concentration of these industries.

Wherever industry had survived the first wave of closures and had succeeded in attracting new businesses and branches of industry, decline was mitigated. The British consumer goods industry shrank overall noticeably less and more slowly than the heavy industries of the North. With the exploitation of North Sea oil near Aberdeen, Scotland was even able to open up a new industrial centre. The crisis of the Scottish steelworks and shipyards around Glasgow was also offset to a certain extent by the arrival of new electronics companies, which in 1986 employed as many as 43,000 people.[5] In general, the 1990s marked a phase in which new economic structures emerged in the northern regions of Britain and decline was compensated for in some places by new growth impulses. Major cities such as Manchester, Sheffield, Newcastle, Liverpool and Glasgow 'reinvented' themselves. They succeeded in attracting not only the growth areas of financial services but also public sector offices and company headquarters, thus creating new job opportunities. However, this did not happen overnight. Typically, it took more than a decade, and in many places twenty years or more, for the transformation of local economic structures to translate into corresponding employment growth. Liverpool is a notable example of this: 95,000 industrial jobs disappeared between 1971 and 1984 but employment in the service sector (especially call centres, banks, insurance and tourism) only began to grow ten years later and by 2001 amounted to just 50,000 new jobs.[6]

None of the old industrial cities succeeded in the mid term in completely compensating for the loss of jobs caused by the structural fracture of the 1970s and 1980s. The highly aggregated data relating to major regions do not allow us to name clear winners and losers of this structural transformation or to identify local shifts in social spaces in detail. For this, we have to zoom in closer, so to speak. However, it is clear that the disparities between the housing and social environments of different sections of the population living in the inner cities increased considerably. A regional metropolis such as Manchester, for example, became more visible and attractive as the seat of financial services and as a centre for trade fairs and a city of culture, but in the 1990s the level of unemployment in its poorer areas was still between 25 and 30 per cent. Added to that, long-term unemployment and youth unemployment were characteristic of the city's labour market and it became brandmarked by high levels of criminality.[7]

In Britain, transition zones emerged between the London metropolitan area, which was experiencing a boom in the new financial service sector, and the old core industrial areas of the North. In these new industrial zones, businesses settled and the service sector grew. The West Midlands, for example, especially the Black Country, the conurbation to the north and west of Birmingham, was able to retain its traditionally strong industrial character, and in Wales the centre of industrial employment also shifted from the coal mines and steelworks of the valleys in South Wales to the coastal region around Cardiff. At the same time, industrial or industry-related businesses in the service sector settled along the corridors north and south of the M4 motorway from London to Bristol and Wales and thus continued a trend that had already begun in the boom years. In spite of all these developments, however, a bird's-eye view of the British section of the map of Western Europe shows that the negative traces of deindustrialization were still plainly visible in 2000, thirty years after it began.

Moving east, we can now look at the section of the map of European regions that shows Germany. In the area of former East Germany, in particular, the collapse of most industrial companies after reunification had a similarly devastating effect to that experienced in the northern regions of Britain. A good ten years later than in Britain, in the period between 1994 and 2009, a startling 850,000 jobs in East German industry disappeared. This is equivalent to a decline of 83 per cent. Unemployment figures stood at between 15 and 19 per cent until 2005[8] and a mass exodus also began here, particularly of the younger and better-qualified population, to the former West German states. This was a level of regional mobility that in real figures far exceeded the development in Britain.[9] After 1990, it led to a deepening of the regional divide in Germany. A striking North–South divide had already been visible in West Germany in the 1980s, where deindustrialization had first hit the industrial coastal regions of the North-West. Hamburg, Bremen, parts of Lower Saxony and Schleswig-Holstein had the highest rates of unemployment in the whole country in the ten years following the closure of most shipyards and the rationalization of jobs in the dockyards. Here too, unemployment figures peaked in 1986–7. Bremen led the way with 16 per cent, followed by Hamburg with more than 14 per cent and Lower Saxony with 12 per cent, whereas rates in the southern federal states were between 6 and 8 per cent.[10] The only other area to be similarly hit was the traditional coal- and steel-producing state, the Saarland, with 14 per cent. This North–South divide became entrenched during the 1990s, in spite of the fact that unemployment figures sank at federal state level, albeit more slowly than in Britain. At this time, the situation on the labour market remained precarious in certain older industrial areas: the south of lower Saxony, the Baltic coast, the Saarland and Western Palatinate. They were soon joined by another large area, the Ruhr, whose cities now had unemployment rates of between 13 and 17 per cent. It had already lost more than 10 per cent of its population between 1970 and 1990[11] and was now hit again by this employment crisis. Finally, the economic crisis of 1992–4 also left its mark on the labour market south of the river Main. The industrial areas of upper and central Franconia (around Nuremberg and Schweinfurt) and the metropolitan region of Mannheim subsequently suffered unemployment levels of over 10 per cent for the first time.[12]

The visible effects of structural change in the industrial regions of West Germany proved to be similar to those in Britain. Some industrial communities attempted to create jobs by developing new growth sectors and adopting completely new images to attract investors, whereas in other districts the negative social impacts of structural change became strikingly concentrated. Local differences between communities, urban districts and smaller regions that were 'dynamic' and those that had been 'left behind' increased and became even more entrenched after the turn of the millennium. In the Ruhr region, for example, the establishment of new industries remained an exception. This resulted particularly in northern cities such as Gelsenkirchen, Bottrop and Recklinghausen from the region of Emscher-Lippe, which was dependent on a single industry, falling clearly behind their counterparts Essen, Bochum and Dortmund in the *Hellweg* zone (a long-established urban area named after an old trade route) with their transregional company headquarters, universities, administrative centres and so on.[13] Again, only a look at a detailed map will reveal the dramatic shifts in social spaces.

The southern and south-western regions of former West Germany, in contrast, are distinguished by the fact that here deindustrialization frequently took place as a complex structural change affecting industries and services equally. They profited from the fact that coal and steel production had scarcely played a role in the industrial development of the region. Although a comprehensive shift in employment structures still took place here, jobs lost in industry could be replaced effortlessly by new jobs. Within a short time, all these regions could be counted among the winners within the European Economic Area in respect of the dynamics of growth. The highly industrialized region of the central upper Rhine (the area south of Karlsruhe), for example, lost only 8.7 per cent of its jobs in industry between 1980 and 1994. This was the result, among other things, of new companies being founded which were able to fill the gap in the labour market created by rationalization and bankruptcy.[14]

The economic geography of France was also fundamentally changed by deindustrialization. In a similar way to London, Paris expanded much more quickly than most other regions in France, attracting above all the best-paid jobs in the new private service sector and the expanding public sector. Industry in Paris, in contrast, declined more drastically than in the rest of France. Between 1982 and 2006, jobs in manufacturing declined by 43 per cent, whereas the decline in other urban centres was 'only' 23 per cent.[15] At the same time, those few areas in the country dedicated almost solely to industry suffered a prolonged structural crisis whose extent and social consequences (unemployment, poverty, labour migration) can be compared to the most drastic situations in Britain and East Germany. This was especially true for the heavy-industry region of Lorraine (around Longwy, Metz and Thionville), the North (Region Nord-Pas-de-Calais) and the coastal areas in the South and West (La Ciotat and Marseille, Nantes and Brest) that depended on shipbuilding and the docks. Other industrial areas such as Alsace, the Rhône-Alpes region (Lyons, Grenoble), the Midi-Pyrénées (around Toulouse) and Normandy were able to survive in a similar way to West Germany, since new businesses connected with industry-related services made up for the decline of older sectors in the region.[16]

France became a model of the *fabbrica diffusa*, mostly small and medium-sized factories spread throughout the country. To be more precise, rural France, *la France profonde* north of a line stretching between La Rochelle and Grenoble, was becoming less agricultural and more strongly industrial, whereas in the south of the country and in the Parisian metropolis, public services and locally oriented services (tourism, health, retail) dominated. This was the continuation after 1975 of an earlier development that had spread in rural and small-town France during the boom years of 1948 to 1973, largely with the growth of the consumer goods industry. The migration of industry into former rural regions came with a significant trend towards gentrification in urban centres. In both middle-class and previously poorer areas of the large cities, a section of the population gradually began to gather that had higher incomes and/or wealth at their disposal as well as economic or political decision-making power and educational capital.[17]

Let us briefly summarize the similarities that this view of the regions of Western Europe has revealed. First, disparities in growth and development intensified at this regional level and caused initially growing, then stagnating regional inequality in terms of the disposition of capital, job opportunities and infrastructure. Second, deindustrialization took place mainly in the mono-industrial areas of iron and steel, coal mining, textiles and shipbuilding as a regional crisis of industry-based social structures. The loss of industrial jobs marked the beginning of a structural crisis lasting more than twenty years, whose typical characteristics were mass unemployment, the spread of absolute and relative poverty and the marginalization of 'losers' in the regional adjustment process. Third, the regional distribution of groups of the working population shifted and, during the period studied here, those employed in industry, especially blue-collar workers, increasingly moved to small towns and rural communities or to the suburbs and margins of urban centres. At the end of the twentieth century, the term 'rural structures' no longer referred to areas shaped by agriculture but to living and housing conditions shaped by wage labour on the fringe of urban centres or outside them.

As a result, the socio-spatial coordinates of industrial labour changed in the long term and with them the entire social space of the three nation-states in our study. I will now leave the regions and turn to smaller-scale processes in order to discover the finer structures of these socio-spatial changes.

Structural change in industrial areas

A closer view of the microstructures of social and economic spaces shows concentrations of business relations, social networks and common socio-cultural factors which have been described as local clusters of companies, specific milieus, modern business landscapes and small-scale social spaces. Social scientists and historians agree that these clusters contribute significantly to understanding social and economic change, but depending on the tradition of the discipline,

282

they have tended to be studied from an economic, social or political-cultural perspective. In social and economic historical research on the nineteenth century in particular, industrial districts play an important role as the smallest socio-spatial units of industrialization,[18] because they can reveal the regionally specific dynamics of its first and second waves. These districts are founded on mostly local groups of highly specialized small and medium-sized companies cooperating and competing with each other. Classic examples are cutlery manufacturers in Sheffield and Solingen; clock-makers in the Black Forest and the French Jura; the manufacturers of locks and fittings and later security systems in and around Wolverhampton; the textile machine factories in Rochdale, Lancashire; the furniture industry in East Westphalia-Lippe; upholstery in the Coburg area; and carpets in and around Kidderminster in Britain.

The companies in these districts depended for their success and survival on the presence of skilled workers who had close local connections, several of whom had founded their own firms that then became traditional family businesses.[19] Their success in the market was based essentially on a labour culture that was firmly rooted to the local area, which assured work of a high standard and trusted in a constant incremental practice of innovation. The close embeddedness of these businesses in local networks and social structures was of extreme importance. They enhanced the scope for economic adaptability and/or innovation.

Alongside these companies, often in close geographical proximity and working in close cooperation with them, other industrial districts emerged which were dominated by corporations and large companies. They employed mostly unskilled workers and attempted to control the whole manufacturing process or to concentrate it under one roof and were intent on securing their dominant position in the local labour market. However, this dominance prevented the development of mutually beneficial partnerships with small and medium-sized companies beyond the narrow circle of suppliers or specialist engineering firms and led to hierarchical relationships between the different local economic actors. The development or establishment of other branches of industry also tended to be hindered by the local dominance of branch leaders. This type of industrial region evolved typically around the coal, steel and chemical industries and grew in overall importance with the rise of mass production. In the period of growth after World War II, they sidelined the old type of industrial districts mentioned above. These were eclipsed by large-scale industry, which was in less need of a foothold in local structures and was able to meet its demand for qualified workers by means of attractive wages and company social benefits.[20] Consumer goods factories (from vehicle manufacturing to food factories) which had sprung up on greenfield sites after 1945 often fitted this model of the major industries. In the economic geography of all three countries, these two types of industrial districts frequently co-existed and developed in direct regional proximity.

In the third industrial revolution, small and medium-sized companies, and with them the older industrial districts, regained their appeal.[21] Economic and social scientists became interested first in the rise of industrial districts in the 'Third Italy', far away from the industrial triangle of Milan, Genoa and Turin, and then also in microregions in Britain, France and West Germany.[22] They soon struck lucky, particularly in South and South-West Germany, with the discovery of 'hidden champions'. These were (global) market leaders in specialized products frequently to be found in regions that looked back on long traditions of employment in industry and traditional craft trades and had developed corresponding social structures and local labour cultures.[23] They proved to be particularly adaptable in the post-boom transformation phase because they were more able to respond to the new demands of flexible quality production than the large companies designed for mass production. The map of these regional labour cultures is remarkably small-scale in all three countries. In their study of small and medium-sized West German companies, Hermann Kotthoff and Josef Reindl identified these sector-specific industrial districts as a particularly important framework for business strategies and company regimes.[24] So, for example, the furniture industry in East Westphalia-Lippe still had a semi-agrarian business tradition in the late 1980s. Here, strong trade union interests and cooperative company politics combined with the industrial traditions of medium-sized companies. The centres of the South-West German metalworking and mechanical engineering industries were able for their part to mobilize specific local capital and labour resources. In Breisgau, for example, the small-scale engineering industry relied for its success on being embedded in rural structures that were still shaped by agriculture and which ensured the continuing development of skilled industrial labour by workers and engineers alike. Further examples in Germany are the metal and textile industries of the western Münsterland, the various small-scale industrial centres in Bavaria outside the metropolitan regions of Munich, Augsburg and Nuremberg, as well as the Allgäu region and the areas around Ingolstadt and Schweinfurt. Similar forms of production-oriented cooperation also existed in urban trade union centres such as around Stuttgart or in the Rhine/Main area near Frankfurt. The economic flexibility of these medium-sized industrial districts in former West Germany was proven in the economic crises after the 1990s, at a time when internationally the location advantages of this form of locally connected, medium-sized production networks were once again being called into question.[25]

In France and Britain, industrial districts were also created and re-created, albeit to a lesser extent than in West Germany or Italy. For France, there is a list of such districts (*pays*), which ultimately reached equal standing with the larger industrial centres as they in turn gradually lost significance, but it is only meaningful for anyone familiar with the regions.[26] In Britain, quantitative indicators make it possible to identify a hundred such local, industry-based business clusters at the beginning of the twenty-first century. In many cases, they continue the traditions of older industrial districts and are therefore to be found particularly in the Midlands (East and West) and in the North-West (Lancashire).[27] The heart of the older industrial districts mentioned above around Wolverhampton and Walsall, Kidderminster and Rochdale survived the setbacks of the early 1980s. Some elements of the socio-cultural embeddedness of these British industrial districts have already been encountered above. The traditional family businesses in the lock and key industry in Wolverhampton, for example, were closely tied to local social cultures. They had a tradition of (male) skilled work, a distinctly local attachment as regards company social policies and business philanthropy, as well as close ties within families and over generations between workers and companies, as the examples in the two previous chapters have shown. This kind of industrial region provided a structure for social advancement, working careers and family relations for local and immigrant labour, thus in turn stabilizing local company regimes.[28]

In the course of industrial restructuring, however, new industrial zones emerged. These include the new regional centres of the car industry already mentioned in chapter 7 in the context of changing company regimes: the Saarland and the Nord-Pas-de-Calais concentrated around Valenciennes and border areas between Germany and France and France and Belgium respectively (see figure 8.2). In Britain, Birmingham had become the centre of the car industry in the postwar era with a regional network of component supplier companies growing up around it. In all four of these regions, the new clusters of businesses at least partially filled the gaps left by the crisis-ridden

Figure 8.2 An aerial view of Smartville Hambach.

While industry was disappearing from major cities, new production plants emerged, particularly in more rural areas, such as near the small town of Hambach in Lorraine. In 1997, Daimler-Benz opened a new car factory here, Smartville Hambach. The workshops of the supplier and logistics factories are arranged around the cross-shaped central buildings where the final assembly of the Smart model is carried out. This arrangement is intended to guarantee the smooth running of 'just-in-time' production. Daimler AG and the other factories in Hamburg are surrounded by fields and forests and today they employ 1,600 people.

decline of the old industries, such as the coal and steel industry in the Saarland and the north of France, and the large stand-alone factories of British car manufacturers in Birmingham. The strategy of attracting component factories to locate close to the assembly plants of the large car manufacturers provided the initial trigger for these regional centres.[29] Similar centres can be found around various large car factories in all three countries: for example, in the south of Lower Saxony around the VW factory in Wolfsburg, in the Stuttgart area around the main Daimler-Benz factory and at the BMW plant in Munich.

The main feature of these new production areas of the automobile industry, therefore, is the fact that large factories with over 2,000 workers co-exist with small or medium-sized factories serving as their primary, secondary or tertiary suppliers. In 2005 in the region of northern France, they accounted for 31,338 employees in 148 different factories. The largest factories employed up to 6,000 people, the smallest fewer than fifty. Two-thirds of them lived in the old mining neighbourhoods nearby.[30]

These examples show socio-spatial continuity particularly clearly. Local labour markets for industrial workers materialized which, although requiring a variety of skills and offering different wage profiles, were generally oriented towards the large auto manufacturers. Particularly in their early phases, the recruitment policies of the new companies profited from the high level of unemployment in the area.[31] This was also the case particularly in those British and French districts where, for example, incoming Japanese companies combined low wages with long-term job prospects in order to secure the loyalty of local workforces. As chapter 7 has shown, this was sometimes successful, but by no means always. In many of the older industrial areas, strong local ties survived which strengthened social relations and morale in the workplace. This is one reason why in the older centres of skilled industrial work there was, for example, still a trade union presence which, as it were, migrated to the new companies as a claim to democratic participation.

There is no doubt that these regenerated industrial districts were of particular importance in the transition phase of the 1980s and 1990s. First, the local labour cultures which had been handed down and cultivated there provided significant potential for industrial production to adapt flexibly to new market conditions and technological openings. This socio-spatial constellation created favourable conditions for business strategies and cooperative company regimes as well as for the spread and further development of knowledge and competencies. Second, regional interconnectedness supported the social embeddedness of capital. The social integration of medium-sized companies in particular continued to play an important role in this, although, as we have seen, it was weakened or displaced by opposing trends towards financialization and the concentration of capital. Third, German companies can be said to have exploited the opportunities offered by the dual education system to use and promote the locally and regionally available knowledge and experience of industrial labour. The knowledge traditions of local industrial cultures in France and Britain, on the other hand, were notably less well placed after the changes in their respective education systems. Fourth, it should be remembered that industrial districts shaped primarily by small and medium-sized businesses profited from the regional tradition of company cooperation. During the crises and changes after the late 1970s, this tradition allowed the flexibility essential for economic survival and successful adjustment to the new markets. Fifth, French sociologists have reported a trend in France (it is not clear whether it also applies to Britain and Germany) whereby beyond the structural crisis of the old industrial regions, deindustrialization triggered a polarization of socio-spatial structures throughout the country. Not only factories but also industrial workers and white-collar workers in the private sector gradually disappeared from the large and medium-sized cities. They tended to live either in more suburban or rural areas or in new or old industrial districts at some distance from the regional and urban centres.

From satellite towns to 'problem neighbourhoods' and terraced housing estates

Zooming in even closer to the urban neighbourhoods, residential areas and streets near industrial factories shows that they were also significantly hit by the upheavals resulting from deindustrialization. They were additionally affected by the regional differences that emerged with the overall economic changes. In general, it can be said that into the 1970s all three countries maintained a legacy from the era of industrialization, namely a fundamental division of social space separating the working-class areas in medium-sized and large cities from middle-class residential areas. Even the new residential districts for the rising middle classes that were expanding fast in the twentieth century were nearly always built at a distance from older or more recent working-class areas. Industrial class society came closer together only in small-scale village or inner-city environments.

The rise of the socio-moral principle of 'social mixing'[32] was one of the side effects of the postwar boom and a long-term consequence of the national mobilization of all three societies in the two world wars. The devastation of World War II also offered opportunities to do justice to the egalitarian principles of a democratic welfare state in terms of socio-spatial arrangements. Consequently, the three decades between 1950 and 1980 were the heyday of social housing subsidized or financed by the public purse.[33] The funding strategies adopted by governments and public administrations were very different but still all bear traces of a fundamental tension between promoting individual home ownership, on the one hand, particularly in the form of owner-occupied detached houses, and funding rented housing by building new or renovating old building stock to alleviate the housing shortage, on the other. This remained a constant theme of social policy in the 1950s and 1960s. It was the second arm of public housing policy, rented accommodation, that was initially relevant for the majority of the constantly growing number of industrial workers, while the purchase of residential property was still reserved for the privileged few. Only in rural and small-town regions did industrial workers frequently live in their own homes, which were often inherited. The structural outcomes of postwar social housing – the satellite towns, high-rise estates and compact rental housing complexes in the redeveloped residential areas of industrial cities – radically changed the housing situation of urban industrial workers particularly during the 1960s and 1970s (see figure 8.3).[34]

In all three countries, advocates of modern concrete structures prevailed, not least for financial reasons. This resulted in monotonous uniformity in cities except for in their old, historical centres and the representative buildings of the inner cities.[35] However, it also led to the disappearance of the nineteenth-century working-class slums and their catastrophic housing conditions, to the filling of gaps left by bombsites in the industrial centres and to the erection of numerous new cities and suburbs which provided housing both for industrial workers and for the growing army of white-collar workers in the service industries and administration. It was indeed blue- and white-collar workers and low-level civil servants who moved into social housing, *sozialen Wohnungsbau, habitations à loyer modéré* (HLM), as well as those young families who benefited from preferential housing allocation. The social mix usually corresponded to the proportion of the various professional and status groups of lower and

289

Figure 8.3   Model of the Cité Colonel-Fabien.

The Cité Colonel-Fabien is a large estate in Saint-Denis, north of Paris, named after a French resistance fighter. It was designed by the distinguished architect André Lurçat in close cooperation with the local communist mayor. It is an example of how closely connected municipal urban planning and modern architecture could be in some cases. During the years of its construction, the character of Saint-Denis was determined by the metalworking industry, referenced here, for example, at the back of the model by a factory with a chimney and a sawtooth roof. During the boom period, this type of large estate on the edge of Paris was a design for a bright future. Nowadays, they are the epitome of failure. Saint-Denis was one of the major hotspots during the riots in the suburbs in 2005.

middle incomes in the local population. These estates rarely housed anyone with a higher income, assets or property to inherit. The quality of the buildings and the interiors of these new flats and estates varied but it can be said that the architectural incompetence of the British surpassed French negligence and German jerry building. The chronicle of scandals in this era of architecture and town planning is long and well documented but it hides an essential factor relevant here, namely that this kind of socio-spatial environment built at the time of industrial expansion was only ten, occasionally only five and rarely as much as fifteen years old when in many industrial cities it was made redundant by deindustrialization.

In the 1980s, there was a moderate to radical change of course in social housing policy in all three countries. Funding for new social housing was cut, the public sector largely limited itself to maintaining existing affordable housing, and at the same time housing policy and its public funding were driven by the new principle of home ownership.[36] In all three countries, this led to the rise of new mass markets for acquiring property by means of mortgages, tax subsidies and other types of public sponsorship.[37] The Conservative government in Britain, for example, introduced the policy of the 'right to buy' for tenants to purchase the council properties they lived in. Given that the asking prices were extremely reasonable, this turned out to be one of the party's most popular policies, with far-reaching socio-spatial consequences.[38] In addition, and sometimes at the same time as the upsurge in urban social housing, more people than ever before in all three countries dreamed of owning their own homes, in the shape of a detached house preferably with a garden. Realizing this dream, however, did not erase the gross social differences between the working class, lower middle class and upper middle class. Studies on Germany use the term 'small workers' house' (*Arbeiterkleinhaus*).[39] In France, the average living space of this kind of house occupied by a working-class family of four was 88 m². [40] Centre-right parties and governments in particular promoted this dream by offering public subsidies, tax concessions and credit relief.[41]

At the end of the expansion phase of social housing in 1979, 48 per cent of industrial workers in Britain were tenants, mostly living in council houses, while 52 per cent owned their own houses or flats or were paying off mortgages.[42] The trend towards home ownership was far more advanced here than on the continent. A special survey carried out by the statistics office INSEE in France showed that in 1973 36.6 per cent of workers owned their own homes.[43] For Germany, figures are available for 1972 showing that 31.3 per

291

cent of those in the category of 'worker' were owners of their own homes.[44]

The trend towards home ownership continued among industrial workers until the turn of the millennium, but there were clear differences between the three countries. This was mainly to do with different structures in housing development and property acquisition. Terraced housing, the standard type of housing since the nineteenth century, was still dominant in Britain, whereas in France and Germany detached or semi-detached houses were widespread. In Germany, the proportion of those living in rented accommodation was notably higher than in the other two countries and high-rise tenement blocks were common, even outside large cities. In Britain, detached and terraced houses made up 83 per cent of the total housing stock; in France, the figure was 58 per cent; and in reunified Germany it was only 39 per cent.[45] It is not surprising, therefore, that the trend towards home ownership amongst ordinary workers persisted particularly in Britain. According to the Labour Force Survey, in 2000, fewer than every fifth labourer or mid-level employee in industry rented their home whereas 64 per cent had already purchased their own home, but were still paying a mortgage; 16 per cent were in full ownership.[46] This development was much slower and regionally patchy in Germany. In former West Germany, 35 per cent of workers owned their own homes in 1998, and in this group there were far more skilled workers than semi-skilled or unskilled workers or labour migrants.[47] The difference between urban centres and the suburbs was also significant. According to a West German study of blue- and white-collar workers in North Rhine Westphalia, Hessen and Rhineland Palatinate in 1999–2000, a clear majority of those interviewed still lived as tenants: 66 per cent of unskilled and semi-skilled workers and just under 57 per cent of skilled workers. This proportion was much higher amongst urban dwellers, namely 79 per cent and 69 per cent respectively.[48] In France, the number of owners or buyers of homes also increased between 1975 and 1996, here by more than 50 per cent. Detached houses (*maisons individuelles*) owned by workers were located mostly in the suburban-rural fringe areas of the country and, as in Germany, significantly fewer migrants owned their own homes.

Deindustrialization and the practical application of the principle of home ownership were both trend reversals. After the mid-1970s, they caused dramatic changes in the socio-spatial structures in many places in the three countries. To put it drastically, the social order in the public housing estates erected mainly on the edge of cities during the boom years decayed even faster than the buildings themselves. The correlation is particularly striking in metropolitan areas. At the end of the 1990s, the 'problem neighbourhoods' and 'social hotspots' in France and Britain were typically located on the outskirts of large cities such as London, Liverpool, Manchester, Paris, Strasbourg and Lyons. The new, densely built high-rise blocks and satellite towns survived the crisis of 'social mixing' that also began in the mid-1970s either with difficulty or not at all. The wave of privatization caused rapid internal social differentiation within the apartment blocks and social housing neighbourhoods everywhere.[49] Properties that had become socially stigmatized and/or were inconveniently located, poorly constructed or in any way substandard remained in the hands of the local housing associations while the better properties moved into private ownership. Younger people, higher earners and salaried employees, in particular, left social housing in droves and were replaced by 'problem families' and people on welfare. Ten years was sufficient for many housing blocks to become places where social deviance and poverty were concentrated. The principle of 'social mixing' fell by the wayside.

The crisis-ridden older industrial regions presented a somewhat different picture. In Britain, the structural fracture of the 1980s robbed swift privatization of its economic foundations so that the strong nationwide trend towards home ownership was not visible in these areas. In the small town of Featherstone (17,000 inhabitants) in the coal mining area of Yorkshire, for example, in 1991 40 per cent of the population still lived as tenants in local council houses and only 55 per cent were homeowners.[50] The socially mixed public housing estates, however, also gradually lost both their structural and social substance – the abrupt end to collective prospects shattered their social order. Local studies at the beginning of the 1990s show that unemployment amongst former miners in the region was high, and figures from two collieries in Doncaster in Yorkshire conform to the general trend: 25 per cent of former miners were unemployed and 23 per cent were on long-term sick leave.[51] Given the difficulties faced by industrial labourers in finding employment locally, it is hardly surprising that the old industrial areas were also centres of youth unemployment. A wave of heroin and alcohol abuse became a huge threat to the local social order in the mid-1990s throughout these mining districts and led to a three- to sixfold rise in crime rates in the second half of the decade, with daily burglaries and car thefts.[52] Developments in the new and old working-class areas of Liverpool, Manchester and Glasgow were similar (see figure 8.4).

Figure 8.4 Youth – hopes for the future dashed: still from the film *Sweet Sixteen* (GB, 2002; director: Ken Loach).

This still from Ken Loach's film *Sweet Sixteen*, released in British cinemas in 2002, shows two young men outside tenements near Glasgow. The decline of shipbuilding has left deep scars here. The youths are recognizable as 'working class' by their tracksuits and baseball caps. Liam (on the left) begins to deal in drugs to give his mother, who is in prison, a better life. He becomes more and more entangled in the situation and it becomes increasingly hopeless. Ken Loach is a chronicler of the British working class in times of deindustrialization (see above, chapter 2). He shows the lack of prospects for young people in a city which only a few decades ago had been one of the world's most important shipbuilding centres.

The housing estates in the newly built satellite towns of the major French cities underwent similar developments. A much higher proportion of migrants in the *classes populaires* meant, however, that ethnic segregation was far more significant than in Britain, where migrants from the Caribbean and South Asia were concentrated mainly in Greater London and a few other major cities. Social protests erupted in the early 1980s on both sides of the Channel and attracted a great deal of public attention. The connection between these riots or *émeutes* and industrial economic upheaval, however, was increasingly forgotten.[53]

Changes in residential neighbourhoods were generally less drastic in those areas that were affected primarily by shifts in employment structures and to a lesser extent by the loss of jobs, especially jobs in industry. In these areas in particular, continuing economic opportunities made it possible for blue- and white-collar workers with secure jobs to own their own homes, either by purchasing the social housing or company housing they lived in or by moving into the growing semi-urban conurbations along motorways and railways. Here again, the price of land and building costs regulated social distribution according to income and background.

Social mixing, the epitome of dreams of harmony from social planners, was rapidly abandoned in the rundown apartment blocks of satellite towns, as explained above. However, this does not mean that it did not exist. But it was more likely to be found in the terraced housing estates of the semi-urban spaces and fringe zones that were becoming typical for the industrialized regions of all three countries.[54] The places workers moved into epitomized the advertising brochures of mortgage banks and building societies, the *Bausparkassen* and *caisses agricoles*. In 1980s France and Germany, estates of this kind mushroomed on the outskirts of urban conurbations and in rural areas and in these decades became centres of modest social advancement.[55] French studies show that some buyers of these houses were previously tenants on nearby social housing estates.[56] The people who settled in these areas were mostly white-collar workers, public sector employees, supervisors, *Meister* and skilled workers, but also technicians and engineers, in other words an upwardly mobile section of the *classes populaires*. In the contemporary political language of the time, they were often termed members of the middle classes, *Mittelschichten*, *classes moyennes*, but in France and Britain they still tended to regard themselves as belonging to the working classes or *classes populaires*.[57] Socio-statistical studies on greater Paris in 1990 identified such *quartiers populaires*. They found they were inhabited by a good 30 per cent of the population, not only workers but also especially white-collar workers, technicians and engineers.[58]

It can be concluded that in all three countries industrial workers increasingly belonged to the large community of property owners on which politicians envisaged the future stability of society to be based. This was the case, however, only for higher earners in the working class. They became owners of houses and flats that around the turn of the millennium were located predominantly in small towns and rural areas. This meant that as it diminished in size but rose in society, the industrial working class became at the same time a social class on the periphery. The end of social housing construction and the crisis in the newly developed neighbourhoods simultaneously deepened the social divide within the *classes populaires*, since links to those who moved into the dilapidated social housing blocks became weaker. The social problems prevailing there meant that in all three countries their residents were increasingly categorized as ethnically (or even racially) 'foreign' or morally inferior. In Britain, the category of the 'under-class', recently imported from the US, became a favourite argument in political and intellectual debates.[59] The same debates took place in France and Germany but with a much less positive response. The semantic and discriminatory divide between Turkish-Kurdish labour migrants in Germany and North African migrants in France and their 'indigenous' counterparts deepened after the 1980s. This was accentuated since the proportion of immigrants in the 'problem neighbourhoods', or *zones urbaines sensibles* as they were officially called in French, was far above the regional average.[60]

Double absence: transit spaces

With economic processes becoming increasingly international, the careers of many working in industry as fitters, technicians, engineers and managers began to include periods working abroad. Their international connections, assets and professional contacts can reasonably be considered as an extension of their socio-spatial world. It is not clear, however, how far this is also true for the numerous labour migrants who came to France, Germany and Britain in the 1960s, 1970s and even 1980s, often with very little or no capital in terms of knowledge, work experience or wealth. What role did migration play in the reshaping of social spaces when industrial jobs became rare and the economic advantages that made them seem so attractive in the boom phase diminished or even disappeared completely?

In order to adequately judge the socio-spatial effects of migration in the three countries studied here, we have first to recall its extent and duration. There were considerable differences in the share of foreign labour migrants depending on the branch of industry, but at the end of the postwar boom it was on average 15 per cent in France and 17 per cent in West Germany. Only some of these new industrial workers remained in the long term, mostly unskilled and semi-skilled workers. Before recruitment was halted in 1974, the proportion of foreign workers returning home from France and Germany was more than 30 per cent.[61] This meant that in the 1960s and 1970s a not insignificant number in both countries were living in social transit spaces. Some stayed in industry for a limited period of five to ten years and then either returned to their home countries or moved into non-industrial jobs. However, even these industrial workers in transit left their mark in socio-spatial terms. Separate social spaces emerged in rundown areas on the edge of working-class neighbourhoods, with shared lodgings, hostels, boarding houses and cheap accommodation. All of these spaces were marked to a certain extent by the hope of returning home and the sense of a provisional solution, even though their residents often spent half of their working lives there before they were able to go back or move into social spaces with stronger family, religious or cultural ties.

As has been suggested above, the situation for labour migrants in manufacturing changed significantly after 1974. France and Germany officially ended recruitment abroad and British citizens of the Commonwealth faced tighter entry restrictions. As a result, many migrants seriously considered the option of returning home. In France and Germany, they were disproportionately affected by the mass redundancies and social plans following the crises in the coal, steel and textile industries. After the economic crisis at the beginning of the 1980s, both France and Germany offered financial incentives for foreign workers to return home as a component of government measures to alleviate mass unemployment. Fewer migrants made use of this opportunity than originally hoped, but those who did were frequently those who had been living in provisional accommodation in the transit spaces. Now that they were slightly older and had sometimes been working in industry for more than ten years, these unskilled and semi-skilled workers attempted to avoid the threat of unemployment by using the state repatriation grants as start-up capital for a new working life in their home country. This was the case, for example, for more than 23,000 Algerians who turned their back on France between 1984 and 1988 and returned to their

297

homeland.[62] In Germany, 13,700 foreign workers, 12,000 of them Turkish labour migrants, made use of these repatriation grants after their introduction in 1983–4.[63]

The Algerian sociologist Abdelmalek Sayad proposed the term 'double absence' to describe the lack of socio-cultural belonging experienced by labour migrants from Algeria who came to France during the period of our study.[64] This contradicted an optimistic view, widespread especially among sociologists of migration, which inferred a 'double presence' from the biographical connection of two separate social and geographical spaces and emphasized the social, economic and cultural gains of the migration experience over the risks of loss. The 'illusion of return' was an essential element of this double absence, not only for North African labour migrants. Studies in Germany show that it was also true for Turkish migrants who had been working for more than fifteen years in Germany. In 1985, 80 per cent of the interviewees still expressed the wish to return home, and twenty years later the figure was still more than 40 per cent.[65]

The traditional transit spaces of labour migrants employed in industry were also changed by deindustrialization. Living space close to the factories gradually disappeared and labour migrants increasingly moved with their families to newly built or vacant social housing. With respect to the trend towards home ownership described above, the majority of them were 'latecomers' who, in labour and housing markets that were both shrinking, struggled with disadvantages such as a lack of professional qualifications and financial assets. This was evident in the striking concentration of foreign workers living in cramped, poor-quality accommodation and on housing estates. In these unpopular areas with their poor reputations, they encountered more recent migrants and other social groups forced out of the open housing market into precarious social and financial situations.[66]

A comparative study of the history of Turkish migration colonies in Colmar and Bamberg between 1970 and 1995 provides more details of the consequences of deindustrialization for migrants' social spaces.[67] In Bamberg, the continuity of local industrial employment ensured that the vast majority of Turkish workers kept their jobs during the recessions of 1973–4 and 1980–2 and mostly lived with their families in socially mixed neighbourhoods nearby. Their integration into the local working cultures survived the disruptions of the two oil crises, and the Turkish 'colony' of nearly 1,400 people became an integral part of the local working-class community. In Colmar, on the other hand, the Turkish-Kurdish migrants were mostly illegal immigrants or had claimed political asylum after the recruitment ban of 1974 and their living and working conditions continued to be unstable and precarious. For the majority of these unqualified migrants, it was extremely difficult to enter into the world of permanent employment, and very few of them succeeded. In this case, typical transit spaces evolved, in which the social experience of double absence was concentrated and continued to influence the lives and opportunities of the second and even third generations.

In Britain, migrants were far less significant in industrial work in real figures than in France and Germany. An average of 5 to 6 per cent of industrial workers were foreigners or British citizens from the Commonwealth. They were also more concentrated in a limited number of centres than in the other two countries. Apart from Inner and Greater London, where the proportion of foreigners in certain areas was more than 33 per cent (Brent, Newham, Tower Hamlets, Hackney, Brixton and Slough), the main centres were Bradford for South Asian migrants and Birmingham and Liverpool, especially Toxteth, for migrants from the Caribbean.[68] The result of this concentration was that in Britain neighbourhoods soon developed in which these migrant groups were either dominant or at least strongly represented.

What is common to all three countries, however, is that there was a statistically significant presence of migrants in the crisis zones of the social housing estates and squalid satellite towns of the last industrial expansion. Migrant households and families had to struggle with the negative consequences of discrimination in the housing market and at the same time with the risks of unstable employment for unskilled and semi-skilled workers. Related media coverage and political treatment thus highlighted the ethnic dimension of the conflicts and problems that were typically concentrated in these areas. The transit spaces of industrial society had become the new problem zones of the service society.

The end of socio-moral milieus and the crisis of local working cultures

Until the 1980s, the working-class areas of industrial cities were also the regional centres of trade union and left-wing political culture. Most of these neighbourhoods were firmly in the hands of the Labour Party in Britain, the SPD in West Germany and the PCF or, as from 1971, the PS in France, and left-wing administrations supported the local culture of their voters with rooms, staff and

299

finances. Social clubs, the local union building, sports clubs, music clubs and other leisure organizations were largely integrated into these networks. Although these 'socio-moral milieus'[69] were always able to mobilize only a minority of party members, trade unionists and activists locally, they had an overall influence on these neighbourhoods and social spaces. These socio-spatial configurations were more widespread in Britain than in France or Germany, because many industrial regions, especially in the North, the Midlands and Wales, had a long and unbroken political tradition. In France and Germany, many of the industrial regions were not as old, the number of migrants was consistently much higher and the political tradition of labour movement cultures was much weaker or had been overlaid by war or the Nazi dictatorship.[70] The fact that political mobilization after 1968 strengthened local left-wing working-class culture in these industrial locations is frequently overlooked. It was responsible, for example, for generational change among activists and expanding the membership base of the left-wing parties and trade unions. In many smaller Catholic industrial communities in France and Germany, the left-wing parties were not able to win municipal majorities before the 1970s.[71] What happened to this 'socio-moral milieu' following deindustrialization has not yet been fully studied. In Germany especially, there are very few regional studies which examine the transformation of regional patterns of social and political order in more detail.[72]

When established socio-cultural routines were hit with all the force of deindustrialization as a local structural crisis, the situation was relatively clear and unambiguous. In these cases, the local working-class milieu disintegrated very swiftly. Waves of redundancies and factory closures, migration, youth unemployment and long-term unemployment transformed the previously work-centred areas of the old industrial regions into the problem zones of urban social policy. Reports and contemporary eyewitnesses from industrial cities in the north of Britain in particular emphasize the speed with which the social and moral fabric in these areas collapsed. Left-wing local councils found themselves increasingly compelled to manage social emergencies and growing poverty as best they could.[73] The workers' parties reacted very differently to this crisis of left-wing politics in the old industrial cities. The increasing social inequality between the winners and losers of the upheavals translated locally into increasing tensions between the different groups of voters and neighbourhoods. In those areas where labour migrants had for the most part taken over the poorly paid or unpopular industrial jobs

300

in the final phase of the boom, hostile racist and nationalist currents emerged that challenged the local integration policies of left-wing communities.

The political outcome of these local conflicts varied considerably. Even if no direct path can be traced from the end of local working cultures to the right-wing populist mobilization of the working classes/ *classes populaires* observed in all three countries in the last ten years, the erosion of these local political cultures ushered in a phase when new political actors entered the local arena and shifted the benchmarks of political-cultural orientation for the remaining workers. 'Green' political activists fighting against environmental devastation and pollution, Muslim activists in the previously 'red' left-wing strongholds of French, British and West German suburbs; right-wing nationalist activists with a blatantly xenophobic programme; social and economic liberal reformers with wide-ranging visions of a post-industrial future – all these new political actors were operating at a local level at the same time as the upheavals in those areas where deindustrialization had sparked a crisis of local working cultures. The old hegemony of left-wing, socialist or social-reformist cultures was based on a specific work ethos and work *habitus*, comprising willingness to do hard and tiring physical labour, respect for skilled work and professional qualifications, adherence to strict gender-specific roles and the division of labour at work and in the home and an appreciation of solidarity and equality. The decline of industrial jobs at that time and the prospect of these jobs disappearing completely in the future also undermined the collective and cohesive nature of this work culture.[74]

The situation was very different in the satellite towns and expanding provincial and rural housing areas in which, as we have seen above, an increasing number of industrial workers were living. Here, other socio-cultural influences and older rural connections, traditional church or religious affiliations or, in the case of the labour migrants, shared countries or regions of origin were just as important as the traditions of nation-specific trade union and left-wing labour movement cultures.[75] In any case, the industrial districts that were relatively successful in the upheaval phase kept their expressly regional-specific characteristics. Different occupational groups and 'socio-moral milieus' passed on the traditional norms described above: hard industrial work, solidarity and so on. In most cases, these work cultures, however, spread across class boundaries and were clearly related to the region. Their (party) political character differed locally and, given the shifts in the occupational composition of regional workers, tended to become weaker. The few studies that exist emphasize above all local connections and the distance from left-wing urban areas and their values.[76]

It has been said for France that this meant the disappearance of the *classe ouvrière* as a socio-cultural milieu from the social spaces of industrial regions and that the workers of the 1990s considered themselves to be more part of regional or local social structures. There is indeed evidence to support the idea that the category of *classe ouvrière* was no longer appropriate and that the term *classes populaires* is more suited to conveying the socio-cultural common-alities in neighbouring households of male industrial workers and technicians and female workers in (low-level) administrative, retail or health professions.[77] In the case of industrial districts, such common-alities often condense into clearly defined work cultures. In chapter 7, it also became clear that these local work cultures in turn play an important role in defending or extending participation and social citizenship in the working world. The 'small world of the companies' expanded to become local social spaces with strong connections and networks. In every company, regional work cultures, mostly politically unremarkable and consensus-oriented, whether they were 'alliances for work' in small and medium-sized companies or cooper-ative working societies, proved to be a mainstay for the continuation of labour-related participation.

These patterns of socio-moral order were threatened when capital and management withdrew from their mutual obligations, either because local companies were taken over by larger corporations or international financial investors who installed new management and severed local ties, or because local competition was used by management as an excuse to withdraw cooperative concessions and 'blackmail' its workers. It was essential for the political-cultural basis of these local work cultures that 'good work' in the form of well-performing, recognized companies with fair working conditions and good wages was secured in the region. The industrial areas still characterized by the *classes populaires* were gradually transformed into zones of precarious service jobs or practically unattainable dream jobs for academic professionals. This eventually undermined the socio-moral foundations of the regional cohesion that had survived the collapse of the old industrial social spaces.

The socio-spatial consequences of deindustrialization are, as I hope has become clear, extremely diverse and cannot be reduced to regional disparities, segregation and gentrification, even if these are factors which enjoy considerable media attention. In conclusion, I

302

would like again to highlight three phenomena which better explain the social mix in both the old and the new industrial towns and regions.

First, as we have seen, industrial work and life retreated into peripheral areas. This 'peripheralization' can be traced back to both the departure of large industries from urban centres and the relocation of new industries in small-town and rural areas and was accompanied by workers moving to live on the edge of cities or in smaller towns or even villages. It was largely responsible for promoting the simultaneous reinvention of all three countries as service societies whose centres were located in core metropolitan areas. They in turn experienced a cultural and economic boost through gentrification and the cultivation of an urban image, such as by means of 'signature' buildings and tourist attractions. There was a seamless link between this displacement of industrial normality to the edges of cities and the 'provinces' and the socio-spatial order of the bourgeois nineteenth century and its symbolic-cultural evaluation of locations.[78] The neglect of public spaces in the *zones urbaines sensibles*, to quote the politically correct term used by French urban planners, and the retreat of state authority from them, may have caught the attention of the media but comprised only a part of this much wider socio-spatial process. Peripheralization or marginalization also refers to a symbolic downgrading, sensitively perceived by those affected as exclusion. A section of the *classes populaires* found themselves once again marginalized, made to appear invisible and deprived of their social recognition by the socio-spatial consequences of deindustrialization.

Second, during the deindustrialization phase, industrial workers moved up into the circle of house and property owners. This was especially true for qualified industrial labourers who belonged to the core workforce of the shrinking industrial companies, but also for families and households with more than one source of income. New opportunities were opened up here by the increase in female employment in the new service industries. Many of these households purchased their property with the help of cheap mortgages, incurring substantial debts. The emergence of corresponding residential areas for the lower middle class – *die untere Mittelschicht*, as is the popular term in German, or the *classes populaires* – has been well documented, especially for France. As the labour markets shifted towards the various service industries, they provided a socio-spatial anchor.[79] Without it, the kind of socio-spatial neglect occurred that was demonstrated so clearly to local authorities or local politicians

303

and the wider public by the suburban problem neighbourhoods and ruins of mono-industrial cities (of which there were in fact very few).

Contrary to the expectations of the social democratic upward mobility programmes in the period of expansion, socio-spatial mixing in an increasingly socially mobile society did not occur. The majority of the working class remained relegated to a place in the lower half of the three national social spaces in terms of their living and housing conditions. We should not ignore the fact that most of the labour migrants who had left their original transit spaces also found a place in these settlements and neighbourhoods. During the period studied here, they were zones of relative socio-spatial stability. They acted as anchors[80] also because of the growth in daily and weekly commuting between home and work – a trend that was equally strong in all three countries. The number of commuters increased in the last three decades of the twentieth century and into the twenty-first century, as did the length of the commute.[81]

Third, in all three countries, with very few exceptions, the large industrial conurbations disappeared. In the heyday of industrialization between 1880 and 1970, they had become areas where spaces of industrial production and social spaces dominated by industry were closely interconnected. The industrial regions of the coal, steel and textile industries, but also the large automobile factories, were examples of these compact industrial working environments. The industrial districts of the digital age, on the other hand, are much more strongly influenced by the same spatial structures that have always been characteristic of small-scale rural industrial areas: that is, provincial settlement patterns with mixed economic structures and close networking between the various socio-economic groups. One main reason why these new smaller industrial areas adopted quite different forms in our three countries is connected to the conditions of their respective nation-specific frameworks. There is an absence of detailed socio-historical studies of the socio-cultural basis for this third phenomenon. A wealth of research work awaits social historians here.

CONCLUSION

The history of deindustrialization as a history of contemporary problems

What legacies have the upheavals of deindustrialization left to contemporary societies in Western Europe? What political challenges and openings ensue from the analyses in the previous chapters of this book? A history of society in the recent past cannot avoid engaging with these kinds of questions and thus straying slightly from the field of historical research. At the end of each of the previous eight chapters, I attempted to identify the continuities that stretch forward into the present, but as a conclusion to this study, I would like to highlight once again the aspects which it has revealed particularly clearly.

For the first time for a long while, deindustrialization produced winners and losers in Western European societies. The highly effective 'elevator effect' (Beck) of the postwar economic boom had lifted nearly all professional groups and classes onto higher levels of income and social security and provided them with educational opportunities and consumer choices. At the end of the 1980s, however, it failed. From then on, it was not only inequality of income that increased but also social risks such as unemployment and income and asset poverty. At the same time, the combination of substandard housing and unsatisfactory jobs became a reality of life, not for the majority but for a considerable section of the population in Western Europe. It was particularly the loss of well-paid jobs in industry that caused the failure of this 'elevator' to continue working for everyone, since there were by far too few jobs in the new service industries, they were frequently poorly paid, provided no job security and did not always offer even what could be considered partial job satisfaction. No sooner had most traces of a proletarian way of life been eliminated in all three Western European countries than a new age of precarity dawned.

Although I have repeatedly addressed the socio-historical contours of this new constellation in this book, it was not my main priority. This was because it emerged that it was the industrial world itself that was a source of strong forces of stability firmly counteracting these new tendencies. In fact, Western European industry generally remained an area of stable employment where, thanks to higher productivity, wages at a similar level of qualification were higher than those in the service industries. While there was only modest growth in real wages, the quality of work and the level of employment security created a gulf between those employed in industry and those who were forced to give up industrial work and secure their livelihoods in the new service industries. This latter trend was particularly marked where industrial production had shrunk swiftly and dramatically, leading to mass redundancies, where there were large-scale reductions in work-related social benefits and social rights and where the proportion of unskilled jobs in production remained relatively high. This was the case in many regions in Britain, whereas in France and Germany the overall situation had developed differently from the outset.

At the beginning of the twenty-first century, the decision of successive British governments to promote radical deindustrialization together with a change of course in social policy was still being admired and praised as 'bold' by many Western European polit-icians. The then apparent positive effects of the British pathway on the labour market encouraged governments on the continent to follow suit, although less widely and more carefully. However, success also came at a high social cost. Precarious living and working conditions became everyday reality for many members of the working classes to an extent unparalleled in France and Germany. Britain's departure from social citizenship widened the gap that separated it from the latter two countries – long before Brexit.

The social forces promoting stability in industrial labour were strongest where technological innovations had caused far-reaching changes both in the organization of work and in the products themselves. Time and again in the course of this study, it has become apparent that the scope for action as businesses and companies switched to flexible production of high-quality goods was relatively wide and that both sides, capital and labour, frequently used it pragmatically, adapting to the particular situation. Company regimes in the 1980s and 1990s, for example, were constantly changing in all three countries in what could be described as experimental conditions. Responsibilities and participation rights were redistributed between the various groups of employees, and technical or production-specific knowledge and experience were reappraised. Company hierarchies generally became flatter and workers were entrusted with a wider range of tasks and responsibilities. In Germany, a model of high-quality production prevailed in the majority of export-oriented businesses and a well-qualified core workforce was given extensive participation and partial co-management rights. In France and Britain, in contrast, the trend developed towards new forms of Taylorized work based on computerized production, communication and control systems. Yet even where the traditional division of labour between technicians, skilled workers and semi-skilled workers was maintained and knowledge and competencies were redistributed only to a limited extent, it was possible for company regimes based on cooperation and recognition to be established. The fact that the company they belonged to was repeatedly cited as a positive reference point in the reports and interviews with industrial workers demonstrates its significance both for social integration and as an anchor of continuity in their lives.

The conditional nature of the data available and the wide variety of company regimes that existed do not permit definitive answers, but they do permit the tentative conclusion that the satisfaction of many workers with their new industrial jobs was also connected with a sense of social recognition and (relative) social security. The improved image of many industrial businesses was therefore not only the result of successful public relations or of the contrast with the negative labour and socio-political balance sheet of many new service industries. It would appear beyond question that even in this period of upheaval the demands of the workforce for participation and recognition were compatible with the profit expectations of capital investors.

It is by no means a new phenomenon for there to be an increase in workers' appreciation of the company they are attached to. This was frequently the case in times of mass redundancies and economic instability. What was new now in this post-boom phase was that to a far greater extent than in the past this appreciation was closely connected to the effective representation of interests by trade unions or at the workplace. This expansion of workers' representation rights is a clear development during this phase which is frequently overlooked. It led to the end of the absolute rule of management and entrepreneurs, particularly in medium-sized and smaller companies, even though this was not the case across the board. Britain and France marked the two opposite extremes of the political organization of worker participation in terms of collective bargaining regulations. The decisive factor in the real world of industrial work in all three countries was undeniably the extent of collective worker participation. Democratic participation at company level developed parallel to the technological and organizational upheavals in industrial production and is an important legacy of this transitional period.

The question of whether factories mutated into 'workhouses' or became 'cooperative working societies' gained in significance also because representation of the collective interests of industrial workers became progressively weaker on the political level. Social integration in a company became an antidote to social divisions and the lack of participation on the macro level of society. As the frontiers of a society became increasingly unclear – were they national, European, Western or even global? – disillusionment with its social order (or lack of it) grew.

Above, I described the gradual withdrawal of the established industrial workforce from the political stage and their role as mainly passive spectators in the conflicts occurring since the beginning of the twenty-first century. In spite of national differences, it is clear that industrial workers steadily disassociated themselves from the left-wing political parties and from political parties and politics in general. Further traces of this crisis of political representation lead more or less directly to current political protest movements and right-wing populist mobilization in Western Europe today. Referring to the analyses of French social scientists, I emphasized that an important element of this crisis of representation was that the problems and experiences of industrial workers became 'invisible'. My approach to this analysis was more from the angle of cultural and political history, while my thesis pertaining to the 'peripheralization' of the social space of industrial workers provides it with a socio-historical basis.

The structural change in the social geography of work and housing is one of the 'silent revolutions' which we have encountered several times in this book, although I have only been able to deal briefly with its cultural significance. Here, further studies are necessary. The influence of the exodus of the *classes populaires* from urban centres and the settlement of many households and families of industrial workers on the outskirts of large cities or in the sprawling suburbs is still felt today. In all three countries, the 'elevator effect' has survived in the area of home ownership, resulting in a growing number of workers becoming part of the property-owning society on whose stability the democratic parties of Western Europe have increasingly come to rely. Some of these households of workers and mid-level employees committed to high, long-term payments in order to fulfil this dream. The ongoing effects of this financial commitment to the acquisition of property and the perpetuation of the dependencies, imponderables and fears resulting from it also require further detailed study.

The increasing number of workers owning their own home also points to a further 'revolutionary social change' that reaches into the present day. The 'farewell to the industrial labourer' was also realized in concrete terms as the disintegration of a compact socio-cultural milieu revolving around the male production worker. The figure of the male shift worker and sole wage earner in the steelworks, mines and automobile factories swiftly lost its significance, not only in terms of numbers. The massive wave of early retirement also heralded a swift end to a milieu-defining social icon. This change of behaviour and role models took place either as a quiet and largely conflict-free shift in the attitudes of younger age groups (particularly in Germany and Britain), or as a more conflict-laden confrontation between typical generational attitudes (particularly in France).

This was accompanied by a gradual and silent change in family and household structures. First impressions suggest that relatively little changed within the *classes populaires* because, more frequently than in the dynamic period of growth after World War II, the subsequent generation of workers also came from the families of workers or low-level white-collar workers. As in the generation of their parents, most spouses found their partners in the same or similar social class and with similar education. However, an increasing number of partnerships appeared between male industrial workers and female white-collar workers, who, for their part, were employed in various service sectors and, in contrast to their mothers, had equivalent qualifications to their husbands or partners. To a much greater extent than the male members of their households, the wives, mothers and daughters worked part-time. They were still strongly represented within the unskilled and semi-skilled workforce, but the proportion of women with professional qualifications was slowly but steadily increasing. As wages stagnated and financial commitments continued, women's contribution to the household income gradually became just as relevant as that of their husbands, fathers and brothers. As a result, the social space of the *classes populaires* developed into a meeting point of different kinds of male and female professional experience and of industrial work and old and new service jobs. The extent of this social space's homogeneity was determined more than ever by local and regional circumstances, such as shared origins and standards of education, local and regional connections, traditions of socio-moral milieu formation and labour relations.

At the end of the upheaval phase and beyond, the *classes populaires* were courted from every side as part of the 'broad political centre' which has been seen in all the three countries since the 1990s (earlier in Germany) as the epicentre of a nation beyond class boundaries. They have, however, remained at a clear distance in cultural, social and economic terms from the 'better-off' middle classes of the academic professional world, whereby this line cannot easily be drawn either at the top or at the bottom of this category. In all three countries, the *classes populaires* took up the greater part of the lower half of social space without lending it a specific identity or even cohesion through cultural characteristics, joint political organizations or shared styles of consumption. They made use of the increasing opportunities for cultural consumption (private television/ leisure activities) and profited from the higher degree of freedom to shape their leisure styles. Their entry into the social logic of subtle distinctions is certainly one of the basic shifts in the social spaces of Western Europe and still has an impact today. It was, however, only indirectly connected to the process of deindustrialization since it was much more closely bound to the dynamics of consumption, media use and education.

In this connection, national cultural frameworks continued to have a crucial influence. They determined the symbolic stakes and gains in the social evaluation of cultural practices.[1] The collapse of the fixed dividing lines between high culture and entertainment, middle-class and popular culture, that occurred on a large scale in all three countries during the last three decades of the twentieth century brought diversity to the sphere of socially accepted cultural forms. But it also marked the start of a complex race for symbolic recognition of lifestyles and consumption opportunities, subtle distinctions and cultural prestige in the social world. The *classes populaires* of all three countries entered this race under the worst possible conditions. They did not have the necessary education to provide general validity to their own preferences as an expression of legitimate culture and at the same time they found themselves confronted by a constant process of re-evaluation and re-appropriation of popular forms of culture by the avant-garde academic middle class. They would remain on the losing side until political reinterpretations changed the rules of the game. This began to happen after the breakdown of social democratic and communist counter-cultures when alternative regional, national and also ethnic-religious patterns became increasingly popular with the *classes populaires* as a contrast to the dominant models of a Western-style liberal cosmopolitan global culture.[2]

From the discussion so far, it might be assumed that the upheaval phase of deindustrialization described in this book has not yet come to an end even today, some fifty years after it began. This leads to the question of whether there are hiatuses which would justify designating the three decades from 1970 to 2000 as a separate epoch and distinguishing them from the present. The question is naturally typical for historians, but my response to it also concerns our analyses of the present. My answer is in the affirmative. Beyond the lines of continuity discernible in the problems and forces of stability, there is clear evidence of characteristics singular to this epoch. One example would be the diverse protests and social mobilizations against established hierarchies and authority that particularly affected the world of work in the early years of deindustrialization as a consequence of the 1968 'revolution'. Traces of political 'rebellion' against hierarchical company regimes and lack of recognition particularly of semi-skilled and unskilled workers can be followed back to the 1970s. The development of alternatives to Taylorist factory organization and the programmes aimed at 'humanizing' work are similar genuine products of the time, as is the expansion of social citizenship in all three countries and the extension of co-determination rights in France and Germany. The last wave of labour migration and the integration of the first and second generation of labour migrants also belong to the singularities of this transformation phase. Taken collectively, the weight of the industrial world, its actors and problems was much greater in the 1970s and 1980s than it was after the turn of the millennium, and many of the changes analysed here that resulted from deindustrialization came to a provisional end in the 1990s. By 2000 at the latest, all three countries had taken their leave of old industrial labour. The widespread conversion of the industrial age into an object of museum and historical interest is a cultural indicator of this break, while the qualitative and quantitative stabilization of industries and their employment figures in the course of the noughties is an economic indicator. The boom of the New Economy which began in the 1990s points to new expectations of the future and interpretations of society. Many of our present-day problems only arose later than or independently of the readjustment process described here. The rapid success of the internet after 1995, for example, has created

311

a wealth of new social phenomena, new political communication patterns and overall a profound structural change in Western Europe and worldwide. A vast gulf divides us from social worlds without social media, the internet or smartphones.

A further argument concerns generations. In the 1980s, the fall in the number of industrial jobs led to those born before 1935 leaving work in rapid succession, and in 2000, only a minority of young people, predominantly men, were on the path towards a new industrial career. The reduction in industrial jobs and the practice of early retirement meant that the importance of industrial work as an underlying experience declined significantly. Finally, the chronology of political events also suggests taking the millennium as the beginning of a new epoch dividing the immediate history of our present from the longer post-boom phase of upheaval. When in 1997 and 1998 two social democrats, Tony Blair and Gerhard Schröder, came to power in Britain and Germany respectively, they both made a conscious break with the past of their political parties. Their economic policy focussed on developing the service sector, and the fact that the Labour Party and the SPD were oriented towards the new upwardly mobile middle classes allowed the old relations of patronage and representation between the *classes populaires* and the two left-wing parties to erode still further. In France, the disastrous election defeat of the socialist presidential candidate Lionel Jospin in 2002 documented a similar break with workers' political representation.

The reorientation in politics, everyday communication and generational experience since the end of the twentieth century outlined here thus speaks in favour of describing the period between 1970 and 2000 as a specific transitional period during which a primarily industrial social order gave way to a clearly more pluralist social order with three equally strong sectors of the economy: public services, private services and industrial production. A social history of this latter period will have to take into account the dependencies and continuities that connect the late twentieth century with our present, but it will for its part have to develop new methods and perspectives to do justice to the dynamics of the last twenty years.

In conclusion, I would like to return to the open concept of 'history of society' that I advocated at the beginning of this book, because it permits transnational macro processes and regional or even local microstructures to be analysed in equal measure. However, the question of both their respective weighting and their mutual interdependence remains open. Even though as the starting point of my study I chose a basic economic process that undoubtedly applies to all developed capitalist industrial countries and which was in addition steered by central economic policy regulations (customs duties, product norms, etc.) at the European level and only secondarily at a national level, I constantly encountered social consequences and structurings that were distinctly specific to a certain region and/or location. For this reason, I have attempted to investigate different types of local constellations from the perspective of a 'history of society' and to assess the scope for social responses to economic challenges. In this sense, the book provides arguments in favour of a small-scale mapping of European industrial regions in transition and disassociates itself from attempts to identify variants of capitalism solely specific to individual nations. Foreign investors, for example, were more likely to be guided by regional than by national considerations when making their investment decisions, and company regimes were more likely to be determined by internal factors or regional influences than by national regulations. However, this method of argumentation reached its limits when it came to the legal regulation of educational qualifications, welfare benefits and employment contracts. In these cases, the extent of national regulation remained crucial and imposed relatively tight restrictions on the range of local variations.

Nevertheless, it would be a mistake to summarize the results of this study in three separate 'national' chapters. It would disregard the significance of transnational, Western European trends to the same extent as it would the influence of regional and local constellations. The fact that the national level has returned to centre stage in such a dramatic fashion has less to do with the social processes analysed here and more with the political developments apparent in Britain, France and Germany since the turn of the millennium. Wars, terror attacks and humanitarian interventions involving all three countries clearly foregrounded national concerns. The transformation of the European Union into a neoliberal modernizing machine based on the consensus of administrators, shareholders, managers and politicians of all political parties, but whose role in providing a space for the development of social citizenship is minimal, has downgraded the European project to a mere business cooperative of European elites. This trend was reinforced by the banking crisis and the crisis of the euro after 2008. These are all reasons why debates about alternative social and economic policies amongst social scientists have reverted to the level of nation-states. It is there that today's populist protest movements formulate expressly nationalist demands. While Western Europe may, therefore, still provide the structural frame of reference, we are repeatedly taken beyond local and regional references by the past experience of actors and returned to the level of nation-states and their societies. How this should be assessed and whether it will remain the case in the future are questions that lie outside the remit of historians.

NOTES

Introduction: Perspectives on a history of Western European society after the boom

1 Particularly prominent, of course, Thomas Piketty, *Capital in the Twenty-First Century*, Cambridge, MA, 2013.
2 Pierre Rosanvallon, *Society of Equals*, Boston, 2013.
3 Ibid., pp. 303–6.
4 This applies to classical contemporary history as well as to social history, but not to the history of ideas and culture and cultural studies in general, and certainly not to literature. A prime example from the field of social history is Peter Laslett, *The World We Have Lost: England before the Industrial Age*, 4th edition, London, 2004 [1966]. However, such nostalgia-suspect approaches do not fit with a critical social history that should not seal itself off from the present.
5 See also Anselm Doering-Manteuffel and Lutz Raphael, *Nach dem Boom. Perspektiven auf die Zeitgeschichte seit 1970*, 3rd edition, Göttingen, 2012; Sebastian Voigt (ed.), *After the Boom: Continuity and Change in the Western Industrialized World after 1970*, Toronto, 2021.
6 Published so far: Anselm Doering-Manteuffel et al. (eds), *Vorgeschichte der Gegenwart. Dimensionen des Strukturbruchs nach dem Boom*, Göttingen, 2016; Tobias Gerstung, *Stapellauf für ein neues Zeitalter. Die Industriemetropole Glasgow im revolutionären Wandel nach dem Boom (1960–2000)*, Göttingen, 2016; Fernando Esposito (ed.), *Zeitenwandel. Transformationen geschichtlicher Zeitlichkeit nach dem Boom*, Göttingen, 2017; Raphael Emanuel Dorn, *Alle in Bewegung. Räumliche Mobilität in der Bundesrepublik Deutschland 1980–2010*, Göttingen, 2018; Arne Hordt, *Kumpel, Kohle und Krawall*, Göttingen, 2018; Ingo Köhler, *Auto-Identitäten. Marketing, Konsum und Produktbilder des Automobils nach dem Boom*, Göttingen, 2018; Arndt Neumann, *Unternehmen Hamburg. Eine Geschichte der neoliberalen Stadt*, Göttingen, 2018.

315

7 Andreas Wirsching, *Der Preis der Freiheit. Geschichte Europas in unserer Zeit*, Munich, 2012.

8 A view of the wider European context of the decades after 1990 is provided by Philipp Ther, *Europe since 1989: A History*, Princeton, 2016.

9 E.J. Hobsbawm, 'From Social History to the History of Society', in *Daedalus* 100/1 (1971), pp. 20–45.

10 Hans-Ulrich Wehler, *Deutsche Gesellschaftsgeschichte*, vol. 1, 4th edition, Munich, 2006, p. 6.

11 This applies not only to 'society', of course, but also to all other principal research terms in historical and social science analysis.

12 For example: Colin Crouch, *Social Change in Western Europe*, Oxford, 2004; Hartmut Kaelble, *A Social History of Europe, 1945–2000*, New York and Oxford, 2013. Britain of course opted out of the EU in 2016 with effect from January 2020.

13 Siegfried Kracauer, *History: The Last Things before the Last*, Oxford, 1969, p. 125.

14 Ibid., p. 97.

15 Michael J. Piore and Charles F. Sabel, *The Second Industrial Divide: Possibilities for Prosperity*, New York, 1984.

16 Stéphane Beaud and Michel Pialoux, *Retour sur la condition ouvrière. Enquête aux usines Peugeot de Sochaux-Montbéliard*, Paris, 1999.

17 Hermann Kotthoff, '"Betriebliche Sozialordnung" als Basis ökonomischer Leistungsfähigkeit', in Jens Beckert and Christoph Deutschmann (eds), *Wirtschaftssoziologie*, Wiesbaden, 2010, pp. 428–46.

18 Rosanvallon, *Society of Equals*; Axel Honneth, *The Struggle for Recognition*, Oxford, 1995.

19 Pierre Bourdieu et al., *The Weight of the World: Social Suffering in Contemporary Societies*, Cambridge and Stanford, CA, 1999, pp. 123–9.

20 Olivier Schwartz, 'Peut-on parler des classes populaires?', in *La Vie des idées* (13 September 2011) : http://www.laviedesidees.fr/Peut-on-parler-des-classes.html.

21 Andreas Wirsching, 'Konsum statt Arbeit? Zum Wandel von Individualität in der modernen Massengesellschaft', in *Vierteljahrshefte für Zeitgeschichte* 57 (2009), pp. 171–99.

22 The data collected here on 12,000 first West German then also East German households provides comprehensive information on the socio-economic situation and on the life courses and attitudes of a representative cross-section of the population resident in Germany. A database was created from this entire data which contains information on working households in West Germany from 1984 to 2000. In it, information has been collected on all households, including partners and children, who were questioned for at least ten working years and who belonged to those workers and who for at least half of these working years were eligible for social insurance or had been unemployed in the previous or following years. This database contains data on more than 3,000 people

in West Germany. In the following, it will be cited as *Arbeiterhaushalte in Westdeutschland 1984–2000*. On the use of representative surveys for historical research, see Raphael Emanuel Dorn, *Alle in Bewegung. Räumliche Mobilität in der Bundesrepublik Deutschland 1980–2010*, Göttingen, 2018, pp. 23–31.

Chapter 1 Industrial labour in Western Europe after the economic boom from the perspective of political economy

1 Michel Hau, 'Introduction', in Jean-Claude Daumas et al. (eds), *La désindustrialization: une fatalité?* Besançon, 2017, pp. 7–16, here p. 7.
2 This definition follows Royce Logan Turner, 'Introduction', in idem (ed.), *The British Economy in Transition: From the Old to the New?*, London and New York, 1995, pp. 1–22, here p. 10.
3 Werner Plumpe and André Steiner, 'Der Mythos von der postindustriellen Welt', in idem (eds), *Der Mythos von der postindustriellen Welt. Wirtschaftlicher Strukturwandel in Deutschland 1960–1990*, Göttingen, 2016, pp. 7–14.
4 André Steiner, 'Abschied von der Industrie? Wirtschaftlicher Strukturwandel in West- und Ostdeutschland seit den 1960er Jahren', in ibid., pp. 15–54, here p. 52.
5 Rainer Metz, 'Volkswirtschaftliche Gesamtrechnungen', in Thomas Rahlf (ed.), *Deutschland in Zahlen. Zeitreihen zur Historischen Statistik*, Bonn, 2015, pp. 186–99, here pp. 192–6.
6 See Philipp Ther, *Europe since 1989: A History*, Princeton, 2016.
7 Joachim Schild and Henrik Uterwedde, *Frankreich. Politik, Wirtschaft, Gesellschaft*, 2nd edition, Wiesbaden, 2006, p. 144; Michael Kitson, 'Failure Followed by Success or Success Followed by Failure? A Re-examination of British Economic Growth since 1949', in Roderick Floud and Paul Johnson (eds), *Structural Change and Growth, 1939–2000*, Cambridge, 2004, pp. 27–56, here p. 33.
8 Peter Dicken, *Global Shift: Reshaping the Global Economic Map in the 21st Century*, 4th edition, London et al., 2006, pp. 317–54; idem, *Global Shift: Mapping the Changing Contours of the World Economy*, 6th edition, New York and London, 2011, pp. 301–30.
9 The figures in the official statistics would have to be adjusted to obtain a realistic assessment of the importance of the industrial sector in the three countries studied. Figures for France are provided by Lilas Demmou, 'Le recul de l'emploi industriel en France entre 1980 et 2007. Ampleur et principaux déterminants: un état des lieux', in *Economie et statistique* 438–40 (2010), pp. 273–96, here p. 275.
10 Lionel Nesta, 'Désindustrialization ou mutation industrielle?', in *Economie et statistique* 438–40 (2010), pp. 297–301, here pp. 298–9.
11 For example, the 1973 Multifibre Agreement and the 1995 GATT Uruguay Agreement.

12 See Dicken, *Global Shift: Reshaping the Global Economic Map*, pp. 337, 338 and 339.
13 Cf. Yves Mény et al. (eds), *The Politics of Steel: Western Europe and the Steel Industry in the Crisis Years (1974–1984)*, Berlin, 1987; Karl Lauschke, *Die halbe Macht. Mitbestimmung in der Eisen- und Stahlindustrie 1945 bis 1989*, Essen, 2007, pp. 231–330.
14 Ther, *Europe since 1989: A History*; Andreas Wirsching, *Der Preis der Freiheit. Geschichte Europas in unserer Zeit*, Munich, 2012, pp. 236–41 and 250–60.
15 The number of recorded company branches and subsidiary companies in Britain, France and Germany rose from 229 in 1985 to 841 in 2000. See Tony Elger and Chris Smith, *Assembling Work: Remaking Factory Regimes in Japanese Multinationals in Britain*, New York, 2005, p. 88, table 3.1.
16 OECD, *Measuring Globalisation*, vol. 1, Geneva, 2001, pp. 107, 108, 345 and 351.
17 Nicholas Comfort, *The Slow Death of British Industry: A Sixty-Year Suicide, 1952–2012*, London, 2013, p. 172.
18 Ulrich Jürgens and Hans Klingel, 'Internationalisierung als Struktur und Strategie im Werkzeugmaschinenbau – Das Beispiel der Firma Trumpf', in Pamela Meil (ed.), *Globalisierung industrieller Produktion. Strategien und Strukturen*, Frankfurt/M. et al., 1996, pp. 27–56, here p. 32.
19 See *Filigran 2015/16*, annual report of the TRUMPF Group: https://www.trumpf.com/filestorage/TRUMPF_Master/Corporate/Annual_report/Archive/TRUMPF_Geschaeftsbericht_2015_2016.pdf.
20 My own calculations based on the ILO database on industrial employment. These figures there are in turn based on official estimates: https://www.ilo.org/global/statistics-and-databases/lang--en/index.htm.
21 OECD, 'Value Added by Activity' (2018): https://data.oecd.org/natincome/value-added-by-activity.htm.
22 This figure is from Eurostat – the Statistical Office of the European Union.
23 Again my own calculations based on the ILO database of industrial employment. Official estimates are used similarly by Jean-Louis Dayan, 'L'emploi en France depuis trente ans', in Olivier Marchand (ed.), *L'emploi, nouveaux enjeux*, Paris, 2000, pp. 17–24, here p. 20.
24 For an overview, see Schild and Uterwedde, *Frankreich*, pp. 138–218.
25 Comparative ILO data from the same period cannot be used for Germany because of reunification. Again these are my own calculations based on the ILO database for 1972 and 1982 for the first phase and the data of the German Federal Office of Statistics for 1980, 1990 and 2000 for the second and third phases.
26 Ingo Köhler, *Auto-Identitäten. Marketing, Konsum und Produktbilder des Automobils nach dem Boom*, Göttingen, 2018.
27 Pascal Brocard and Carole Donada, *La chaîne de l'équipement automobile*, Paris, 2003, pp. 13–46.

28 Ibid., pp. 31–2.
29 Christian Marx, 'Der Aufstieg multinationaler Konzerne. Umstrukturierungen und Standortkonkurrenz in der westeuropäischen Chemieindustrie', in Anselm Doering-Manteuffel et al. (eds), *Vorgeschichte der Gegenwart. Dimensionen des Strukturbruchs nach dem Boom*, Göttingen, 2016, pp. 197–216; Christian Marx and Morten Reitmayer, 'Zwangslagen und Handlungsspielräume. Der Wandel von Produktionsmodellen in der westdeutschen Chemieindustrie im letzten Drittel des 20. Jahrhunderts', in *Archiv für Sozialgeschichte* 56 (2016), pp. 297–334.
30 Christian Marx, 'Between National Governance and the Internationalization of Business: The Case of Four Major West German Producers of Chemicals, Pharmaceuticals and Fibres, 1945–2000', in *Business History* 27 (2017), pp. 1–30; Jürgen Kädtler, 'German Chemical Giants' Business and Social Models in Transition: Financialisation as a Management Strategy', in *Transfer* 15 (2009), pp. 229–49.
31 Ralf Ahrens, 'Eine alte Industrie vor neuen Herausforderungen. Aufbrüche und Niedergänge im ost- und westdeutschen Maschinenbau seit den 1960er Jahren', in Plumpe and Steiner (eds), *Der Mythos von der postindustriellen Welt*, pp. 55–119; Mike Geddes and Anne Green, 'Engineering: Company Strategies and Public Policy in an Industry in Crisis', in Turner (ed.), *The British Economy in Transition*, pp. 123–41.
32 Hermann Simon, *Hidden Champions of the 21st Century: Lessons from 500 of the World's Best Unknown Companies*, Boston, 1996.
33 *Annuaire statistique de la France* 104 (1999), p. 125.
34 Ulrich Widmaier (ed.), *Der deutsche Maschinenbau in den neunziger Jahren*, Frankfurt/M. and New York, 2000.
35 *Annuaire statistique de la France* 89 (1986), p. 346; 106 (2001), p. 437.
36 Textiles: 1984: 11.2 per cent; 2000: 5.6 per cent; clothing: 1984: 12.5 per cent; 2000: 13 per cent; mechanical engineering: 1984: 9.2 per cent; 2000: 6.2 per cent. See *Statistisches Jahrbuch für die Bundesrepublik Deutschland 1986*, p. 170; 2002, p. 190.
37 Manuel Castells, *The Information Age: Economy, Society, and Culture*, vol. 1: *The Rise of the Network Society*, 2nd edition, Chichester, 2010, pp. 28–76.
38 Arndt Neumann, *Unternehmen Hamburg. Eine Geschichte der neoliberalen Stadt*, Göttingen, 2018, p. 198.
39 Widmaier (ed.), *Der deutsche Maschinenbau in den neunziger Jahren*, p. 119.
40 Uwe Jürgenhake and Beate Winter, *Neue Produktionskonzepte in der Stahlindustrie. Ökonomisch-technischer Wandel und Arbeitskräfteeinsatz in der Eisen- und Stahlindustrie und seine Auswirkungen auf die Arbeitsorganization und -gestaltung sowie die betriebliche Aus- und Weiterbildung*, Dortmund, 1992, pp. 65–106, figures: p. 68.
41 Franck Cochoy et al., 'Comment l'écrit travaille l'organisation: le cas

des normes ISO 9000', in *Revue française de sociologie* 39 (1998), pp. 673–99.

42 Günter Spur et al., *Automatisierung und Wandel der betrieblichen Arbeitswelt*, Berlin, 1993, p. 144.

43 Brocard and Donada, *La chaîne de l'équipement automobile*, p. 145.

44 Ibid., p. 87.

45 Gerold Ambrosius, *Wirtschaftsraum Europa. Vom Ende der Nationalökonomien*, Frankfurt/M., 1996.

46 Stefan Eich and Adam Tooze, 'The Great Inflation', in Anselm Doering-Manteuffel et al. (eds), *Vorgeschichte der Gegenwart. Dimensionen des Strukturbruchs nach dem Boom*, Göttingen, 2016, pp. 173–96.

47 Jean-Jacques Becker and Pascal Ory, *Crises et alternances (1974–1995)*, Paris, 1998, p. 297.

48 Ibid., p. 294.

49 Eich and Tooze, 'The Great Inflation', pp. 188–91.

50 The nationalization law of 11 February 1982 covered the companies CGE, Saint-Gobain, Péchiney Ugine Kuhlmann, Rhône-Poulenc, Thomson-Brandt and Usinor-Sacilor. Further nationalizations affected the defence companies Dassault and Matra.

51 Comfort, *The Slow Death of British Industry*, pp. 113, 118, 119.

52 Ibid., pp. 123–45.

53 Andreas Wirsching, *Abschied vom Provisorium, 1982–1990*, Munich, 2006, p. 256.

54 Nick von Tunzelmann, 'Technology in Postwar Britain', in Roderick Floud and Paul Johnson (eds), *Structural Change and Growth, 1939–2000*, Cambridge, 2004, pp. 299–331, here p. 304.

55 Wolfgang Streeck, 'The Crisis in Context: Democratic Capitalism and Its Contradictions', in Armin Schäfer (ed.), *Politics in the Age of Austerity*, Cambridge, 2013, pp. 262–302.

56 Anselm Doering-Manteuffel and Lutz Raphael, *Nach dem Boom. Westeuropäische Zeitgeschichte seit 1970*, 3rd edition, Göttingen, 2011, pp. 27, 71–4.

57 See especially the contributions in Paul Windolf (ed.), *Finanzmarkt-Kapitalismus. Analysen zum Wandel von Produktionsregimen*, Wiesbaden, 2005; similarly for the French regulation school: Michel Aglietta, *Le capitalisme de demain*, Paris, 1998; Robert Boyer, *The Political Economy of Capitalisms*, Singapore, 2022; for a summary of the critique, see Michael Faust et al., *Das kapitalmarktorientierte Unternehmen. Externe Erwartungen, Unternehmenspolitik, Personalwesen und Mitbestimmung*, Berlin, 2011, pp. 401–20.

58 The following is adapted from Paul Windolf, 'Was ist Finanzmarkt-Kapitalismus?', in idem (ed.), *Finanzmarkt-Kapitalismus*, pp. 20–57.

59 Karina Becker, *Die Bühne der Bonität. Wie mittelständische Unternehmen auf die neuen Anforderungen des Finanzmarkts reagieren*, Baden-Baden, 2009.

60 Hartmut Berghoff, 'Varieties of Financialization? Evidence from German Industry in the 1990s', in *Business History Review* 90 (2016), pp. 81–108, here p. 85.

61 On Germany, see Saskia Freye, 'Neue Managerkarrieren im deutschen Kapitalismus?', in *Leviathan* 41 (2013), pp. 57–93.

62 Wolfgang Streeck, *Buying Time: The Delayed Crisis of Democratic Capitalism*, London and New York, 2014.

63 Robert Boyer, 'How and Why Capitalisms Differ', in *Economy and Society* 34 (2005), pp. 509–57.

64 On France: François Morin and Eric Rigamonti, 'Évolution et structure de l'actionnariat en France', in *Revue française de gestion* 141 (2002), pp. 155–81; Daniel Baudru and Med Kechidi, 'Les investisseurs institutionnels étrangers. Vers la fin du capitalisme à la française?', in *Revue d'économie financière* 48 (1998), pp. 93–105; Laurent Commaille, 'Das Ende des französischen Modells. Die Eisen- und Stahlindustrie im späten 20. Jahrhunderts', in Morten Reitmayer (ed.), *Unternehmen am Ende des goldenen Zeitalters. Die 1970er Jahre in unternehmens- und wirtschaftshistorischer Perspektive*, Essen, 2008, pp. 129–45. On Germany: Berghoff, 'Varieties of Financialization?'; Jürgen Beyer, 'Die Strukturen der Deutschland AG. Ein Rückblick auf ein Modell der Unternehmenskontrolle', in Ralf Ahrens et al. (eds), *Die 'Deutschland AG'. Historische Annäherungen an den bundesdeutschen Kapitalismus*, Essen, 2013, pp. 31–56; Susanne Lütz, 'Von der Infrastruktur zum Markt? Der deutsche Finanzsektor zwischen Deregulierung und Reregulierung', in Windolf (ed.), *Finanzmarkt-Kapitalismus*, pp. 294–315.

65 Marx and Reitmayer, 'Zwangslagen und Handlungsspielräume', p. 323; Comfort, *The Slow Death of British Industry*, p. 181.

66 Kädtler, 'German Chemical Giants' Business and Social Models in Transition', pp. 237–46.

67 Faust et al., *Das kapitalmarktorientierte Unternehmen*.

68 Klaus Dörre, 'Das flexible-marktzentrierte Produktionsmodell. Gravitationszentrum eines neuen Kapitalismus', in idem and Bernd Röttger (eds), *Das neue Marktregime. Konturen eines nachfordistischen Produktionsmodells*, Hamburg, 2003, pp. 7–34.

69 Gary Herrigel, 'Roles and Rules: Ambiguity, Experimentation and New Forms of Stakeholderism in Germany', in *Industrial Relations* 15 (2008), pp. 111–32.

70 Josef Mooser, 'Abschied von der "Proletarität". Sozialstruktur und Lage der Arbeiterschaft in der Bundesrepublik in historischer Perspektive', in Werner Conze and M. Rainer Lepsius (eds), *Sozialgeschichte der Bundesrepublik Deutschland. Beiträge zum Kontinuitätsproblem*, 2nd edition, Stuttgart, 1984, pp. 143–66.

71 Serge Paugam, *Le salarié de la précarité. Les nouvelles formes de l'intégration professionnelle*, Paris, 2000.

72 My own calculations (1995 only former West Germany) based on the

Socio-Economic Panel (SOEP): https://www.diw.de/en/diw_02.c.221178
.en/about_soep.html.

73 Christine Trampusch, 'Institutional Resettlement: The Case of Early
Retirement in Germany', in Wolfgang Streeck and Kathleen Ann Thelen
(eds), *Beyond Continuity: Institutional Change in Advanced Political
Economies*, Oxford and New York, 2005, pp. 203–28.

74 Günther Schmid and Frank Oschmiansky, 'Arbeitsmarktpolitik und
Arbeitslosenversicherung', in Manfred G. Schmidt (ed.), *Bundesrepublik
Deutschland, 1982–1989. Finanzielle Konsolidierung und institutionelle
Reform*, Baden-Baden, 2005, pp. 237–88.

75 Thomas Raithel, *Jugendarbeitslosigkeit in der Bundesrepublik.
Entwicklung und Auseinandersetzung während der 1970er und 1980er
Jahre*, Munich, 2012.

76 Arthur McIvor, *Working Lives: Work in Britain since 1945*, Basingstoke,
2013, p. 260.

77 Figures based on my own calculations from the ILO database on industrial employment: International Labour Organization: statistics and
databases: https://www.ilo.org/global/statistics-and-databases/lang--en
/index.htm.

78 Reinhard Pollak, *Kaum Bewegung, viel Ungleichheit. Eine Studie zu
sozialem Auf- und Abstieg in Deutschland*, Berlin, 2010; Ivan Reid,
Class in Britain, Cambridge et al., 1998, pp. 111–19; Stéphanie Dupays,
'En un quart du siècle, la mobilité sociale a peu évolué', in *Données
sociales. La société française*, Paris, 2006, pp. 343–9.

Chapter 2   Farewell to class struggle and fixed social structures

1 Pierre Bourdieu, *In Other Words: Essays Towards a Reflexive Sociology*,
Stanford, CA, and Cambridge, 1990, p. 53.

2 Morten Reitmayer, *Elite. Sozialgeschichte einer politisch-gesellschaftlichen
Idee in der frühen Bundesrepublik*, Munich, 2009, pp. 32–42, with
reference to Pierre Bourdieu, *Outline of a Theory of Practice*, Cambridge,
1977.

3 Philipp Ther, *Europe since 1989: A History*, Princeton, 2016; idem,
'Der Neoliberalismus' Version 1.0, in *Docupedia Zeitgeschichte* (5
July 2016): https://docupedia.de/zg/Ther_neoliberalismus_v1_de_2016;
Philip Plickert, *Wandlungen des Neoliberalismus. Eine Studie zu
Entwicklung und Ausstrahlung der 'Mont Pèlerin Society'*, Stuttgart,
2008; Serge Audier, *Néo-libéralisme(s). Une archéologie intellectuelle*,
Paris, 2012.

4 Daniel T. Rodgers, *Age of Fracture*, Cambridge, MA, 2012, pp. 270–1.

5 Zygmunt Bauman, *Liquid Modernity*, London, 2000, pp. 1–15.

6 Wiebke Wiede, 'Subjekt und Subjektivierung', Version 1.0, in *Docupedia-
Zeitgeschichte* (10 December 2014): https://docupedia.de/zg/Wiede
_subjekt_und_subjektivierung_v1_de_2014.

7 See François Cusset, *La décennie. Le grand cauchemar des années 1980*, Paris, 2013, pp. 90–100; Horst-Eberhard Richter, *Sich der Krise stellen: Reden, Aufsätze, Interviews*, Reinbek bei Hamburg, 1981.

8 Jim Tomlinson, 'Inventing "Decline": The Falling behind of the British Economy in the Postwar Years', in *The Economic History Review* 49 (1996), pp. 731–57.

9 Volker Hauff and Fritz W. Scharpf, *Modernisierung der Volkswirtschaft. Technologiepolitik als Strukturpolitik*, Frankfurt/M., 1975.

10 See chapter 1. Jean Fourastié, *Le grand espoir du XXe siècle. Progrès technique, progrès économique, progrès social*, Paris, 1949; for a critical classification, see Daniel Speich Chassé, *Die Erfindung des Bruttosozialprodukts. Globale Ungleichheit in der Wissensgeschichte der Ökonomie*, Göttingen, 2013.

11 Olaf Bach, *Die Erfindung der Globalisierung. Entstehung und Wandel eines zeitgeschichtlichen Grundbegriffs*, Frankfurt/M., 2013.

12 E.P. Thompson, *The Making of the English Working Class*, London, 1968; Gareth Stedman Jones, *Languages of Class: Studies in English Working-Class History, 1832–1982*, Cambridge, 1996.

13 Arthur Marwick, *Class: Image and Reality in Britain, France and the US since 1930*, 2nd edition, London, 1990; David Cannadine, *Class in Britain*, New Haven, 1998.

14 Paul Nolte, *Die Ordnung der deutschen Gesellschaft. Selbstentwurf und Selbstbeschreibung im 20. Jahrhundert*, Munich, 2000.

15 Rüdiger Hachtmann, *Industriearbeit im 'Dritten Reich'. Untersuchungen zu den Lohn- und Arbeitsbedingungen in Deutschland 1933–1945*, Göttingen, 1989; Dietmar Süß, *'Ein Volk, ein Reich, ein Führer'. Die deutsche Gesellschaft im Dritten Reich*, Munich, 2017, pp. 84–97.

16 Nolte, *Die Ordnung der deutschen Gesellschaft*, pp. 351–61.

17 Pierre Rosanvallon, *Le peuple introuvable. Histoire de la représentation démocratique en France*, Paris, 1998.

18 Louis Chauvel and Franz Schultheis, 'Le sens d'une dénégation: l'oubli des classes sociales en Allemagne et en France', in *Mouvements* 26 (2003), pp. 17–26.

19 Franz Schultheis, 'Repräsentationen des sozialen Raumes im interkulturellen Vergleich', in *Berliner Journal für Soziologie* 6 (1996), pp. 43–68.

20 Alain Desrosières and Laurent Thévenot, *Les catégories socioprofessionelles*, Paris, 1992.

21 Chauvel and Schultheis, 'Le sens d'une dénégation', pp. 22–3.

22 John H. Goldthorpe and Keith Hope, *The Social Grading of Occupations: A New Approach and Scale*, Oxford, 1974.

23 Kerstin Brückweh, *Menschen zählen. Wissensproduktion durch britische Volkszählungen und Umfragen vom 19. Jahrhundert bis ins digitale Zeitalter*, Berlin and Boston, 2015, pp. 151–8; for a comparable survey of standard classification systems, see Ivan Reid, *Class in Britain*, Cambridge et al., 1998, pp. 245–56.

24 Cannadine, *Class in Britain*, pp. 163–89.
25 Schultheis, 'Repräsentationen des sozialen Raumes im interkulturellen Vergleich'.
26 Helmut Schelsky, 'Die Bedeutung des Schichtungsbegriffs für die Analyse der gegenwärtigen deutschen Gesellschaft' (1953), in idem, *Auf der Suche nach der Wirklichkeit*, Düsseldorf, 1965, pp. 331–6; cf. Nolte, *Die Ordnung der deutschen Gesellschaft*, pp. 330–5.
27 Chauvel and Schultheis, 'Le sens d'une dénégation', p. 21.
28 Ibid., pp. 17–18.
29 Gerhard Schulze, *The Experience Society*, London, 2005; Ulrich Beck, *Risk Society: Towards a New Modernity*, London, 1992; Daniel Bell, *The Coming of Post-Industrial Society*, New York, 1973; Manuel Castells, *The Information Age: Economy, Society, and Culture*, vol. 1: *The Rise of the Network Society*, 2nd edition, Chichester, 2010.
30 Sarah K. Haßdenteufel, *Neue Armut, Exklusion, Prekarität. Armutspolitische Debatten um Armut in Frankreich und der Bundesrepublik Deutschland 1970–1990*, Berlin and Boston, 2019.
31 John Welshman, *Underclass: A History of the Excluded, 1880–2000*, London and New York, 2006; Lydia Morris, *Dangerous Classes: The Underclass and Social Citizenship*, London and New York, 1994.
32 Ulla Plener (ed.), *Die Treuhand. Der Widerstand in den Betrieben der DDR, die Gewerkschaften (1990–1994)*, Berlin, 2011.
33 Stéphane Beaud and Michel Pialoux, *Retour sur la condition ouvrière. Enquête aux usines Peugeot de Sochaux-Montbéliard*, Paris, 1999.
34 Eric Shaw, 'Labourism: Myths and Realities', in Kevin Hickson et al. (eds), *The Struggle for Labour's Soul: Understanding Labour's Political Thought since 1945*, London and New York, 2004, pp. 187–205.
35 Geoff Eley, *Forging Democracy: The History of the Left in Europe, 1850–2000*, Oxford and New York, 2002.
36 Mark Wickham-Jones, 'The New Left', in Hickson et al. (eds), *The Struggle for Labour's Soul*, pp. 24–46.
37 Dominique Andolfatto and Dominique Labbé, *La CGT. Organization et audience depuis 1945*, Paris, 1997; Guy Groux and René Mouriaux, *La CGT. Crises et alternatives*, Paris, 1992; Bernard Pudal, *Prendre parti. Pour une sociologie historique du PCF*, Paris, 1989; Stéphane Courtois and Marc Lazar, *Histoire du Parti Communiste Français*, Paris, 1995.
38 Anne-Marie Hetzel and Claire Bernard, *Le syndicalisme à mots découverts. Dictionnaire des fréquences (1971–1990)*, Paris, 1998, pp. 7, 62–5 and 178–82.
39 François Mitterrand, *La Rose au poing*, Paris, 1973, cited in Henri Rey, *La gauche et les classes populaires. Histoire et actualité d'une mésentente*, Paris, 2004, p. 114: 'Ainsi que le rappelle le programme du Part socialiste, la destruction réelle et complète de tous les modes d'exploitation de l'homme par l'homme suppose l'avènement de la démocratie économique dont le point de départ reste l'appropriation

collective des grands moyens de productions, d'investissement et d'échange.'

40 Pierre Lévêque, *Histoire des forces politiques en France*, Paris, 1997, pp. 104–21.

41 Michel Pialoux and Florence Weber, 'La gauche et les classes populaires. Réflexions sur un divorce', in *Mouvements* 23 (2002), pp. 9–21; Rey, *La gauche et les classes populaires*, pp. 96–112.

42 See Geoffrey Foote, *The Labour Party's Political Thought: A History*, Basingstoke, 1997; see also Hickson et al. (eds), *The Struggle for Labour's Soul*.

43 Shaw, 'Labourism'.

44 Oliver Nachtwey, *Marktsozialdemokratie. Die Transformation von SPD und Labour Party*, Wiesbaden, 2009.

45 For example, a poll in 1997 showed 56 per cent of skilled workers and 60 per cent of unskilled and semi-skilled workers voting Labour and 29 per cent and 25 per cent respectively voting Conservative: see Reid, *Class in Britain*, p. 205.

46 Figures in Hans Günter Hockerts (ed.), *Bundesrepublik Deutschland, 1966–1974. Eine Zeit vielfältigen Aufbruchs*, Baden-Baden, 2006, p. 113; and Peter Lösche and Franz Walter, *Die SPD. Klassenpartei – Volkspartei – Quotenpartei. Zur Entwicklung der Sozialdemokratie von Weimar bis zur deutschen Vereinigung*, Darmstadt, 1992, pp. 164 and 166.

47 Stefan Wannenwetsch, '"In Gottes Namen, wenn es sich nicht verhindern läßt." – "Arbeiter" als Problem für die DGB-Gewerkschaften "nach dem Boom"', Süddeutschen Kolloquium zur Zeitgeschichte Stuttgart, 1 June 2018, version 4 June 2018. I am grateful to Herr Wannenwetsch for his kind permission to quote from his lecture which is a section of his doctoral thesis: Stefan Wannenwetsch, *'Es gibt noch Arbeiter in Deutschland'. Zur Transformation der Kategorie Arbeiter in der westdeutschen Arbeiternehmergesellschaft*, University of Tübingen, 2019.

48 John Kirk, *Twentieth-Century Writing and the British Working Class*, Cardiff, 2003; Sally R. Munt (ed.), *Cultural Studies and the Working Class: Subject to Change*, London, 2000; Nicolas Hatzfeld et al., 'Le travail au cinéma. Un réapprentissage de la réalité sociale', in *Esprit* (July 2006), pp. 78–99; Nicolas Hatzfeld, 'Figures filmiques d'ouvrières. Travail, genre et dignité, variations sur une trilogie classique (1962–2011)', in *Clio* 38 (2013), pp. 79–96.

49 Nicolas Hatzfeld et al., 'L'ouvrier en personne, une irruption dans le cinéma documentaire (1961–1974)', in *Le mouvement social* 226 (2009), pp. 67–78.

50 My thanks to Pascal Licher for researching filmography on the topic of industrial workers in Germany (1970–2000).

51 Werkkreis Literatur der Arbeitswelt (ed.), *25 Jahre Widerstand Wahrheit Kritik*, Munich, 1995.

52 Robert Linhart, *The Assembly Line*, London, 1981.

53 Marcel Durand, *Grain de sable sous le capot*, 2nd edition, Marseille, 2006 [1990]; Daniel Martinez, *Carnets d'un intérimaire*, Marseille, 2003.

54 A broad historical review of this topic area is lacking. See, however, Knud Andresen, *Triumpherzählungen. Wie Gewerkschafterinnen und Gewerkschafter über ihre Erinnerungen sprechen*, Essen, 2014, pp. 130–62; John Kirk et al. (eds), *Changing Work and Community Identities in European Regions: Perspectives on the Past and Present*, Houndmills et al., 2011; Tim Strangleman, '"Smokestack Nostalgia", "Ruin Porn", or Working-Class Obituary: The Role and Meaning of Deindustrial Representation', in *International Labor and Working-Class History* 84 (2013), pp. 23–37.

55 Sarah Vanessa Losego, *Fern von Afrika. Die Geschichte der nordafrikanischen 'Gastarbeiter' im französischen Industrierevier von Longwy (1945–1990)*, Cologne, 2009, p. 422.

56 Ibid., pp. 432–59.

57 Jean-Louis Tornatore, 'L'invention de la Lorraine industrielle', in *Ethnologie française* 35 (2005), pp. 679–89.

58 Dirk van Laak, 'Alltagsgeschichte', in Michael Maurer (ed.), *Neue Themen und Methoden der Geschichtswissenschaft*, Stuttgart, 2003, pp. 14–80; Kristin Ross, *May '68 and Its Afterlives*, Chicago, 2002; Dennis L. Dworkin, *Cultural Marxism in Postwar Britain: History, the New Left, and the Origins of Cultural Studies*, Durham, NC, 1997, pp. 182–218.

59 Tim Strangleman et al., 'Introduction to Crumbling Cultures: Deindustrialization, Class, and Memory', in *International Labor and Working-Class History* 84 (2013), pp. 7–22.

60 Strangleman, '"Smokestack Nostalgia"', pp. 26–7.

61 Kirk, *Twentieth-Century Writing*, pp. 83–90.

62 Cited in John Tulloch, *Television Drama: Agency, Audience and Myth*, London, 1990, p. 278.

63 Gunter Wallraff, *Lowest of the Low*, London, 1988.

64 *Ganz unten* (1986), director: Jörg Gfrörer.

65 Luc Boltanski and Ève Chiapello, *The New Spirit of Capitalism*, London, 2005, pp. 38–40, 385–482.

66 Owen Jones, *Chavs: The Demonization of the Working Class*, London and New York, 2012.

67 Louis Chauvel, 'La déstabilisation du système des positions sociales', in Hugues Lagrange (ed.), *L'épreuve des inégalités*, Paris, 2006, pp. 91–112, here p. 99.

68 Beaud and Pialoux, *Retour sur la condition ouvrière*, pp. 14–16.

69 Thompson, *The Making of the English Working Class*.

70 Rainer Geißler and Sonja Weber-Menges, '"Natürlich gibt es heute noch Schichten!" Bilder der modernen Sozialstruktur in den Köpfen

der Menschen', in Helmut Bremer and Andrea Lange-Vester (eds), *Soziale Milieus und Wandel der Sozialstruktur. Die gesellschaftlichen Herausforderungen und die Strategien der sozialen Gruppen*, Wiesbaden, 2006, pp. 102–27.

Chapter 3 Political history from below: labour conflict and new social movements

1 Karl Marx and Friedrich Engels, *Manifesto of the Communist Party*: https://www.marxists.org/archive/marx/works/1848/communist -manifesto/ch01.htm#007.
2 Michel Pigenet and Danielle Tartakowsky (eds), *Histoire des mouvements sociaux en France. De 1814 à nos jours*, Paris, 2014; Guya Accornero and Olivier Fillieule (eds), *Social Movement Studies in Europe: The State of the Art*, Oxford, 2016; Olivier Fillieule et al. (eds), *Penser les mouvements sociaux. Conflits sociaux et contestations dans les sociétés contemporaines*, Paris, 2010.
3 Erik Neveu, 'Médias et protestation collective', in Fillieule et al. (eds), *Penser les mouvements sociaux*, pp. 245–64.
4 Michel Pigenet and Danielle Tartakowsky, 'Institutionnalisation et mobilisations au temps de l'État social (années 1930–années 1970)', in idem (eds), *Histoire des mouvements sociaux*, pp. 337–54.
5 Colin Crouch, *Social Change in Western Europe*, Oxford, 2004, pp. 34–6.
6 Ken Lunn, 'Complex Encounters: Trade Unions, Immigration and Racism', in John McIlroy et al. (eds), *The High Tide of British Trade Unionism: Trade Unions and Industrial Politics, 1964–79*, Monmouth, 2007, pp. 70–90.
7 Xavier Vigna, *L'insubordination ouvrière dans les années 68. Essai d'histoire politique*, 2nd edition, Rennes, 2008, pp. 25–87.
8 The 'Grenelle Agreement', which paved the way for the end of the 'May unrest', was negotiated between the government, business associations and the trade unions in the Ministry of Labour, whose Paris offices were situated in the rue de Grenelle. See Geneviève Dreyfus-Armand et al. (eds), *Les années 68. Le temps de la contestation*, Brussels, 2000; Ingrid Gilcher-Holtey, *'Die Phantasie an die Macht'. Mai 68 in Frankreich*, 2nd edition, Frankfurt/M., 2001.
9 Vigna, *L'insubordination ouvrière dans les années 68*, pp. 13–14.
10 Walter Hüls, *Betriebsbesetzungen und Gewerkschaftskonzeption der CFDT. Praxis und Theorie des Projektes 'autogestion' in der Zeit von 1968–1978*, Rossdorf, 1983. On the 'LIP affair', see Donald Reid, *Opening the Gates: The Lip Affair, 1968–1981*, London, 2018, and the detailed article on the French Wikipedia site: https://fr.wikipedia.org /wiki/Affaire_Lip. In 2007, Thomas Faverjon made a film documentary, *Fils de Lip*, on the blockade of the self-managed factory.

11 Hélène Hatzfeld, *Faire de la politique autrement. Les expériences inachevées des années 1970*, Paris, 2005; idem, 'De l'autogestion à la démocratie participative', in Marie-Hélène Bacqué and Yves Sintomer (eds), *La démocratie participative. Histoire et généalogie*, Paris, 2011, pp. 51–61.

12 Hüls, *Betriebsbesetzungen und Gewerkschaftskonzeption der CFDT*, p. 7.

13 *Echos* – CFDT, No. 60, cited in Vigna, *L'insubordination ouvrière dans les années 68*, p. 107; on imitators, see ibid., pp. 107–11.

14 Jean-Jacques Becker and Pascal Ory, *Crises et alternances (1974–1995)*, Paris, 1998, pp. 60–1; Vigna, *L'insubordination ouvrière dans les années 68*, pp. 301–24.

15 John McIlroy and Alan Campbell, 'The High Tide of Trade Unionism: Mapping Industrial Politics, 1964–79', in McIlroy et al. (eds), *The High Tide of British Trade Unionism*, pp. 93–130, here p. 100.

16 See McIlroy et al. (eds), *The High Tide of British Trade Unionism*; especially: John McIlroy, 'Notes on the Communist Party and Industrial Politics', pp. 216–58, and idem, '"Always Outnumbered, Always Outgunned": The Trotskyists and the Trade Unions', pp. 259–96.

17 Jim Phillips, 'The 1972 Miners' Strike: Popular Agency and Industrial Politics in Britain', in *Contemporary British History* 20 (2006), pp. 187–207; Andy Beckett, *When the Lights Went Out: Britain in the Seventies*, London, 2010, pp. 53–87.

18 Beckett, *When the Lights Went Out*, pp. 53–87.

19 Andrew John Richards, *Miners on Strike: Class Solidarity and Division in Britain*, Oxford, 1996, p. 124.

20 The figure for 1979 is from McIlroy and Campbell, 'The High Tide of British Trade Unionism', p. 122.

21 Beckett, *When the Lights Went Out*, pp. 464–97.

22 Ibid., p. 464.

23 Andrew Thorpe, 'The Labour Party and the Trade Unions', in McIlroy et al. (eds), *The High Tide of British Trade Unionism*, pp. 133–50.

24 Udo Achten, *Zorn und Unzufriedenheit genügen nicht. Die Septemberstreiks 1969*, Berlin, 2016; Peter Birke, *Wilde Streiks im Wirtschaftswunder. Arbeitskämpfe, Gewerkschaften und soziale Bewegungen in der Bundesrepublik und Dänemark*, Frankfurt/M., 2007.

25 Hans Otto Hemmer et al. (eds), *Geschichte der Gewerkschaften in der Bundesrepublik Deutschland. Von den Anfängen bis heute*, Cologne, 1990, p. 87.

26 Knud Andresen, *Gebremste Radikalisierung. Die IG Metall und ihre Jugend 1968 bis in die 1980er Jahre*, Göttingen, 2016.

27 Jürgen Peters and Holger Gorr (eds), *In freier Verhandlung. Dokumente zur Geschichte der Tarifpolitik der IG Metall 1945–2002*, 2nd edition, Göttingen, 2009, p. 942.

28 Walther Müller-Jentsch (ed.), *Konfliktpartnerschaft. Akteure und Institutionen industrieller Beziehungen*, Munich and Mering, 1991.

29 In April 1983, 500,000 people took part in the Easter marches. On 22 October that year, 1 million people were demonstrating on the streets of Bonn, Berlin and Hamburg. See Andreas Wirsching, *Abschied vom Provisorium, 1982–1990*, Munich, 2006, pp. 99–101.

30 Karl Lauschke, *Die halbe Macht. Mitbestimmung in der Eisen- und Stahlindustrie 1945 bis 1989*, Essen, 2007, p. 303.

31 Sophie Camard, 'Comment interpréter les statistiques des grèves?', in *Genèses* 47 (2002), pp. 107–22.

32 For further figures on this international trend, see Hagen Lesch, 'Arbeitskämpfe und Strukturwandel im internationalen Vergleich', in *IW-Trends – Vierteljahresschrift zur empirischen Wirtschaftsforschung aus dem Institut der deutschen Wirtschaft Köln* 32 (2005), no. 2, pp. 1–17, here p. 4, table 1.

33 Gérard Noiriel and Benaceur Azzaoui, *Vivre et lutter à Longwy*, Paris, 1980, p. 18.

34 Étienne Penissat, 'Les occupations de locaux dans les années 1960–1970. Processus sociohistoriques de "réinvention" d'un mode d'action', in *Genèses* 59 (2005), pp. 71–93.

35 Sarah Vanessa Losego, *Fern von Afrika. Die Geschichte der nordafrikanischen 'Gastarbeiter' im französischen Industrierevier von Longwy (1945–1990)*, Cologne, 2009, pp. 414–28.

36 Ingrid Hayes, 'Les limites d'une médiation militante: l'expérience de Radio Lorraine Coeur d'Acier, Longwy 1979–1980', in *Actes de la recherche en sciences sociales* 196/7 (2013), pp. 84–101.

37 Losego, *Fern von Afrika*, pp. 450–95.

38 Not all districts were involved in the strike. The majority of miners in the Nottinghamshire, Staffordshire and Derbyshire coalfields did not take part, whereas those in other regions (Yorkshire, Scotland, Northumberland and Wales) followed the NUM's call to strike.

39 For a critical view of the literature, see Arne Hordt, *Von Scargill zu Blair? Der britische Bergarbeiterstreik 1984–85 als Problem einer europäischen Zeitgeschichtsschreibung*, Frankfurt/M., 2013; a brief description can be found in Arthur Marwick, *British Society since 1945*, 4th edition, London et al., 2003, pp. 282–8. See also Jörg Arnold, 'Vom Verlierer zum Gewinner – und zurück', in *Geschichte und Gesellschaft* 42 (2016), pp. 266–97.

40 For the sequence of events, see Andy McSmith, *No Such Thing as Society: Britain in the Turmoil of the 1980s*, London, 2011, pp. 152–70.

41 Richards, *Miners on Strike*, pp. 50–4.

42 Marwick, *British Society since 1945*, p. 394.

43 Richards, *Miners on Strike*, pp. 149–54.

44 John E. Kelly, 'British Trade Unionism 1979–89: Change, Continuity and Contradictions', in *Work, Employment & Society* 4 (1990), pp. 29–65;

Duncan Gallie (ed.), *Trade Unionism in Recession*, Oxford, 1996; Chris Howell, 'Unforgiven: British Trade Unionism in Crisis', in Andrew Martin and George Ross (eds), *The Brave New World of European Labor: European Trade Unions at the Millennium*, New York, 1999, pp. 26–74.

45 Richards, *Miners on Strike*.

46 Lauschke, *Die halbe Macht*, p. 313.

47 Cited in Arne Hordt, *Kumpel, Kohle und Krawall*, Göttingen, 2018, p. 205.

48 Lauschke, *Die halbe Macht*, p. 321.

49 Ibid., p. 324.

50 Ibid., pp. 231–56.

51 Hemmer et al. (eds), *Geschichte der Gewerkschaften in der Bundesrepublik Deutschland*, p. 486.

52 Cited in Peters and Gorr (eds), *In freier Verhandlung*, p. 621.

53 'Stenografische Berichte des Deutschen Bundestages, 10. Wahlperiode, 70. Sitzung, Freitag, 4. Mai 1984', p. 4985, cited in ibid., p. 646.

54 For the trade union view, see ibid., pp. 619–36.

55 Paul Bagguley, 'The Moral Economy of Anti-Poll Tax Protest', in Colin Barker (ed.), *To Make Another World: Studies in Protest and Collective Action*, Aldershot et al., 1996, pp. 7–24; Rodney Barker, 'Legitimacy in the United Kingdom: Scotland and the Poll Tax', in *British Journal of Political Science* 22 (1992), pp. 521–33; Paul Hoggett and Danny Burns, 'The Revenge of the Poor: The Anti-Poll Tax Campaign in Britain', in *Critical Social Policy* 11 (1991), pp. 95–110.

56 McSmith, *No Such Thing as Society*, pp. 277–8.

57 Clifford John T. Stott and John Drury, 'Crowds, Context and Identity: Dynamic Categorization Processes in the "Poll Tax Riot"', in *Human Relations* 53 (2000), pp. 247–73.

58 See the detailed account on the English Wikipedia page 'Anti-Poll Tax Unions': https://en.wikipedia.org/wiki/Anti-Poll_Tax_Unions.

59 Wolfgang Streeck, *Buying Time: The Delayed Crisis of Democratic Capitalism*, London, 2014.

60 Margaret Thatcher in the *Daily Telegraph*, 1 April 1980, cited in Charles Docherty, *Steel and Steelworkers: The Sons of Vulcan*, London, 1983, p. 218.

61 Lynsey Hanley, *Estates: An Intimate History*, London, 2012, pp. 97–147.

62 Michel Kokoreff, 'L'émeute urbaine', in Pigenet and Tartakowsky (eds), *Histoire des mouvements sociaux*, pp. 733–43; François Dubet, *La galère. Jeunes en survie*, Paris, 2003.

63 Alain Bertho, Le temps des émeutes, Paris, 2009; La Documentation française, *Enquêtes sur les violences urbaines: comprendre les émeutes de novembre 2005*, Paris, 2007: https://www.vie-publique.fr/rapport /29083-enquetes-sur-les-violences-urbaines-comprendre-les-emeutes-de -novembre.

64 For the 1981 Toxteth riots, see https://en.wikipedia.org/wiki/1981
_Toxteth_riots.
65 Stéphane Beaud and Michel Pialoux, *Violences urbaines, violence sociale.
Genèse des nouvelles classes dangereuses*, Paris, 2006; Stéphane Beaud,
80% au bac ... et après? Les enfants de la démocratisation scolaire,
Paris, 2003.
66 Beaud and Pialoux, *Violences urbaines, violence sociale*, pp. 347–8.
67 Ferdinand Sutterlüty, 'The Hidden Morale of the 2005 French and
2011 English Riots', in *Thesis Eleven* 121 (2014), pp. 38–56; Stephen
Reicher and Clifford John T. Stott, *Mad Mobs and Englishmen? Myths
and Realities of the 2011 Riots*, New York, 2011; Pierre Rosanvallon,
Society of Equals, Boston. 2013.
68 Reicher and Stott, *Mad Mobs and Englishmen?*
69 At first glance, the major exception to the picture of the encroaching alienation of social protests from the world of work drawn above seems to be
France, where in 1995 and 2003 there were major nationwide strikes and
mass protests against the governments' pension reform plans. They were
triggered by plans for reform and cuts in social services by the respective
governments. In 1995, Alain Juppé's Republican government put forward
a plan for a comprehensive reform of the social security system, but then
only forced through a structural reform of public sector pensions. In
2003, Jean-Pierre Raffarin's UMP government gradually increased the
number of years of contributions required for a pension without deduc-
tions. However, these protests were all borne by public sector workers
and the state transport sector, whereas private sector workers, and thus
(almost) all industrial workers, remained at best sympathetic spectators.
70 See in general Müller-Jentsch (ed.), *Konfliktpartnerschaft*.
71 Laure Pitti, 'Grèves ouvrières versus luttes de l'immigration. Une controverse entre historiens', in *Ethnologie française* 31 (2001), pp. 465–76.
72 See the French Wikipedia entry 'Cellatex': https://fr.wikipedia.org/wiki
/Cellatex.
73 Georges Ubbiali, 'Mémoires des luttes', in *Politix* 74 (2006), pp. 189–98;
Steve Jefferys, 'Forward to the Past? Ideology and Trade Unionism in
France and Britain', in Craig Phelan (ed.), *The Future of Organized
Labour: Global Perspectives*, Oxford and New York, 2007, pp. 209–42,
here pp. 229–30; Richard Detje et al., 'Gewerkschaftliche Kämpfe gegen
Betriebsschließungen – ein Anachronismus?', in *WSI Mitteilungen* 59
(2008), pp. 238–45.

Chapter 4   Industrial citizens and wage earners: labour relations, social benefits and wages

1 Union Européenne and Commission Européenne (eds), *Au-delà de
l'emploi. Transformations du travail et devenir du droit du travail en
Europe*, Paris, 1999.

2 Alain Supiot, *Beyond Employment: Changes in Work and the Future of Labour Law in Europe*, Oxford, 2001, pp. 1–2.

3 Ibid., p. 228.

4 T.H. Marshall, *Sociology at the Crossroads and Other Essays*, London, 1963, p. 98.

5 Colin Crouch, *Social Change in Western Europe*, Oxford, 2004, pp. 34–6.

6 On the historical specifics of Fordism, especially in the first half of the twentieth century, see Adelheid von Saldern, '"Alles ist möglich". Fordism – ein visionäres Ordnungsmodell des 20. Jahrhunderts', in Lutz Raphael (ed.), *Theorien und Experimente der Moderne. Europäische Gesellschaften im 20. Jahrhundert*, Cologne et al., 2012, pp. 155–92; Adelheid von Saldern and Rüdiger Hachtmann, 'Das fordistische Jahrhundert. Eine Einleitung', in *Zeithistorische Forschungen/Studies in Contemporary History*, online edition, 6/2 (2009): http://www .zeithistorische-forschungen.de/2-2009/id=4508; print edition: pp. 174–85.

7 Robert Castel, *Les métamorphoses de la question sociale. Une chronique du salariat*, Paris, 1995, Part II: 'Du contrat au statut', pp. 213–384.

8 John McIlroy, 'Ten Years of New Labour: Workplace Learning, Social Partnership and Union Revitalization in Britain', in *British Journal of Industrial Relations* 46 (2008), pp. 283–313; Ralf Hoffrogge, 'Engineering New Labour: Trade Unions, Social Partnership and the Stabilization of British Neoliberalism', in *Journal of Labor and Society* 21 (2018), pp. 301–16.

9 Paul Davies and Mark Freedland, *Labour Legislation and Public Policy: A Contemporary History*, Oxford et al., 2006.

10 See ibid. and idem, *Towards a Flexible Labour Market: Labour Legislation and Regulation since the 1990s*, Oxford, 2007.

11 Idem, *Towards a Flexible Labour Market*, p. 7.

12 Reinhard Richardi, 'Arbeitsverfassung und Arbeitsrecht', in Hans Günter Hockerts (ed.), *Bundesrepublik Deutschland, 1966–1974. Eine Zeit vielfältigen Aufbruchs*, Baden-Baden, 2006, pp. 225–76; Thomas Blanke, 'Koalitionsfreiheit und Tarifautonomie. Rechtliche Grundlagen und Rahmenbedingungen der Gewerkschaften in Deutschland', in Wolfgang Schroeder and Bernhard Weßels (eds), *Die Gewerkschaften in Politik und Gesellschaft der Bundesrepublik Deutschland. Ein Handbuch*, Wiesbaden, 2003, pp. 144–73.

13 Manfred Weiss, 'Die Entwicklung der Arbeitsbeziehungen aus arbeitsrechtlicher Sicht', in *Industrielle Beziehungen* 20 (2013), pp. 393–417; Gerd Bender, 'Herausforderung Tarifautonomie. Normative Ordnung als Problem', in Thomas Duve and Stefan Ruppert (eds), *Rechtswissenschaft in der Berliner Republik*, Berlin, 2018, pp. 697–725.

14 Davies and Freedland, *Towards a Flexible Labour Market*, pp. 25–7.

15 Eric Batstone, *The Reform of Workplace Industrial Relations: Theory, Myth and Evidence*, Oxford, 1988, pp. 77–111.

16 Ibid., pp. 78f.

17 Barbara Kersley, *Inside the Workplace: Findings from the 2004 Workplace Employment Relations Survey*, Milton Park et al., 2006, p. 110.

18 Figures for 2003 in Thomas Amossé, 'Mythes et réalités de la syndicalisation en France', in *Premières Synthèses* 44/2 (2004), pp. 1–5, here pp. 2f.

19 Dominique Andolfatto and Dominique Labbé, *La CGT. Organization et audience depuis 1945*, Paris, 1997, pp. 266 and 269.

20 Bernhard Ebbinghaus, 'Die Mitgliederentwicklung deutscher Gewerkschaften im historischen und internationalen Vergleich', in Schroeder and Weßels (eds), *Die Gewerkschaften in Politik und Gesellschaft der Bundesrepublik Deutschland*, pp. 174–203, here p. 182.

21 Jürgen Peters and Holger Gorr (eds), *In freier Verhandlung. Dokumente zur Geschichte der Tarifpolitik der IG Metall 1945–2002*, 2nd edition, Göttingen, 2009, pp. 942f.

22 Ebbinghaus, 'Die Mitgliederentwicklung deutscher Gewerkschaften im historischen und internationalen Vergleich', p. 182.

23 Reinhard Bahnmüller, *Stabilität und Wandel der Entlohnungsformen. Entgeltsysteme und Entgeltpolitik in der Metallindustrie, in der Textil- und Bekleidungsindustrie und im Bankgewerbe*, Munich and Mering, 2001, tables pp. 50 and 52.

24 Ingrid Artus, *Krise des deutschen Tarifsystems. Die Erosion des Flächentarifvertrags in Ost und West*, Wiesbaden, 2001.

25 Ibid., pp. 505–22; see also Weiss, 'Die Entwicklung der Beziehungen aus arbeitsrechtlicher Sicht'.

26 Neil Millward et al., *All Change at Work? British Employment Relations 1980–1998, as Portrayed by the Workplace Industrial Relations Survey Series*, New York, 2000, p. 109.

27 Amossé, 'Mythes et réalités de la syndicalisation en France', p. 4.

28 Pierre Saint-Jevin, 'Les résultats des élections aux comités d'entreprises en 1977 et l'état de l'institution en novembre 1978', in *Revue française des affaires sociales* 33 (1979), pp. 161–270, here p. 169; Olivier Jacod, *Les élections aux comités d'entreprise de 1989 à 2004*, Paris, 2008, p. 17.

29 Baptiste Giraud, 'Au-delà du déclin. Difficultés, rationalisation et réinvention du recours à la grève dans les stratégies confédérales des syndicats', in *Revue française de science politique* 56 (2006), pp. 943–68.

30 Richardi, 'Arbeitsverfassung und Arbeitsrecht', pp. 257–62; Werner Milert and Rudolf Tschirbs, *Die andere Demokratie. Betriebliche Interessenvertretung in Deutschland, 1848 bis 2008*, Essen, 2012, pp. 462–75.

31 Anke Hassel and Thorsten Schulten, 'Globalization and the Future of Central Collective Bargaining: The Example of the German Metal Industry', in *Economy and Society* 27 (1998), pp. 486–522, here p. 489.

32 Horst-Udo Niedenhoff, *Betriebsratswahlen. Eine Analyse der Betriebsratswahlen von 1975 bis 2006*, Cologne, 2007, p. 25.

33 Wolfgang Rudolph and Wolfram Wassermann, *Betriebsräte im Wandel. Aktuelle Entwicklungsprobleme gewerkschaftlicher Betriebspolitik im Spiegel der Betriebsratswahlen*, Münster, 1996, p. 7.

34 Niedenhoff, *Betriebsratswahlen*, p. 35.

35 For British and West German developments up to the early 1980s, see the overview in Knuth Dohse et al., *Reorganisation der Arbeit in der Automobilindustrie. Konzepte, Regelungen, Veränderungstendenzen in den USA, Großbritannien und der Bundesrepublik Deutschland. Ein Materialbericht*, Berlin, 1984.

36 Cf. the case analysed by Hermann Kotthoff and Josef Reindl in *'Fitneßtraining'. Betriebliche Reorganisation in Saarland*, Saarbrucken, 1999, p. 39.

37 Bahnmüller, *Stabilität und Wandel der Entlohnungsformen*, p. 62.

38 Ibid., pp. 74–6.

39 Ibid., p. 146.

40 Peter Jauch and Werner Schmidt, *Industrielle Beziehungen im Umbruch. Die Regulierung von Lohn, Gehalt und Arbeitszeit in Deutschland und Großbritannien*, Munich and Mering, 2000, p. 36.

41 Jean-Pierre Durand, 'Introduction: The Diversity of Employee Relationships', in idem et al. (eds), *Teamwork in the Automobile Industry: Radical Change or Passing Fashion?*, Basingstoke, 1999, pp. 1–34, here p. 28.

42 Jauch and Schmidt, *Industrielle Beziehungen im Umbruch*, p. 47.

43 Adrien Friez and Martine Julhès, 'Séries longues sur les salariés. Édition 1998', in *Résultats. Emploi-revenues* 605 (1998), pp. 1–89, here p. 10.

44 Richardi, 'Arbeitsverfassung und Arbeitsrecht', pp. 242f.

45 Ulrich Zachert, *Beendigungstatbestände im internationalen Vergleich. Eine normative und empirische Bestandsaufnahme*, Baden-Baden, 2004, pp. 12–20 and 43–52.

46 Ibid., p. 75.

47 Davies and Freedland, *Labour Legislation and Public Policy*, pp. 211 and 381–5.

48 Ibid., pp. 220–30 and 380–5.

49 Millward et al., *All Change at Work?*, p. 40.

50 Ingrid Tucci, *Les descendants des Immigrés en France et en Allemagne: des destins contrastés. Participation au marché du travail, formes d'appartenance et modes de mise à distance sociale*, dissertation, Humboldt University of Berlin, 2008.

51 Steve Jefferys, *Liberté, Egalité and Fraternité at Work: Changing French Employment Relations and Management*, Houndmills et al., 2003, pp. 99f.

52 See the overview tables in Peters and Gorr (eds), *In freier Verhandlung*, p. 948.

53 Ibid., p. 950.

54 Anna Pollert, '"Team Work" on the Assembly Line: Contradiction and the Dynamics of Union Resilience', in Peter Ackers et al. (eds), *The New Workplace and Trade Unionism*, London and New York, 1996, pp. 178–209, here p. 201.

55 Jauch and Schmidt, *Industrielle Beziehungen im Umbruch*, p. 36.

56 In Britain in 1974 with the Health and Safety at Work Act; in France in 1982 with the *Loi Auroux*, which prescribed health and safety committees; in Germany with the Occupational Safety Act of 1973.

57 Dietrich Bethge, 'Arbeitsschutz', in Manfred G. Schmidt (ed.), *Bundesrepublik Deutschland, 1982–1989. Finanzielle Konsolidierung und institutionelle Reform*, Baden-Baden, 2005, pp. 197–236.

58 Zachert, *Beendigungszustände im internationalen Vergleich*, pp. 19, 51, 82.

59 Lutz Leisering and Christian Marschallek, 'Zwischen Wohlfahrtsstaat und Wohlfahrtsmarkt. Alterssicherung und soziale Ungleichheit', in Hans Günter Hockerts and Winfried Süß (eds), *Soziale Ungleichheit im Sozialstaat. Die Bundesrepublik Deutschland und Großbritannien im Vergleich*, Munich, 2010, pp. 89–116, here p. 94.

60 Cornelius Torp, *Gerechtigkeit im Wohlfahrtsstaat. Alter und Alterssicherung in Deutschland und Großbritannien von 1945 bis heute*, Göttingen, 2015, pp. 145–7.

61 Rodney Lowe, *The Welfare State in Britain since 1945*, 3rd edition, Basingstoke et al., 2007, pp. 307f.; Jefferys, *Liberté, Egalité and Fraternité at Work*, p. 147.

62 Lowe, *The Welfare State in Britain since 1945*, p. 337.

63 Ibid., p. 343; Torp, *Gerechtigkeit im Wohlfahrtsstaat*, pp. 197–212.

64 Günther Schmid and Frank Oschmiansky, 'Arbeitsmarktpolitik und Arbeitslosenversicherung', in Schmidt (ed.), *Bundesrepublik Deutschland, 1982–1989*, pp. 237–88, here p. 264.

65 Jefferys, *Liberté, Egalité and Fraternité at Work*, p. 149.

66 The recommendations of the so-called Hartz Commission were implemented in four laws (Hartz I–IV) in 2002 and 2003: the first and second *Gesetz für moderne Dienstleistungen am Arbeitsmarkt*, 23 December 2002, the third and fourth *Gesetz für moderne Dienstleistungen am Arbeitsmarkt*, 23 and 24 December 2003.

67 Wolfgang Schroeder and Samuel Greef, 'Gewerkschaften und Arbeitsbeziehungen nach dem Boom', in Anselm Doering-Manteuffel et al. (eds), *Vorgeschichte der Gegenwart. Dimensionen des Strukturbruchs nach dem Boom*, Göttingen, 2016, pp. 245–70, here p. 265.

Chapter 5   Skilled work, production knowledge and educational capital: conflicts of interpretation and readjustments

1 See, e.g., 'Kommission für Zukunftsfragen der Freistaaten Bayern und Sachsen' (1998), cited in Hermann Kocyba, 'Wissensbasierte

Selbststeuerung. Die Wissensgesellschaft als arbeitspolitisches Kontrollszenario', in Wilfried Konrad (ed.), *Wissen und Arbeit. Neue Konturen von Wissensarbeit*, Münster, 1999, pp. 92–119, here p. 92.

2 Martina Heßler, 'Die Halle 54 bei Volkswagen und die Grenzen der Automatisierung. Überlegungen zum Mensch-Maschine-Verhältnis in der industriellen Produktion der 1980er-Jahre', in *Zeithistorische Forschungen/Studies in Contemporary History*, online edition: 11/1 (2014): https://zeithistorische-forschungen.de/1-2014/id=4996; print edition: pp. 56–76.

3 Maurice Halbwachs, *Les classes sociales*, Paris, 2008, pp. 91–103.

4 Karl Marx, *Capital*, vol. 1, in Karl Marx and Friedrich Engels (eds), *Collected Works*, vol. 35, London, 1987, pp. 422f.

5 Gerhard Ritter and Klaus Tenfelde, *Geschichte der Arbeiter und der Arbeiterbewegung in Deutschland seit dem Ende des 18. Jahrhunderts*, Bonn, 1992, pp. 431–2; see also ibid., pp. 298–353.

6 Wolf-Dietrich Greinert, *Berufsqualifizierung und dritte industrielle Revolution. Eine historisch-vergleichende Studie zur Entwicklung der klassischen Ausbildungssysteme*, Baden-Baden, 1999, pp. 53–79.

7 Gérard Noiriel, *Workers in French Society in the 19th and 20th Centuries*, Oxford, 1990.

8 John Sheldrake and Sarah Vickerstaff, *The History of Industrial Training in Britain*, Aldershot, 1987, pp. 4–18.

9 Bernard Charlot and Madeleine Figeat, *Histoire de la formation des ouvriers 1789–1984*, Paris, 1985; Greinert, *Berufsqualifizierung und dritte industrielle Revolution*, pp. 66–9.

10 Wolf-Dietrich Greinert, *Das 'deutsche System' der Berufsausbildung. Geschichte, Organisation, Perspektiven*, 2nd edition, Baden-Baden, 1995, pp. 61–102.

11 For contemporary diagnoses, see Nico Stehr, '"Wissensgesellschaften" oder die Zerbrechlichkeit moderner Gesellschaften', in Konrad (ed.), *Wissen und Arbeit*, pp. 13–23; see also Manfred Moldaschl (ed.), *Wissensökonomie und Innovation. Beiträge zur Ökonomie der Wissensgesellschaft*, Marburg, 2010.

12 Gary S. Becker, *Human Capital*, Chicago, 1964.

13 Brigitta Bernet, 'Dein Hirn, dein Kapital', *Zeit Online*, 3 July 2014: http://pdf.zeit.de/2014/28/wissensgesellschaft-brigitta-bernet-schweiz.pdf.

14 Colin Crouch, 'Skill Formation Systems', in Stephen Ackroyd et al. (eds), *The Oxford Handbook of Work and Organization*, Oxford, 2005, pp. 95–114, here pp. 96–7.

15 Martin Baethge, 'Entwicklungstendenzen in der Beruflichkeit – neue Befunde aus der industriesoziologischen Forschung', in *Zeitschrift für Berufs- und Wirtschaftspädagogik. Beihefte* 100 (2004), pp. 336–47; Martin Baethge, 'The German "Dual System" of Training in Transition: Current Problems and Perspectives', in Peter Berg (ed.), *Creating*

Competitive Capacity: Labor Market Institutions and Workplace Practices in Germany and the United States, Berlin, 2000, pp. 101–18.

16 David W. Soskice and Wolfgang Franz, *The German Apprenticeship System*, Berlin, 1994; Horst Kern and Charles F. Sabel, 'Verblaßte Tugenden. Zur Krise des deutschen Produktionsmodells', in Nils Beckenbach and Werner von Treeck (eds), *Umbrüche gesellschaftlicher Arbeit*, Göttingen, 1994, pp. 605–24; Wolfgang Streeck, 'Skills and the Limits of Neo-Liberalism: The Enterprise of the Future as a Place of Learning', in *Work, Employment & Society* 3 (1989), pp. 89–104; Kathleen Ann Thelen, 'Institutionen und sozialer Wandel. Die Entwicklung der beruflichen Bildung in Deutschland', in Jens Beckert et al. (eds), *Transformationen des Kapitalismus. Festschrift für Wolfgang Streeck zum sechzigsten Geburtstag*, Frankfurt/M. 2006, pp. 399–424.

17 For an analysis of the political history of the reforms, see Marius R. Busemeyer, *Wandel trotz Reformstau. Die Politik der beruflichen Bildung seit 1970*, Frankfurt/M., 2009; summarized in idem, 'Die Sozialpartner und der Wandel in der Politik der beruflichen Bildung seit 1970', in *Industrielle Beziehungen. Zeitschrift für Arbeit, Organisation und Management* 3 (2016), pp. 273–94.

18 This phrase comes from Greinert, *Berufsqualifizierung und dritte industrielle Revolution*, p. 46.

19 Greinert, *Das 'deutsche System' der Berufsausbildung*, pp. 100–3.

20 Ibid., p. 100.

21 Karl Ulrich Mayer, 'Ausbildungswege und Berufskarrieren', in *Forschung im Dienst von Praxis und Politik. Festveranstaltung zum 25jährigen Bestehen des Bundesinstituts für Berufsbildung am 7. und 8. September 1995. Dokumentation*, Berlin, 1996, pp. 113–45.

22 This is at least suggested by empirical studies on the development of the vocational training system in Germany during the final three decades of the twentieth century. See Greinert, *Das 'deutsche System' der Berufsausbildung*; Busemeyer, *Wandel trotz Reformstau*.

23 Thomas Raithel, *Jugendarbeitslosigkeit in der Bundesrepublik. Entwicklung und Auseinandersetzung während der 1970er und 1980er Jahre*, Munich, 2012, pp. 69–103.

24 Gerhard Bosch, 'Zur Zukunft der dualen Berufsausbildung in Deutschland', in idem (ed.), *Das Berufsbildungssystem in Deutschland*, Wiesbaden, 2010, pp. 37–62.

25 Ibid., p. 45.

26 Greinert, *Das 'deutsche System' der Berufsausbildung*, p. 123.

27 Sirikit Krone, 'Aktuelle Probleme der Berufsausbildung in Deutschland', in Gerhard Bosch (ed.), *Das Berufsbildungssystem in Deutschland*, Wiesbaden, 2010, pp. 19–36, here p. 24.

28 Sheldrake and Vickerstaff, *The History of Industrial Training in Britain*, pp. 32–43.

29 Ibid., pp. 26–42; Paul Ryan, 'Apprenticeship in Britain – Tradition

and Innovation', in Thomas Deißinger (ed.), *Berufliche Bildung zwischen nationaler Tradition und globaler Entwicklung. Beiträge zur vergleichenden Berufsbildungsforschung*, Baden-Baden, 2001, pp. 133–58; Roy Canning, 'Vocational Education and Training in Scotland: Emerging Models of Apprenticeship', in ibid., pp. 159–80.

30 These figures have been taken from the Labour Force Survey of 1979, UK Social Data Archive [UK SDA] Study Number 1756: Labour Force Survey (LFS) 1979.

31 John McIlroy, 'Ten Years of New Labour: Workplace Learning, Social Partnership and Union Revitalization in Britain', in *British Journal of Industrial Relations* 46 (2008), pp. 283–313; Ryan, 'Apprenticeship in Britain'; Canning, 'Vocational Education and Training in Scotland'.

32 These is the conclusion of studies of the Social Change and Economic Life Initiative (SCELI). See Alan Felstead et al., *Work Skills in Britain 1986–2001*, Nottingham, 2002; Roger Penn et al. (eds), *Skill and Occupational Change*, Oxford and New York, 1994.

33 This only applies to workers in industry and construction; my calculations based on the Labour Force Survey 1979 and 2000 UK SDA Study Number 1756 (LFS 1979) and 5857 (LFS 2000).

34 Paul Willis, *Learning to Labour: How Working Class Kids Get Working Class Jobs*, London, 1977.

35 Cf. the interviews with young skilled workers at the end of the 1990s in the SOFI study. SOFI Archiv Facharbeiterstudie, Interviews WD01F02, MS01F01j, MS01F04, PK01F03. See Peter Kupka, 'Arbeit und Subjektivität bei industriellen Facharbeitern', in *Beiträge zur Arbeitsmarkt- und Berufsforschung* 240 (2002), pp. 99–113.

36 Charlot and Figeat, *Histoire de la formation des ouvriers 1789–1984*.

37 Jens Schriewer, 'Alternativen in Europa: Frankreich. Lehrlingsausbildung unter dem Anspruch von Theorie und Systematik', in Herwig Blankertz (ed.), *Enzyklopädie Erziehungswissenschaften, Bd 9: Sekundarstufe II, Teil 1: Handbuch*, Stuttgart, 1982, pp. 250–85.

38 Stéphane Beaud, *80% au bac – et après? Les enfants de la démocratisation scolaire*, Paris, 2003; idem and Michel Pialoux, *Retour sur la condition ouvrière. Enquête aux usines Peugeot de Sochaux-Montbéliard*, Paris, 1999.

39 Armelle Gorgeu and René Mathieu, 'La place des diplômes dans la carrière des ouvriers de la filière automobile', in *Formation emploi* 105 (2009), pp. 37–51.

40 Nicolas Hatzfeld, *Les gens d'usine. 50 ans d'histoire à Peugeot-Sochaux*, Paris, 2002; Beaud and Pialoux, *Retour sur la condition ouvrière*.

41 Examples of this can be found for the Hewlett-Packard factory in Grenoble in the archive of the research project *Enquête Emploi salarié et conditions de vie* and for the Peugeot factory in Sochaux also in Beaud and Pialoux, *Retour sur la condition ouvrière*, pp. 111–60.

42 Christoph Deutschmann, 'Latente Funktionen der Institution des Berufs',

in Marita Jacob and Peter Kupka (eds), *Perspektiven des Berufskonzepts. Die Bedeutung des Berufs für Ausbildung und Arbeitsmarkt*, Nuremberg, 2005, pp. 3–16.

43 Pierre Bourdieu and Luc Boltanski, 'The Educational System and the Economy: Titles and Jobs', in Charles C. Lemert (ed.), *French Sociology*, New York, 1981, pp. 141–51.

44 Hilary Steedman, 'A Decade of Skill Formation in Britain and Germany', in *Journal of Education and Work* 11 (1998), pp. 77–94.

45 Idem, 'Vocational Training in France and Britain: Mechanical and Electrical Craftsmen', in *National Institute Economic Review* 126 (1988), pp. 57–70.

46 Idem et al., 'Intermediate Skills in the Workplace: Development, Standards and Supply in Britain, France and Germany', in *National Institute Economic Review* 136 (1991), pp. 60–76; idem and Karin Wagner, 'Nationale Ausbildungssysteme und ihr Einfluss auf das betriebliche Ausbildungs- und Rekrutierungsverhalten von Unternehmen', in *Arbeit – Beispiele für ihre Humanisierung. Erfahrungen, Berichte, Analysen* 17 (2008), pp. 268–82; Geoff Mason et al., 'Productivity, Product Quality and Workforce Skills: Food Processing in Four European Countries', in *National Institute Economic Review* 147 (1994), pp. 62–83; Karin Wagner and Geoff Mason, 'Restructuring of Automotive Supply-Chains: The Role of Workforce Skills in Germany and Britain', in *International Journal of Automotive Technology and Management* 5 (2005), pp. 378–410.

47 Burkart Lutz, 'Bildungssystem und Beschäftigungssystem in Deutschland und Frankreich. Zum Einfluss des Bildungssystems auf die Gestaltung betrieblicher Arbeitskräftestrukturen', in Hans-Gerhard Mendius et al. (eds), *Betrieb, Arbeitsmarkt, Qualifikation*, Frankfurt/M., 1976, pp. 83–151; Marc Maurice et al., *Politique d'éducation et organisation industrielle en France et en Allemagne. Essai d'analyse sociétale*, Paris, 1982.

48 Wagner and Mason, 'Restructuring of Automotive Supply-Chains', p. 394.

49 Malcolm Anderson and John Fairley, 'The Politics of Industrial Training in the United Kingdom', in *Journal of Public Policy* 3 (1983), pp. 191–207, here p. 200.

50 Sigbert Jon Prais, *Productivity, Education and Training: An International Perspective*, Cambridge, 1995; Mary O'Mahony, 'Employment, Education and Human Capital', in Roderick Floud and Paul Johnson (eds), *Structural Change and Growth, 1939–2000*, Cambridge, 2004, pp. 112–33; Hilary Steedman, 'Do Work-Force Skills Matter?', in *British Journal of Industrial Relations* 31 (1993), pp. 285–92.

51 Hilary Steedman and Karin Wagner, 'A Second Look to Productivity, Machinery and Skills in Germany and Britain', in *National Institute Economic Review* 122 (1987), pp. 84–95; Steedman et al., 'Intermediate Skills in the Workplace'; Hilary Steedman, 'A Decade of Skill Formation

in Britain and Germany', in *Journal of Education and Work* 11 (1998), pp. 77–94.

52 Wagner and Mason, 'Restructuring of Automotive Supply-Chains', pp. 397–8.

53 Gorgeu and Mathieu, 'La place des diplômes dans la carrière des ouvriers de la filière automobile'.

54 See Alain Lattard, 'Das Prinzip Alternanz – Zum Versuch der Modernisierung des bürokratischen Ausbildungsmodells', in Greinert, *Berufsqualifizierung und dritte industrielle Revolution*, pp. 120–31.

55 Armelle Gorgeu and René Mathieu, 'La déqualification ouvrière en question', in *Formation emploi* 103 (2008), pp. 83–100.

56 SOFI Archiv: files on: Kompetenzerweiterung; Trendreport.

57 Quoted in Crouch, 'Skill Formation Systems', p. 105.

58 These calculations are based on my SOEP database *Arbeiterhaushalte in Westdeutschland 1984–2001*.

59 Sonja Weber-Menges, *'Arbeiterklasse' oder Arbeitnehmer? Vergleichende empirische Untersuchung zu Soziallage, Lebenschancen und Lebensstilen von Arbeitern und Angestellten in Industriebetrieben*, Wiesbaden, 2004, p. 209.

60 Michael Lacher, 'Bildungsferne und Weiterbildungsnähe – ein Gegensatz?', in *Zeitschrift für Berufs- und Wirtschaftspädagogik. Beihefte* 86 (1990), pp. 309–24; Michael Lacher et al., *Die Fort- und Weiterbildung von Montagearbeitern/-innen: Voraussetzungen und Perspektiven am Beispiel der Volkswagen AG*, Recklinghausen, 1987.

61 Hasso von Henninges, *Ausbildung und Verbleib von Facharbeitern. Eine empirische Analyse für die Zeit von 1980 bis 1989*, Nuremberg, 1991.

62 REFA is the acronym for Reichsausschuß für Arbeitszeitermittlung (Reich Committee for Working Time Determination), founded in 1924, which has since undergone many name changes while retaining its acronym. Since 1977, REFA has been called the Verband für Arbeitsstudien und Betriebsorganisation (Association for Work Design, Business Organization and Business Development) and is situated in Darmstadt.

63 Hermann Kotthoff and Josef Reindl, 'Fitneßtraining'. *Betriebliche Reorganisation im Saarland*, Saarbrücken, 1999, p. 25.

64 Reported in ibid.; see also Rick Delbridge, *Life on the Line in Contemporary Manufacturing: The Workplace Experience of Lean Production and the 'Japanese' Model*, Oxford and New York, 1998; Michael Schumann et al., *Trendreport Rationalisierung. Automobilindustrie, Werkzeugmaschinenbau, chemische Industrie*, Berlin, 1994; Jean-Pierre Durand and Nicolas Hatzfeld, 'The Effectiveness of Tradition: Peugeot's Sochaux Factory', in Jean-Pierre Durand et al. (eds), *Teamwork in the Automobile Industry: Radical Change or Passing Fashion?*, Basingstoke, 1999, pp. 173–201, and further texts in this collection; Beaud and Pialoux, *Retour sur la condition ouvrière*.

65 Cited in Barry Wilkinson et al., 'The Iron Fist in the Velvet Glove:

Management and Organization in Japanese Manufacturing Transplants in Wales', in *Journal of Management Studies* 32 (1995), pp. 819–30, here p. 825.

66 Examples in Delbridge, *Life on the Line in Contemporary Manufacturing*, p. 91.

67 Durand and Hatzfeld, 'The Effectiveness of Tradition', pp. 188–9.

68 Wilfried Glißmann and Klaus Peters, *Mehr Druck durch mehr Freiheit. Die neue Autonomie in der Arbeit und ihre paradoxen Folgen*, Hamburg, 2001.

69 Jörg Flecker et al., 'The Sexual Division of Labour in Process Manufacturing: Economic Restructuring, Training and "Women's Work"', in *European Journal of Industrial Relations* 4 (1998), pp. 7–34.

Chapter 6 Life courses, work and unemployment in times of upheaval

1 Some sections of this chapter have been previously published as 'Arbeitsbiographien "nach dem Boom": Lebensläufe und Berufserfahrungen britischer, französischer und westdeutscher Industriearbeiter und -arbeiterinnen von 1970 bis 2000', in *Geschichte und Gesellschaft* 43 (2017), pp. 32–67.

2 This is not the case in Britain. See studies by Selena Todd, *The People: The Rise and Fall of the Working Class 1910–2010*, London, 2010; David Hall, *Working Lives: The Forgotten Voices of Britain's Post-War Working Class*, London, 2012; Arthur McIvor, *Working Lives: Work in Britain since 1945*, Basingstoke, 2013.

For Germany, see studies on trade union officials by Wolfgang Hindrichs et al., *Der lange Abschied vom Malocher. Sozialer Umbruch in der Stahlindustrie und die Rolle der Betriebsräte von 1960 bis in die neunziger Jahre*, Essen, 2000; Knut Andresen, *Triumpherzählungen. Wie Gewerkschafterinnen und Gewerkschafter über ihre Erinnerungen sprechen*, Essen, 2014. For France, see Jean-Pierre Terrail, *Destins ouvriers. La fin d'une classe?*, Paris, 1990.

3 Cf. Wiebke Wiede, 'Subjekt und Subjektivierung', Version 1.0, in *Docupedia-Zeitgeschichte* (10 December 2014): https://docupedia.de/zg/Wiede_subjekt_und_subjektivierung_v1_de_2014.

4 Pierre Bourdieu, 'The Biographical Illusion', in Richard J. Parmentier and Greg Urban (eds), *Working Papers and Proceedings of the Center for Psychosocial Studies*, no. 14 (1987), pp. 1–7.

5 Ulfert Herlyn et al., *Neue Lebensstile in der Arbeiterschaft? Eine empirische Untersuchung in zwei Industriestädten*, Opladen, 1994; Claudine Attias-Donfut, 'Generationenwechsel und sozialer Wandel', in Renate Köcher and Joachim Schild (eds), *Wertewandel in Deutschland und Frankreich*, Opladen, 1998, pp. 173–206.

6 For the basic concepts, see the critical comment in Hannah Brückner and Karl Ulrich Mayer, 'De-Standardization of the Life Course: What

It Might Mean? And If It Means Anything, Whether It Actually Took Place?', in *Advances in Life Course Research* 9 (2005), pp. 27–53, here pp. 27–35. Surveys of the empirical research on Germany can be found in Steffen Hillmert and Karl Ulrich Mayer (eds), *Geboren 1964 und 1971. Neuere Untersuchungen zu Ausbildungs- und Berufschancen in Westdeutschland*, Wiesbaden, 2004.

7 See, however, Karl Ulrich Mayer and Glenn R. Carroll, 'Jobs and Classes: Structural Constraints on Career Mobility', in *European Sociological Review* 3 (1987), pp. 14–38.

8 Max Weber, 'Objective Possibility and Adequate Causation in the Historical Causal Approach', in idem, *Collected Methodological Writings*, eds Hans Henrik Bruun and Sam Whimster, London, 2012, pp. 169–84.

9 The following databases were used: my own database *Arbeiterhaushalte in Westdeutschland 1984–2001* created on the basis of the Socio-Economic Panel (SOEP); Labour Force Survey from the UK Social Data Archive (UK SDA) Study Number 1758 (LFS 1975), 5876 (LFS 1995), 5857 (LFS 2000); life-history interviews in the UK Social Data Archive UK SDA SN 4938: *Families and Social Mobility: A Comparative Study, 1985–1988*; the British Library Sounds Collection interview series *Lives in Steel* and *Food: From Source to Salespoint*; life-history interviews from the inquiry *Emploi salarié et conditions de vie*, FNSP and CNRS, 1996–9, in the archive of the Centre Maurice Halbwachs (CMH), Paris.

10 Cf. Josef Mooser, *Arbeiterleben in Deutschland 1900–1970*, Frankfurt/M., 1984, pp. 61–73.

11 Figures for France from Claude Thélot, 'L'évolution de la mobilité sociale dans chaque génération', in *Economie et statistique* 161 (1983), pp. 3–21, here p. 12; for Germany, my calculations are based on figures in Mooser, *Arbeiterleben in Deutschland 1900–1970*, p. 106, table 16.

12 In the LFS for 1975, only 3.6 per cent of industrial and construction workers had a migrant background. See UK SDA, Study Number 1758 (LFS 1975), my calculations.

13 A good third of the industrial workers born after 1939 who were interviewed by Wilfried Deppe changed jobs several times after finishing their apprenticeship – a further third did so once. For those trained in traditional trades, the figure was higher, and in the case of unskilled workers every one in eight changed jobs very frequently (between three and seven times): Wilfried Deppe, *Drei Generationen Arbeiterleben*, Göttingen, 1982, pp. 281f., 313 and 341.

14 Burkart Lutz, 'Konfliktpotential und sozialer Konsens. Die Geschichte des industriellen Systems der BRD im Spiegel des Schicksals einer Generation', in Otthein Rammstedt and Gert Schmidt (eds), *BRD ade!*, Frankfurt/M., 1992, pp. 101–22.

15 On the trade union careers of this age cohort, see Andresen, *Triumpherzählungen*, pp. 59–95, 116–29; Hindrichs et al., *Der lange Abschied vom Malocher*, pp. 105–24; Christian Corouge and Michel

Pialoux, 'Engagement et désengagement militant aux usines Peugeot de Sochaux dans les années 1980 et 1990', in *Actes de la recherche en sciences sociales* 196/197 (2013), pp. 20–33; Alain Chenu, 'Les ouvriers et leurs carrières: enracinement et mobilités', in *Sociétés contemporaines* (1993), pp. 79–92.

16 Karl Lauschke, *Die Hoesch-Arbeiter und ihr Werk. Sozialgeschichte der Dortmunder Westfalenhütte während der Jahre des Wiederaufbaus 1945–1966*, Essen, 2000, pp. 142–73; Hindrichs et al., *Der lange Abschied vom Malocher*, pp. 43–89.

17 Robert Castel, *Les métamorphoses de la question sociale*, Paris, 1995, pp. 323–84.

18 Jenny Pleinen, *Die Migrationsregime Belgiens und der Bundesrepublik seit dem Zweiten Weltkrieg*, Göttingen, 2012, p. 101.

19 Christine von Oertzen, *Teilzeitarbeit und die Lust am Zuverdienen. Geschlechterpolitik und gesellschaftlicher Wandel in Westdeutschland 1948–1969*, Göttingen, 1999.

20 John H. Goldthorpe et al., *The Affluent Worker in the Class Structure*, Cambridge, 1969; for the historicization of this research, see Jon Lawrence, 'Social-Science Encounters and the Negotiation of Difference in early 1960s' England', in *History Workshop Journal* 77 (2014), pp. 215–39; Mike Savage, *Identities and Social Change in Britain since 1940: The Politics of Method*, Oxford and New York, 2010; and for a critical secondary analysis and follow-up study, Fiona Devine, *Affluent Workers Revisited: Privatism and the Working Class*, Edinburgh, 1992.

21 Arthur Marwick, *British Society since 1945*, 4th edition, London et al., 2003, pp. 124–40.

22 In 1970, 9 per cent of unskilled workers were registered unemployed: McIvor, *Working Lives*, p. 243.

23 Louis Chauvel, *Le destin des générations*, 2nd edition, Paris, 2010, p. 66.

24 Thomas Amossé and Olivier Chardon, 'Les travailleurs non qualifiés: une nouvelle classe sociale?', in *Economie et statistique* 393/4 (2006), pp. 203–27, here p. 209.

25 Michel Cézard, 'Les ouvriers', in *INSEE première* 455 (1996), pp. 1–4, here p. 2.

26 Thomas Raithel, *Jugendarbeitslosigkeit in der Bundesrepublik. Entwicklung und Auseinandersetzung während der 1970er und 1980er Jahre*, Munich, 2012, p. 16.

27 This is the figure for 2001. See Olivier Chardon, 'Les transformations de l'emploi non qualifié depuis vingt ans', in *INSEE première* 796 (2001), pp. 1–4, here p. 3.

28 Stéphanie Dupays, 'En un quart du siècle, la mobilité sociale a peu évolué', in *Données sociales. La société française*, Paris, 2006, pp. 343–9.

29 Anne-Françoise Molinié, 'Industrial Workforce Decline and Renewal', in *INSEE Studies* 43 (2000), pp. 1–17, here p. 5.

30 Ibid., p. 8.

31 Stéphane Beaud and Michel Pialoux, *Retour sur la condition ouvrière. Enquête aux usines Peugeot de Sochaux-Montbéliard*, Paris, 1999, pp. 111–57.

32 Rachid Benattig, 'Les retours assistés dans les pays d'origine: une enquête en Algérie', in *Revue européenne des migrations internationales* 5 (1989), pp. 79–102.

33 Chardon, 'Les transformations de l'emploi non qualifié depuis vingt ans', p. 3.

34 Nicolas Hatzfeld, 'L'individualisation des carrières à l'epreuve', in *Sociétés contemporaines* 54 (2004), pp. 15–33; Stéphane Beaud and Michel Pialoux, 'Jeunes ouvrier(e)s à l'usine', in *Travail, genre et sociétés* 8 (2002), pp. 73–103.

35 Beaud and Pialoux, *Retour sur la condition ouvrière*, pp. 293–332.

36 Abdallah Jelidi, in Laurence Bagot (ed.), *Ceux de Billancourt*, Ivry-sur-Seine, 2015, pp. 99–112.

37 On the situation for labour migrants, see Fanny Mikol and Chloé Tavan, 'La mobilité professionnelle des ouvriers et employés immigrés', in *Données sociales: La société française* 12 (2006), pp. 351–9; Chloé Tavan, 'Migration et trajectoires professionnelles, une approche longitudinale', in *Economie et statistique* 393/4 (2006), pp. 81–99; Anne-Sophie Bruno, 'Analyser le marché du travail par les trajectoires individuelles. Le cas des migrants de Tunisie en région parisienne pendant les Trente Glorieuses', in *Vingtième Siècle. Revue d'histoire* 121 (2014), pp. 35–47.

38 The project was based at the CMH in Paris. My thanks to Serge Paugam for giving me access to his research data.

39 Serge Paugam, *Le salarié de la précarité. Les nouvelles formes de l'intégration professionnelle*, Paris, 2000.

40 These are my calculations based on the ILO, which is in turn based on official figures.

41 Ivan Reid, *Class in Britain*, Cambridge, 1998, p. 83.

42 Ibid., p. 260.

43 See the company agreements reached for works closures of British Steel in the Modern Records Archives of the University of Warwick, MSS.365/BSC/55 (Ebbw Vale, 1978), MSS.365/BSC/58 (Hartlepool, 1977), MSS.365/BSC/60 (Corby, 1980).

44 McIvor, *Working Lives*, p. 242.

45 Royce Logan Turner, *Coal Was Our Life: An Essay on Life in a Yorkshire Former Pit Town*, Sheffield, 2000, pp. 22 and 27.

46 Hall, *Working Lives*, p. 460.

47 The average annual income of those with new jobs sank from £24,000 to £18,728; see Owen Jones, *Chavs: The Demonization of the Working Class*, London and New York, 2012, p. 151.

48 My calculations based on the Labour Force Survey, UK SDA, Study Number (= SN) 1758 (LFS 1975), SN 5876 (LFS 1995), SN 5857 (LFS 2000).

49 Low wages are defined here in relative terms as wages that are less than two-thirds of average gross wages. See Robert Solow, 'The German Story', in Gerhard Bosch and Claudia Weinkopf (eds), *Low-Wage Work in Germany*, New York, 2008, pp. 1–14, here p. 5.

50 Geoff Mason et al., 'Low Pay, Labour Market Institutions, and Job Quality in the United Kingdom', in Caroline Lloyd et al. (eds), *Low-Wage Work in the United Kingdom*, New York, 2008, pp. 41–95, here p. 46, table 2.2. The equivalent figures for West Germany in 1995 are a total of 8.9 per cent of low-paid workers in manufacturing and 13.2 per cent of skilled workers. See Gerhard Bosch and Thorsten Kalina, 'Low-Wage Work in Germany: An Overview', in Bosch and Weinkopf (eds), *Low-Wage Work in Germany*, pp. 19–112, tables 33 and 37.

51 See the series of interviews with workers in the British steel industry in the British Library: British Library Sounds Collection: *Lives in Steel*.

52 Ibid. Interview Lyn Bendle, C 532/055, part 5/6.

53 John Sheldrake and Sarah Vickerstaff, *The History of Industrial Training in Britain*, Aldershot, 1987; Hilary Steedman, *The State of Apprenticeship in 2010*, London, 2010.

54 My calculations based on data from Christoph Weischer, *Sozialstrukturanalyse*, Wiesbaden, 2011, p. 234.

55 For the SOEP and the database created from its figures, see above, Introduction, note 22.

56 The following age cohorts were defined: year of birth 1945 and earlier [1]; year of birth 1946 to 1955 [2]; year of birth 1956 to 1965 [3]; year of birth 1966 to 1969 [4]; and year of birth 1970 to 1979 [5]. This differentiation allows changes in the labour market for different age groups to be more clearly detected and situations specific to the generations to be identified. All the following calculations are my own based on the SOEP 1984–2001: *Lebensläufe aus (Industrie) arbeiterhaushalten*.

57 A total of 94 women: 62 with a German family background and 32 of Turkish origin.

58 A total of 473 German and 163 non-German men. They make up 74 per cent and 26 per cent respectively of all the male life stories evaluated. This means the life stories of migrants are overrepresented in my sample, since they comprise 'only' 17.2 per cent of the 3,565 cases documented in my database, *Arbeiterhaushalte in Westdeutschland 1984–2001*, itself based on the SOEP.

59 In most cases, there was no change of job at all and this category was used to analyse particular preconditions of precarious jobs and job insecurity.

60 Construction (10.2 per cent), metalworking (9.6 per cent), chemicals (5.1 per cent), automobile construction (4.3 per cent), machine engineering (4.3 per cent), electronics (2.4 per cent), wood and furniture manufacturing (2.6 per cent).

61 SOEP PID 85201, 85202.
62 SOEP PID 572101.
63 Paugam, *Le salarié de la précarité*, pp. 296f.
64 See Karin Hunn, '*Nächstes Jahr kehren wir zurück …* '. *Die Geschichte der türkischen 'Gastarbeiter' in der Bundesrepublik*, Göttingen, 2005.
65 Cornelius Torp, *Gerechtigkeit im Wohlfahrtsstaat. Alter und Alterssicherung in Deutschland und Großbritannien von 1945 bis heute*, Göttingen, 2015, p. 269.
66 Gerd Mutz et al., *Diskontinuierliche Erwerbsverläufe. Analysen zur postindustriellen Arbeitslosigkeit*, Opladen, 1995.
67 See also Lothar Lappe, *Berufsperspektiven junger Facharbeiter. Eine qualitative Längsschnittanalyse zum Kernbereich westdeutscher Industriearbeit*, Frankfurt/M., 1993; Hasso von Henninges, *Ausbildung und Verbleib von Facharbeitern. Eine empirische Untersuchung für die Zeit von 1980 bis 1989*, Nuremberg, 1991.
68 These figures are based on the monthly net wage (converted into euros) provided by the respective surveys carried out by the SOEP. They were then adjusted for inflation to exclude depreciation. See SOEP PID 110101, my figures for 1984, 1998 and 2006.
69 SOEP PID 110101.
70 Ibid. A monthly net income of between €1,063 in 1990 and a peak of €2,659 in 2000.
71 SOEP PID 57205
72 SOEP PID 563701.
73 A third of the women in this sample belonged to this category: 94 out of 275 women of German origin and 39 out of 130 women of Turkish origin.
74 From 2000 to 2004, her income was approximately €1,800–€1,200, up to €1,500 when adjusted for inflation; cf. SOEP PID 565403.
75 Ibid.
76 Sonja Weber-Menges, '*Arbeiterklasse' oder Arbeitnehmer? Vergleichende empirische Untersuchung zu Soziallage, Lebenschancen und Lebensstilen von Arbeitern und Angestellten in Industriebetrieben*, Wiesbaden, 2004, pp. 144f.
77 Reid, *Class in Britain*, p. 130; Alain Chenu, *L'archipel des employés*, Paris, 1990, pp. 175–7.
78 See my database *Arbeiterhaushalte in Westdeutschland 1984–2001*.
79 Partially transcribed interview with M. Kenyon in British Library Sounds Collection: *Food: From Source to Salespoint*, C821/120/01-03.
80 SOEP PID 4057(01-03).
81 For West Germany, see Nicole Mayer-Ahuja, *Wieder dienen lernen? Vom westdeutschen 'Normalarbeitsverhältnis' zu prekärer Beschäftigung seit 1973*, Berlin, 2003.
82 Philipp Ther, *Europe since 1989: A History*, Princeton, 2016.

Chapter 7 Transformations in company regimes

1 Arnold Picot et al., *Die grenzenlose Unternehmung. Information, Organisation, Management*, Wiesbaden, 1996. American edition: Rolf Wigand et al., *Information, Organization and Management: Expanding Markets and Corporate Boundaries*, New York, 1997.

2 Luc Boltanski and Ève Chiapello, *The New Spirit of Capitalism*, London, 2005.

3 Picot et al., *Die grenzenlose Unternehmung*, p. 447.

4 Hermann Simon, *Hidden Champions of the 21st Century: Lessons from 500 of the World's Best Unknown Companies*, Boston, 1996, pp. 195–244.

5 James P. Womack et al., *The Machine That Changed the World: The Story of Lean Production*, Boulder, CO, 1991. On the concrete Japanese conditions, see Ulrich Jürgens, 'Lean Production in Japan: Myth and Reality', in Wolfgang Littek and Tony Charles (eds), *The New Division of Labour: Emerging Forms of Work Organisation in International Perspective*, Berlin and New York, 1995, pp. 349–66.

6 Uwe Dombrowski and Tim Mielke (eds), *Ganzheitliche Produktionssysteme. Aktueller Stand und zukünftige Entwicklungen*, Heidelberg, 2015.

7 Serge Paugam, *Le salarié de la précarité. Les nouvelles formes de l'intégration professionnelle*, Paris, 2000.

8 Ibid., pp. 235–50. The tapes and transcripts of all the interviews in this study were kindly made available to me by the author. They are cited in the following as *Emploi salarié et conditions de vie*, Centre Maurice Halbwachs (CMH), Paris.

9 Interview Company no. 11, Monsieur Raoul, in *Emploi salarié et conditions de vie*, CMH, Paris.

10 Paugam, *Le salarié de la précarité*, p. 249.

11 Ibid., pp. 95–125. This correlation is even higher for better-qualified workers.

12 Pierre Rosanvallon, *Society of Equals*, Boston, 2013, pp. 255–8.

13 Christoph Deutschmann, *Postindustrielle Industriesoziologie. Theoretische Grundlagen, Arbeitsverhältnisse und soziale Identitäten*, Weinheim, 2002, pp. 126–39.

14 Charles Heckscher, 'From Bureaucracy to Networks', in Stephen Edgell et al. (eds), *The SAGE Handbook of Sociology, Work and Employment*, Los Angeles, 2016, pp. 245–61.

15 Deutschmann, *Postindustrielle Industriesoziologie*, p. 140.

16 Cf. Peter Hinrichs, *Um die Seele des Arbeiters. Arbeitspsychologie, Industrie- und Betriebssoziologie in Deutschland 1871–1945*, Cologne, 1981; Gertraude Krell, *Vergemeinschaftende Personalpolitik. Normative Personallehren, Werksgemeinschaft, NS-Betriebsgemeinschaft, betriebliche Partnerschaft, Japan, Unternehmenskultur*, Munich, 1994.

17 The expression 'factory regimes' can be found, for example, in Michael

Burawoy, *Manufacturing Consent: Changes in the Labor Process under Monopoly Capitalism*, Chicago, 1979, p. 23.

18 Ralph Darlington, *The Dynamics of Workplace Unionism: Shop Stewards' Organization in Three Merseyside Plants*, London and New York, 1994; John E. Kelly, *Rethinking Industrial Relations: Mobilization, Collectivism and Long Waves*, London and New York, 2006.

19 Martin Kuhlmann and Michael Schumann, 'What's Left of Workers' Solidarity? Workplace Innovation and Workers' Attitudes towards the Firm', in *Research in the Sociology of Work* 10 (2001), pp. 189–214.

20 Thomas Coutrot, 'L'entreprise néolibérale: la cooperation forcée', in idem, *L'entreprise néo-libérale, nouvelle utopie capitaliste? Enquête sur les modes d'organisation du travail*, Paris, 1998, pp. 219–53, here p. 241.

21 Michael Faust and Jürgen Kädtler, 'Die Finanzialisierung von Unternehmen', in *Kölner Zeitschrift für Soziologie und Sozialpsychologie* 70 (2018), pp. 167–94.

22 Thomas Welskopp, *Unternehmen Praxisgeschichte. Historische Perspektiven auf Kapitalismus, Arbeit und Klassengesellschaft*, Tübingen, 2014, pp. 181–9.

23 Hermann Kotthoff, *Betriebsräte und Bürgerstatus. Wandel und Kontinuität betrieblicher Mitbestimmung*, Munich and Mering, 1994, p. 31.

24 This is demonstrated with the example of Peugeot by Stéphane Beaud and Michel Pialoux, *Retour sur la condition ouvrière. Enquête aux usines Peugeot de Sochaux-Montbéliard*, Paris, 1999.

25 Nicolas Hatzfeld, *Les gens d'usine. 50 ans d'histoire à Peugeot-Sochaux*, Paris, 2002, pp. 351–548; Rick Delbridge, *Life on the Line in Contemporary Manufacturing: The Workplace Experience of Lean Production and the 'Japanese' Model*, Oxford and New York, 1998; Horst Kern and Michael Schumann, *Das Ende der Arbeitsteilung? Rationalisierung in der industriellen Produktion: Bestandsaufnahme, Trendbestimmung*, Munich, 1984; Michael Schumann et al., *Trendreport Rationalisierung. Automobilindustrie, Werkzeugmaschinenbau, chemische Industrie*, Berlin, 1994; Andrew Scott, *Willing Slaves? British Workers under Human Resource Management*, Cambridge and New York, 1994; Beaud and Pialoux, *Retour sur la condition ouvrière*.

26 Wolfgang Lecher and Hans-Wolfgang Platzer, 'Europäische Betriebsräte', in Wolfgang Schroeder and Bernhard Weßels (eds), *Die Gewerkschaften in Politik und Gesellschaft der Bundesrepublik Deutschland. Ein Handbuch*, Wiesbaden, 2003, pp. 588–613; Wolfgang Streeck, 'Industrial Citizenship under Regime Competition: The Case of the European Works Councils', in *Journal of European Public Policy* 4 (1997), pp. 643–64; Paul Marginson et al., 'The Impact of European Works Councils on Management Decision-making in UK and US-based Multinationals: A Case Study Comparison', in *British Journal of Industrial Relations*

42 (2004), pp. 209–33; Michael Whittall and Hermann Kotthoff, 'Les comités d'entreprise européens, des zones libres de syndicats', in *La Revue de l'Ires* 68 (2011), pp. 207–36; Harald Stöger, *Abstieg oder Aufbruch? Europäische Betriebsräte zwischen Marginalisierung und transnationalem Einfluss*, Vienna, 2011.

27 Hermann Simon, *Hidden Champions of the 21st Century: Success Strategies of Unknown World Market Leaders*, Dordrecht et al., 2009, pp. 257, 258.

28 Werner Milert and Rudolf Tschirbs, *Die andere Demokratie. Betriebliche Interessenvertretung in Deutschland. 1848 bis 2008*, Essen, 2012.

29 On the strong tradition of community-building company ideologies, see Krell, *Vergemeinschaftende Personalpolitik*, pp. 85–205. See also Hinrichs, *Um die Seele des Arbeiters*, pp. 146–207.

30 Ingrid Artus, *Betriebe ohne Betriebsrat. Informelle Interessenvertretung in Unternehmen*, Frankfurt/M. et al., 2006; idem, *Interessenhandeln jenseits der Norm. Mittelständische Betriebe und prekäre Dienstleistungsarbeit in Deutschland und Frankreich*, Frankfurt/M. and New York 2008; Hermann Kotthoff and Josef Reindl, *Die soziale Welt kleiner Betriebe. Wirtschaften, Arbeiten und Leben im mittelständischen Industriebetrieb*, Göttingen, 1990.

31 Marshall remarks on a lack of 'moral community' and a 'sense of obligation'. Quoted from Kotthoff, *Betriebsräte und Bürgerstatus*, p. 332. Counter-examples can be found, particularly in small and medium-sized companies.

32 Neil Millward et al., *All Change at Work? British Employment Relations 1980–1998, as Portrayed by the Workplace Industrial Relations Survey Series*, New York, 2000, p. 109.

33 Karl Lauschke, *Die Hoesch-Arbeiter und ihr Werk. Sozialgeschichte der Dortmunder Westfalenhütte während der Jahre des Wiederaufbaus 1945–1966*, Essen, 2000, pp. 142–74; Thomas Welskopp, 'Soziale Kontinuität im institutionellen Wandel. Arbeits- und industrielle Beziehungen in der deutschen und amerikanischen Eisen- und Stahlindustrie von der Jahrhundertwende bis zu den 1960er Jahren', in Matthias Frese and Michael Prinz (eds), *Politische Zäsuren und gesellschaftlicher Wandel*, Paderborn, 1996, pp. 217–267; Serge Bonnet, *L'homme du fer*, 2nd edition, Nancy, 1987.

34 See Wolfgang Hindrichs et al., *Der lange Abschied vom Malocher. Sozialer Umbruch in der Stahlindustrie und die Rolle der Betriebsräte von 1960 bis in die neunziger Jahre*, Essen, 2000; Uwe Jürgenhake and Beate Winter, *Neue Produktionskonzepte in der Stahlindustrie. Ökonomisch-technischer Wandel und Arbeitskräfteeinsatz in der Eisen- und Stahlindustrie und seine Auswirkungen auf die Arbeitsorganisation und -gestaltung sowie die betriebliche Aus- und Weiterbildung*, Dortmund, 1992.

35 Kern and Schumann, *Das Ende der Arbeitsteilung?*, pp. 137–234; Schumann et al., *Trendreport Rationalisierung*, pp. 371–457.

36 For an example of a precise description of local work cultures, see Kotthoff and Reindl, *Die soziale Welt kleiner Betriebe*, pp. 324–53; Beaud and Pialoux, *Retour sur la condition ouvrière*; Wolfgang Schäfer, *Die Fabrik auf dem Dorf. Studien zum betrieblichen Sozialverhalten ländlicher Industriearbeiter*, Göttingen, 1991.

37 This can be credited mainly to the international research group GERPISA and its ongoing publications and conferences. See http://gerpisa.org/actes/actes_index.html.html.

38 See Hatzfeld, *Les gens d'usine*, pp. 395, 400, 404f. and 408–53.

39 See Nicolas Hatzfeld, 'Organisation du travail, repères pour une histoire comparée (1945–2000)', in Jacqueline Costa-Lascoux (ed.), *Renault sur Seine*, Paris, 2007, pp. 37–53.

40 Jean-Pierre Durand, 'Introduction: The Diversity of Employee Relationships', in idem et al. (eds), *Teamwork in the Automobile Industry: Radical Change or Passing Fashion?*, Basingstoke, 1999, pp. 1–34, here pp. 19–20.

41 Cf. for VW Ulrich Jürgens, 'The Development of Volkswagen's Industrial Model, 1967–1995', in Michel Freyssenet (ed.), *One Best Way? Trajectories and Industrial Models of the World's Automobile Producers*, Oxford, 1998, pp. 273–310; Kern and Schumann, *Das Ende der Arbeitsteilung?*, pp. 40–116; Martina Heßler, 'Die Halle 54 bei Volkswagen und die Grenzen der Automatisierung. Überlegungen zum Mensch-Maschine-Verhältnis in der industriellen Produktion der 1980er-Jahre', in: *Zeithistorische Forschungen*, online edition 11/1 (2014): https://zeithistorische-forschungen.de/1-2014/id=4996; print edition: pp. 56–76.

42 Christian Kleinschmidt, *Der produktive Blick. Wahrnehmung amerikanischer und japanischer Management- und Produktionsmethoden durch deutsche Unternehmer 1950–1985*, Berlin, 2002; Leo Kissler, *Toyotismus in Europa. Schlanke Produktion und Gruppenarbeit in der deutschen und französischen Automobilindustrie*, Frankfurt/M. and New York, 1996.

43 Cf. Koichi Shimizu, 'A New Toyotaism?', in Freyssenet (ed.), *One Best Way?*, pp. 63–90; Jürgens, 'Lean Production in Japan'.

44 Pascal Brocard and Carole Donada, *La chaîne de l'équipement automobile*, Paris, 2003, pp. 13–26.

45 Durand et al. (eds), *Teamwork in the Automobile Industry*, with case studies on Peugeot's European factories (Jean-Pierre Durand and Nicolas Hatzfeld, 'The Effectiveness of Tradition: Peugeot's Sochaux Factory', in ibid., pp. 173–201), Renault (Michel Freyssenet, 'Transformations in the Teamwork at Renault', in ibid., pp. 202–17), General Motors (Paul Stewart, 'The Negotiation of Change in the Evolution of the Workplace towards a New Production Model at Vauxhall (General Motors) UK', in ibid., pp. 236–53), Rover (Andrew Mair, 'The Introduction of Teamwork at Rover Group's Stamping Plant', in ibid., pp. 254–86), Daimler-Benz

(Detlef Gerst et al., 'Group Work in the German Automobile Industry – The Case of Mercedes-Benz', in ibid., pp. 366–94) und VW (Anne Labit, 'Group Working at Volkswagen: An Issue for Negotiation between Trade Unions and Management', in ibid., pp. 395–411).

46 Cf. Durand, 'The Diversity of Employee Relationships'.

47 Paul Stewart et al., 'Les ouvriers de Vauxhall face à la lean production', in Le mouvement social 217 (2006), pp. 33–52.

48 Beaud and Pialoux, Retour sur la condition ouvrière, pp. 333–74.

49 Ibid. See also Christian Corouge and Michel Pialoux, 'Chronique Peugeot', in Actes de la recherche en sciences sociales 57/58 (1985), pp. 108–28.

50 Armelle Gorgeu et al., 'Une forme moderne de gestion paternaliste', in idem, Organisation du travail et gestion de la main-d'œuvre dans la filière automobile, Paris, 1998, pp. 27–40, here p. 38.

51 Jean-Pierre Durand et al., 'The Transformation of Employee Relations in the Automobile Industry?', in idem (eds), Teamwork in the Automobile Industry, pp. 412–45.

52 Tony Charles, 'The New Division of Labour in Europe', in Littek and Charles (eds), The New Division of Labour, pp. 235–61, here pp. 250f.

53 Tommaso Pardi, 'Travailler chez Toyota. De l'emploi à vie à la course à la survie', in La Revue de l'Ires 62 (2009), pp. 39–70, here p. 39; idem, 'Crise et rejet de la greffe Toyota à Valenciennes?', in Le journal de l'école de Paris du management 99 (2013), pp. 29–36, here p. 29.

54 Jürgens, 'The Development of Volkswagen's Industrial Model'; Klaus Dörre, Kampf um Beteiligung. Arbeit, Partizipation und industrielle Beziehungen im flexiblen Kapitalismus. Eine Studie aus dem Soziologischen Forschungsinstitut Göttingen (SOFI), Wiesbaden, 2002.

55 Gerst et al., 'Group Work in the German Automobile Industry – The Case of Mercedes-Benz', p. 366; see also Durand et al., 'The Transformation of Employee Relations in the Automobile Industry?'

56 Felix Fitzroy and Kornelius Kraft, 'Mitarbeiterbeteiligung und Produktivität. Eine ökonometrische Untersuchung', in Zeitschrift für Betriebswirtschaft 55 (1985), pp. 21–36; Lothar Kamp and Nikolaus Simon, 'Mitbestimmung als Faktor nachhaltiger Unternehmensentwicklung', in WSI Mitteilungen 56 (2005), pp. 459–64.

57 Most case studies on supplier factories are from the 1990s, when more stable structures had formed after the wave of production outsourcing and rationalization. See Dörre, Kampf um Beteiligung; Hermann Kotthoff and Josef Reindl, 'Fitneßtraining'. Betriebliche Reorganisation im Saarland, Saarbrücken, 1999; Delbridge, Life on the Line in Contemporary Manufacturing; Gorgeu et al., Organisation du travail et gestion de la main-d'œuvre dans la filière automobile.

58 Kotthoff and Reindl, 'Fitneßtraining', p. 21.

59 Ibid., p. 22.

60 Ibid., pp. 28 (longer quote) and 29.

61 Ibid., pp. 43–5.
62 Ibid., pp. 46–50.
63 Ibid., p. 57.
64 Delbridge, *Life on the Line in Contemporary Manufacturing*, pp. 24–31.
65 Ibid., p. 24.
66 Armelle Gorgeu and René Mathieu, 'La place des diplômes dans la carrière des ouvriers de la filière automobile', in *Formation emploi* 105 (2009), pp. 37–51.
67 Idem, 'Les suppressions d'emploi dans la filière automobile. L'impact negatif sur les conditions de travail et la qualification ouvrière', in *Formation emploi* 124 (2013), pp. 87–103.
68 Ibid., p. 116.
69 Ibid., p. 117.
70 On large companies, cf. Britta Rehder, *Betriebliche Bündnisse für Arbeit in Deutschland. Mitbestimmung und Flächentarif im Wandel*, Frankfurt/M., 2003.
71 Cornelia Girndt, *Anwälte, Problemlöser, Modernisierer. Betriebsratsreportagen*, Gütersloh, 1997.
72 Kotthoff and Reindl, *Die soziale Welt kleiner Betriebe*, pp. 82–117.
73 Ibid., pp. 187–212.
74 Kotthoff, *Betriebsräte und Bürgerstatus*, p. 91.
75 Ibid., p. 161.
76 John Black et al., 'Clinging to Collectivism? Some Ethnographic Shop-Floor Evidence from the British Lock Industry 1979–98', in *The International Journal of Human Resource Management* 10 (1999), pp. 941–57; Anne-Marie Greene, *Voices from the Shop Floor: Dramas of the Employment Relationship*, Burlington, VT, 2001; idem et al., *Lost Narratives? From Paternalism to Team-Working in a Lock Manufacturing Firm*, Wolverhampton, 2000.
77 Greene, *Voices from the Shop Floor*, pp. 56–60.
78 This term seems appropriate having read the contemporary management press and the journalistic traces left here by these two successful managers, Rudd and McGovern.
79 Greene, *Voices from the Shop Floor*, pp. 81–106.
80 A study on West Germany even spoke of 'shock tactics' news coming 'as a bombshell': Dörre, *Kampf um Beteiligung*, p. 60.
81 Ibid., p. 22.
82 Ibid., p. 371; Michael Faust et al., *Das kapitalmarktorientierte Unternehmen. Externe Erwartungen, Unternehmenspolitik, Personalwesen und Mitbestimmung*, Berlin, 2011.
83 Thomas Amossé and Thomas Coutrot, 'Socio-productive Models in France: An Empirical Dynamic Overview, 1992–2004', in *Industrial and Labour Relations Review* 64 (2011), pp. 786–817, here p. 798.
84 Stephan Voswinkel and Gabriele Wagner, 'Die Person als Leistungskraft: Anerkennungspolitiken in Organisationen', in *Leviathan: Berliner*

Zeitschrift für Sozialwissenschaft (special issue) 40/4 (2012), pp. 591–608; Manfred Moldaschl and Gerd-Günter Voß, *Subjektivierung von Arbeit*, Munich, 2002; Gerd-Günter Voß, 'Die Entgrenzung von Arbeit und Arbeitskraft', in *Mitteilungen aus der Arbeitsmarkt- und Berufsforschung* 31 (1998), pp. 473–87.

85 Klaus Dörre et al., 'Zwischen Firmenbewusstsein und Wachstumskritik', in idem (eds), *Das Gesellschaftsbild der LohnarbeiterInnen. Soziologische Untersuchungen in ost- und westdeutschen Industriebetrieben*, Hamburg, 2013, pp. 198–261.

Chapter 8 Industrial districts, social spaces, 'problem neighbourhoods' and owner-occupier areas: social spaces and deindustrialization

1 Karl Schlögel, *In Space We Read Time: On the History of Civilization and Geopolitics*, Chicago, 2016.

2 Tobias Gerstung, *Stapellauf für ein neues Zeitalter. Die Industriemetropole Glasgow im revolutionären Wandel nach dem Boom (1960–2000)*, Göttingen, 2016; Arndt Neumann, *Unternehmen Hamburg. Eine Geschichte der neoliberalen Stadt*, Göttingen, 2018; Jon Murden, '"City of Change and Challenge": Liverpool since 1945', in John Belchem (ed.), *Liverpool 800: Culture, Character & History*, Liverpool, 2006, pp. 393–485.

3 Tim Strangleman, '"Smokestack Nostalgia", "Ruin Porn" or Working-Class Obituary: The Role and Meaning of Deindustrial Representation', in *International Labor and Working-Class History* 84 (2013), pp. 23–37.

4 All data from Arthur Marwick, *British Society since 1945*, 4th edition, London et al., 2003, pp. 248f., 254 and 423.

5 Ibid., pp. 246f.

6 Murden, '"City of Change and Challenge"', pp. 431 and 479.

7 Benito Giordano and Laura Twomey, 'Economic Transitions: Restructuring Local Labour Markets', in Jamie Peck and Kevin Ward (eds), *City of Revolution: Restructuring Manchester*, Manchester et al., 2006, pp. 50–75, here p. 71.

8 Figures from Bundesagentur für Arbeit, *Arbeitsmarkt in Deutschland. Analytikreport der Statistik*, April 2009, n.p.; Raphael Emanuel Dorn, *Alle in Bewegung. Räumliche Mobilität in der Bundesrepublik Deutschland 1980–2010*, Göttingen, 2018, p. 173.

9 Dorn, *Alle in Bewegung*, pp. 89–148.

10 Bundesagentur für Arbeit, *Arbeitsmarkt in Deutschland*, n.p.

11 For figures for parishes in the municipal area of the Ruhr (*Kommunalverband Ruhrgebiet*) (1970–1987), see Bernhard Butzin, 'Regional Life Cycles and Problems of Revitalisation in the Ruhr', in Trevor Wild and Philip N. Jones (eds), *De-Industrialisation and New Industrialisation in Britain and Germany*, London, 1991, pp. 186–98, here p. 194.

12 *Bundesarbeitsblatt* 1 (1998), pp. 81f.

13 Stefan Goch, *Eine Region im Kampf mit dem Strukturwandel. Bewältigung von Strukturwandel und Strukturpolitik im Ruhrgebiet*, Essen, 2002; idem, 'Betterment without Airs: Social, Cultural and Political Consequences of Deindustrialization in the Ruhr', in *International Review of Social History* 47 (2002), pp. 87–111.

14 Knud Andresen, *Triumpherzählungen. Wie Gewerkschafterinnen und Gewerkschafter über ihre Erinnerungen sprechen*, Essen, 2014, pp. 156–8.

15 Cyrille van Puymbroek and Robert Reynard, 'Répartition géographique des emplois', in *INSEE première* 1278 (2010), pp. 1–4, here p. 4.

16 Hervé Le Bras and Emmanuel Todd, *Le mystère français*, Paris, 2013, p. 155.

17 Nicole Tabard, 'Des quartiers pauvres aux banlieues aisées. Une représentation sociale du territoire', in *Economie et statistique* 270 (1993), pp. 5–22; Alain Chenu and Nicole Tabard, 'Les transformations socio-professionnelles du territoire français, 1982–1990', in *Population* 48 (1993), pp. 1735–69.

18 Rainer Fremdling and Richard H. Tilly (eds), *Industrialisierung und Raum. Studien zur regionalen Differenzierung im Deutschland des 19. Jahrhunderts*, Stuttgart, 1979.

19 Andrew Popp and John F. Wilson, 'The Emergence and Development of Industrial Districts in Industrialising England, 1750–1914', in Giacomo Becattini et al. (eds), *A Handbook of Industrial Districts*, Cheltenham and Northampton, 2009, pp. 43–57.

20 On the long-term dualism of German industrial structures, cf. Gary Herrigel, *Industrial Constructions: The Sources of German Industrial Power*, Cambridge, MA, et al., 2009.

21 Becattini et al. (eds), *A Handbook of Industrial Districts*.

22 Popp and Wilson, 'The Emergence and Development of Industrial Districts in Industrialising England, 1750–1914'; Georges Benko and Bernard Pecqueur, 'Industrial Districts and the Governance of Local Economies: The French Example', in Becattini et al. (eds), *A Handbook of Industrial Districts*, pp. 501–11.

23 Hermann Simon, *Hidden Champions of the 21st Century: Success Strategies of Unknown World Market Leaders*, Dordrecht et al., 2009, pp. 271–4.

24 Hermann Kotthoff and Josef Reindl, *Die soziale Welt kleiner Betriebe. Wirtschaften, Arbeiten und Leben im mittelständischen Industriebetrieb*, Göttingen, 1990, pp. 324–40.

25 For a regional case study, cf. Marc Bonaldo, *Resiliente Region Stuttgart? Anpassung und Innovation regionaler Industriekultur 'nach dem Boom'*, dissertation, University of Trier, 2019.

26 See the map in Le Bras and Todd, *Le mystère français*, p. 160. In 2009, such peripheral regional clusters were, for example, Vimeu (mouth of

the Seine) in Picardy, Choletais (border area between the *départements* of Vendée and Anjo) and the region surrounding the city of Roanne. Ibid., pp. 159 and 161. On the industrial districts in close geographical proximity to the urban centres of Toulouse, Lyons, Bordeaux and Strasbourg and Greater Paris, see Benko and Pecqueur, 'Industrial Districts and the Governance of Local Economies', p. 506.

27 Lisa de Propris, 'The Empirical Evidence of Industrial Districts in Great Britain', in Becattini et al. (eds), *A Handbook of Industrial Districts*, pp. 360–80, here p. 369.

28 Nicolas Renahy et al., 'Deux âges d'émigration ouvrière. Migration et sédentarité dans un village industriel', in *Population* 58 (2006), pp. 707–38.

29 Stéphane Humbert et al., *Le secteur automobile en Nord-Pas-de-Calais*, Lille, 2007, p. 19.

30 Ibid.

31 Armelle Gorgeu and René Mathieu, 'La place des diplômes dans la carrière des ouvriers de la filière automobile', in *Formation emploi* 105 (2009), pp. 37–51; Armelle Gorgeu et al., *Organisation du travail et gestion de la main-d'œuvre dans la filière automobile*, Paris, 1998; Tony Elger and Chris Smith, 'New Town, New Capital, New Workplace? The Employment Relations of Japanese Inward Investors in a West Midlands New Town', in *Economy and Society* 27 (1998), pp. 523–53.

32 Tilman Harlander and Gerd Kuhn (eds), *Soziale Mischung in der Stadt. Case Studies – Wohnungspolitik in Europa – Historische Analyse*, Stuttgart, 2012.

33 Günther Schulz (ed.), *Wohnungspolitik im Sozialstaat. Deutsche und europäische Lösungen, 1918–1960*, Düsseldorf, 1993; Peter Kramper, *Neue Heimat. Unternehmenspolitik und Unternehmensentwicklung im gewerkschaftlichen Wohnungs- und Städtebau 1950–1982*, Stuttgart, 2008; Rodney Lowe, *The Welfare State in Britain since 1945*, 3rd edition, Basingstoke et al., 2007, pp. 246–71; Guy Groux and Cathérine Lévy, *La possession ouvrière. Du taudis à la propriété (XIXe–XXe siècle)*, Paris, 1993.

34 On Germany, see Adelheid von Saldern, *Häuserleben. Zur Geschichte städtischen Arbeiterwohnens vom Kaiserreich bis heute*, 2nd edition, Bonn, 1997, pp. 351–62 and 379–84.

35 On Britain, see Lynsey Hanley's impressive *Estates: An Intimate History*, London, 2012.

36 For Germany, see Tilman Harlander, 'Wohnungspolitik', in Martin H. Geyer (ed.), *Geschichte der Sozialpolitik in Deutschland seit 1945. 1974–1982 Bundesrepublik Deutschland. Neue Herausforderungen, neue Unsicherheiten*, Baden-Baden, 2008, pp. 823–50; idem, 'Wohnungspolitik', in Manfred G. Schmidt (ed.), *Bundesrepublik Deutschland, 1982–1989. Finanzielle Konsolidierung und institutionelle*

Reform, Baden-Baden, 2005, pp. 683–712. For Britain, see Lowe, *The Welfare State in Britain since 1945*, pp. 365–75 and 428–31.

37 Pierre Bourdieu and Rosine Christin, 'La construction du marché. Le champs administratif et la production de la "politique du logement"', in *Actes de la recherche en sciences sociales* 81/82 (1990), pp. 65–85.

38 Lowe, *The Welfare State in Britain since 1945*, pp. 365–9.

39 Saldern, *Häuserleben*, pp. 440f.

40 Michel Verret, *L'espace ouvrier*, Paris, 1979, p. 193.

41 For Britain, see Lowe, *The Welfare State in Britain since 1945*, pp. 264, 267 and 366f.; Martin J. Daunton, *A Property-Owning Democracy? Housing in Britain*, London, 1987. For Germany: Clemens Zimmermann, 'Wohnungspolitik – Eigenheim für alle?', in Tilman Harlander and Harald Bodenschatz (eds), *Villa und Eigenheim. Suburbaner Städtebau in Deutschland*, Stuttgart, 2001, pp. 330–49. And for France: Groux and Lévy, *La possession ouvrière*.

42 My calculations based on the Labour Force Survey [LFS] 1979, in UK Social Data Archive Study [UK SDA] Study Number 1756 (LFS 1979).

43 The study is cited in Verret, *L'espace ouvrier*, p. 193.

44 Karin Kurz, 'Soziale Ungleichheiten beim Übergang zu Wohneigentum', in *Zeitschrift für Soziologie* 1 (2000), pp. 27–43, here p. 30.

45 As of 1995, figures for the three countries in *Annuaire statistique de la France* 105 (2000), p. 256.

46 My calculations based on the Labour Force Survey in UK Social Data Archive Study Number 5857 (LFS 2000).

47 Kurz, 'Soziale Ungleichheiten beim Übergang zu Wohneigentum', pp. 30 and 37.

48 Sonja Weber-Menges, *'Arbeiterklasse' oder Arbeitnehmer? Vergleichende empirische Untersuchung zu Soziallage, Lebenschancen und Lebensstilen von Arbeitern und Angestellten in Industriebetrieben*, Wiesbaden, 2004, p. 165.

49 Sylvie Tissot, '"Une discrimination informelle"? Usage du concept de mixité sociale dans la gestion des attributions de logements HLM', in *Actes de la recherche en sciences sociales* 159 (2005), pp. 54–69; Olivier Masclet, 'Du "bastion" au "ghetto". Le communisme municipal en butte à l'immigration', in *Actes de la recherche en sciences sociales* 159 (2005), pp. 10–25.

50 Royce Logan Turner, *Coal Was Our Life: An Essay on Life in a Yorkshire Former Pit Town*, Sheffield, 2000, p. 32.

51 Ibid., p. 27.

52 Ibid., pp. 196–212.

53 See above, chapter 5.

54 Harlander and Bodenschatz (eds), *Villa und Eigenheim*, with numerous case studies for Germany.

55 Pierre Bourdieu, *The Social Structures of the Economy*, Cambridge, 2003.

56 Marie Cartier, *La France des "petits-moyens"*. *Enquête sur la banlieue pavillonnaire*, Paris, 2008, pp. 53, 54.

57 See ibid., pp. 38–67; cf. also Mike Savage et al., 'Ordinary, Ambivalent and Defensive: Class Identities in the Northwest of England', in *Sociology* 35 (2001), pp. 875–92.

58 Edmond Préteceille, 'La ségrégation contre la cohésion sociale: la métropole parisienne', in Hugues Lagrange (ed.), *L'épreuve des inégalités*, Paris, 2006, pp. 195–246, here pp. 225–7.

59 John Welshman, *Underclass: A History of the Excluded, 1880–2000*, London and New York, 2006.

60 Ingrid Tucci, *Les descendants des Immigrés en France et en Allemagne: des destins contrastés. Participation au marché du travail, formes d'appartenance et modes de mise à distance sociale*, dissertation, University of Berlin, 2008, pp. 136–41.

61 Helen Baykara-Krumme, 'Returning, Staying or Both? Mobility Patterns among Elderly Turkish Migrants after Retirement', in *Transnational Social Review* 3 (2013), pp. 11–29, here p. 13.

62 Rachid Benattig, 'Le devenir des Algériens rentrés avec l'aide à la réinsertion', in *Revue européenne des migrations internationales* 4 (1988), pp. 97–113; idem, 'Les retours assistés dans les pays d'origine: une enquête en Algérie', in *Revue européenne des migrations internationales* 5 (1989), pp. 79–102.

63 Jan Motte, 'Gedrängte Freiwilligkeit. Arbeitsmigration, Betriebspolitik und Rückkehrförderung 1983/84', in idem et al. (eds), *50 Jahre Bundesrepublik, 50 Jahre Einwanderung. Nachkriegsgeschichte als Migrationsgeschichte*, Frankfurt/M. and New York, 1999, pp. 165–83; Karin Hunn, *'Nächstes Jahr kehren wir zurück…'. Die Geschichte der türkischen 'Gastarbeiter' in der Bundesrepublik*, Göttingen, 2005, pp. 478–91.

64 Abdelmalek Sayad, *The Suffering of the Immigrant*, Cambridge, 2004.

65 Claudia Diehl and Elisabeth Liebau, 'Turning back to Turkey – Or Turning the Back on Germany? Remigration Intentions and Behavior of Turkish Immigrants in Germany between 1984 and 2001', in *Zeitschrift für Soziologie* 44/1 (2015), pp. 22–41, here p. 31.

66 Pierre Bourdieu et al., *The Weight of the World: Social Suffering in Contemporary Society*, Cambridge and Stanford, CA, 1999, pp. 23–129.

67 Gaby Straßburger, 'Türkische Migrantenkolonien in Deutschland und Frankreich', in *Archiv für Sozialgeschichte* 42 (2002), pp. 173–89; idem et al., *Die türkischen Kolonien in Bamberg und Colmar. Ein deutsch–französischer Vergleich sozialer Netzwerke von Migranten im interkulturellen Kontext*, Online-Schriftenreihe Turkologie und Türkeikunde, vol. 1, Bamberg, 2000.

68 Marwick, *British Society since 1945*, p. 389.

69 M. Rainer Lepsius, *Demokratie in Deutschland. Soziologisch-historische Konstellationsanalysen*, Göttingen, 1993.

70 Stefan Goch, *Sozialdemokratische Arbeiterbewegung und Arbeiterkultur im Ruhrgebiet. Eine Untersuchung am Beispiel Gelsenkirchen, 1948–1975*, Düsseldorf, 1990.

71 For the Ruhr, cf. Wolfgang Hindrichs et al., *Der lange Abschied vom Malocher. Sozialer Umbruch in der Stahlindustrie und die Rolle der Betriebsräte von 1960 bis in die neunziger Jahre*, Essen, 2000.

72 Arne Hordt, *Kumpel, Kohle und Krawall*, Göttingen, 2018; Neumann, *Unternehmen Hamburg*; Dietmar Süß, *Kumpel und Genossen. Arbeiterschaft, Betrieb und Sozialdemokratie in der bayerischen Montanindustrie 1945 bis 1976*, Berlin and Boston, 2003.

73 Murden, '"City of Change and Challenge"'; Karen Evans et al., *A Tale of Two Cities: Global Change, Local Feeling and Everday Life in the North of England*, London, 2003.

74 Danièle Linhart, 'D'un monde à l'autre: la fermeture d'une entreprise', in *La Revue de l'Ires* 47 (2005), pp. 81–94.

75 Wolfgang Schäfer, *Die Fabrik auf dem Dorf. Studien zum betrieblichen Sozialverhalten ländlicher Industriearbeiter*, Göttingen, 1991.

76 Werner Kudera, 'Lebenskunst auf niederbayerisch. Schichtarbeiter in einem ländlichen Industriebetrieb', in Projektgruppe 'Alltägliche Lebensführung' (ed.), *Alltägliche Lebensführung. Arrangements zwischen Traditionalität und Modernisierung*, Wiesbaden, 1995, pp. 121–70; Florence Weber, *Le travail à-côté. Une ethnographie des perceptions*, Paris, 2009.

77 Olivier Schwartz, 'Peut-on parler des classes populaires?' in *La Vie des idées*, 13 September 2011: http://www.laviedesidees.fr/Peut-on-parler -des-classes.html.

78 Bourdieu calls this 'site effects'. See *The Weight of the World*, pp. 159–68.

79 Wilhelm Heitmeyer et al. (eds), *Die Krise der Städte. Analysen zu den Folgen desintegrativer Stadtentwicklung für das ethnisch-kulturelle Zusammenleben*, Frankfurt/M., 1999.

80 Cartier, *La France des 'petits-moyens'*.

81 Detailed data on Germany are provided by Dorn, *Alle in Bewegung*, pp. 63 and 123.

Conclusion: The history of deindustrialization as a history of contemporary problems

1 Brigitte Le Roux et al., 'Class and Cultural Division in the UK', in *Sociology* 42 (2008), pp. 1049–71; Mike Savage, *Social Class in the 21st Century*, London, 2015; Gérard Mauger, 'Bourdieu et les classes populaires. L'ambivalence des cultures dominées', in Philippe Coulangeon (ed.), *Trente ans après 'La distinction' de Pierre Bourdieu*, Paris, 2013, pp. 243–54; Olivier Schwartz, 'Peut-on parler des classes populaires?', in *La Vie des idées*, 13 September 2011 : http://www .laviedesidees.fr/Peut-on-parler-des-classes.html.

2 This cultural dimension of increasing inequality again requires its own study from the perspective of cultural and political history. For a pertinent sociological view, see Andreas Reckwitz, *The Society of Singularities: On the Structural Transformation of Modernity*, London, 2020.

SOURCES AND LITERATURE

1 Databases, statistics, archival documents

Annuaire statistique de la France.
Annual Abstracts of Statistics.
Archive of the Centre Maurice Halbwachs (CMH): *Emploi salarié et conditions de vie*, FNSP and CNRS, 1996–9.
British Library Sounds Collection:
Food: From Source to Salespoint.
Lives in Steel.
International Labour Organization: statistics and databases. ILO statistics by sectors and countries: https://www.ilo.org/global/statistics-and-databases/lang--en/index.htm.
Socio-Economic Panel (SOEP): database *Arbeiterhaushalte in Westdeutschland 1984–2001.*
SOFI Archiv Göttingen. Files: Facharbeiterstudie; Kompetenzweiterung; Trendreport.
Statistisches Jahrbuch für die Bundesrepublik Deutschland.
TRUMPF Group, *Filigran 2015/2016*, annual report: https://www.trumpf.com/filestorage/TRUMPF_Master/Corporate/Annual_report/Archive/TRUMPF_Geschaeftsbericht_2015_2016.pdf.
UK Social Data Archive (UK SDA):
Study Number (SN) 1756: Labour Force Survey (LFS) 1979.
SN 1758: LFS 1975.
SN 5876: LFS 1995.
SN 5857: LFS 2000.
SN 4938: *Families and Social Mobility: A Comparative Study, 1985–1988.*
Wikipedia (English):
'1981 England Riots': https://en.wikipedia.org/wiki/1981_England_riots.
'Anti-Poll Tax Unions': https://en.wikipedia.org/wiki/Anti-Poll_Tax_Unions.
'Toxteth Riots': https://en.wikipedia.org/wiki/1981_Toxteth_riots.

Wikipedia (French):
'Affaire LIP': https://fr.wikipedia.org/wiki/Affaire_Lip.
'Cellatex': https://fr.wikipedia.org/wiki/Cellatex.
'Émeutes dans les banlieues françaises depuis les années 1970': https://fr.wikipedia.org/wiki/%C3%89meutes_dans_les_banlieues_fran%C3%A7aises_depuis_les_ann%C3%A9es_1970.

2 Literature

Accornero, Guya, and Olivier Fillieule (eds), *Social Movement Studies in Europe: The State of the Art*, Oxford, 2016.

Achten, Udo, *Zorn und Unzufriedenheit genügen nicht. Die Septemberstreiks 1969*, Berlin, 2016.

Aglietta, Michel, *Le capitalisme de demain*, Paris, 1998.

Ahrens, Ralf, 'Eine alte Industrie vor neuen Herausforderungen. Aufbrüche und Niedergänge im ost- und westdeutschen Maschinenbau seit den 1960er Jahren', in Werner Plumpe and André Steiner (eds), *Der Mythos von der postindustriellen Welt. Wirtschaftlicher Strukturwandel in Deutschland 1960–1990*, Göttingen, 2016, pp. 55–119.

Ambrosius, Gerold, *Wirtschaftsraum Europa. Vom Ende der Nationalökonomien*, Frankfurt/M., 1996.

Amossé, Thomas, 'Mythes et réalités de la syndicalisation en France', in *Premières Synthèses* 44/2 (2004), pp. 1–5.

Amossé, Thomas, and Olivier Chardon, 'Les travailleurs non qualifiés: une nouvelle classe sociale?', in *Economie et statistique* 393/4 (2006), pp. 203–27.

Amossé, Thomas, and Thomas Coutrot, 'Socio-productive Models in France: An Empirical Dynamic Overview, 1992–2004', in *Industrial and Labour Relations Review* 64 (2011), pp. 786–817.

Anderson, Malcolm, and John Fairley, 'The Politics of Industrial Training in the United Kingdom', in *Journal of Public Policy* 3 (1983), pp. 191–207.

Andolfatto, Dominique, and Dominique Labbé, *La CGT. Organization et audience depuis 1945*, Paris, 1997.

Andresen, Knud, *Triumpherzählungen. Wie Gewerkschafterinnen und Gewerkschafter über ihre Erinnerungen sprechen*, Essen, 2014.

Andresen, Knud, *Gebremste Radikalisierung. Die IG Metall und ihre Jugend 1968 bis in die 1980er Jahre*, Göttingen, 2016.

Arnold, Jörg, 'Vom Verlierer zum Gewinner – und zurück', in *Geschichte und Gesellschaft* 42 (2016), pp. 266–97.

Artus, Ingrid, *Krise des deutschen Tarifsystems. Die Erosion des Flächentarifvertrags in Ost und West*, Wiesbaden, 2001.

Artus, Ingrid, *Betriebe ohne Betriebsrat. Informelle Interessenvertretung in Unternehmen*, Frankfurt/M. et al., 2006.

Artus, Ingrid, *Interessenhandeln jenseits der Norm. Mittelständische Betriebe und prekäre Dienstleistungsarbeit in Deutschland und Frankreich*, Frankfurt/M. and New York, 2008.

Attias-Donfut, Claudine, 'Generationenwechsel und sozialer Wandel', in

Renate Köcher and Joachim Schild (eds), *Wertewandel in Deutschland und Frankreich*, Opladen, 1998, pp. 173–206.

Audier, Serge, *Néo-libéralisme(s). Une archéologie intellectuelle*, Paris, 2012.

Bach, Olaf, *Die Erfindung der Globalisierung. Entstehung und Wandel eines zeitgeschichtlichen Grundbegriffs*, Frankfurt/M., 2013.

Baethge, Martin, 'The German "Dual System" of Training in Transition: Current Problems and Perspectives', in Peter Berg (ed.), *Creating Competitive Capacity: Labor Market Institutions and Workplace Practices in Germany and the United States*, Berlin, 2000, pp. 101–18.

Baethge, Martin, 'Entwicklungstendenzen in der Beruflichkeit – neue Befunde aus der industriesoziologischen Forschung', in *Zeitschrift für Berufs- und Wirtschaftspädagogik. Beihefte* 100 (2004), pp. 336–47.

Bagguley, Paul, 'The Moral Economy of Anti-Poll Tax Protest', in Colin Barker (ed.), *To Make Another World: Studies in Protest and Collective Action*, Aldershot et al., 1996, pp. 7–24.

Bagot, Laurence (ed.), *Ceux de Billancourt*, Ivry-sur-Seine, 2015.

Bahnmüller, Reinhard, *Stabilität und Wandel der Entlohnungsformen. Entgeltsysteme und Entgeltpolitik in der Metallindustrie, in der Textil- und Bekleidungsindustrie und im Bankgewerbe*, Munich and Mering, 2001.

Barker, Rodney, 'Legitimacy in the United Kingdom: Scotland and the Poll Tax', in *British Journal of Political Science* 22 (1992), pp. 521–33.

Batstone, Eric, *The Reform of Workplace Industrial Relations: Theory, Myth and Evidence*, Oxford, 1988.

Baudru, Daniel, and Med Kechidi, 'Les investisseurs institutionnels étrangers. Vers la fin du capitalisme à la française?', in *Revue d'économie financière* 48 (1998), pp. 93–105.

Bauman, Zygmunt, *Liquid Modernity*, London, 2000.

Baykara-Krumme, Helen, 'Returning, Staying or Both? Mobility Patterns among Elderly Turkish Migrants after Retirement', in *Transnational Social Review* 3 (2013), pp. 11–29.

Beaud, Stéphane, *80% au bac ... et après? Les enfants de la démocratisation scolaire*, Paris, 2003.

Beaud, Stéphane, and Michel Pialoux, *Retour sur la condition ouvrière. Enquête aux usines Peugeot de Sochaux-Montbéliard*, Paris, 1999.

Beaud, Stéphane, and Michel Pialoux, 'Jeunes ouvrier(e)s à l'usine', in *Travail, genre et sociétés* 8 (2002), pp. 73–103.

Beaud, Stéphane, and Michel Pialoux, *Violences urbaines, violence sociale. Genèse des nouvelles classes dangereuses*, Paris, 2006.

Beck, Ulrich, *Risk Society: Towards a New Modernity*, London, 1992.

Becker, Gary S., *Human Capital*, Chicago, 1964.

Becker, Jean-Jacques, and Pascal Ory, *Crises et alternances (1974–1995)*, Paris, 1998.

Becker, Karina, *Die Bühne der Bonität. Wie mittelständische Unternehmen auf die neuen Anforderungen des Finanzmarkts reagieren*, Baden-Baden, 2009.

Beckett, Andy, *When the Lights Went Out: Britain in the Seventies*, London, 2010.

Bell, Daniel, *The Coming of Post-Industrial Society*, New York, 1973.

Benattig, Rachid, 'Le devenir des Algériens rentrés avec l'aide à la réinsertion', in *Revue européenne des migrations internationales* 4 (1988), pp. 97–113.

Benattig, Rachid, 'Les retours assistés dans les pays d'origine: une enquête en Algérie', in *Revue européenne des migrations internationales* 5 (1989), pp. 79–102.

Bender, Gerd, 'Herausforderung Tarifautonomie. Normative Ordnung als Problem', in Thomas Duve and Stefan Ruppert (eds), *Rechtswissenschaft in der Berliner Republik*, Berlin, 2018, pp. 697–725.

Benko, Georges, and Bernard Pecqueur, 'Industrial Districts and the Governance of Local Economies: The French Example', in Giacomo Becattini et al. (eds), *A Handbook of Industrial Districts*, Cheltenham and Northampton, 2009, pp. 501–11.

Berghoff, Hartmut, 'Varieties of Financialization? Evidence from German Industry in the 1990s', in *Business History Review* 90 (2016), pp. 81–108.

Bernet, Brigitta, 'Dein Hirn, dein Kapital', *Zeit Online*, 3 July 2014: http://pdf.zeit.de/2014/28/wissensgesellschaft-brigitta-bernet-schweiz.pdf.

Bertho, Alain, Le temps des émeutes, Paris, 2009.

Bethge, Dietrich, 'Arbeitsschutz', in Manfred G. Schmidt (ed.), *Bundesrepublik Deutschland, 1982–1989. Finanzielle Konsolidierung und institutionelle Reform*, Baden-Baden, 2005, pp. 197–236.

Beyer, Jürgen, 'Die Strukturen der Deutschland AG. Ein Rückblick auf ein Modell der Unternehmenskontrolle', in Ralf Ahrens et al. (eds), *Die 'Deutschland AG'. Historische Annäherungen an den bundesdeutschen Kapitalismus*, Essen, 2013, pp. 31–56.

Birke, Peter, *Wilde Streiks im Wirtschaftswunder. Arbeitskämpfe, Gewerkschaften und soziale Bewegungen in der Bundesrepublik und Dänemark*, Frankfurt/M., 2007.

Black, John, et al., 'Clinging to Collectivism? Some Ethnographic Shop-Floor Evidence from the British Lock Industry 1979–98', in *The International Journal of Human Resource Management* 10 (1999), pp. 941–57.

Blanke, Thomas, 'Koalitionsfreiheit und Tarifautonomie. Rechtliche Grundlagen und Rahmenbedingungen der Gewerkschaften in Deutschland', in Wolfgang Schroeder and Bernhard Weßels (eds), *Die Gewerkschaften in Politik und Gesellschaft der Bundesrepublik Deutschland. Ein Handbuch*, Wiesbaden, 2003, pp. 144–73.

Boltanski, Luc, and Ève Chiapello, *The New Spirit of Capitalism*, London, 2005.

Bonaldo, Marc, *Resiliente Region Stuttgart? Anpassung und Innovation regionaler Industriekultur 'nach dem Boom'*, dissertation, University of Trier, 2019.

Bonnet, Serge, *L'homme du fer*, 2nd edition, Nancy, 1987.

Bosch, Gerhard, 'Zur Zukunft der dualen Berufsausbildung in Deutschland', in idem (ed.), *Das Berufsbildungssystem in Deutschland*, Wiesbaden, 2010, pp. 37–62.

Bosch, Gerhard, and Thorsten Kalina, 'Low-Wage Work in Germany: An

Overview', in Gerhard Bosch and Claudia Weinkopf (eds), *Low-Wage Work in Germany*, New York, 2008, pp. 19–112.

Bourdieu, Pierre, *Outline of a Theory of Practice*, Cambridge, 1977.

Bourdieu, Pierre, 'The Biographical Illusion', in Richard J. Parmentier and Greg Urban (eds), *Working Papers and Proceedings of the Center for Psychosocial Studies*, 14 (1987), pp. 1–7.

Bourdieu, Pierre, *In Other Words: Essays Towards a Reflexive Sociology*, Stanford, CA, and Cambridge, 1990.

Bourdieu, Pierre, *The Social Structures of the Economy*, Cambridge, 2003.

Bourdieu, Pierre, and Luc Boltanski, 'The Educational System and the Economy: Titles and Jobs', in Charles C. Lemert (ed.), *French Sociology*, New York, 1981, pp. 141–51.

Bourdieu, Pierre, and Rosine Christin, 'La construction du marché. Le champs administratif et la production de la "politique du logement"', in *Actes de la recherche en sciences sociales* 81/82 (1990), pp. 65–85.

Bourdieu, Pierre, et al., *The Weight of the World: Social Suffering in Contemporary Societies*, Cambridge and Stanford, CA, 1999.

Boyer, Robert, 'How and Why Capitalisms Differ', in *Economy and Society* 34 (2005), pp. 509–57.

Boyer, Robert, *The Political Economy of Capitalisms*, Singapore, 2022.

Brocard, Pascal, and Carole Donada, *La chaîne de l'équipement automobile*, Paris, 2003.

Brückner, Hannah, and Karl Ulrich Mayer, 'De-Standardization of the Life Course: What It Might Mean? And If It Means Anything, Whether It Actually Took Place?', in *Advances in Life Course Research* 9 (2005), pp. 27–53.

Brückweh, Kerstin, *Menschen zählen. Wissensproduktion durch britische Volkszählungen und Umfragen vom 19. Jahrhundert bis ins digitale Zeitalter*, Berlin and Boston, 2015.

Bruno, Anne-Sophie, 'Analyser le marché du travail par les trajectoires individuelles. Le cas des migrants de Tunisie en région parisienne pendant les Trente Glorieuses', in *Vingtième Siècle. Revue d'histoire* 121 (2014), pp. 35–47.

Bundesagentur für Arbeit, *Arbeitsmarkt in Deutschland. Analytikreport der Statistik*, April 2009.

Burawoy, Michael, *Manufacturing Consent: Changes in the Labor Process under Monopoly Capitalism*, Chicago, 1979.

Busemeyer, Marius R., *Wandel trotz Reformstau. Die Politik der beruflichen Bildung seit 1970*, Frankfurt/M., 2009.

Busemeyer, Marius R., 'Die Sozialpartner und der Wandel in der Politik der beruflichen Bildung seit 1970', in *Industrielle Beziehungen. Zeitschrift für Arbeit, Organisation und Management* 3 (2016), pp. 273–94.

Butzin, Bernhard, 'Regional Life Cycles and Problems of Revitalisation in the Ruhr', in Trevor Wild and Philip N. Jones (eds), *De-Industrialisation and New Industrialisation in Britain and Germany*, London, 1991, pp. 186–98.

Camard, Sophie, 'Comment interpréter les statistiques des grèves?', in *Genèses* 47 (2002), pp. 107–22.

Cannadine, David, *Class in Britain*, New Haven, 1998.

Canning, Roy, 'Vocational Education and Training in Scotland: Emerging Models of Apprenticeship', in Thomas Deißinger (ed.), *Berufliche Bildung zwischen nationaler Tradition und globaler Entwicklung. Beiträge zur vergleichenden Berufsbildungsforschung*, Baden-Baden, 2001, pp. 159–80.

Cartier, Marie, *La France des "petits-moyens". Enquête sur la banlieue pavillonnaire*, Paris, 2008.

Castel, Robert, *Les métamorphoses de la question sociale. Une chronique du salariat*, Paris, 1995.

Castells, Manuel, *The Information Age: Economy, Society, and Culture*, vol. 1: *The Rise of the Network Society*, 2nd edition, Chichester, 2010.

Cézard, Michel, 'Les ouvriers', in *INSEE première* 455 (1996), pp. 1–4.

Chardon, Olivier, 'Les transformations de l'emploi non qualifié depuis vingt ans', in *INSEE première* 796 (2001), pp. 1–4.

Charles, Tony, 'The New Division of Labour in Europe', in Wolfgang Littek and Tony Charles (eds), *The New Division of Labour: Emerging Forms of Work Organisation in International Perspective*, Berlin and New York, 1995, pp. 235–61.

Charlot, Bernard, and Madeleine Figeat, *Histoire de la formation des ouvriers 1789–1984*, Paris, 1985.

Chauvel, Louis, 'La déstabilisation du système des positions sociales', in Hugues Lagrange (ed.), *L'épreuve des inégalités*, Paris, 2006, pp. 91–112.

Chauvel, Louis, *Le destin des générations*, 2nd edition, Paris, 2010.

Chauvel, Louis, and Franz Schultheis, 'Le sens d'une dénégation: l'oubli des classes sociales en Allemagne et en France', in *Mouvements* 26 (2003), pp. 17–26.

Chenu, Alain, *L'archipel des employés*, Paris, 1990.

Chenu, Alain, 'Les ouvriers et leurs carrières: enracinement et mobilités', in *Sociétés contemporaines* (1993), pp. 79–92.

Chenu, Alain, and Nicole Tabard, 'Les transformations socioprofessionnelles du territoire français, 1982–1990', in *Population* 48 (1993), pp. 1735–69.

Cochoy, Franck, et al., 'Comment l'écrit travaille l'organisation: le cas des normes ISO 9000', in *Revue française de sociologie* 39 (1998), pp. 673–99.

Comfort, Nicholas, *The Slow Death of British Industry: A Sixty-Year Suicide, 1952–2012*, London, 2013.

Commaille, Laurent, 'Das Ende des französischen Modells. Die Eisen- und Stahlindustrie im späten 20. Jahrhunderts', in Morten Reitmayer (ed.), *Unternehmen am Ende des goldenen Zeitalters. Die 1970er Jahre in unternehmens- und wirtschaftshistorischer Perspektive*, Essen, 2008, pp. 129–45.

Corouge, Christian, and Michel Pialoux, 'Chronique Peugeot', in *Actes de la recherche en sciences sociales* 57/58 (1985), pp. 108–28.

Corouge, Christian, and Michel Pialoux, 'Engagement et désengagement militant aux usines Peugeot de Sochaux dans les années 1980 et 1990', in *Actes de la recherche en sciences sociales* 196/197 (2013), pp. 20–33.

Courtois, Stéphane, and Marc Lazar, *Histoire du Parti Communiste Français*, Paris, 1995.

Coutrot, Thomas, 'L'entreprise néolibérale: la cooperation forcée', in idem, *L'entreprise néo-libérale, nouvelle utopie capitaliste? Enquête sur les modes d'organisation du travail*, Paris, 1998, pp. 219–53.

Crouch, Colin, *Social Change in Western Europe*, Oxford, 2004.

Crouch, Colin, 'Skill Formation Systems', in Stephen Ackroyd et al. (eds), *The Oxford Handbook of Work and Organization*, Oxford, 2005, pp. 95–114.

Cusset, François, *La décennie. Le grand cauchemar des années 1980*, Paris, 2013.

Darlington, Ralph, *The Dynamics of Workplace Unionism: Shop Stewards' Organization in Three Merseyside Plants*, London and New York, 1994.

Daunton, Martin J., *A Property-Owning Democracy? Housing in Britain*, London, 1987.

Davies, Paul, and Mark Freedland, *Labour Legislation and Public Policy: A Contemporary History*, Oxford et al., 2006.

Davies, Paul, and Mark Freedland, *Towards a Flexible Labour Market: Labour Legislation and Regulation since the 1990s*, Oxford, 2007.

Dayan, Jean-Louis, 'L'emploi en France depuis trente ans', in Olivier Marchand (ed.), *L'emploi, nouveaux enjeux*, Paris, 2000, pp. 17–24.

de Propris, Lisa, 'The Empirical Evidence of Industrial Districts in Great Britain', in Becattini et al. (eds), *A Handbook of Industrial Districts*, pp. 360–80.

Delbridge, Rick, *Life on the Line in Contemporary Manufacturing: The Workplace Experience of Lean Production and the 'Japanese' Model*, Oxford and New York, 1998.

Demmou, Lilas, 'Le recul de l'emploi industriel en France entre 1980 et 2007. Ampleur et principaux déterminants: un état des lieux', in *Economie et statistique* 438–40 (2010), pp. 273–96.

Deppe, Wilfried, *Drei Generationen Arbeiterleben*, Göttingen, 1982.

Desrosières, Alain, and Laurent Thévenot, *Les catégories socioprofessionelles*, Paris, 1992.

Detje, Richard, et al., 'Gewerkschaftliche Kämpfe gegen Betriebsschließungen – ein Anachronismus?', in *WSI Mitteilungen* 59 (2008), pp. 238–45.

Deutschmann, Christoph, *Postindustrielle Industriesoziologie. Theoretische Grundlagen, Arbeitsverhältnisse und soziale Identitäten*, Weinheim, 2002.

Deutschmann, Christoph, 'Latente Funktionen der Institution des Berufs', in Marita Jacob and Peter Kupka (eds), *Perspektiven des Berufskonzepts. Die Bedeutung des Berufs für Ausbildung und Arbeitsmarkt*, Nuremberg, 2005, pp. 3–16.

Devine, Fiona, *Affluent Workers Revisited: Privatism and the Working Class*, Edinburgh, 1992.

Dicken, Peter, *Global Shift: Reshaping the Global Economic Map in the 21st Century*, 4th edition, London et al., 2006.

Dicken, Peter, *Global Shift: Mapping the Changing Contours of the World Economy*, 6th edition, New York and London, 2011.

Diehl, Claudia, and Elisabeth Liebau, 'Turning back to Turkey – Or Turning the Back on Germany? Remigration Intentions and Behavior of Turkish Immigrants in Germany between 1984 and 2001', in *Zeitschrift für Soziologie* 44/1 (2015), pp. 22–41.

Docherty, Charles, *Steel and Steelworkers: The Sons of Vulcan*, London, 1983.

La Documentation française, *Enquêtes sur les violences urbaines: comprendre les émeutes de novembre 2005*, Paris, 2007: https://www.vie-publique .fr/rapport/29083-enquetes-sur-les-violences-urbaines-comprendre-les -emeutes-de-novembre.

Doering-Manteuffel, Anselm, and Lutz Raphael, *Nach dem Boom. Perspektiven auf die Zeitgeschichte seit 1970*, 3rd edition, Göttingen, 2012.

Dohse, Knuth, et al., *Reorganisation der Arbeit in der Automobilindustrie. Konzepte, Regelungen, Veränderungstendenzen in den USA, Großbritannien und der Bundesrepublik Deutschland. Ein Materialbericht*, Berlin, 1984.

Dombrowski, Uwe, and Tim Mielke (eds), *Ganzheitliche Produktionssysteme. Aktueller Stand und zukünftige Entwicklungen*, Heidelberg, 2015.

Dorn, Raphael Emanuel, *Alle in Bewegung. Räumliche Mobilität in der Bundesrepublik Deutschland 1980–2010*, Göttingen, 2018.

Dörre, Klaus, *Kampf um Beteiligung. Arbeit, Partizipation und industrielle Beziehungen im flexiblen Kapitalismus. Eine Studie aus dem Soziologischen Forschungsinstitut Göttingen (SOFI)*, Wiesbaden, 2002.

Dörre, Klaus, 'Das flexible-marktzentrierte Produktionsmodell. Gravitationszentrum eines neuen Kapitalismus', in idem and Bernd Röttger (eds), *Das neue Marktregime. Konturen eines nachfordistischen Produktionsmodells*, Hamburg, 2003, pp. 7–34.

Dörre, Klaus, et al., 'Zwischen Firmenbewusstsein und Wachstumskritik', in idem (eds), *Das Gesellschaftsbild der LohnarbeiterInnen. Soziologische Untersuchungen in ost- und westdeutschen Industriebetrieben*, Hamburg, 2013, pp. 198–261.

Dreyfus-Armand, Geneviève, et al. (eds), *Les années 68. Le temps de la contestation*, Brussels, 2000.

Dubet, François, *La galère. Jeunes en survie*, Paris, 2003.

Dupays, Stéphanie, 'En un quart du siècle, la mobilité sociale a peu évolué', in *Données sociales. La société française*, Paris, 2006, pp. 343–9.

Durand, Jean-Pierre, 'Introduction: The Diversity of Employee Relationships', in Jean-Pierre Durand et al. (eds), *Teamwork in the Automobile Industry: Radical Change or Passing Fashion?*, Basingstoke, 1999, pp. 1–34.

Durand, Jean-Pierre, and Nicolas Hatzfeld, 'The Effectiveness of Tradition: Peugeot's Sochaux Factory', in Jean-Pierre Durand et al. (eds), *Teamwork in the Automobile Industry: Radical Change or Passing Fashion?*, Basingstoke, 1999, pp. 173–201.

Durand, Jean-Pierre, et al. (eds), *Teamwork in the Automobile Industry: Radical Change or Passing Fashion?*, Basingstoke, 1999.

Durand, Jean-Pierre, et al., 'The Transformation of Employee Relations in the

Automobile Industry?', in Jean-Pierre Durand et al. (eds), *Teamwork in the Automobile Industry: Radical Change or Passing Fashion?*, Basingstoke, 1999, pp. 412–45.

Durand, Marcel, *Grain de sable sous le capot*, 2nd edition, Marseille, 2006 [1990].

Dworkin, Dennis L., *Cultural Marxism in Postwar Britain: History, the New Left, and the Origins of Cultural Studies*, Durham, NC, 1997.

Ebbinghaus, Bernhard, 'Die Mitgliederentwicklung deutscher Gewerkschaften im historischen und internationalen Vergleich', in Wolfgang Schroeder and Bernhard Weßels (eds), *Die Gewerkschaften in Politik und Gesellschaft der Bundesrepublik Deutschland. Ein Handbuch*, Wiesbaden, 2003, pp. 174–203.

Eich, Stefan, and Adam Tooze, 'The Great Inflation', in Anselm Doering-Manteuffel et al. (eds), *Vorgeschichte der Gegenwart. Dimensionen des Strukturbruchs nach dem Boom*, Göttingen, 2016, pp. 173–96.

Eley, Geoff, *Forging Democracy: The History of the Left in Europe, 1850–2000*, Oxford and New York, 2002.

Elger, Tony, and Chris Smith, 'New Town, New Capital, New Workplace? The Employment Relations of Japanese Inward Investors in a West Midlands New Town', in *Economy and Society* 27 (1998), pp. 523–53.

Elger, Tony, and Chris Smith, *Assembling Work: Remaking Factory Regimes in Japanese Multinationals in Britain*, New York, 2005.

Esposito, Fernando (ed.), *Zeitenwandel. Transformationen geschichtlicher Zeitlichkeit nach dem Boom*, Göttingen, 2017.

Evans, Karen, et al., *A Tale of Two Cities: Global Change, Local Feeling and Everday Life in the North of England*, London, 2003.

Faust, Michael, and Jürgen Kädtler, 'Die Finanzialisierung von Unternehmen', in *Kölner Zeitschrift für Soziologie und Sozialpsychologie* 70 (2018), pp. 167–94.

Faust, Michael, et al., *Das kapitalmarktorientierte Unternehmen. Externe Erwartungen, Unternehmenspolitik, Personalwesen und Mitbestimmung*, Berlin, 2011.

Felstead, Alan, et al., *Work Skills in Britain 1986–2001*, Nottingham, 2002.

Fillieule, Olivier, et al. (eds), *Penser les mouvements sociaux. Conflits sociaux et contestations dans les sociétés contemporaines*, Paris, 2010.

Fitzroy, Felix, and Kornelius Kraft, 'Mitarbeiterbeteiligung und Produktivität. Eine ökonometrische Untersuchung', in *Zeitschrift für Betriebswirtschaft* 55 (1985), pp. 21–36.

Flecker, Jörg, et al., 'The Sexual Division of Labour in Process Manufacturing: Economic Restructuring, Training and "Women's Work"', in *European Journal of Industrial Relations* 4 (1998), pp. 7–34.

Foote, Geoffrey, *The Labour Party's Political Thought: A History*, Basingstoke, 1997.

Fourastié, Jean, *Le grand espoir du XXe siècle. Progrès technique, progrès économique, progrès social*, Paris, 1949.

Fremdling, Rainer, and Richard H. Tilly (eds), *Industrialisierung und Raum.*

Studien zur regionalen Differenzierung im Deutschland des 19. Jahrhunderts, Stuttgart, 1979.

Freye, Saskia, 'Neue Managerkarrieren im deutschen Kapitalismus?', in *Leviathan* 41 (2013), pp. 57–93.

Freyssenet, Michel, 'Transformations in the Teamwork at Renault', in Jean-Pierre Durand et al. (eds), *Teamwork in the Automobile Industry: Radical Change or Passing Fashion?*, Basingstoke, 1999, pp. 202–17.

Friez, Adrien, and Martine Julhès, 'Séries longues sur les salariés. Édition 1998', in *Résultats. Emploi-revenues* 605 (1998), pp. 1–89.

Gallie, Duncan (ed.), *Trade Unionism in Recession*, Oxford, 1996.

Geddes, Mike, and Anne Green, 'Engineering: Company Strategies and Public Policy in an Industry in Crisis', in Royce Logan Turner (ed.), *The British Economy in Transition: From the Old to the New?*, London and New York, 1995, pp. 123–41.

Geißler, Rainer, and Sonja Weber-Menges, '"Natürlich gibt es heute noch Schichten!" Bilder der modernen Sozialstruktur in den Köpfen der Menschen', in Helmut Bremer and Andrea Lange-Vester (eds), *Soziale Milieus und Wandel der Sozialstruktur. Die gesellschaftlichen Herausforderungen und die Strategien der sozialen Gruppen*, Wiesbaden, 2006, pp. 102–27.

Gerst, Detlef, et al., 'Group Work in the German Automobile Industry – The Case of Mercedes-Benz', in Jean-Pierre Durand et al. (eds), *Teamwork in the Automobile Industry: Radical Change or Passing Fashion?*, Basingstoke, 1999, pp. 366–94.

Gerstung, Tobias, *Stapellauf für ein neues Zeitalter. Die Industriemetropole Glasgow im revolutionären Wandel nach dem Boom (1960–2000)*, Göttingen, 2016.

Gilcher-Holtey, Ingrid, *'Die Phantasie an die Macht'. Mai 68 in Frankreich*, 2nd edition, Frankfurt/M., 2001.

Giordano, Benito, and Laura Twomey, 'Economic Transitions: Restructuring Local Labour Markets', in Jamie Peck and Kevin Ward (eds), *City of Revolution: Restructuring Manchester*, Manchester et al., 2006, pp. 50–75.

Giraud, Baptiste, 'Au-delà du déclin. Difficultés, rationalisation et réinvention du recours à la grève dans les stratégies confédérales des syndicats', in *Revue française de science politique* 56 (2006), pp. 943–68.

Girndt, Cornelia, *Anwälte, Problemlöser, Modernisierer. Betriebsratsreportagen*, Gütersloh, 1997.

Glißmann, Wilfried, and Klaus Peters, *Mehr Druck durch mehr Freiheit. Die neue Autonomie in der Arbeit und ihre paradoxen Folgen*, Hamburg, 2001.

Goch, Stefan, *Sozialdemokratische Arbeiterbewegung und Arbeiterkultur im Ruhrgebiet. Eine Untersuchung am Beispiel Gelsenkirchen, 1948–1975*, Düsseldorf, 1990.

Goch, Stefan, 'Betterment without Airs: Social, Cultural and Political Consequences of Deindustrialization in the Ruhr', in *International Review of Social History* 47 (2002), pp. 87–111.

Goch, Stefan, *Eine Region im Kampf mit dem Strukturwandel. Bewältigung von Strukturwandel und Strukturpolitik im Ruhrgebiet*, Essen, 2002.

Goldthorpe, John H., and Keith Hope, *The Social Grading of Occupations: A New Approach and Scale*, Oxford, 1974.

Goldthorpe, John H., et al., *The Affluent Worker in the Class Structure*, Cambridge, 1969.

Gorgeu, Armelle, and René Mathieu, 'La déqualification ouvrière en question', in *Formation emploi* 103 (2008), pp. 83–100.

Gorgeu, Armelle, and René Mathieu, 'La place des diplômes dans la carrière des ouvriers de la filière automobile', in *Formation emploi* 105 (2009), pp. 37–51.

Gorgeu, Armelle, and René Mathieu, 'Les suppressions d'emploi dans la filière automobile. L'impact négatif sur les conditions de travail et la qualification ouvrière', in *Formation emploi* 124 (2013), pp. 87–103.

Gorgeu, Armelle, et al., *Organisation du travail et gestion de la main-d'œuvre dans la filière automobile*, Paris, 1998.

Greene, Anne-Marie, *Voices from the Shop Floor: Dramas of the Employment Relationship*, Burlington, VT, 2001.

Greene, Anne-Marie, et al., *Lost Narratives? From Paternalism to Team-Working in a Lock Manufacturing Firm*, Wolverhampton, 2000.

Greinert, Wolf-Dietrich, *Das 'deutsche System' der Berufsausbildung. Geschichte, Organisation, Perspektiven*, 2nd edition, Baden-Baden, 1995.

Greinert, Wolf-Dietrich, *Berufsqualifizierung und dritte industrielle Revolution. Eine historisch-vergleichende Studie zur Entwicklung der klassischen Ausbildungssysteme*, Baden-Baden, 1999.

Groux, Guy, and Cathérine Lévy, *La possession ouvrière. Du taudis à la propriété (XIXe–XXe siècle)*, Paris, 1993.

Groux, Guy, and René Mouriaux, *La CGT. Crises et alternatives*, Paris, 1992.

Hachtmann, Rüdiger, *Industriearbeit im 'Dritten Reich'. Untersuchungen zu den Lohn- und Arbeitsbedingungen in Deutschland 1933–1945*, Göttingen, 1989.

Halbwachs, Maurice, *Les classes sociales*, Paris, 2008.

Hall, David, *Working Lives: The Forgotten Voices of Britain's Post-War Working Class*, London, 2012.

Hanley, Lynsey, *Estates: An Intimate History*, London, 2012.

Harlander, Tilman, 'Wohnungspolitik', in Manfred G. Schmidt (ed.), *Bundesrepublik Deutschland, 1982–1989. Finanzielle Konsolidierung und institutionelle Reform*, Baden-Baden, 2005, pp. 683–712.

Harlander, Tilman, 'Wohnungspolitik', in Martin H. Geyer (ed.), *Geschichte der Sozialpolitik in Deutschland seit 1945. 1974–1982 Bundesrepublik Deutschland. Neue Herausforderungen, neue Unsicherheiten*, Baden-Baden, 2008, pp. 823–50.

Harlander, Tilman, and Harald Bodenschatz (eds), *Villa und Eigenheim. Suburbaner Städtebau in Deutschland*, Stuttgart, 2001.

Harlander, Tilman, and Gerd Kuhn (eds), *Soziale Mischung in der Stadt. Case Studies – Wohnungspolitik in Europa – Historische Analyse*, Stuttgart, 2012.

Haßdenteufel, Sarah K., *Neue Armut, Exklusion, Prekarität. Armutspolitische*

Debatten um Armut in Frankreich und der Bundesrepublik Deutschland 1970–1990, Berlin and Boston, 2019.

Hassel, Anke, and Thorsten Schulten, 'Globalization and the Future of Central Collective Bargaining: The Example of the German Metal Industry', in *Economy and Society* 27 (1998), pp. 486–522.

Hatzfeld, Hélène, *Faire de la politique autrement. Les expériences inachevées des années 1970*, Paris, 2005.

Hatzfeld, Hélène, 'De l'autogestion à la démocratie participative', in Marie-Hélène Bacqué and Yves Sintomer (eds), *La démocratie participative. Histoire et généalogie*, Paris, 2011, pp. 51–61.

Hatzfeld, Nicolas, *Les gens d'usine. 50 ans d'histoire à Peugeot-Sochaux*, Paris, 2002.

Hatzfeld, Nicolas, 'L'individualisation des carrières à l'épreuve', in *Sociétés contemporaines* 54 (2004), pp. 15–33.

Hatzfeld, Nicolas, 'Organisation du travail, repères pour une histoire comparée (1945–2000)', in Jacqueline Costa-Lascoux (ed.), *Renault sur Seine*, Paris, 2007.

Hatzfeld, Nicolas, 'Figures filmiques d'ouvrières. Travail, genre et dignité, variations sur une trilogie classique (1962–2011)', in *Clio* 38 (2013), pp. 79–96.

Hatzfeld, Nicolas, et al., 'Le travail au cinéma. Un réapprentissage de la réalité sociale', in *Esprit* (July 2006), pp. 78–99.

Hatzfeld, Nicolas, et al., 'L'ouvrier en personne, une irruption dans le cinéma documentaire (1961–1974)', in *Le mouvement social* 226 (2009), pp. 67–78.

Hau, Michel, 'Introduction', in Jean-Claude Daumas et al. (eds), *La désindustrialization: une fatalité?* Besançon, 2017, pp. 7–16.

Hauff, Volker and Fritz W. Scharpf, *Modernisierung der Volkswirtschaft. Technologiepolitik als Strukturpolitik*, Frankfurt/M., 1975.

Hayes, Ingrid, 'Les limites d'une médiation militante: l'expérience de Radio Lorraine Coeur d'Acier, Longwy 1979–1980', in *Actes de la recherche en sciences sociales* 196/7 (2013), pp. 84–101.

Heckscher, Charles, 'From Bureaucracy to Networks', in Stephen Edgell et al. (eds), *The SAGE Handbook of Sociology, Work and Employment*, Los Angeles, 2016, pp. 245–61.

Heitmeyer, Wilhelm, et al. (eds), *Die Krise der Städte. Analysen zu den Folgen desintegrativer Stadtentwicklung für das ethnisch-kulturelle Zusammenleben*, Frankfurt/M., 1999.

Hemmer, Hans Otto, et al. (eds), *Geschichte der Gewerkschaften in der Bundesrepublik Deutschland. Von den Anfängen bis heute*, Cologne, 1990.

Herlyn, Ulfert, et al., *Neue Lebensstile in der Arbeiterschaft? Eine empirische Untersuchung in zwei Industriestädten*, Opladen, 1994.

Herrigel, Gary, 'Roles and Rules: Ambiguity, Experimentation and New Forms of Stakeholderism in Germany', in *Industrial Relations* 15 (2008), pp. 111–32.

Herrigel, Gary, *Industrial Constructions: The Sources of German Industrial Power*, Cambridge, MA, et al., 2009.

Heßler, Martina, 'Die Halle 54 bei Volkswagen und die Grenzen der Automatisierung. Überlegungen zum Mensch-Maschine-Verhältnis in der industriellen Produktion der 1980er-Jahre', in *Zeithistorische Forschungen/ Studies in Contemporary History*, online edition: 11/1 (2014): https:// zeithistorische-forschungen.de/1-2014/id=4996; print edition: pp. 56–76.

Hetzel, Anne-Marie, and Claire Bernard, *Le syndicalisme à mots découverts. Dictionnaire des fréquences (1971–1990)*, Paris, 1998.

Hillmert, Steffen, and Karl Ulrich Mayer (eds), *Geboren 1964 und 1971. Neuere Untersuchungen zu Ausbildungs- und Berufschancen in Westdeutschland*, Wiesbaden, 2004.

Hindrichs, Wolfgang, et al., *Der lange Abschied vom Malocher. Sozialer Umbruch in der Stahlindustrie und die Rolle der Betriebsräte von 1960 bis in die neunziger Jahre*, Essen, 2000.

Hinrichs, Peter, *Um die Seele des Arbeiters. Arbeitspsychologie, Industrie- und Betriebssoziologie in Deutschland 1871–1945*, Cologne, 1981.

Hockerts, Hans Günter (ed.), *Bundesrepublik Deutschland, 1966–1974. Eine Zeit vielfältigen Aufbruchs*, Baden-Baden, 2006.

Hoffrogge, Ralf, 'Engineering New Labour: Trade Unions, Social Partnership and the Stabilization of British Neoliberalism', in *Journal of Labor and Society* 21 (2018), pp. 301–16.

Hoggett, Paul, and Danny Burns, 'The Revenge of the Poor: The Anti-Poll Tax Campaign in Britain', in *Critical Social Policy* 11 (1991), pp. 95–110.

Honneth, Axel, *The Struggle for Recognition*, Oxford, 1995.

Hordt, Arne, *Von Scargill zu Blair? Der britische Bergarbeiterstreik 1984–85 als Problem einer europäischen Zeitgeschichtsschreibung*, Frankfurt/M., 2013.

Hordt, Arne, *Kumpel, Kohle und Krawall*, Göttingen, 2018.

Howell, Chris, 'Unforgiven: British Trade Unionism in Crisis', in Andrew Martin and George Ross (eds), *The Brave New World of European Labor: European Trade Unions at the Millennium*, New York, 1999, pp. 26–74.

Hüls, Walter, *Betriebsbesetzungen und Gewerkschaftskonzeption der CFDT. Praxis und Theorie des Projektes 'autogestion' in der Zeit von 1968–1978*, Rossdorf, 1983.

Humbert, Stéphane, et al., *Le secteur automobile en Nord-Pas-de-Calais*, Lille, 2007.

Hunn, Karin, *'Nächstes Jahr kehren wir zurück ... '. Die Geschichte der türkischen 'Gastarbeiter' in der Bundesrepublik*, Göttingen, 2005.

Jacod, Olivier, *Les élections aux comités d'entreprise de 1989 à 2004*, Paris, 2008.

Jauch, Peter, and Werner Schmidt, *Industrielle Beziehungen im Umbruch. Die Regulierung von Lohn, Gehalt und Arbeitszeit in Deutschland und Großbritannien*, Munich and Mering, 2000.

Jefferys, Steve, *Liberté, Egalité and Fraternité at Work: Changing French Employment Relations and Management*, Houndmills et al., 2003.

Jefferys, Steve, 'Forward to the Past? Ideology and Trade Unionism in France and Britain', in Craig Phelan (ed.), *The Future of Organized Labour: Global Perspectives*, Oxford and New York, 2007, pp. 209–42.

Jones, Owen, *Chavs: The Demonization of the Working Class*, London and New York, 2012.

Jürgenhake, Uwe, and Beate Winter, *Neue Produktionskonzepte in der Stahlindustrie. Ökonomisch-technischer Wandel und Arbeitskräfteeinsatz in der Eisen- und Stahlindustrie und seine Auswirkungen auf die Arbeitsorganization und -gestaltung sowie die betriebliche Aus- und Weiterbildung*, Dortmund, 1992.

Jürgens, Ulrich, 'Lean Production in Japan: Myth and Reality', in Wolfgang Littek and Tony Charles (eds), *The New Division of Labour: Emerging Forms of Work Organisation in International Perspective*, Berlin and New York, 1995, pp. 349–66.

Jürgens, Ulrich, 'The Development of Volkswagen's Industrial Model, 1967–1995', in Michel Freyssenet (ed.), *One Best Way? Trajectories and Industrial Models of the World's Automobile Producers*, Oxford, 1998, pp. 273–310.

Jürgens, Ulrich, and Hans Klingel, 'Internationalisierung als Struktur und Strategie im Werkzeugmaschinenbau – Das Beispiel der Firma Trumpf', in Pamela Meil (ed.), *Globalisierung industrieller Produktion. Strategien und Strukturen*, Frankfurt/M. et al., 1996, pp. 27–56.

Kädtler, Jürgen, 'German Chemical Giants' Business and Social Models in Transition: Financialisation as a Management Strategy', in *Transfer* 15 (2009), pp. 229–49.

Kaelble, Hartmut, *A Social History of Europe, 1945–2000*, New York and Oxford, 2013.

Kamp, Lothar, and Nikolaus Simon, 'Mitbestimmung als Faktor nachhaltiger Unternehmensentwicklung', in *WSI Mitteilungen* 56 (2005), pp. 459–64.

Kelly, John E., 'British Trade Unionism 1979–89: Change, Continuity and Contradictions', in *Work, Employment & Society* 4 (1990), pp. 29–65.

Kern, Horst, and Charles F. Sabel, 'Verblaßte Tugenden. Zur Krise des deutschen Produktionsmodells', in Nils Beckenbach and Werner von Treeck (eds), *Umbrüche gesellschaftlicher Arbeit*, Göttingen, 1994, pp. 605–24.

Kern, Horst, and Michael Schumann, *Das Ende der Arbeitsteilung? Rationalisierung in der industriellen Produktion: Bestandsaufnahme, Trendbestimmung*, Munich, 1984.

Kersley, Barbara, *Inside the Workplace: Findings from the 2004 Workplace Employment Relations Survey*, Milton Park et al., 2006.

Kirk, John, *Twentieth-Century Writing and the British Working Class*, Cardiff, 2003.

Kirk, John, et al. (eds), *Changing Work and Community Identities in European Regions: Perspectives on the Past and Present*, Houndmills et al., 2011.

Kissler, Leo, *Toyotismus in Europa. Schlanke Produktion und Gruppenarbeit in der deutschen und französischen Automobilindustrie*, Frankfurt/M. and New York, 1996.

Kitson, Michael, 'Failure Followed by Success or Success Followed by Failure?

A Re-examination of British Economic Growth since 1949', in Roderick Floud and Paul Johnson (eds), *Structural Change and Growth, 1939–2000*, Cambridge, 2004, pp. 27–56.

Kleinschmidt, Christian, *Der produktive Blick. Wahrnehmung amerikanischer und japanischer Management- und Produktionsmethoden durch deutsche Unternehmer 1950–1985*, Berlin, 2002.

Kocyba, Hermann, 'Wissensbasierte Selbststeuerung. Die Wissensgesellschaft als arbeitspolitisches Kontrollszenario', in Wilfried Konrad (ed.), *Wissen und Arbeit. Neue Konturen von Wissensarbeit*, Münster, 1999, pp. 92–119.

Köhler, Ingo, *Auto-Identitäten. Marketing, Konsum und Produktbilder des Automobils nach dem Boom*, Göttingen, 2018.

Kokoreff, Michel, 'L'émeute urbaine', in Michel Pigenet and Danielle Tartakowsky (eds), *Histoire des mouvements sociaux en France. De 1814 à nos jours*, Paris, 2014, pp. 733–43.

Kotthoff, Hermann, *Betriebsräte und Bürgerstatus. Wandel und Kontinuität betrieblicher Mitbestimmung*, Munich and Mering, 1994.

Kotthoff, Hermann, '"Betriebliche Sozialordnung" als Basis ökonomischer Leistungsfähigkeit', in Jens Beckert and Christoph Deutschmann (eds), *Wirtschaftssoziologie*, Wiesbaden, 2010, pp. 428–46.

Kotthoff, Hermann, and Josef Reindl, *Die soziale Welt kleiner Betriebe. Wirtschaften, Arbeiten und Leben im mittelständischen Industriebetrieb*, Göttingen, 1990.

Kotthoff, Hermann, and Josef Reindl, *'Fitneßtraining'. Betriebliche Reorganisation in Saarland*, Saarbrucken, 1999.

Kracauer, Siegfried, *History: The Last Things before the Last*, Oxford, 1969.

Kramper, Peter, *Neue Heimat. Unternehmenspolitik und Unternehmensentwicklung im gewerkschaftlichen Wohnungs- und Städtebau 1950–1982*, Stuttgart, 2008.

Krell, Gertraude, *Vergemeinschaftende Personalpolitik. Normative Personallehren, Werksgemeinschaft, NS-Betriebsgemeinschaft, betriebliche Partnerschaft, Japan, Unternehmenskultur*, Munich, 1994.

Krone, Sirikit, 'Aktuelle Probleme der Berufsausbildung in Deutschland', in Gerhard Bosch (ed.), *Das Berufsbildungssystem in Deutschland*, Wiesbaden, 2010.

Kudera, Werner, 'Lebenskunst auf niederbayerisch. Schichtarbeiter in einem ländlichen Industriebetrieb', in Projektgruppe 'Alltägliche Lebensführung' (ed.), *Alltägliche Lebensführung. Arrangements zwischen Traditionalität und Modernisierung*, Wiesbaden, 1995, pp. 121–70.

Kuhlmann, Martin, and Michael Schumann, 'What's Left of Workers' Solidarity? Workplace Innovation and Workers' Attitudes towards the Firm', in *Research in the Sociology of Work* 10 (2001), pp. 189–214.

Kupka, Peter, 'Arbeit und Subjektivität bei industriellen Facharbeitern', in *Beiträge zur Arbeitsmarkt- und Berufsforschung* 240 (2002), pp. 99–113.

Kurz, Karin, 'Soziale Ungleichheiten beim Übergang zu Wohneigentum', in *Zeitschrift für Soziologie* 1 (2000), pp. 27–43.

Labit, Anne, 'Group Working at Volkswagen: An Issue for Negotiation between Trade Unions and Management', in Jean-Pierre Durand et al. (eds), *Teamwork in the Automobile Industry: Radical Change or Passing Fashion?*, Basingstoke, 1999, pp. 395–411.

Lacher, Michael, 'Bildungsferne und Weiterbildungsnähe – ein Gegensatz?', in *Zeitschrift für Berufs- und Wirtschaftspädagogik. Beihefte* 86 (1990), pp. 309–24.

Lacher, Michael, et al., *Die Fort- und Weiterbildung von Montagearbeitern/-innen: Voraussetzungen und Perspektiven am Beispiel der Volkswagen AG*, Recklinghausen, 1987.

Lappe, Lothar, *Berufsperspektiven junger Facharbeiter. Eine qualitative Längsschnittanalyse zum Kernbereich westdeutscher Industriearbeit*, Frankfurt/M., 1993.

Lauschke, Karl, *Die Hoesch-Arbeiter und ihr Werk. Sozialgeschichte der Dortmunder Westfalenhütte während der Jahre des Wiederaufbaus 1945–1966*, Essen, 2000.

Lauschke, Karl, *Die halbe Macht. Mitbestimmung in der Eisen- und Stahlindustrie 1945 bis 1989*, Essen, 2007.

Lawrence, Jon, 'Social-Science Encounters and the Negotiation of Difference in early 1960s England', in *History Workshop Journal* 77 (2014), pp. 215–39.

Le Bras, Hervé, and Emmanuel Todd, *Le mystère français*, Paris, 2013.

Le Roux, Brigitte, et al., 'Class and Cultural Division in the UK', in *Sociology* 42 (2008), pp. 1049–71.

Lecher, Wolfgang, and Hans-Wolfgang Platzer, 'Europäische Betriebsräte', in Wolfgang Schroeder and Bernhard Weßels (eds), *Die Gewerkschaften in Politik und Gesellschaft der Bundesrepublik Deutschland. Ein Handbuch*, Wiesbaden, 2003, pp. 588–613.

Leisering, Lutz, and Christian Marschallek, 'Zwischen Wohlfahrtsstaat und Wohlfahrtsmarkt. Alterssicherung und soziale Ungleichheit', in Hans Günter Hockerts and Winfried Süß (eds), *Soziale Ungleichheit im Sozialstaat. Die Bundesrepublik Deutschland und Großbritannien im Vergleich*, Munich, 2010, pp. 89–116.

Lepsius, M. Rainer, *Demokratie in Deutschland. Soziologisch-historische Konstellationsanalysen*, Göttingen, 1993.

Lesch, Hagen, 'Arbeitskämpfe und Strukturwandel im internationalen Vergleich', in *IW-Trends – Vierteljahresschrift zur empirischen Wirtschaftsforschung aus dem Institut der deutschen Wirtschaft Köln* 32 (2005), no. 2, pp. 1–17.

Lévêque, Pierre, *Histoire des forces politiques en France*, Paris, 1997.

Linhart, Danièle, 'D'un monde à l'autre: la fermeture d'une entreprise', in *La Revue de l'Ires* 47 (2005), pp. 81–94.

Linhart, Robert, *The Assembly Line*, London, 1981.

Lösche, Peter, and Franz Walter, *Die SPD. Klassenpartei – Volkspartei – Quotenpartei. Zur Entwicklung der Sozialdemokratie von Weimar bis zur deutschen Vereinigung*, Darmstadt, 1992.

Losego, Sarah Vanessa, *Fern von Afrika. Die Geschichte der nordafrikanischen 'Gastarbeiter' im französischen Industrierevier von Longwy (1945–1990)*, Cologne, 2009.

Lowe, Rodney, *The Welfare State in Britain since 1945*, 3rd edition, Basingstoke et al., 2007.

Lunn, Ken, 'Complex Encounters: Trade Unions, Immigration and Racism', in John McIlroy et al. (eds), *The High Tide of British Trade Unionism: Trade Unions and Industrial Politics, 1964–79*, Monmouth, 2007, pp. 70–90.

Lutz, Burkart, 'Bildungssystem und Beschäftigungssystem in Deutschland und Frankreich. Zum Einfluss des Bildungssystems auf die Gestaltung betrieblicher Arbeitskräftestrukturen', in Hans-Gerhard Mendius et al. (eds), *Betrieb, Arbeitsmarkt, Qualifikation*, Frankfurt/M., 1976, pp. 83–151.

Lutz, Burkart, 'Konfliktpotential und sozialer Konsens. Die Geschichte des industriellen Systems der BRD im Spiegel des Schicksals einer Generation', in Otthein Rammstedt and Gert Schmidt (eds), *BRD ade!*, Frankfurt/M., 1992, pp. 101–22.

Lütz, Susanne, 'Von der Infrastruktur zum Markt? Der deutsche Finanzsektor zwischen Deregulierung und Reregulierung', in Paul Windolf (ed.), *Finanzmarkt-Kapitalismus. Analysen zum Wandel von Produktionsregimen*, Wiesbaden, 2005, pp. 294–315.

Mair, Andrew, 'The Introduction of Teamwork at Rover Group's Stamping Plant', in Jean-Pierre Durand et al. (eds), *Teamwork in the Automobile Industry: Radical Change or Passing Fashion?*, Basingstoke, 1999, pp. 254–86.

Marginson, Paul, et al., 'The Impact of European Works Councils on Management Decision-making in UK and US-based Multinationals: A Case Study Comparison', in *British Journal of Industrial Relations* 42 (2004), pp. 209–33.

Marshall, T.H., *Sociology at the Crossroads and Other Essays*, London, 1963.

Martinez, Daniel, *Carnets d'un intérimaire*, Marseille, 2003.

Marwick, Arthur, *Class: Image and Reality in Britain, France and the US since 1930*, 2nd edition, London, 1990.

Marwick, Arthur, *British Society since 1945*, 4th edition, London et al., 2003.

Marx, Christian, 'Der Aufstieg multinationaler Konzerne. Umstrukturierungen und Standortkonkurrenz in der westeuropäischen Chemieindustrie', in Anselm Doering-Manteuffel et al. (eds), *Vorgeschichte der Gegenwart. Dimensionen des Strukturbruchs nach dem Boom*, Göttingen, 2016, pp. 197–216.

Marx, Christian, 'Between National Governance and the Internationalization of Business: The Case of Four Major West German Producers of Chemicals, Pharmaceuticals and Fibres, 1945–2000', in *Business History* 27 (2017), pp. 1–30.

Marx, Christian, and Morten Reitmayer, 'Zwangslagen und Handlungsspielräume. Der Wandel von Produktionsmodellen in der westdeutschen Chemieindustrie im letzten Drittel des 20. Jahrhunderts', in *Archiv für Sozialgeschichte* 56 (2016), pp. 297–334.

Marx, Karl, *Capital*, vol. 1, in Karl Marx and Friedrich Engels (eds), *Collected Works*, vol. 35, London, 1987.

Marx, Karl, and Friedrich Engels, *Manifesto of the Communist Party*: https://

www.marxists.org/archive/marx/works/1848/communist-manifesto/ch01
.htm#007.

Masclet, Olivier, 'Du "bastion" au "ghetto". Le communisme municipal en
butte à l'immigration', in *Actes de la recherche en sciences sociales* 159
(2005), pp. 10–25.

Mason, Geoff, et al., 'Productivity, Product Quality and Workforce Skills: Food
Processing in Four European Countries', in *National Institute Economic
Review* 147 (1994), pp. 62–83.

Mason, Geoff, et al., 'Low Pay, Labour Market Institutions, and Job Quality
in the United Kingdom', in Caroline Lloyd et al. (eds), *Low-Wage Work in
the United Kingdom*, New York, 2008, pp. 41–95.

Mauger, Gérard, 'Bourdieu et les classes populaires. L'ambivalence des cultures
dominées', in Philippe Coulangeon (ed.), *Trente ans après 'La distinction' de
Pierre Bourdieu*, Paris, 2013, pp. 243–54.

Maurice, Marc, et al., *Politique d'éducation et organisation industrielle en
France et en Allemagne. Essai d'analyse sociétale*, Paris, 1982.

Mayer, Karl Ulrich, 'Ausbildungswege und Berufskarrieren', in *Forschung im
Dienst von Praxis und Politik. Festveranstaltung zum 25 jährigen Bestehen
des Bundesinstituts für Berufsbildung am 7. und 8. September 1995.
Dokumentation*, Berlin, 1996, pp. 113–45.

Mayer, Karl Ulrich, and Glenn R. Carroll, 'Jobs and Classes: Structural
Constraints on Career Mobility', in *European Sociological Review* 3 (1987),
pp. 14–38.

Mayer-Ahuja, Nicole, *Wieder dienen lernen? Vom westdeutschen
'Normalarbeitsverhältnis' zu prekärer Beschäftigung seit 1973*, Berlin, 2003.

McIlroy, John, 'Notes on the Communist Party and Industrial Politics', in
John McIlroy et al. (eds), *The High Tide of British Trade Unionism: Trade
Unions and Industrial Politics, 1964–79*, Monmouth, 2007, pp. 216–58.

McIlroy, John, '"Always Outnumbered, Always Outgunned": The Trotskyists
and the Trade Unions', in John McIlroy et al. (eds), *The High Tide of
British Trade Unionism: Trade Unions and Industrial Politics, 1964–79*,
Monmouth, 2007, pp. 259–96.

McIlroy, John, 'Ten Years of New Labour: Workplace Learning, Social
Partnership and Union Revitalization in Britain', in *British Journal of
Industrial Relations* 46 (2008), pp. 283–313.

McIlroy, John, and Alan Campbell, 'The High Tide of Trade Unionism:
Mapping Industrial Politics, 1964–79', in John McIlroy et al. (eds), *The
High Tide of British Trade Unionism: Trade Unions and Industrial Politics,
1964–79*, Monmouth, 2007, pp. 93–130.

McIvor, Arthur, *Working Lives: Work in Britain since 1945*, Basingstoke,
2013.

McSmith, Andy, *No Such Thing as Society: Britain in the Turmoil of the
1980s*, London, 2011.

Ményr, Yves, et al. (eds), *The Politics of Steel: Western Europe and the Steel
Industry in the Crisis Years (1974–1984)*, Berlin, 1987.

Metz, Rainer, 'Volkswirtschaftliche Gesamtrechnungen', in Thomas Rahlf (ed.), *Deutschland in Zahlen. Zeitreihen zur Historischen Statistik*, Bonn, 2015, pp. 186–99.

Mikol, Fanny, and Chloé Tavan, 'La mobilité professionnelle des ouvriers et employés immigrés', in *Données sociales: La société française* 12 (2006), pp. 351–9.

Milert, Werner, and Rudolf Tschirbs, *Die andere Demokratie. Betriebliche Interessenvertretung in Deutschland, 1848 bis 2008*, Essen, 2012, pp. 462–75.

Millward, Neil, et al., *All Change at Work? British Employment Relations 1980–1998, as Portrayed by the Workplace Industrial Relations Survey Series*, New York, 2000.

Mitterrand, François, *La Rose au poing*, Paris, 1973.

Moldaschl, Manfred (ed.), *Wissensökonomie und Innovation. Beiträge zur Ökonomie der Wissensgesellschaft*, Marburg, 2010.

Moldaschl, Manfred, and Gerd-Günter Voß, *Subjektivierung von Arbeit*, Munich, 2002.

Molinié, Anne-Françoise, 'Industrial Workforce Decline and Renewal', in *INSEE Studies* 43 (2000), pp. 1–17.

Mooser, Josef, 'Abschied von der "Proletarität". Sozialstruktur und Lage der Arbeiterschaft in der Bundesrepublik in historischer Perspektive', in Werner Conze and M. Rainer Lepsius (eds), *Sozialgeschichte der Bundesrepublik Deutschland. Beiträge zum Kontinuitätsproblem*, 2nd edition, Stuttgart, 1984, pp. 143–66.

Mooser, Josef, *Arbeiterleben in Deutschland 1900–1970*, Frankfurt/M., 1984.

Morin, François, and Eric Rigamonti, 'Évolution et structure de l'actionnariat en France', in *Revue française de gestion* 141 (2002), pp. 155–81.

Morris, Lydia, *Dangerous Classes: The Underclass and Social Citizenship*, London and New York, 1994.

Motte, Jan, 'Gedrängte Freiwilligkeit. Arbeitsmigration, Betriebspolitik und Rückkehrförderung 1983/84', in idem et al. (eds), *50 Jahre Bundesrepublik, 50 Jahre Einwanderung. Nachkriegsgeschichte als Migrationsgeschichte*, Frankfurt/M. and New York, 1999, pp. 165–83.

Müller-Jentsch, Walther (ed.), *Konfliktpartnerschaft. Akteure und Institutionen industrieller Beziehungen*, Munich and Mering, 1991.

Munt, Sally R. (ed.), *Cultural Studies and the Working Class: Subject to Change*, London, 2000.

Murden, Jon, '"City of Change and Challenge": Liverpool since 1945', in John Belchem (ed.), *Liverpool 800: Culture, Character & History*, Liverpool, 2006, pp. 393–485.

Mutz, Gerd, et al., *Diskontinuierliche Erwerbsverläufe. Analysen zur postindustriellen Arbeitslosigkeit*, Opladen, 1995.

Nachtwey, Oliver, *Marktsozialdemokratie. Die Transformation von SPD und Labour Party*, Wiesbaden, 2009.

Nesta, Lionel, 'Désindustrialization ou mutation industrielle?' in *Economie et statistique* 438–40 (2010), pp. 297–301.

Neumann, Arndt, *Unternehmen Hamburg. Eine Geschichte der neoliberalen Stadt*, Göttingen, 2018.

Neveu, Erik, 'Médias et protestation collective', in Olivier Fillieule et al. (eds), *Penser les mouvements sociaux. Conflits sociaux et contestations dans les sociétés contemporaines*, Paris, 2010, pp. 245–64.

Niedenhoff, Horst-Udo, *Betriebsratswahlen. Eine Analyse der Betriebsratswahlen von 1975 bis 2006*, Cologne, 2007.

Noiriel, Gérard, *Workers in French Society in the 19th and 20th Centuries*, Oxford, 1990.

Noiriel, Gérard, and Benaceur Azzaoui, *Vivre et lutter à Longwy*, Paris, 1980.

Nolte, Paul, *Die Ordnung der deutschen Gesellschaft. Selbstentwurf und Selbstbeschreibung im 20. Jahrhundert*, Munich, 2000.

OECD, *Measuring Globalisation*, vol. 1, Geneva, 2001.

O'Mahony, Mary, 'Employment, Education and Human Capital', in Roderick Floud and Paul Johnson (eds), *Structural Change and Growth, 1939–2000*, Cambridge, 2004, pp. 112–33.

Pardi, Tommaso, 'Travailler chez Toyota. De l'emploi à vie à la course à la survie', in *La Revue de l'Ires* 62 (2009), pp. 39–70.

Pardi, Tommaso, 'Crise et rejet de la greffe Toyota à Valenciennes?', in *Le journal de l'école de Paris du management* 99 (2013), pp. 29–36.

Paugam, Serge, *Le salarié de la précarité. Les nouvelles formes de l'intégration professionnelle*, Paris, 2000.

Penissat, Étienne, 'Les occupations de locaux dans les années 1960–1970. Processus sociohistoriques de "réinvention" d'un mode d'action', in *Genèses* 59 (2005), pp. 71–93.

Penn, Roger, et al. (eds), *Skill and Occupational Change*, Oxford and New York, 1994.

Peters, Jürgen, and Holger Gorr (eds), *In freier Verhandlung. Dokumente zur Geschichte der Tarifpolitik der IG Metall 1945–2002*, 2nd edition, Göttingen, 2009.

Phillips, Jim, 'The 1972 Miners' Strike: Popular Agency and Industrial Politics in Britain', in *Contemporary British History* 20 (2006), pp. 187–207.

Pialoux, Michel, and Florence Weber, 'La gauche et les classes populaires. Réflexions sur un divorce', in *Mouvements* 23 (2002), pp. 9–21.

Pigenet, Michel, and Danielle Tartakowsky (eds), *Histoire des mouvements sociaux en France. De 1814 à nos jours*, Paris, 2014.

Pigenet, Michel, and Danielle Tartakowsky, 'Institutionnalisation et mobilisations au temps de l'État social (années 1930–années 1970)', in idem (eds), *Histoire des mouvements sociaux en France. De 1814 à nos jours*, Paris, 2014, pp. 337–54.

Piketty, Thomas, *Capital in the Twenty-First Century*, Cambridge, MA, 2013.

Pitti, Laure, 'Grèves ouvrières versus luttes de l'immigration. Une controverse entre historiens', in *Ethnologie française* 31 (2001), pp. 465–76.

Pleinen, Jenny, *Die Migrationsregime Belgiens und der Bundesrepublik seit dem Zweiten Weltkrieg*, Göttingen, 2012.

Plener, Ulla (ed.), *Die Treuhand. Der Widerstand in den Betrieben der DDR, die Gewerkschaften (1990–1994)*, Berlin, 2011.

Plickert, Philip, *Wandlungen des Neoliberalismus. Eine Studie zu Entwicklung und Ausstrahlung der 'Mont Pèlerin Society'*, Stuttgart, 2008.

Plumpe, Werner, and André Steiner, 'Der Mythos von der postindustriellen Welt', in idem (eds), *Der Mythos von der postindustriellen Welt. Wirtschaftlicher Strukturwandel in Deutschland 1960–1990*, Göttingen, 2016.

Pollak, Reinhard, *Kaum Bewegung, viel Ungleichheit. Eine Studie zu sozialem Auf- und Abstieg in Deutschland*, Berlin, 2010.

Pollert, Anna, '"Team Work" on the Assembly Line: Contradiction and the Dynamics of Union Resilience', in Peter Ackers et al. (eds), *The New Workplace and Trade Unionism*, London and New York, 1996, pp. 178–209.

Popp, Andrew, and John F. Wilson, 'The Emergence and Development of Industrial Districts in Industrialising England, 1750–1914', in Giacomo Becattini et al. (eds), *A Handbook of Industrial Districts*, Cheltenham and Northampton, 2009, pp. 43–57.

Prais, Sigbert Jon, *Productivity, Education and Training: An International Perspective*, Cambridge, 1995.

Préteceille, Edmond, 'La ségrégation contre la cohésion sociale: la métropole parisienne', in Hugues Lagrange (ed.), *L'épreuve des inégalités*, Paris, 2006, pp. 195–246.

Pudal, Bernard, *Prendre parti. Pour une sociologie historique du PCF*, Paris, 1989.

Raithel, Thomas, *Jugendarbeitslosigkeit in der Bundesrepublik. Entwicklung und Auseinandersetzung während der 1970er und 1980er Jahre*, Munich, 2012.

Reckwitz, Andreas, *The Society of Singularities: On the Structural Transformation of Modernity*, London, 2020.

Rehder, Britta, *Betriebliche Bündnisse für Arbeit in Deutschland. Mitbestimmung und Flächentarif im Wandel*, Frankfurt/M., 2003.

Reicher, Stephen, and Clifford John T. Stott, *Mad Mobs and Englishmen? Myths and Realities of the 2011 Riots*, New York, 2011.

Reid, Donald, *Opening the Gates: The Lip Affair, 1968–1981*, London, 2018.

Reid, Ivan, *Class in Britain*, Cambridge et al., 1998.

Reitmayer, Morten, *Elite. Sozialgeschichte einer politisch-gesellschaftlichen Idee in der frühen Bundesrepublik*, Munich, 2009.

Renahy, Nicolas, et al., 'Deux âges d'émigration ouvrière. Migration et sédentarité dans un village industriel', in *Population* 58 (2006), pp. 707–38.

Rey, Henri, *La gauche et les classes populaires. Histoire et actualité d'une mésentente*, Paris, 2004.

Richardi, Reinhard, 'Arbeitsverfassung und Arbeitsrecht', in Hans Günter Hockerts (ed.), *Bundesrepublik Deutschland, 1966–1974. Eine Zeit vielfältigen Aufbruchs*, Baden-Baden, 2006, pp. 225–76.

Richards, Andrew John, *Miners on Strike: Class Solidarity and Division in Britain*, Oxford, 1996.

Richter, Horst-Eberhard, *Sich der Krise stellen: Reden, Aufsätze, Interviews*, Reinbek bei Hamburg, 1981.

Ritter, Gerhard, and Klaus Tenfelde, *Geschichte der Arbeiter und der*

Arbeiterbewegung in Deutschland seit dem Ende des 18. Jahrhunderts, Bonn, 1992.

Rodgers, Daniel T., *Age of Fracture*, Cambridge, MA, 2012.

Rosanvallon, Pierre, *Le peuple introuvable. Histoire de la représentation démocratique en France*, Paris, 1998.

Rosanvallon, Pierre, *Society of Equals*, Boston, 2013.

Ross, Kristin, *May '68 and Its Afterlives*, Chicago, 2002.

Rudolph, Wolfgang, and Wolfram Wassermann, *Betriebsräte im Wandel. Aktuelle Entwicklungsprobleme gewerkschaftlicher Betriebspolitik im Spiegel der Betriebsratswahlen*, Münster, 1996.

Ryan, Paul, 'Apprenticeship in Britain – Tradition and Innovation', in Thomas Deißinger (ed.), *Berufliche Bildung zwischen nationaler Tradition und globaler Entwicklung. Beiträge zur vergleichenden Berufsbildungsforschung*, Baden-Baden, 2001, pp. 133–58.

Saint-Jevin, Pierre, 'Les résultats des élections aux comités d'entreprises en 1977 et l'état de l'institution en novembre 1978', in *Revue française des affaires sociales* 33 (1979), pp. 161–270.

Savage, Mike, *Identities and Social Change in Britain since 1940: The Politics of Method*, Oxford and New York, 2010.

Savage, Mike, *Social Class in the 21st Century*, London, 2015.

Savage, Mike, et al., 'Ordinary, Ambivalent and Defensive: Class Identities in the Northwest of England', in *Sociology* 35 (2001), pp. 875–92.

Sayad, Abdelmalek, *The Suffering of the Immigrant*, Cambridge, 2004.

Schäfer, Wolfgang, *Die Fabrik auf dem Dorf. Studien zum betrieblichen Sozialverhalten ländlicher Industriearbeiter*, Göttingen, 1991.

Schelsky, Helmut, 'Die Bedeutung des Schichtungsbegriffs für die Analyse der gegenwärtigen deutschen Gesellschaft' (1953), in idem, *Auf der Suche nach der Wirklichkeit*, Düsseldorf, 1965, pp. 331–6.

Schild, Joachim, and Henrik Uterwedde, *Frankreich. Politik, Wirtschaft, Gesellschaft*, 2nd edition, Wiesbaden, 2006.

Schlögel, Karl, *In Space We Read Time: On the History of Civilization and Geopolitics*, Chicago, 2016.

Schmid, Günther, and Frank Oschmiansky, 'Arbeitsmarktpolitik und Arbeitslosenversicherung', in Manfred G. Schmidt (ed.), *Bundesrepublik Deutschland, 1982–1989. Finanzielle Konsolidierung und institutionelle Reform*, Baden-Baden, 2005, pp. 237–88.

Schriewer, Jens, 'Alternativen in Europa: Frankreich. Lehrlingsausbildung unter dem Anspruch von Theorie und Systematik', in Herwig Blankertz (ed.), *Enzyklopädie Erziehungswissenschaften, Bd 9: Sekundarstufe II, Teil 1: Handbuch*, Stuttgart, 1982, pp. 250–85.

Schroeder, Wolfgang, and Samuel Greef, 'Gewerkschaften und Arbeitsbeziehungen nach dem Boom', in Anselm Doering-Manteuffel et al. (eds), *Vorgeschichte der Gegenwart. Dimensionen des Strukturbruchs nach dem Boom*, Göttingen, 2016, pp. 245–70.

Schultheis, Franz, 'Repräsentationen des sozialen Raumes im interkulturellen Vergleich', in *Berliner Journal für Soziologie* 6 (1996), pp. 43–68.

Schulz, Günther (ed.), *Wohnungspolitik im Sozialstaat. Deutsche und europäische Lösungen, 1918–1960*, Düsseldorf, 1993.

Schulze, Gerhard, *The Experience Society*, London, 2005.

Schumann, Michael, et al., *Trendreport Rationalisierung. Automobilindustrie, Werkzeugmaschinenbau, chemische Industrie*, Berlin, 1994.

Schwartz, Olivier, 'Peut-on parler des classes populaires?', in *La Vie des idées* (13 September 2011) : http://www.laviedesidees.fr/Peut-on-parler-des-classes.html.

Scott, Andrew, *Willing Slaves? British Workers under Human Resource Management*, Cambridge and New York, 1994.

Shaw, Eric, 'Labourism: Myths and Realities', in Kevin Hickson et al. (eds), *The Struggle for Labour's Soul: Understanding Labour's Political Thought since 1945*, London and New York, 2004, pp. 187–205.

Sheldrake, John, and Sarah Vickerstaff, *The History of Industrial Training in Britain*, Aldershot, 1987.

Simon, Hermann, *Hidden Champions of the 21st Century: Lessons from 500 of the World's Best Unknown Companies*, Boston, 1996.

Simon, Hermann, *Hidden Champions of the 21st Century: Success Strategies of Unknown World Market Leaders*, Dordrecht et al., 2009.

Solow, Robert, 'The German Story', in Gerhard Bosch and Claudia Weinkopf (eds), *Low-Wage Work in Germany*, New York, 2008, pp. 1–14.

Soskice, David W., and Wolfgang Franz, *The German Apprenticeship System*, Berlin, 1994.

Speich Chassé, Daniel, *Die Erfindung des Bruttosozialprodukts. Globale Ungleichheit in der Wissensgeschichte der Ökonomie*, Göttingen, 2013.

Spur, Günter, et al., *Automatisierung und Wandel der betrieblichen Arbeitswelt*, Berlin, 1993.

Stedman Jones, Gareth, *Languages of Class: Studies in English Working-Class History, 1832–1982*, Cambridge, 1996.

Steedman, Hilary, 'Vocational Training in France and Britain: Mechanical and Electrical Craftsmen', in *National Institute Economic Review* 126 (1988), pp. 57–70.

Steedman, Hilary, 'A Decade of Skill Formation in Britain and Germany', in *Journal of Education and Work* 11 (1998), pp. 77–94.

Steedman, Hilary, 'Do Work-Force Skills Matter?', in *British Journal of Industrial Relations* 31 (1993), pp. 285–92.

Steedman, Hilary, *The State of Apprenticeship in 2010*, London, 2010.

Steedman, Hilary, and Karin Wagner, 'A Second Look to Productivity, Machinery and Skills in Germany and Britain', in *National Institute Economic Review* 122 (1987), pp. 84–95.

Steedman, Hilary, and Karin Wagner, 'Nationale Ausbildungssysteme und ihr Einfluss auf das betriebliche Ausbildungs- und Rekrutierungsverhalten von Unternehmen', in *Arbeit – Beispiele für ihre Humanisierung. Erfahrungen, Berichte, Analysen* 17 (2008), pp. 268–82.

Steedman, Hilary, et al., 'Intermediate Skills in the Workplace: Development, Standards and Supply in Britain, France and Germany', in *National Institute Economic Review* 136 (1991), pp. 60–76.

Stehr, Nico, "'Wissensgesellschaften" oder die Zerbrechlichkeit moderner Gesellschaften', in Wilfried Konrad (ed.), *Wissen und Arbeit. Neue Konturen von Wissensarbeit*, Münster, 1999, pp. 13–23.

Steiner, André, 'Abschied von der Industrie? Wirtschaftlicher Strukturwandel in West- und Ostdeutschland seit den 1960er Jahren', in Wener Plumpe and André Steiner (eds), *Der Mythos von der postindustriellen Welt. Wirtschaftlicher Strukturwandel in Deutschland 1960–1990*, Göttingen, 2016, pp. 15–54.

Stewart, Paul, 'The Negotiation of Change in the Evolution of the Workplace towards a New Production Model at Vauxhall (General Motors) UK', in Jean-Pierre Durand et al. (eds), *Teamwork in the Automobile Industry: Radical Change or Passing Fashion?*, Basingstoke, 1999, pp. 236–53.

Stewart, Paul, et al., 'Les ouvriers de Vauxhall face à la lean production', in *Le mouvement social* 217 (2006), pp. 33–52.

Stöger, Harald, *Abstieg oder Aufbruch? Europäische Betriebsräte zwischen Marginalisierung und transnationalem Einfluss*, Vienna, 2011.

Stott, Clifford John T., and John Drury, 'Crowds, Context and Identity: Dynamic Categorization Processes in the "Poll Tax Riot"', in *Human Relations* 53 (2000), pp. 247–73.

Strangleman, Tim, "'Smokestack Nostalgia", "Ruin Porn", or Working-Class Obituary: The Role and Meaning of Deindustrial Representation', in *International Labor and Working-Class History* 84 (2013), pp. 23–37.

Strangleman, Tim, et al., 'Introduction to Crumbling Cultures: Deindustrialization, Class, and Memory', in *International Labor and Working-Class History* 84 (2013), pp. 7–22.

Straßburger, Gaby, 'Türkische Migrantenkolonien in Deutschland und Frankreich', in *Archiv für Sozialgeschichte* 42 (2002), pp. 173–89.

Straßburger, Gaby, et al., *Die türkischen Kolonien in Bamberg und Colmar. Ein deutsch–französischer Vergleich sozialer Netzwerke von Migranten im interkulturellen Kontext*, Online-Schriftenreihe Turkologie und Türkeikunde, vol. 1, Bamberg, 2000.

Streeck, Wolfgang, 'Skills and the Limits of Neo-Liberalism: The Enterprise of the Future as a Place of Learning', in *Work, Employment & Society* 3 (1989), pp. 89–104.

Streeck, Wolfgang, 'Industrial Citizenship under Regime Competition: The Case of the European Works Councils', in *Journal of European Public Policy* 4 (1997), pp. 643–64.

Streeck, Wolfgang, 'The Crisis in Context: Democratic Capitalism and Its Contradictions', in Armin Schäfer (ed.), *Politics in the Age of Austerity*, Cambridge, 2013, pp. 262–302.

Streeck, Wolfgang, *Buying Time: The Delayed Crisis of Democratic Capitalism*, London and New York, 2014.

Supiot, Alain, *Beyond Employment: Changes in Work and the Future of Labour Law in Europe*, Oxford, 2001.

Süß, Dietmar, *Kumpel und Genossen. Arbeiterschaft, Betrieb und*

Sozialdemokratie in der bayerischen Montanindustrie 1945 bis 1976, Berlin and Boston, 2003.

Süß, Dietmar, *'Ein Volk, ein Reich, ein Führer'. Die deutsche Gesellschaft im Dritten Reich*, Munich, 2017.

Sutterlüty, Ferdinand, 'The Hidden Morale of the 2005 French and 2011 English Riots', in *Thesis Eleven* 121 (2014), pp. 38–56.

Tabard, Nicole, 'Des quartiers pauvres aux banlieues aisées. Une représentation sociale du territoire', in *Economie et statistique* 270 (1993), pp. 5–22.

Tavan, Chloé, 'Migration et trajectoires professionnelles, une approche longitudinale', in *Economie et statistique* 393/4 (2006), pp. 81–99.

Terrail, Jean-Pierre, *Destins ouvriers. La fin d'une classe?*, Paris, 1990.

Thelen, Kathleen Ann, 'Institutionen und sozialer Wandel. Die Entwicklung der beruflichen Bildung in Deutschland', in Jens Beckert et al. (eds), *Transformationen des Kapitalismus. Festschrift für Wolfgang Streeck zum sechzigsten Geburtstag*, Frankfurt/M. 2006, pp. 399–424.

Thélot, Claude, 'L'évolution de la mobilité sociale dans chaque génération', in *Economie et statistique* 161 (1983), pp. 3–21.

Ther, Philipp, 'Der Neoliberalismus' Version 1.0, in *Docupedia Zeitgeschichte* (5 July 2016): https://docupedia.de/zg/Ther_neoliberalismus_v1_de_2016.

Ther, Philipp, *Europe since 1989: A History*, Princeton, 2016.

Thompson, E.P., *The Making of the English Working Class*, London, 1968.

Tissot, Sylvie, '"Une discrimination informelle"? Usage du concept de mixité sociale dans la gestion des attributions de logements HLM', in *Actes de la recherche en sciences sociales* 159 (2005), pp. 54–69.

Todd, Selena, *The People: The Rise and Fall of the Working Class 1910–2010*, London, 2010.

Tomlinson, Jim, 'Inventing "Decline": The Falling behind of the British Economy in the Postwar Years', in *The Economic History Review* 49 (1996), pp. 731–57.

Tornatore, Jean-Louis, 'L'invention de la Lorraine industrielle', in *Ethnologie française* 35 (2005), pp. 679–89.

Torp, Cornelius, *Gerechtigkeit im Wohlfahrtsstaat. Alter und Alterssicherung in Deutschland und Großbritannien von 1945 bis heute*, Göttingen, 2015.

Trampusch, Christine, 'Institutional Resettlement: The Case of Early Retirement in Germany', in Wolfgang Streeck and Kathleen Ann Thelen (eds), *Beyond Continuity: Institutional Change in Advanced Political Economies*, Oxford and New York, 2005, pp. 203–28.

Tucci, Ingrid, *Les descendants des Immigrés en France et en Allemagne: des destins contrastés. Participation au marché du travail, formes d'appartenance et modes de mise à distance sociale*, dissertation, Humboldt University of Berlin, 2008.

Tulloch, John, *Television Drama: Agency, Audience and Myth*, London, 1990.

Turner, Royce Logan, 'Introduction', in idem (ed.), *The British Economy in Transition: From the Old to the New?*, London and New York, 1995, pp. 1–22.

Turner, Royce Logan, *Coal Was Our Life: An Essay on Life in a Yorkshire Former Pit Town*, Sheffield, 2000.

Ubbiali, Georges, 'Mémoires des luttes', in *Politix* 74 (2006), pp. 189–98.

Union Européenne and Commission Européenne (eds), *Au-delà de l'emploi. Transformations du travail et devenir du droit du travail en Europe*, Paris, 1999.

van Laak, Dirk, 'Alltagsgeschichte', in Michael Maurer (ed.), *Neue Themen und Methoden der Geschichtswissenschaft*, Stuttgart, 2003, pp. 14–80.

van Puymbroek, Cyrille, and Robert Reynard, 'Répartition géographique des emplois', in *INSEE première* 1278 (2010), pp. 1–4.

Verret, Michel, *L'espace ouvrier*, Paris, 1979.

Vigna, Xavier, *L'insubordination ouvrière dans les années 68. Essai d'histoire politique*, 2nd edition, Rennes, 2008.

von Henninges, Hasso, *Ausbildung und Verbleib von Facharbeitern. Eine empirische Analyse für die Zeit von 1980 bis 1989*, Nuremberg, 1991.

von Oertzen, Christine, *Teilzeitarbeit und die Lust am Zuverdienen. Geschlechterpolitik und gesellschaftlicher Wandel in Westdeutschland 1948–1969*, Göttingen, 1999.

von Saldern, Adelheid, *Häuserleben. Zur Geschichte städtischen Arbeiterwohnens vom Kaiserreich bis heute*, 2nd edition, Bonn, 1997.

von Saldern, Adelheid, '"Alles ist möglich". Fordism – ein visionäres Ordnungsmodell des 20. Jahrhunderts', in Lutz Raphael (ed.), *Theorien und Experimente der Moderne. Europäische Gesellschaften im 20. Jahrhundert*, Cologne et al., 2012, pp. 155–92.

von Saldern, Adelheid, and Rüdiger Hachtmann, 'Das fordistische Jahrhundert. Eine Einleitung', in *Zeithistorische Forschungen/Studies in Contemporary History*, online edition, 6/2 (2009): http://www.zeithistorische-forschungen.de/2-2009/id=4508; print edition: pp. 174–85.

von Tunzelmann, Nick, 'Technology in Postwar Britain', in Roderick Floud and Paul Johnson (eds), *Structural Change and Growth, 1939–2000*, Cambridge, 2004, pp. 299–331.

Voß, Gerd-Günter, 'Die Entgrenzung von Arbeit und Arbeitskraft', in *Mitteilungen aus der Arbeitsmarkt- und Berufsforschung* 31 (1998), pp. 473–87.

Voswinkel, Stephan, and Gabriele Wagner, 'Die Person als Leistungskraft: Anerkennungspolitiken in Organisationen', in *Leviathan: Berliner Zeitschrift für Sozialwissenschaft* (special issue) 40/4 (2012), pp. 591–608.

Wagner, Karin, and Geoff Mason, 'Restructuring of Automotive Supply-Chains: The Role of Workforce Skills in Germany and Britain', in *International Journal of Automotive Technology and Management* 5 (2005), pp. 378–410.

Wallraff, Gunter, *Lowest of the Low*, London, 1988.

Wannenwetsch, Stefan, *'Es gibt noch Arbeiter in Deutschland'. Zur Transformation der Kategorie Arbeiter in der westdeutschen Arbeiternehmergesellschaft*, dissertation, University of Tübingen, 2019.

Weber, Florence, *Le travail à-côté. Une ethnographie des perceptions*, Paris, 2009.

Weber, Max, 'Objective Possibility and Adequate Causation in the Historical Causal Approach', in idem, *Collected Methodological Writings*, eds Hans Henrik Bruun and Sam Whimster, London, 2012, pp. 169–84.

Weber-Menges, Sonja, *'Arbeiterklasse' oder Arbeitnehmer? Vergleichende empirische Untersuchung zu Soziallage, Lebenschancen und Lebensstilen von Arbeitern und Angestellten in Industriebetrieben*, Wiesbaden, 2004.

Wehler, Hans-Ulrich, *Deutsche Gesellschaftsgeschichte*, vol. 1, 4th edition, Munich, 2006.

Weischer, Christoph, *Sozialstrukturanalyse*, Wiesbaden, 2011.

Weiss, Manfred, 'Die Entwicklung der Arbeitsbeziehungen aus arbeitsrechtlicher Sicht', in *Industrielle Beziehungen* 20 (2013), pp. 393–417.

Welshman, John, *Underclass: A History of the Excluded, 1880–2000*, London and New York, 2006.

Welskopp, Thomas, *Unternehmen Praxisgeschichte. Historische Perspektiven auf Kapitalismus, Arbeit und Klassengesellschaft*, Tübingen, 2014.

Werkkreis Literatur der Arbeitswelt (ed.), *25 Jahre Widerstand Wahrheit Kritik*, Munich, 1995.

Whittall, Michael, and Hermann Kotthoff, 'Les comités d'entreprise européens, des zones libres de syndicats', in *La Revue de l'Ires* 68 (2011), pp. 207–36.

Wickham-Jones, Mark, 'The New Left', in Kevin Hickson et al. (eds), *The Struggle for Labour's Soul: Understanding Labour's Political Thought since 1945*, London and New York, 2004, pp. 24–46.

Widmaier, Ulrich (ed.), *Der deutsche Maschinenbau in den neunziger Jahren*, Frankfurt/M. and New York, 2000.

Wiede, Wiebke, 'Subjekt und Subjektivierung', Version 1.0, in *Docupedia-Zeitgeschichte* (10 December 2014): https://docupedia.de/zg/Wiede _subjekt_und_subjektivierung_v1_de_2014.

Wigand, Rolf, et al., *Information, Organization and Management: Expanding Markets and Corporate Boundaries*, New York, 1997.

Wilkinson, Barry, et al., 'The Iron Fist in the Velvet Glove: Management and Organization in Japanese Manufacturing Transplants in Wales', in *Journal of Management Studies* 32 (1995), pp. 819–30.

Willis, Paul, *Learning to Labour: How Working Class Kids Get Working Class Jobs*, London, 1977.

Windolf, Paul (ed.), *Finanzmarkt-Kapitalismus. Analysen zum Wandel von Produktionsregimen*, Wiesbaden, 2005.

Windolf, Paul, 'Was ist Finanzmarkt-Kapitalismus?', in idem (ed.), *Finanzmarkt-Kapitalismus. Analysen zum Wandel von Produktionsregimen*, Wiesbaden, 2005, pp. 20–57.

Wirsching, Andreas, *Abschied vom Provisorium, 1982–1990*, Munich, 2006.

Wirsching, Andreas, 'Konsum statt Arbeit? Zum Wandel von Individualität in der modernen Massengesellschaft', in *Vierteljahrshefte für Zeitgeschichte* 57 (2009), pp. 171–99.

Wirsching, Andreas, *Der Preis der Freiheit. Geschichte Europas in unserer Zeit*, Munich, 2012.

Womack, James P., et al., *The Machine That Changed the World: The Story of Lean Production*, Boulder, CO, 1991.

Zachert, Ulrich, *Beendigungstatbestände im internationalen Vergleich. Eine normative und empirische Bestandsaufnahme*, Baden-Baden, 2004.

Zimmermann, Clemens, 'Wohnungspolitik – Eigenheim für alle?', in Tilman Harlander and Harald Bodenschatz (eds), *Villa und Eigenheim. Suburbaner Städtebau in Deutschland*, Stuttgart, 2001, pp. 330–49.

INDEX

Printed and bound by CPI Group (UK) Ltd, Croydon, CR0 4YY

22/04/2024

14487252-0001